THE PARTICIPATORY CULTURES HANDBOOK

How did we get from Hollywood to YouTube? What makes Wikipedia so different from a traditional encyclopedia? Has blogging dismantled journalism as we know it?

Our media landscape has undergone a seismic shift as digital technology has fostered the rise of "participatory culture," in which knowledge is originated, created, distributed, and evaluated in radically new ways. *The Participatory Cultures Handbook* is an indispensable, interdisciplinary guide to this rapidly changing terrain. With short, accessible essays from leading geographers, political scientists, communication theorists, game designers, activists, policy makers, physicists, and poets, this volume will introduce students to the concept of participatory culture, explain how researchers approach participatory culture studies, and provide original examples of participatory culture in action. Topics include crowdsourcing, crisis mapping, grid computing, digital activism in authoritarian countries, collaborative poetry, collective intelligence, participatory budgeting, and the relationship between video games and civic engagement.

New essays by:

Daren C. Brabham, Helen Burgess, Clay Calvert, Mia Consalvo, Kelly Czarnecki, Aaron Delwiche, David M. Faris, Dieter Fuchs, Owen Gallagher, Clive Goodinson, Alexander Halavais, Cynthia Hawkins, John Heaven, Jennifer Jacobs Henderson, The Janissary Collective, Henry Jenkins, Barry Joseph, Christopher M. Kelty, Pierre Lévy, Sophia B. Liu, Rolf Luehrs, Alice Mattoni, Patrick Meier, Jason Mittell, Sarah Pearce, Donatella della Porta, W. James Potter, Howard Rheingold, Suzanne Scott, Benjamin Stokes, Thomas Swiss, Paul A. Taylor, Will Venters, Jen Ziemke.

Aaron Delwiche is an associate professor in the Department of Communication at Trinity University in San Antonio, Texas.

Jennifer Jacobs Henderson is an associate professor and chair of the Department of Communication at Trinity University in San Antonio, Texas.

THE PARTICIPATORY CULTURES HANDBOOK

Edited by Aaron Delwiche
and Jennifer Jacobs Henderson

Routledge
Taylor & Francis Group

NEW YORK AND LONDON

First published 2013
by Routledge
711 Third Avenue, New York, NY 10017

Simultaneously published in the UK
by Routledge
2 Park Square, Milton Park, Abingdon, Oxon OX14 4RN

Routledge is an imprint of the Taylor & Francis Group, an informa business

Library of Congress Cataloging in Publication Data
The participatory cultures handbook / edited by Aaron Delwiche and
Jennifer Henderson.
    p. cm.
Includes bibliographical references and index.
ISBN 978-0-415-88223-1 (hbk.) – ISBN 978-0-415-50609-0 (pbk.) –
ISBN 978-0-203-11792-7 (ebook) 1. Information technology–Social aspects.
2. Online social networks. 3. Social media. 4. Social participation. 5. Culture.
I. Delwiche, Aaron Alan. II. Henderson, Jennifer Jacobs.
HM851.P363 2012
302.30285–dc23   2011048598

ISBN: 978-0-415-88223-1 (hbk)
ISBN: 978-0-415-50609-0 (pbk)
ISBN: 978-0-203-11792-7 (ebk)

Typeset in Bembo
by Cenveo Publisher Services

SFI Certified Sourcing
www.sfiprogram.org
SFI-00453

Printed and bound in the United States of America
by Edwards Brothers, Inc.

To everyone who believed in the power of participation
long before the rise of the Internet.

CONTENTS

CONTRIBUTORS

Peter Blank is interested in social identity research on different digital profiles (network profiles, userIDs, game avatars, customer profiles) that reveals how people's identities are (per)formed through specific footings, switchings and contexts in mediated society. He works both as a media/language teacher and media consultant.

Daren C. Brabham is an Assistant Professor in the School of Journalism and Mass Communication and a faculty fellow in the Center for Urban and Regional Studies at the University of North Carolina at Chapel Hill. He teaches and conducts research in the areas of new media and public relations. Among the first to publish research on the crowdsourcing model, his work has appeared in journals such as: *Convergence*; *Information, Communication & Society*; and *First Monday*.

Watson Brown is a student in the Indiana University Department of Telecommunications, and is a founding contributor to the Janissary Collective.

Helen Burgess is an Assistant Professor of English at the University of Maryland Baltimore County, where she teaches a variety of classes in new media and digital literacies. She is co-author of the 2008 interactive DVD-ROM *Biofutures: Owning Body Parts and Information* and editor of the online new media and net art journal *Hyperrhiz: New Media Cultures*.

Clay Calvert is Professor and Brechner Eminent Scholar in Mass Communication and the Director of the Marion B. Brechner First Amendment Project at the University of Florida in Gainesville. He has authored or co-authored more than 100 published law journal articles, as well as dozens of op-ed commentaries. Professor Calvert is co-author, along with Don R. Pember, of the media law textbook *Mass Media Law* (McGraw Hill, 17th edn, 2011), and is author of *Voyeur Nation: Media, Privacy, and Peering in Modern Culture* (Westview Press, 2000).

Mia Consalvo is Canada Research Chair in Game Studies and Design at Concordia University in Montreal. She is the author of *Cheating: Gaining Advantage in Videogames*, and is writing a book about Japan's influence on the videogame industry and game culture. Mia served as product owner for *Eksa: Isle of the Wisekind* with the Singapore-MIT GAMBIT Game Lab, in order to study social interaction in social network games. She has published her written work in *Critical Studies in Media Communication*, *Games & Culture*, *Game Studies*, *Convergence*, and many other journals.

Kelly Czarnecki is a Teen Librarian at ImaginOn in Charlotte, North Carolina. She writes and edits the Gaming Life column for *School Library Journal* and has written numerous articles for library publications. She published *Gaming in Libraries* (Neal Schuman, 2010) and *Digital Storytelling in Practice* (American Library Association, 2009). In her spare time, she enjoys training and competing in triathlons.

Donatella della Porta is Professor of Sociology in the Department of Political and Social Sciences at the European University Institute. Her main research interests concern social movements, political violence, terrorism, corruption, the police, and policies of public order. On these issues she has conducted investigations in Italy, France, Germany, and Spain. In 2011 she has been awarded a five-year ERC advanced scholar grant on "Mobilizing from below: Social Movements and Democratization."

Aaron Delwiche is an Associate Professor in the Department of Communication at Trinity University in San Antonio, Texas. He teaches courses on hacking subcultures, transmedia storytelling, and videogame design and criticism. His experiments with games in the classroom have been covered by publications ranging from *Wired* to the *Guardian* (UK). In 2009, with support from the Lennox Foundation, he organized the lecture series "Reality Hackers: The Next Wave of Media Revolutionaries" and published an anthology of essays related to the series.

Mark Deuze is Associate Professor at the Department of Telecommunications of Indiana University in Bloomington. His most recent book is *Media Life* (2012, Polity Press). He is a part of the Janissary Collective, a writers' group consisting of researchers advocating a militant rejection of disciplinary dogma, and an aggressive pursuit of free thinking beyond traditional theories, paradigms, and methods.

Lindsay Ems is a doctoral student at Indiana University in the Department of Telecommunications. Her research topics aim to explore how social values are expressed in group use of technologies. Her work explores dissent, anarchy, and breakdown in the use of technologies by protesters. She also aims to uncover cultural forces at work in shaping the use of technologies in groups of users like the Amish. Six years of work using media design software programs as a graphic and web designer initiated Lindsay's interest in digital media. This interest grew as she began building physically interactive media systems.

David M. Faris is an Assistant Professor of Political Science at Roosevelt University in Chicago, where he studies the intersection of digital media and politics in the Middle East, democratization, and social movements. His scholarly work has appeared in *Arab Media & Society* and *Middle East Politics*, and he has written for the *Christian Science Monitor*, NPR.org, and the *Daily News Egypt*.

Dieter Fuchs is Professor of Political Science at the University of Stuttgart. His research focuses are the theory of democracy, comparative analyses of political cultures, and support of the European Union. His latest publication is *Cultural Diversity, European Identity and the Legitimacy of the EU* (together with Hans-Dieter Klingemann).

Owen Gallagher is a PhD researcher in the Faculty of Visual Culture at the National College of Art and Design, Dublin. He holds a Masters in Design Communication from the University of Ulster, Derry, and a Bachelor of Design in Digital Media from Letterkenny Institute of Technology. He is the founder of TotalRecut.com, an online remix community and remix video archive, as well as co-founder of the Remix Theory & Praxis international research group (remixstudies.org). He has been lecturing in web, digital media, and design theory for the past five years and currently lectures in web media at Bahrain Polytechnic.

Clive Goodinson brings creative vision and technical expertise worthy of a superhero to Pixton comics, as its co-founder and creator. With an MSc degree from the University of British Columbia, prior to Pixton he spent nearly a decade building interactive content for some of Canada's leading brands and design agencies.

Alexander Halavais is Associate Professor of Interactive Media at Quinnipiac University, as well as serving as the president of the Association of Internet Researchers. His research addresses questions of social change and social media, and particularly how open analytics can promote new forms of social organization. His most recent book, *Search Engine Society*, explores how search changes us. He blogs at http://alex.halavais.net and tweets @halavais.

Cynthia Hawkins is a PhD graduate of the creative writing program at SUNY Binghamton. Her work has appeared in literary journals and magazines such as *Passages North*, *Monkeybicycle*, *ESPN the Magazine*, *Parent:Wise Magazine*, and *Our Stories*, and her entertainment reviews and features have appeared in the *San Antonio Current*, the *Orlando Weekly*, the *Monterey County Weekly*, the *Detroit Metrotimes*, *InDigest Magazine*, and *Strange Horizons*. Cynthia currently works as a freelance writer, contributes regularly at *The Nervous Breakdown* where she is also an Associate Editor of Arts and Culture, and serves as Managing Fiction Editor of *Prick of the Spindle*.

John Heaven manages international eParticipation projects at TuTech Innovation GmbH in Hamburg, including the Pan-European eParticipation Network (PEP-NET) and PARTERRE, an EU project to promote citizen participation in spatial planning. He writes about eParticipation topics regularly on the Pan-European eParticipation (PEP-NET) blog. Before TuTech, John worked for Birmingham City Council, UK, on several eGovernment and eParticipation projects at a customer-facing and policy level.

Jennifer Jacobs Henderson is an Associate Professor and Chair of the Department of Communication at Trinity University in San Antonio, Texas. Dr Henderson is the author of the 2010 book *Defending the Good News: The Jehovah's Witnesses and Their Plan to Expand the First Amendment*. She specializes in issues of media law, the ethics of media, and the use of participatory cultures for political and social action. For more than a decade, she has been researching how voices outside of American mainstream discourse have pressured the government to expand free-speech protections.

Henry Jenkins is the Provost's Professor for Communication, Journalism, Cinematic Art, and Education at the University of Southern California and author/editor of fifteen books, including *Textual Poachers: Television Fans and Participatory Culture*, *Convergence Culture: Where Old and New Media Collide*, and the forthcoming *Spreadable Media: Creating Value and Meaning in a Networked Culture* (with Sam Ford and Joshua Green).

Barry Joseph directs the Online Leadership Program at Global Kids in New York City. Since 2000 he has developed innovative programs in the areas of youth-led online dialogues, videogames as a form of youth media, the application of social networks for social good, and the educational potential of virtual worlds, mobile phones, and alternative assessments models, always seeking to combine youth development practices with the development of high-profile digital media projects that develop 21st century skills and new media literacies. More information can be found at olp-globalkids.org.

Christopher M. Kelty works at UCLA. He is the author of *Two Bits: The Cultural Significance of Free Software* (Duke University Press, 2008).

Pierre Lévy has devoted his professional life to study the phenomenon of digital-based collective intelligence. He has published a dozen books on this subject that have been translated into more than ten languages. He currently teaches at the communication department of the University of Ottawa (Canada), where he holds a Canada Research Chair in Collective Intelligence. Pierre Lévy is fellow of the Royal Society of Canada and has received several awards and academic distinctions. His last book, *The Semantic Sphere. Volume 1: Computation, Cognition and the Information Economy*, was published in 2011 by Wiley.

Nicky Lewis recently completed her Master's coursework in the Department of Telecommunications at Indiana University. Nicky's research interests involve dimensions of participation in mediated environments, including social media and fantasy sports. Now in her first year of PhD studies, she continues her research in social psychology and mediated competition, specifically in the areas of group processes and the trait and motivational differences that exist among users.

Sophia B. Liu is a Mendenhall Postdoctoral Fellow at the US Geological Survey, conducting research on the integration of official and crowdsourced geographic information pertaining to earthquakes. Dr Liu recently finished her PhD at University of Colorado at Boulder in the Technology, Media and Society interdisciplinary program at the Alliance for Technology, Learning and Society (ATLAS) Institute conducting research in the area of crisis informatics. Her dissertation focused on the use of social media pertaining to historically significant crises and the emergence of socially distributed curatorial practices as a way of managing crisis information in the social media landscape.

Rolf Luehrs is head of the Interactive Communication Department at TuTech Innovation GmbH, Hamburg. The department specialises in eDemocracy and eParticipation projects and is one of Germany's leading solution providers in these domains. Rolf has a Diploma in Sociology and has worked for more than a decade in social science, technology assessment, and online research, and has been involved in many national and European research and development projects. He is coordinator of the Pan-European eParticipation Network (PEP-NET) and is CEO and co-founder of DEMOS Gesellschaft für E-Partizipation mbH. Rolf has authored numerous articles in scientific journals, books, and conference proceedings.

Jenna McWilliams is a doctoral student in Indiana University's Learning Sciences program, where her primary focus is on equity, educational policy, and the role of new media technologies in public education. She blogs about education, human rights, gender politics, and queer issues, making edible playdough is hegemonic (http://jennamcwilliams.com).

Alice Mattoni researches activist media practices, public discourse construction, and struggles against precarity. Dr Mattoni is currently a postdoctoral research fellow at the University of Pittsburgh, where she teaches courses on the sociology of social movements and continues her research on grassroots political communication.

Patrick Meier is internationally recognized for his work on the application of new technologies for crisis early warning, humanitarian response, human rights, and civil resistance. He currently serves as Director of Crisis Mapping at Ushahidi. He previously co-founded the International Network of Crisis Mappers and co-directed Harvard University's Program on Crisis Mapping and Early Warning. He is also a distinguished scholar, holding a PhD from the Fletcher School, a Doctoral Fellowship from Stanford University and an MA from Columbia University. He blogs at iRevolution.net and tweets at @patrickmeier.

Jason Mittell is Associate Professor of American Studies and Film & Media Culture at Middlebury College. He is the author of *Genre and Television: From Cop Shows to Cartoons in American Culture* (Routledge, 2004) and *Television and American Culture* (Oxford University Press, 2009). His newest book projects are *Complex Television: The Poetics of Contemporary Television Narrative* and How to Watch TV (co-edited with Ethan Thompson), both forthcoming from NYU Press.

Sarah Pearce was Project Manager for GridPP, the UK's particle physics computing grid, at the time the Large Hadron Collider particle accelerator was switched on. As well as experience as a science project manager, Sarah has also worked as a science adviser to the UK parliament, where among other tasks she was responsible for the first online consultation run by a UK parliamentary committee. Sarah has a PhD in astronomy, and at the time of publication she was Deputy Chief of Astronomy and Space Science at CSIRO, the Australian research organization.

W. James Potter, Professor at the University of California at Santa Barbara, holds one PhD in Communication Studies and another in Instructional Technology. He has served as editor of the *Journal of Broadcasting & Electronic Media* and is the author of more than a hundred scholarly articles and books including *Media Literacy* (now in its 6th edition), *Theory of Media Literacy: A Cognitive Approach, Arguing for a General Framework for Mass Media Scholarship, The 11 Myths of Media Violence, Becoming a Strategic Thinker: Developing Skills for Success,* and the forthcoming *Media Effects.*

Howard Rheingold is a social critic and media theorist who specializes in the Internet, social media, and digital journalism. He coined the phrase "Virtual Community" in a book documenting his experiences with the WELL, and he is also the author of *Smart Mobs: The Next Social Revolution* (2002) and *Tools for Thought: The History and Future of Mind-Expanding Technology* (2000). He currently teaches a course on digital journalism at Stanford University and a course on virtual community at UC Berkeley.

Suzanne Scott is currently a Mellon Digital Scholarship Postdoctoral Fellow in the Center for Digital Learning + Research at Occidental College. Her dissertation, "Revenge of the Fanboy: Convergence Culture and the Politics of Incorporation," explores the gendered tensions underpinning the media industry's embrace of fans within convergence culture. Her work has been published in the anthology *Cylons in America: Critical Studies in Battlestar Galactica,* and the journals *Spectator* and *Transformative Works and Cultures,* where she currently serves on the symposium editorial team.

Laura Speers is completing a PhD in Culture, Media and Creative Industries at King's College London. Laura's research interests lie in the intersection of youth culture, popular music, and new/digital/social media, with a focus on creativity, authenticity, and identity. She is currently researching how young people use the musical genre of hip-hop to make (sense of) their identity, and how these self and social identities are articulated and performed in local and virtual contexts.

Benjamin Stokes investigates and designs civic media, especially to empower individuals and organizations. Previously he co-founded Games for Change, the branch of the serious games movement focused on social issues and nonprofit organizations. He is a PhD student at the Annenberg School for Communication and Journalism at the University of Southern California. He has also worked at the MacArthur Foundation, NetAid/Mercy Corps, and ProQuest/BigChalk.

Thomas Swiss has published two volumes of poems (*Measure*, University of Alabama; *Rough Cut*, University of Illinois) and many volumes of criticism, including recent volumes on new media poetry and poetics (MIT Press) and Bob Dylan (University of Minnesota Press). His poems have been published in *Ploughshares*, *Iowa Review*, *American Scholar*, *New England Review*, *Agni*, *Postmodern Culture*, and so on. He is Professor of Culture and Teaching at the University of Minnesota.

Paul A. Taylor is a Senior Lecturer in Communications Theory at the University of Leeds Institute of Communication Studies. His research interests include critical theories of mass media culture, psychoanalytically influenced media/film theory, and philosophically informed media criticism. He is the General Editor of the *International Journal of Žižek Studies*, and the author of *Hackers: Crime and the Digital Sublime* (1999) and *Žižek and the Media* (2010).

Will Venters is a Lecturer in Information Systems within the Department of Management at the London School of Economics. His research considers the distributed development of distributed systems. This includes researching grid and cloud computing, global systems development practices, outsourcing, and innovation through examining the work practices of those involved in order to better understand how distributed systems emerge. http://personal.lse.ac.uk/venters.

Jen Ziemke is the co-founder of the International Network of Crisis Mappers, the world's largest and most active international community of experts, practitioners, policy makers, technologists, researchers, journalists, scholars, hackers and skilled volunteers engaged at the intersection between humanitarian crises, technology, and crisis mapping. As a recognized thought leader on conflict processes, she is also Assistant Professor of International Relations at John Carroll University and a fellow at the Harvard Humanitarian Initiative. Jen received her PhD from the University of Wisconsin-Madison (Political Science) and undergraduate degree from the University of Michigan. She has hitchhiked 20,000 miles in over a dozen African countries.

ACKNOWLEDGMENTS

We have many people to thank, most notably the amazing collection of scholars who agreed to take part in this venture, many without knowing us at all. Their work on participatory cultures will endure long after the term has gone out of style. The concepts and ideas they set forth in this volume are groundbreaking, important, and accessible. It was easy to edit such fine work.

We would also like to acknowledge our colleagues in the Department of Communication at Trinity University who thoughtfully encouraged and edited the collection from concept to completion.

We would like to thank Trinity University, an institution that has always given us the freedom to research and teach on the boundaries of communication. Without institutional support, we could have never taught courses such as Media Fandoms, Participatory Cultures, or Reality Hackers, and subsequently would have never edited a book such as this. A special thanks to Dr Michael Fischer, Vice President for Academic and Student Affairs, who has always encouraged us to pursue our passions, no matter how far they stray from the mainstream.

Finally, thank you to our families who have lived with this project as long as we have, and have never complained once when we dominated Thanksgiving Dinner with our longwinded diatribes about participation. They are our source of strength and inspiration.

PART I

Introducing Participatory Cultures

1

INTRODUCTION

What is Participatory Culture?

Aaron Delwiche and Jennifer Jacobs Henderson

> Before you lies cyberspace with its teeming communities and the interlaced ramification of its creations, as if all of humankind's memory were deployed in the moment: an immense act of synchronous collective intelligence, converging on the present, a silent bolt of lightning, diverging, an exploding crown of neurons.
>
> (Pierre Lévy, 1997, p. 236)

In 2006, the MacArthur Foundation launched a $50 million initiative exploring the ways digital media were transforming the lives of young people. As part of this project, a research team headed by Henry Jenkins (2006) mapped the rise of "participatory culture" in contemporary society. In *Confronting the Challenges of Participatory Culture: Media Education for the 21st Century*, Jenkins and his colleagues explain that participatory cultures are characterized by "relatively low barriers to artistic expression and civic engagement, strong support for creating and sharing one's creations, and some type of information mentorship whereby what is known by the most experienced is passed along to novices" (p. 7). "A participatory culture," they add, "is also one in which members believe their contributions matter, and feel some degree of social connections with one another (at least they care what other people think about what they have created)" (p. 7).

One only need visit a local coffee shop or public library to see that people of all ages and backgrounds are increasingly active and engaged in participatory networks. Citizens around the world create and distribute messages via online and interpersonal networks at a rapid and ever-accelerating rate. Armed with inexpensive tools for capturing, editing, and organizing, people tap into a vast ocean of real-time data and multimedia content to promote personal and political interests. Functions once monopolized by a handful of hierarchical institutions (e.g. newspapers, television stations, and universities) have been usurped by independent publishers, video-sharing sites, collaboratively sustained knowledge banks, and fan-generated entertainment.

To date, communication scholars and media literacy educators have focused primarily on the implications of participatory creative cultures, but this is just one aspect of a much larger cultural movement. Our world is being transformed by participatory knowledge cultures in which people work together to collectively classify, organize, and build information—a phenomenon that the philosopher Pierre Lévy characterizes as the emergence of collective intelligence. In our daily life, we engage with this form of participatory culture each time we seek guidance from collaboratively updated websites that review books, restaurants, physicians, and college professors. Participatory knowledge cultures flourish on the Internet each time we exchange advice on programming, cooking, graphic design, statistical analysis, or writing style. These knowledge cultures have become an integral part of our lives; they function as prosthetic extensions of our nervous system and we often feel crippled when our access to these networks is curtailed. It is hard to believe that, for most of recorded history, human beings were unable to instantly find answers to questions such as "How long can I safely store cooked chicken in the refrigerator" or "What should I do about a second-degree burn?"

We are also witnessing the accelerated growth of participatory economic and political cultures. According to Yochai Benkler (2006)—former co-director of Harvard's Berkman Center for Internet and Society—cooperative actions "carried out through radically distributed, nonmarket mechanisms that do not depend on proprietary strategies" are radically transforming the information economy (p. 3). Citizen journalists collect and share information to report on news affecting their local communities. Dissidents use distributed communication technologies to organize political opposition in repressive regimes. Humanitarian workers and activists around the globe use geomapping technologies to monitor elections, coordinate relief efforts, and identify looming environmental disasters. Proponents of information transparency have used websites such as WikiLeaks to disseminate formerly secret documents, sparking riots and toppling governments in the process.

These phenomena generate important questions. As individuals, have we lost the right to keep our personal lives and political opinions secret? What happens to anonymity and privacy in an age of ubiquitous connection? What about intellectual property laws that inhibit our ability to access and communicate within these networks? Is it possible that the illusion of participation in this brave new world cloaks fundamental passivity? What if people don't want to participate? Where is the checkbox that allows us to opt out?

Four Phases of Participatory Culture

Academics often think in terms of disciplinary boundaries, but participatory-culture studies are more properly thought of as an emergent, interdisciplinary project. As early tremors rippled across our global media and technology landscapes, scholars across disciplines noticed common patterns and began referencing each other's work. In fact, some of the most useful research on this topic never uses the phrase "participatory culture." For decades, researchers have been writing about contribution, collaboration, and collective knowledge. In an attempt to get a handle on recent scholarship that provides the foundation for this collection, we suggest that participatory culture studies can be divided into four distinct phases.

Phase One. Emergence (1985–1993)

During the second half of the 1980s, our global communication landscape was already beginning to manifest signs of impending transformation. Personal computers had found their way into the living rooms and offices of ordinary citizens, and networking these machines with one another was the next logical step. ARPANET (the precursor to the civilian Internet) grew exponentially on college campuses and military institutions, and virtual communities emerged in dial-up bulletin board systems (BBS), the Whole Earth 'Lectronic Link, and FidoNet. College radio stations, mix tapes, and independent record labels intersected with the underground music scene. Meanwhile, the advent of laser printers and page layout software put small-scale publishing in the hands of ordinary citizens, accelerating the growth of a vibrant zine subculture.

As these changes unfolded, a growing body of academic research challenged the traditional view of citizens and media audiences as largely passive. In the influential *Television Culture* (1987), John Fiske argued that television viewing audiences regularly resisted, subverted, and recoded the meanings of popular entertainment programs—a process he termed "semiotic democracy." Within Fiske's vision, "individuals can become both producers *and* creators, able to reinscribe and recode existing representations" in a public domain that invites everyone to participate "equally in the ongoing process of cultural production" (Katyal, 2006, p. 3). A similar vision of active audiences was articulated by a promising young scholar named Henry Jenkins—a graduate student who worked with Fiske. Analyzing the behaviors of mostly female *Star Trek* fan fiction writers, Jenkins (1988) argued that these women should be thought of as "textual poachers" who reshape the meanings of cultural products to serve their own needs. Deepening these arguments in his book *Textual Poachers: Television Fans and Participatory Culture* (1992), he became one of the most recognizable thinkers associated with fan culture studies. However, as Jenkins is quick to point out, he was part of a larger movement that included Ien Ang's (1985) *Watching Dallas: Soap Opera and the Melodramatic Imagination*, Janice Radway's (1984) *Reading the Romance: Women, Patriarchy, and Popular Literature*, and Camille Bacon-Smith's (1991) *Enterprising Women: Television Fandom and the Creation of Popular Myth*.

Meanwhile, journalists, scholars, and science fiction writers were taking note of the nascent computer subculture. Anticipating themes that would emerge in subsequent definitions of participatory culture, Steven Levy's *Hackers: Heroes of the Computer Revolution* (1984) argued that computer hobbyists and the technology industry itself were influenced by a "hacker ethic" that celebrated access to technology, the free flow of information, decentralized networks, creative expression, and self-actualization. Howard Rheingold—a technology writer and cultural critic who participated actively in the Whole Earth 'Lectronic Link—coined the term "virtual community" in a 1993 book of the same name that explained on-line computer networks to a general audience. In 1987, Microsoft Press published an updated version of Ted Nelson's *Computer Lib/Dream Machines*—a ground-breaking manifesto dedicated to the radical proposition that *everyone* is capable of understanding how to program their own computers.

Phase Two. Waking up to the Web (1994–1998)

Twenty-five years after the Defense Advanced Research Projects Agency began networking mainframe computers and military researchers, the American public began paying attention to what *TIME* magazine referred to as "the strange new world of the Internet." No longer shackled by a clumsy text interface, the advent of graphical web browsers such as Mosaic made it possible for people to easily search the Internet and create their own web pages. Netscape was the most well-known of the new web browsers, and the company's initial public stock offering was wildly successful, kick-starting a speculative technology bubble (the "dot-com bubble") that lasted five years. These transformative years witnessed the birth of the Internet Movie Database (1993), Yahoo (1994), web-based electronic mail (1994), the Linux operating system (1994), Amazon (1994), streaming audio (1995), Craigslist (1995), eBay (1995), and Google (1996).

The scope and speed of these transformations in our media landscape captured the attention of scholars across disciplines. Working at a macroscopic level, the sociologist Manuel Castells mapped the rapidly changing global infrastructure in *The Rise of the Network Society* (1996), *The Power of Identity* (1997), and *End of the Millennium* (1998). His core message—the notion that decentralized participatory networks were transforming the ways we work, learn, and play—was indirectly supported by a series of more locally focused case studies. Stephen Duncombe's (1997) *Notes from Underground: Zines and the Politics of Alternative Culture* argued that emerging networks of amateur publishers represented a "crack in the seemingly impenetrable wall of the system" and could be interpreted as "a culture spawning the next wave of meaningful resistance" (p. 3). Nancy Baym (1985) appropriated ethnographic research methods from the field of anthropology to document the norms, behaviors, and conversational themes of soap opera fans who posted in Usenet forums. In *Life on the Screen: Identity in the Age of the Internet* (1995) the psychologist Sherry Turkle investigated the interactions of gamers in text-based virtual worlds, suggesting that these spaces could be used as tools for identity experimentation and personal growth. These seemingly disparate case studies were united by their authors' bold insistence that seemingly frivolous social networks were worthy of serious scholarly analysis. Duncombe, Baym, and Turkle demonstrated that the practices and cultural expressions of these amateur publishers, soap opera fans, and computer gamers were both interesting and important. If the first wave of researchers had unlocked the door to participatory culture studies, this second wave kicked the door off its hinges entirely.

Phase Three. Push-button Publishing (1999–2004)

Although it is relatively easy to create web pages with HTML, the mystique surrounding computer programming frightened many people away from creating their own web sites. The advent of user-friendly web publishing systems such as Blogger (1999), LiveJournal (1999), and Xanga (2000) almost completely obliterated remaining barriers to entry, increasing the number of potential participants by several orders of magnitude. During these transitional years, we witnessed the emergence of Napster (1999), the game EverQuest (1999), the iPod (2001), the BitTorrent protocol (2001), the social virtual world Second Life (2003), MySpace (2003), Flickr (2004), Yelp (2004), and Facebook (2004). Though some of these platforms have already crumbled or mutated beyond recognition, each represented a significant step forward in the ability of citizens to share, annotate, publish, and remix digital information.

On the academic front, there were two noticeable strands of research on participatory culture during this phase. The first strand was composed of mostly qualitative case studies. Shifting attitudes about what constituted legitimate research topics, combined with increasingly refined tools and methodologies for studying on-line communities, generated a tsunami of fandom studies on topics ranging from *Buffy the Vampire Slayer* (Hill & Calcutt, 2001) and *Doctor Who* (McKee, 2001) to *Hello Kitty* (McVeigh, 2000) and *Pokemon* (Willett, 2004). A second strand explored macroscopic patterns, interconnections, and technological underpinnings of participatory culture. In the English translation of *Collective Intelligence: Mankind's Emerging World in Cyberspace* (1999), the Canadian philosopher Pierre Lévy identified the existence of a "universally distributed intelligence, constantly enhanced, coordinated in real time, and resulting in the effective mobilization of skills" (p. 13). Pointing out that "no one knows everything" and "everyone knows something," Lévy argued that it was now possible to create democratic political structures in which people could participate directly as unique individuals rather than as members of an undifferentiated mass. Howard Rheingold drew similar conclusions in *Smart Mobs: The Next Social Revolution* (2002), predicting that "large numbers of small groups, using the new media to their individual benefit, will create emergent effects that will nourish some existing institutions and ways of life and dissolve others" (p. xiii). Though optimistic about the potential, he also highlighted such risks as the loss of privacy and the deterioration of private life that one might encounter in a world saturated with network connections.

Phase Four. Ubiquitous Connections (2005–2011)

Made possible as a result of widespread broadband Internet connections, the video-sharing site YouTube (2005) introduced global citizens to a meme-filled world of sneezing pandas, awkward pre-teens, and piano-playing felines. Users immediately bent the platform to their own purposes, experimenting with new forms of citizen journalism, creating performance art projects, designing mash-up music videos, and sharing DIY tutorials on a wide range of topics. No longer constrained to print or audio, digital publishing became transmedia publishing. At roughly the same time, mobile phones were evolving into small hand-held computers with powerful multi-media capabilities. The iPhone (2007), the Android operating system (2008), and the iPad (2010) each played a part in this revolution.

During this most recent phase, researchers have tempered their hopes about the positive potential of participatory culture with an acknowledgment of the many challenges that characterize our increasingly networked existence. In *Free Culture: The Nature and Future of Creativity* (2004), the legal scholar Lawrence Lessig argued that a problematic conceptualization of intellectual property undergirds a draconian regulatory framework which stifles creativity, inhibits popular democracy, and limits the autonomy of the very people it is supposed to protect. Yochai Benkler (2006) made a similar case in *The Wealth of Networks*, hailing "new opportunities for how we make and exchange information, knowledge and culture," while calling on his readers to pay close attention to the laws and institutions that influence the "institutional ecology of the digital environment" (p. 2). During this period, Henry Jenkins's (2006) *Convergence Culture* further developed the author's ideas about the intersection of media convergence, participatory culture, and collective intelligence; a cross-over hit, the book helped make these ideas accessible to a general audience. However, noises of doubt emerged from unexpected quarters. In *Alone Together* (2011), Sherry Turkle argued that ubiquitous technology penetrates every nook and cranny of our lives, leaving us alienated and indifferent. "We expect more from technology," she writes, "and less from each other" (p. 113).

About This Book

As we begin dipping our big toe into Pierre Lévy's "knowledge space," we are confronted with exponentially expanding information, connections, and potential. What shall become of that potential is yet to be known. As many authors in this collection suggest, it might be an expansion of creativity, scientific knowledge, civic engagement, and activism. Or, if others are correct, it could spiral into incivility, passivity, and exclusion. While we cannot see the future clearly, we do know that grappling with these participatory cultures requires new ways of speaking about information, new methods of education, and a rethinking of traditional ownership structures.

Just as Lévy describes our current situation as the "knowledge space" set astride the "commodity space," we also see hybrid creator/consumers of media working alongside traditional media producers and the new theories arising from participatory culture (e.g. informationalism, collective intelligence, transmedia narrative) intersecting with traditional understandings of our postmodern condition. Few doubt that this is a time of transition. This book seeks to be both a snapshot of that transition and a speculative probe into possible futures.

When we recruited authors to participate in this collection, we emphasized three principles. First, these chapters are intended to be accessible to all readers, and therefore free of specialist jargon. This does not mean that the ideas are simple. Readers might occasionally need to look up unfamiliar words or references. However, all of the contributors to this collection share a desire to be understood. Second, to the extent possible, all the contributors have steered away from an emphasis on specific technological platforms. Technology ages quickly; today's buzzwords may be forgotten or laughable tomorrow. By the time this book reaches your hands, your technological landscape might look very different than that of 2012. Yet, the underlying principles, patterns, and challenges endure. Third, you will note that this collection synthesizes contributions from a wide range of disciplines. Geographers. Physicists. Economists. Poets. Game designers. Activists.

Computer pioneers. Cartoonists. The world around us is less constrained than ever by disciplinary boundaries, a condition reflected in this collection.

This book is organized into seven sections. These sections explore fan subcultures, participatory creativity, knowledge cultures, civic engagement, activism, and looming challenges on the boundaries of participatory culture. You are welcome to read the chapters in order, though we find it highly unlikely that most readers will do so. The advent of the web, with its decentralized hyperlinks and stream-of-consciousness lateral browsing, highlighted an unspoken truth about the relationship between authors and readers: we have absolutely no control over how you choose to use this book. You, the audience, are unpredictable, and may choose to consume and participate on your own terms.

At the broadest level, this book wrestles with the hopes, the stumbling blocks, and the potential pitfalls of participation in our rapidly changing world. It is both idealistic and realistic; it is both optimistic and cynical. While recognizing that we are hardly on the brink of Utopia, we agree with Pierre Lévy (1997) that "a new communication space is now accessible, and it is now up to us to exploit its most positive potential on an economic, political, cultural, and human level" (p. ix).

The following pages contain essays from some of our favorite thinkers. Many you know by name; others you may not yet have discovered. They are not housed in one discipline, and certainly not in one university. Their commonality lies in their ability to see a world where participation thrives—on-line and off. As a result, we hope that you will bump into ideas you didn't set out to find. All too often readers forget to browse the stacks, turning instead to recommendations, stars, tomatoes, and "likes." When was the last time you found a new favorite author because a book had been placed on the wrong shelf? When was the last time you picked out your next novel based solely on the beautiful lettering on its binding? We hope this volume reminds you of how wonderful it is to stumble across new concepts and beautiful language. And, of course, how important it is to participate.

References

Ang, Ien. 1985. *Watching Dallas: Soap opera and the melodramatic imagination*. London: Methuen.

Bacon-Smith, Camille. 1991. *Enterprising women: Television fandom and the creation of popular myth*. Philadelphia: University of Pennsylvania Press.

Baym, Nancy. 1995. "From practice to culture on Usenet." In S. L. Star (ed.). *The cultures of computing*. Oxford: Blackwell Publishers, pp. 29–52.

Benkler, Yochai. 2006. *The wealth of networks: How social production transforms markets and freedom*. New Haven, CT: Yale University Press.

Castells, Manuel. 1996. *The rise of the network society*. Malden, MA: Blackwell Publishers.

Castells, Manuel. 1997. *The power of identity*. Malden, MA: Blackwell Publishers.

Castells, Manuel. 1998. *End of the millennium*. Malden, MA: Blackwell Publishers.

Duncombe, Stephen. 1997. *Notes from underground: Zines and the politics of alternative culture*. London: Verso.

Fiske, John. 1987. *Television culture*. London: Methuen.

Hill, Annette and Calcutt, Ian. 2001. "Vampire hunters: The scheduling and reception of *Buffy the Vampire Slayer* and *Angel* in the UK," *Intensities: The Journal of Cult Media*, 1(1).

Jenkins, Henry. 1988. "*Star Trek* rerun, read, rewritten: Fan writing as textual poaching," *Critical Studies in Mass Communication*, 5(2): 85–107.

Jenkins, Henry. 1992. *Textual poachers: Television fans & participatory culture*. New York: Routledge.

Jenkins, Henry. 2006. *Convergence culture: Where old and new media collide*. New York: New York University Press.

Jenkins, Henry, Clinton, Katie, Purushotma, Ravi, Robison, Alice J., and Weigel, Margaret. 2009. *Confronting the challenges of participatory culture: Media education for the 21st century*. Chicago, IL: John D. and Catherine T. MacArthur Foundation.

Katyal, Sonia. 2006. "Semiotic disobedience," *Washington University Law Review*, 84(3): 489–571.

Lessig, Lawrence. 2004. *Free culture: The nature and future of creativity*. New York: Penguin Books.

Lévy, Pierre. 1997. *Collective intelligence: Mankind's emerging world in cyberspace*. New York: Plenum Trade.

Levy, Steven. 1984. *Hackers: Heroes of the computer revolution*. New York: Penguin Books.

McKee, Alan. 2001. "Which is the best *Doctor Who* case story? A case study in value judgments outside the academy," *Intensities: The Journal of Cult Media*, 1(1).

McVeigh, Brian. 2000. "How Hello Kitty commodifies the cute, cool and camp: 'Consumotopia' versus 'control' in Japan," *Journal of Material Culture*, 5(2): 225–245.

Nelson, Ted. 1987. *Computer lib/Dream machines*. Redmond, WA: Tempus Books of Microsoft Press.

Radway, Janice. 1984. *Reading the romance: Women, patriarchy, and popular literature*. Chapel Hill: University of North Carolina Press.

Rheingold, Howard. 1993. *The virtual community: Homesteading on the electronic frontier*. Reading, MA: Addison-Wesley Publishing Co.

Rheingold, Howard. 2002. *Smart mobs: The next social revolution*. Cambridge, MA: Perseus Publishing.

Turkle, Sherry. 1995. *Life on the screen: Identity in the age of the Internet*. New York: Simon & Schuster.

Turkle, Sherry. 2011. *Alone together: Why we expect more from technology and less from each other*. New York: Basic Books.

Willett, Rebekkah. 2004. "The multiple identities of *Pokemon* fans." In Joseph Tobin (ed.). *Pikachu's global adventure: The rise and fall of Pokemon*. Durham, NC: Duke University Press, pp. 226–240.

2

THE NEW LEFT AND THE COMPUTER UNDERGROUND

Recovering Political Antecedents of Participatory Culture

Aaron Delwiche

January 1968: Hundreds of students from Caltech University march through the streets of Burbank. They wave banners, torches and picket signs. Some carry guitars. Their chants fill the streets. Young people raise their voices; they demand to be heard. Despite the emotional intensity, everyone is in a good mood. The crowd chants their demands, but they are also laughing. Bystanders smile as they pass. Today, there will be no tear gas. No salt pellets. No riot police. Just pointy ears.

Few in this crowd anticipate the bleak events that will unfold during the months ahead. Demonstrations will erupt around the globe. Three months from now, Martin Luther King Jr. will be slain on the balcony of the Lorraine Motel. Five months from now, not far from this very spot, Robert F. Kennedy will be killed moments after sweeping the California primaries. Tanks will roll into the streets of Paris, Warsaw, Mexico City, Tokyo, and Prague. In the streets of Chicago, riot police will gas protesters and beat journalists with truncheons. By all measures, it will be a very bad year.

At this moment, the students are more concerned with the fate of James T. Kirk, Spock, and the United Federation of Planets. NBC plans to cancel their favorite television program, and the students are outraged. "Draft Spock!" chants one student. "It is totally illogical to cancel Star Trek" proclaims another. And the good news is that—on this issue at least—the students will succeed. *Star Trek* will survive.

This apparently frivolous *Star Trek* demonstration in Burbank is an important moment of cultural history. If passionate fans had failed to save the program, a University of Wisconsin graduate student named Henry Jenkins (1988) might never have published "*Star Trek* rerun, reread, rewritten: Fan writing as textual poaching" in *Critical Studies in Mass Communication*. He wasn't the first communication scholar to challenge obsolete assumptions about passive media audiences, but Jenkins's essay became the basis for the book *Textual Poachers* (1992), sparking a wave of media fandom studies in the process.

The *Star Trek* demonstration is also a useful marker for thinking about the differences between the early and late stages of the 1960s youth movement. The students marching on NBC Universal expressed earnest optimism, cosmopolitan open-mindedness, and peaceful determination. These traits were closely associated with *Star Trek*'s unique brand of liberal futurism, and they were also core values of the early New Left before movement leaders took their eyes off the prize.

FIGURE 2.1 Caltech students protest the cancellation of *Star Trek* in January 1968
Source: photo by Harry Chase/Los Angeles Times Archive/UCLA.

The most exciting thing about this anecdote is the reminder that the grassroots activism and participatory practices expressed by *Star Trek* fans were firmly situated within the cultural and political climate of the 1960s. This is not a coincidence. The values and technologies that characterize contemporary fan subcultures are the direct outgrowth of participatory ideals articulated by the New Left and youth counterculture.

For several decades, researchers have explored fan communities that use social media and online forums to celebrate, decode, and transform beloved media texts (Jenkins, 1992; Mittell, 2003; Gray, 2010). As this area of study emerged, scholars articulated common understandings about participatory culture's characteristics and origins. Working inductively from a rich collection of case studies and local ethnographies, researchers have demonstrated that participatory cultures are characterized by commitment to access, expression, sharing, mentorship, the need to make a difference, and the desire for social connections (Jenkins, *et al.*, 2009). Scholars have also attempted to sketch the recent history of these social groupings. According to the most widely accepted narrative, participatory subcultures became increasingly visible in the 1980s as a result of three intersecting factors: 1) the horizontal integration of media conglomerates, 2) the emergence of technologies enabling the archival, annotation, and recirculation of media content, and 3) the influence of subcultures that celebrate a do-it-yourself (DIY) ethic.

This explanation is compelling and well argued, but it raises certain questions. Why this particular constellation of values? Why does access go hand in hand with expression? How are these terms linked to social connection, sharing, and the desire to make a difference? Where did all of this energy come from?

The established narrative lacks a crucial component: it has no beginning. It is a superhero comic book without an origin story. This absence is remarkable; the missing bits are fascinating.

Just as Peter Parker's fate was determined by a bite from a radioactive spider, and just as Clark Kent's future was shaped by his parents' decision to hurl him across the galaxy, the most exciting elements of our contemporary media landscape are at least partially indebted to a handful of young activists who gathered for a summer retreat at the FDR Camp in Port Huron, Michigan, in 1962.

A Democracy of Individual Participation

Approximately five dozen members of Students for a Democratic Society (SDS) met in Port Huron in 1962 with the goal of producing a searching critique of contemporary politics and culture. Working from a detailed draft authored by Tom Hayden, they produced the *Port Huron Statement*. Eloquent and politically sophisticated, this "unabashedly middle class" document "thoroughly plumbed and analyzed the conditions of mid-century American society" and "shaped the spirit of the new student mood" (Sale, 1973, p. 50).

Authored at the peak of the "American Century" by privileged, well-educated, and mostly white college students, the statement blended familiar political topics (the military industrial complex, racial discrimination, and poverty) with humanistic musings on loneliness, isolation, and dehumanization (Roszak, 1995). In one of the most well-known passages, the authors placed participatory democracy at the center of their analysis:

> We seek the establishment of a democracy of individual participation, governed by two central aims: that the individual share in those social decisions determining the quality and direction of his life; that society be organized to encourage independence in men [*sic*] and provide the media for their common participation.
>
> *(Sale, 1973, p. 52)*

Of course, this dream was not entirely new. Participatory democracy was not invented by a handful of college students in 1962. What was original about the *Port Huron Statement* was the way that Hayden and his co-authors stitched together strands from multiple theoretical traditions; these included John Dewey's vision of active publics (Berman, 1996), C. Wright Mills's (1958) celebration of free associations as the lifeblood of authentic democracy, and community organizing practices pioneered by the Student Nonviolent Coordinating Committee (SNCC) and the civil rights movement (McMillian, 2011). Taken as a whole, it was a bold new vision.

The audacity of this vision was evident in the statement's approach to emerging technologies. Just two years earlier, in his farewell address to the nation, President Dwight D. Eisenhower had warned against the domination of public policy decisions by a scientific-technological elite. SDS leaders shared this concern, but they were hardly Luddites. Recognizing that the problem was technocracy—not technology—they carefully distinguished machines themselves from the "regime of experts" that deployed them. Anticipating the critique that the statement's demands were idealistic and far-fetched, they explained that new technologies were a plausible mechanism for achieving their objectives. Decades before the advent of the Internet, personal computers, and online forums, they called for mechanisms of voluntary association, civic participation, and public information dissemination. They also advanced the radical suggestion that governments could be made more accountable to citizens through the use of decentralized technological structures "based on the vision of man as master of his machines and society."

The Long Sixties (1958–1974)

An opening shot across the bow of the established political order, the *Port Huron Statement* was one the most important developments during the early years of a period that historian Arthur Marwick (1998) terms "the long Sixties." Even from our vantage point on the other side of the millennium, this era is highly mythologized by those on all sides of the political spectrum. Some view the long Sixties as a hedonistic tragedy in which a disrespectful youth movement corrupted society's moral compass and initiated years of cultural decline. Some are more celebratory, arguing that popular uprisings ended an unjust war and made it possible for disenfranchised citizens to participate fully in American democracy. Others hover somewhere near the middle of these two caricatured perspectives.

However, for many people—certainly for most born after Watergate—the decade is shrouded in the grainy cinematography one might find in an old movie. All history is mediated, but—perhaps due to the explosive growth of electronic communication technologies at the very same time—representations of the 1960s seem particularly prone to distortion. For younger, contemporary audiences, the decade is a hazy assemblage of decontextualized and improperly sequenced signifiers: peace signs, martini glasses, long hair, Hendrix at Woodstock, go-go boots, jungle helicopters, and pitched battles in the streets. Like the protagonist in Dylan's "Ballad of a Thin Man," we know something happened then. We just don't know what it was.

History textbooks used in American classrooms are not much help. For the most part, they subordinate intellectual foundations of the student movement to hyperbolic descriptions of "bad drug trips, sexually transmitted diseases, loneliness and violence" (Henretta *et al.*, 2006, p. 893). These books rarely discuss the movement's textured demands, instead reducing the students' political message to the simplistic mantra "peace and love." This collective amnesia should be deeply troubling to serious students of politics and culture. After all, the core values that defined the early student movement—the insistence on authentic participation and humanized technology—were a potent call that echoed around the world.

Consider the global political struggles that erupted in 1968. From Warsaw to Prague, students and artists in the Eastern Bloc agitated for greater intellectual freedom. In France, student uprisings at the University of Nanterre and Sorbonne University triggered protests across all sectors of society, nearly toppling the De Gaulle administration. Medical students occupied the Yasuda Auditorium clock tower at Tokyo University, spreading student strikes and riots to almost 200 universities across Japan (Steinhoff, 1999). In Mexico City, a series of popular demonstrations in support of university autonomy culminated in the Tlatelolco Massacre of nearly four dozen protesters. These were all different struggles, to be sure, but they were all driven by the demand for authentic participation.

In hindsight, this transcendent yearning for political participation was just as important as the ideological polarities undergirding the Cold War during the second half of the 20th century. The philosopher Hannah Arendt (1970) concluded that the New Left's early emphasis on participatory democracy represented "the best in the revolutionary tradition" and "constituted the most significant common denominator of the rebellions in the East and the West" (p. 54). The global desire for meaningful participation is a thread connecting the struggles of 1968 with one another, but it also connects them to the Eastern Bloc upheavals of 1989 and to the more recent wave of protests throughout the Middle East.

Given its importance, one wonders how so many people could forget the deeper stakes that were linked to this moment in our political history. The psychological state known as "trauma" might have something to do with it. Amnesia is one response to deeply disturbing events, and the violent clashes of the late 1960s and early 1970s were nothing if not traumatic. When one

FIGURE 2.2 Students and teachers at the University of Mexico call for greater autonomy (August 1968)

scrutinizes photographs from global popular uprisings of this time, the images are depressingly uniform. Tanks. Tear gas. Riot police. Truncheons splitting skulls. Demonstrators hurling Molotov cocktails. Blood-drenched students mourning the loss of their friends. These signifiers transcend left-wing/right-wing binaries. The underlying message, the immutable truth, is brutal. These are pictures of naked violence; taken together, they constitute a tapestry of repression.

This is where the story takes an interesting turn. Confronted with increasingly intense repression by the state, a fragmented student movement lost its grip on the substantive and procedural aims that defined its early existence. If the state would not respond to demands of its citizens, a different strategy was needed. In 1969, a militant faction of SDS leaders proclaimed themselves the Weathermen, declared war on the United States government, and announced plans to "lead white kids into armed revolution" (Dohrn, 1970). Other factions followed a similar route. In his history of the SDS, Kirkpatrick Sale notes that, in the 1969–70 school year, there were "174 major bombings and attempts on campus, and at least 70 more off-campus incidents associated with the white left – a rate of roughly one a day" (p. 632). In May 1970, following the Kent State massacre, 16 states activated the national guard 26 times at 21 universities, and "30 ROTC buildings on college campuses were burned or bombed at the rate of more than four every single day" (p. 637).

President Nixon, the FBI, and the militant New Left disagreed on almost everything, but they shared a disturbing tendency to reduce political action and revolutionary change to a clash of physical forces. If one were to agree with this philosophical approach—if pitched battles in the streets would determine the ultimate victors of the long 1960s—the established order would seem destined for victory. After all, the state had a near monopoly on guns, tanks, bombs, prisons, and other tools of physical violence. Law and order candidates such as Ronald Reagan used political unrest as a springboard to national power, and it seemed that the movement had truly lost.

Alienated by the violence, the movement's rank-and-file members headed in multiple directions. Many retreated from politics altogether. By 1976, Seymour Lipset was able to say of American college campuses that "students are working hard, are competitively concerned for grades, and pay little heed to politics" (p. xxvii). The New Left's critics welcomed these events as proof that the notion of participatory democracy was little more than a pipe dream. The movement activists had failed to make their vision permanent. In the pages of *Time* magazine, even Tom Hayden wondered "how could we accomplish so much and have so little in the end?" (1977, p. 67).

However, if the optimism that fueled the movement's most noble aspirations had sometimes been exaggerated, Hayden's pessimistic declaration of failure was equally overstated. The story was still unfolding. In understanding the nature of the movement's long-term accomplishments, we can restore the missing gaps in the history of participatory culture.

In suspense thrillers and action movies, one occasionally stumbles across the trope known as "the false protagonist." Throughout the story, the audience follows one protagonist toward his objective. In the final moments, the apparent hero stumbles and fails. As members of the shocked audience, we wonder if this story will surprise us with an unhappy ending. Then, we realize that the writer has tricked us. A secondary character—some friend of the protagonist—emerges from the periphery and saves the day. She casts the ring into the lake of fire. She smuggles the microfilm across the border. We realize that unsung sidekicks were the heroes all along.

Life is not a movie, and the path of cultural and political change is never clear cut. But history is just another story, and popular tropes can aid our interpretations—if only as thought experiments. The movement celebrities and leaders of the New Left played an important role in the struggle, but *they were not the sole protagonists*. Many years later, one of the founding members of the Weather Underground drew the same conclusion in an essay about the movement's tendency to idolize revolutionary figureheads:

> We don't need great revolutionary heroes—they actually get in the way—but ordinary people taking countless small acts such as talking to their neighbors in order to create the mass movements we need for social change.
>
> *(Rudd, 2008, para. 43)*

Indeed, the activists who made the most difference were those who fanned out across the nation, spreading the seeds of participatory culture and radically transforming the world in which we live. They created "free universities, free clinics, food conspiracies, the underground press, collectives, communes, tribal families, [and] alternate vocations" and "even the technology that was the dominant culture's pride came in for rethinking and remaking" (Roszak, 1995, p. xxvii). Personal computers and digital networks— technologies fueling the growth of participatory culture—were the direct outgrowth of these highly political efforts.

Participatory Culture under Our Skin

Stepping back for a moment, we can revisit the intellectual and strategic topography of the movement during the tumultuous years that followed the crackdowns of 1968. Clear-headed observers recognized that a full frontal assault on the establishment was doomed to failure. At the same time that high-profile radicals made headlines with prison breakouts, bank robberies, and bombings, many movement intellectuals adjusted their tactics to the new political reality.

TABLE 2.1 Subversive Power of New Media

Repressive use of media	Emancipatory use of media
Centrally controlled program	Decentralized program
One transmitter, many receivers	Each receiver a potential transmitter
Immobilization of isolated individuals	Mobilization of the masses
Passive consumer behavior	Interaction of those involved, feedback
Depoliticization	A political learning process
Production by specialists	Collective production
Control by property owners or bureaucracy	Social control by self-organization

Source: Enzensberger, Hans Magnus. 1970. "Constituents of a theory of media," *New Left Review*, I(64).

In a prescient article for *New Left Review*, Hans Magnus Enzensberger (1970) mercilessly dissected the left's traditional skepticism of electronic media. "For the first time in history," he argued, "the media are making possible mass participation in a social and socialized productive process, the practical means of which are in the hands of the masses themselves" (p. 15). "Every transistor radio is, by the nature of its construction, at the same time a potential transmitter" but this is "consciously prevented for understandable political reasons" (p. 15). A truly revolutionary plan, he explained "should not require the manipulators to disappear; on the contrary, it must make everyone a manipulator" (p. 20). Although he did not use the phrase "participatory culture," a more concise definition of the term is difficult to imagine.

The Yippie activist Abbie Hoffman (1980) also realized that culture and communication were crucial vehicles for political transformation. Reflecting on this insight several years later, he wrote:

> A modern revolutionary group headed for the television station, not for the factory. Information was more than a news show; it was punches on an IBM card, scratches on magnetic tape, music, sex, family, schools, fashions, architecture. Information was culture, and change in society would come when the information changed. We would make what was irrelevant relevant. What was outrageous, commonplace. Like freaked-out Wobblies, we would build a new culture smack-dab in the burned out shell of the old dinosaur. (p. 86)

And so he did. Declaring that it was time to transform "improper control of communication in this country," Hoffman and Al Bell launched a newspaper called *Youth International Party Line* (*YIPL*) in 1971. In the first issue, Hoffman (1971a) made it very clear that this was a conscious political tactic. "We did *not* turn our backs on the movement for change," he announced. Later, Hoffman (1971b) explained that "we are attempting to bridge the communication gap generated by monopolies like the BELL SYSTEM, and American mass media too" promising to "spread information that we feel cannot be spread adequately through other means" (p. 3).

One of the first examples of what would eventually be termed "the hacking subculture," the *YIPL* supplemented technical blurbs about phone phreaking with short articles exhorting readers to become involved in other areas of the movement. In one issue, Hoffman asked readers to contribute blank cassette tapes that New York-based WPAX could use to create rock, soul, rap, and education tapes that could be shared with "our people serving in Nam" (p. 3). Several months later, anticipating the "user-generated-content" mantra by more than three decades, Hoffman

(1971c) asked readers to send in any information about phones, food, transportation, and enter-tainment with the goal of the publication eventually becoming "totally reader supplied" (p. 1). Subsequent issues (Hoffman, 1972) deputized readers to create their own local chapters of the Youth International Party Line, urging them to "work with health clinics, food coops, libraries, headshops, day care centers, collectives, radio stations, newspapers, bookstores, or *any* communi-cations medium" (p. 1).

The underground press continued to serve as a vital force during this period. The historian John McMillian argues, in *Smoking Typewriters* (2011), that underground newspapers tied to the New Left played an essential role in circulating the movement's message while circumventing mainstream media filters. The underlying technologies—scissors, rubber cement, and the off-set printing revolution enabling "creatively designed layouts, whereby prose could be fitted around swirling drawings and photo collages"—anticipated the cut-and-paste and sampling techniques witnessed in contemporary participatory cultures (p. 7). Many of the newspapers were decentral-ized collectives in which both content and production were opened up to anyone who expressed interest in participating.

Meanwhile, participatory democracy and computers were merging with one another in the form of experimental education. Between 1967 and 1971, an eclectic network of community organizers, educators, and activists coordinated the Midpeninsula Free University (MFU) to foster "the emergence of a new politics, a new religion, a new education, a new economy, and a new version of humanity based on libertarian, democratic, and communitarian values" (Shugart *et al.*, 1967, p. 3). Organized around the principles of participatory democracy articulated by the New Left, the school taught more than 100 courses on topics ranging from "American Radical Movements," "Computers Now," "Gardening for Amateurs," and "Participatory Salad." Many of the hackers and activists affiliated with the MFU eventually became key players in the Silicon Valley's computer revolution. Larry Tesler, who taught the course "How to end the IBM Monopoly," later worked for Apple Computer where he helped build the Apple Lisa and the Macintosh Plus. Jim Warren, who taught courses on intentional communities and "compassion-ate gentleness," co-founded the West Coast Computer Faire and launched the very first monthly software magazine.

Similar efforts were underway in Berkeley, California, as politicized engineers and program-mers pursued the Community Memory project. Their goal was to build "a communications system which allows people to make contact with each other on the basis of mutually expressed interests without having to cede judgment to third parties" (Levy, 1984, p. 156). Described by Steven Levy as "sort of a squashed piano, the height of a Fender Rhodes, with a typewriter key-board instead of a musical one" the Community Memory terminal was deployed in Leopold's Records on Telegraph Avenue and opened up to community access.

Wildly successful with local residents, the conversations enabled by Community Memory were early forerunners of the interactions one might find in online forums and the comments threads of contemporary web sites. There was, however, one crucial difference. In the 1970s, Berkeley residents were pleasantly surprised by technologies that gave them the ability to interact with one another in unprecedented ways. Today, audience members simply *expect* that such conversational tools will be available on even the most mainstream web sites.

Emerging technologies also intersected with political motivations in the nearby Homebrew Computer Club. The organization was co-founded by Fred Moore, a seasoned activist who had been one of the very first students to speak out against the presence of the military on college campuses. In 1959, appalled by compulsory ROTC enrollment policies at UC Berkeley, Moore fasted for two days on the steps of the campus administration building. More than 1300 students signed his petition, lending their support to what some have characterized as "the opening

FIGURE 2.3 Community Memory Tool in Leopold's Records on Berkeley, *ca.* 1975
Source: image courtesy of Computer History Museum.

political act of the 1960s" (Markoff, 2005, p. 38). Nearly fifteen years later, Moore's computer club was a model of participatory culture and information sharing. Participants exchanged algorithms and design concepts, and "one person's idea would spark another person into embarking on a large project" (Levy, 1984, p. 218). At one club meeting in 1975, an engineer named Dan Sokol supplied a fellow hacker with a box of unused Motorola-compatible computer chips. The hacker's name was Steve Wozniak. Working closely with his childhood friend Steve Jobs, Wozniak stitched these chips together into a circuit board that ultimately became the basis for the Apple II computer.

The notion that individual citizens might someday desire their own personal computers was itself revolutionary, but these machines were still disconnected from one another. As computers became more ubiquitous, technology activists focused their attention on ways that individual machines could be linked up with one another to transform "consciousness and community" (Turner, 2005, p. 489). The Defense Advanced Research Projects Agency (DARPA) had demonstrated that computer networks were possible, but their systems were only available to a handful of scientists and military researchers. Computer hobbyists realized that there must be other ways of accomplishing the same thing.

One networking alternative, FidoNet, was developed by Tom Jennings in 1984. A computer programmer with a penchant for punk rock, Jennings designed an open protocol for freely exchanging messages between bulletin board systems. FidoNet rapidly became a global network, and it was one of the first non-military systems that made it possible for users on opposite sides of the world to participate in online forums and exchange electronic mail. A second network took the form of the Whole Earth 'Lectronic Link (WELL). Co-founded by Stewart Brand, editor of the *Whole Earth Catalog* and occasional guest lecturer at the MFU, the WELL offered an early taste of the virtual communities that would capture the American consciousness in the 1990s. The WELL was firmly rooted in participatory culture, with founding principles that included self-governance, community connections, user-driven design, open-endedness, and low barriers to access. Power was deliberately decentralized and the network's programmers carefully embedded "a countercultural conception of community" into the entire fabric of the system (Turner, p. 498).

Putting the Politics Back in Participatory Culture

This essay is not the first attempt to document the cultural and intellectual currents that helped create our contemporary media landscape. Steven Levy (1984) covers similar ground in his book *Hackers: Heroes of the Computer Revolution*, as do John Markoff (2005) in *What the Dormouse Said: How the 60s Counterculture Shaped the Personal Computer Industry* and Fred Turner (2006) in *From Counterculture to Cyberculture*. However, while some theorists acknowledge connections between the counterculture and contemporary participatory culture, they almost always downplay the political dimensions. This is particularly surprising because the notion of participation is intrinsically political.

Jenkins (2002) briefly acknowledges the influence of the New Left's alternative media practices, but he pays little attention to the many similarities between the student movement and contemporary fan subcultures. Turner (2005) goes even further, explicitly arguing that the New Left's emphasis on "building new political parties and engaging in political struggles" was less significant than the counterculture's emphasis on transforming human consciousness.

Tensions between political and cultural segments of the youth movement have been widely documented. The so-called "hippie–yippie split" reflects the truth that some people are more interested in politics than others. But politics and culture are interdependent and inseparable aspects of the human condition. Recognizing that "the political movement and counter-culture are often treated as if they were separate creations of the sixties," Robert Pardun (2001) emphasizes that "they are really different ends of a spectrum of ideas about how to the change the world." In fact, "the political radicals and the cultural radicals were overlapping parts of the same community, resulting in a movement that was very experimental as it challenged authority and tried to change the world" (p. 2).

This was, ultimately, the key to the movement's victory. Even during the 1980s, when the movement appeared to have lost, the New Left's procedural and substantive yearnings found expression in other arenas. Creative cultures flourished beneath the surface of the mainstream media; many of these cultures were nurtured and extended by mimeographed zines. "While the Left was left behind, crumbling and attracting few new converts," writes the cultural historian Stephen Duncombe (1997), "zines and underground culture grew by leaps and bounds" (p. 3). The seemingly apolitical nature of these subcultural projects helped to further embed participatory culture into the practices of daily life. "Unlike a political treatise or a demagogic speech," notes Duncombe, "the politics of culture never announce themselves as political. As we live our lives and take pleasure in our entertainment, the politics expressed through culture become part of us, get under our skin, and become part of our common sense" (p. 175).

"The Marxists are so busy looking for a revolution which could not happen that they miss the fact that another kind of revolution did happen," argued the historian Arthur Marwick (1998). It was a revolutionary transformation "of the material conditions, lifestyles, family relationships, and personal freedoms for the vast majority of ordinary people" (p. 15).

Ultimately, in the ways that matter most, the activists won when no one was paying attention. The fact that so few people registered their accomplishments is a testimony to the depth of the social transformations. As we gaze nervously toward the coming decades, retrieving the lost history of participatory culture is an essential task. In repudiating the myth of the movement's failure, this narrative demonstrates that seemingly idealistic political and cultural objectives *are* attainable. In the words of Mark Rudd—a former member of the Weather Underground who turned his back on violence and became a teacher—"what an individual does, in concert with others, *can* change the world" (2010, p. 313).

It simply takes a long time.

References

Arendt, Hannah. 1970. *On violence*. New York: Harcourt, Brace, Jovanovich.

Berman, Paul. 1996. *A tale of two Utopias: The political journey of the generation of 1968*. New York: W. W. Norton & Company.

Dohrn, Bernardine. 1970. "Weather Underground declaration of a state of war." Wikisource: The Free Library.

Duncombe, Stephen. 1997. *Notes from underground: Zines and the politics of alternative culture*. London: Verso.

Enzensberger, Hans Magnus. 1970. "Constituents of a theory of media," *New Left Review*, I(64): 13–36.

Gray, Jonathan, 2010. *Show sold separately: Promos, spoilers and other media paratexts*. New York: New York University Press.

Hayden, Tom. 1977. "Elegy for the new left." *Time*, August 15.

Henretta, James, Brody, David, and Dumenil, Lynn. 2006. *America: A concise history*. Boston, MA: Bedford/ St. Martin's.

Hoffman, Abbie. 1971a. *Youth International Party Line*, June.

Hoffman, Abbie. 1971b. *Youth International Party Line*, August.

Hoffman, Abbie. 1971c. *Youth International Party Line*, November.

Hoffman, Abbie. 1972. *Youth International Party Line*, May.

Hoffman, Abbie. 1980. *Soon to be a major motion picture*. New York: Perigee Books.

Jenkins, Henry. 1988. "*Star Trek* rerun, read, rewritten: Fan writing as textual poaching," *Critical Studies in Mass Communication*, 5(2): 85–107.

Jenkins, Henry. 1992. *Textual poachers: Television fans and participatory culture*. New York: Routledge.

Jenkins, Henry. 2002. "Interactive audiences? The 'collective intelligence' of media fans." In *Fans, Bloggers, and Gamers Exploring Participatory Culture*. New York: New York University Press.

Jenkins, Henry, Clinton, Katie, Purushotma, Ravi, Robison, Alice J., and Weigel, Margaret. 2009. *Confronting the challenges of participatory culture: Media education for the 21st century*. Chicago, IL: John D. and Catherine T. MacArthur Foundation.

Levy, Steven. 1984. *Hackers: Heroes of the computer revolution*. New York: Penguin Books.

Lipset, Seymour Martin. 1976. *Rebellion in the university*. Chicago, IL: University of Chicago Press.

McMillian, John. 2011. *Smoking typewriters: The sixties underground press and the rise of alternative media in America*. Oxford: Oxford University Press.

Markoff, John. 2005. *What the dormouse said: How the 60s counterculture shaped the personal computer industry*. New York: Viking Penguin.

Marwick, Arthur. 1998. *The sixties: Cultural revolution in Britain, France, Italy, and the United States, c. 1958–c.1974*. Oxford: Oxford University Press.

Midpeninsula Free University. 1967. *Midpeninsula Free University Course Catalog*, fall.

Mills, C. Wright. 1958. *The causes of World War Three*. London: Secker & Warburg.

Mittell, Jason. 2003. "Audiences talking genre: Television talk shows and cultural hierarchies," *Journal of Popular Film and Television*, 31(1): 36–46.

Pardun, Robert. 2001. *Prairie radical: A journey through the sixties*. Los Gatos, CA: Shire Press.

Roszak, Theodore. 1995. *The making of a counterculture: Reflections on the technocratic society and its youthful opposition*. Berkeley, CA: University of California Press.

Rudd, M. 2010. *Underground: My life with SDS and the Weathermen*. New York: Harper.

Sale, Kirkpatrick. 1973. *SDS*. New York: Vintage Books (Random House).

Shugart, Diana, Groen, Fran, Goldman, Judi, Powers, Kathy, and Larimore, Joan. 1967. *Midpeninsula Free University Course Catalog*. Menlo Park, CA: Nowels Publications.

Steinhoff, Patricia.1999. "Student protest in the 1960s." *Social Science Japan*, 15(3): 3–7.

Turner, Fred. 2005. "Where the counterculture met the new economy: The WELL and the origins of virtual community." *Technology and Culture*, 46(3): 485–512.

Turner, Fred. 2006. *From counterculture to cyberculture: Stewart Brand, the Whole Earth Network, and the rise of digital utopianism*. Chicago, IL: University Of Chicago Press.

3

FROM PARTICIPATION TO POWER

Christopher M. Kelty[1]

A 2010 *New Yorker* article by Malcolm Gladwell compared the civil rights activism of the 1960s to contemporary social media activism. He found the claim of a social media revolution wanting, and in particular that, unlike the civil rights activists of the 1960s who risked bodily harm, people who participate via social media in activist causes are engaged in a low-risk activity, unlikely to cause significant change in the world. The reasoning he gave for this was typically Gladwellian in its movement between anecdote and scholarly abstraction. He suggested that, because social media is a "weak tie" phenomenon, it does not demand sacrifice from people; and because sacrifice requires discipline it requires hierarchy; and as hierarchy is opposed to networks, social media must be networks, not hierarchies. The rub, he argued, was that an activism that relies on networks instead of hierarchies privileges adaptability and resilience over strategic and disciplined confrontation. Ergo if we rely on networks in the face of danger, we will not survive. Real change requires disciplined hierarchical organization; resilient adaptability is pyrrhic change. Gladwell concluded:

> The instruments of social media are well suited to making the existing social order more efficient. They are not a natural enemy of the status quo. If you are of the opinion that all the world needs is a little buffing around the edges, this should not trouble you. But if you think that there are still lunch counters out there that need integrating it ought to give you pause.

Predictably, the blogs and tweets were alight for twenty-four to forty-eight hours afterwards as people debated his conclusions, argued the issue and then ultimately moved on to the next issue (a proof in its own way, perhaps, of Gladwell's argument about discipline). But none of the responses asked a simple question: *are networks and hierarchies mutually exclusive*? Gladwell turned these abstract social forms into concrete objects, and he was not alone in doing so. Insisting on such an opposition was a good way to stir up the hornets' nest of social media users; they found no fault, perhaps surprisingly, with the premises of the article, and instead exerted their diffuse uncoordinated energy investigating flaws in the ensuing argument.

Like so much writing about social media, Gladwell's argument (and the discussions that followed) erases distinctions rather than enabling more precise ones. Rather than encouraging the kind of collective, creative exploration and questioning that new media are often credited with, such a discussion blinds people to the possibility of seeing things another way. Are networks and hierarchies mutually exclusive? Are they even the right terms of analysis for what is happening to participation today? What might the right terms be?[2]

Scholarship of the last decade has proliferated terms and concepts to explain the effects of the Internet and new media on participation: terms such as 'peer production' (Benkler, 2006), 'produsage' (Bruns, 2008), 'the wisdom of crowds' (Surowiecki, 2004), "prosumers/prosumption" (Toffler, 1980; Ritzer & Jurgenson, 2010), the 'network society' (Castells, 1996; 2001), 'user-led innovation' (von Hippel, 2005), 'recursive publics' (Kelty, 2008), 'creation capitalism' (Boellstorff, 2008), 'convergence culture' (Jenkins, 2006), 'organized networks' (Rossiter, 2006; Lovink and Rossiter, 2005), 'wikinomics' (Tapscott and Williams, 2006), or 'networked publics' (Varnelis, 2008; boyd, 2008).

Clearly more is at stake than simply whether social media are hierarchical or network forms. But this list also suggests a different analytical problem. All of these terms refer to social media, the Internet, software, fan cultures and "knowledge societies," but *not to each other*: they are the scholarly equivalent of proprietary formats, they lack compatibility, interoperability, or convertibility. In part this is a problem of lingering disciplinary allegiances—each analysis must pay tribute to the terms and debates of the disciplines from which it emerges. And, even in the case where scholars work within closely related disciplines, there is a need, a demand, to invent new terms and to "brand" one's research rather than adopting the terms and practices of another.

What would it mean, therefore, to view participation in a *naturalistic* light: to simply present the practices and organizational formations of participation and ask, "What is that?" How is Facebook different from Linux different from Second Life different from barackobama.com? How are they organized and for whom? Do they interact with each other and how? And can we design a language that allows for comparison across diverse forms of participation today—and possibly across disciplines as well?

The Natural History of Participation

What is participation like today? How has it become newly important with respect to yesterday? Are participatory democracy, audience participation, user-generated content, peer production, participant-observation, crowdsourcing all the same phenomena? If they are different, what characterizes the difference?

One can identify a subtle shift with respect to participation by dwelling on one of the definitions provided by the *Oxford English Dictionary*:

> The process or fact of sharing in an action, sentiment, etc.; (now *esp.*) active involvement in a matter or event, esp. one in which the outcome directly affects those taking part. Freq. with *in*. Cf. *audience participation* at AUDIENCE n. 7d.

In this definition, there is a loop: one participates because the outcome directly affects the one participating. Participatory democracy, by this definition, is not representative but direct—and direct in the sense that participating in democratic politics directly benefits the participant (with the implication that in a government of, by and for the people, it is a benefit to all).

But it is not only the participant's perspective that is at stake today: increasingly, and for obscure reasons, those who provide the capacity for participation expect something as well. Participation is now a two-way street. Governments now *provide* participatory democracy, citizens are *engaged* by the government or corporations, and publics are constituted, consulted, and used to legitimate decision-making. Similarly, organizations regularly solicit not just purchases or opinions, but also participation in innovation, in marketing, and in the creation of lifestyles, cultures, and loyalties.

Whereas participation is at first glance understood to primarily benefit the participants—whether conceived as a collection of individuals or a collective body—at second glance it is clear that participation is now expected to have an effect on the structures, institutions, organizations, or technologies in which one participates. Participation is no longer simply an opening up, an expansion, a liberation, it is now also a principle of improvement, an instrument of change, a creative force. It no longer threatens, but has become a resource: participation has been made *valuable*.

Consider Gladwell's invocation of the civil rights movement. Two kinds of participation were at stake in that moment: participation in the movement itself (through networks of friends, churchgoers, and neighbors) and participation in the process of local and national government itself, namely *enfranchisement* (a core goal of the movement). Civil rights leaders provided a framework for participating in the movement (with elements of both hierarchy and networks) and, as they expanded the networks, the benefits from participation accrued both to individuals and to the movement as it grew. The US government, by contrast, opposed participation by these very citizens—such participation was something to fear, to prevent, to mishandle, or sabotage, whether that meant ignoring local laws concerning lunch counters, or blocking equal access to the voting booth. One organization facilitated and expected returns from participation; the other sought to restrict and delimit participation.

Contrast this with, for instance, the so-called Twitter revolution in Iran. In that case, there are at least three distinct forms of participation at stake: 1) participation in a movement to achieve democratization in Iran that took myriad forms, and consisted of many different structures that might enable that participation; 2) participation in the government of Iran (the goal of the movement); and 3) participation *in Twitter itself*. The first of these benefitted in many ways from the third, but they are not one and the same thing.

In both cases, civil rights and Twitter in Iran, two different questions are collapsed and confused: first, what kinds of participatory structures do organizations, movements, or governments create? This is a question one can ask equally of the civil rights movement, the US and Iranian Governments, and Twitter. The second, however, is how does participation in the civil rights movement, or in Twitter, *affect or transform* the structure of participation in the US or Iranian government? This is a different kind of question, one concerned with the best possible strategies and tactics for achieving change in a particular structure (a national government). It is also a question that could be asked of the civil rights movement or Twitter (i.e. what is the best strategy for changing the structure of participation in Twitter?), assuming one wanted to protest, resist, or transform those organizations. The confusion begins as soon as one sees participation in Twitter as tantamount to participation in the Iranian government. But Twitter encourages participation in particular ways, while the Iranian government discourages it in particular and often brutal ways. Participation is a pluralistic thing, and it helps to distinguish the good from the bad.

The expectation that participation will yield outcomes for both participants and those structuring participation takes many forms; it is impossible to assess the meaning and effect of participation without making some distinctions that might be useful across the range of social reality—and not only in those places where specific technologies or specific forms of organization are present. The goal of distinctions is to produce comparisons that allow one to evaluate claims about what a thing is and what it can do. Such distinctions cannot answer the question of whether Twitter is democratic or not, but they can help articulate why that might not be a meaningful question.

Structure: Platform as Problematization

To understand the difference between forms of participation today, it is necessary to start with the question of organization. To be sure, the concepts of hierarchy, market, and network are important—but they are not the only concepts in play today. As Tarleton Gillespie (2010) has recently pointed out, the major players in new media and social media don't talk much about hierarchies and networks, they talk about "platforms." The work of a term like "platform" is not to refer to real things in the world, but to diagnose. When people use the term "platform" it is a sign that something about our existing terms and understandings of organizations, goals, boundaries, and their structure has been jostled loose—problematized. "Platforms" as Gillespie analyzes them are not websites, not companies, not technologies, nor the "social networks" themselves. The term is rhetorically allied with participation: it raises people up, it levels the field, it structures from below, not from above, and so on. But what it really reveals is a lack of words and concepts for making sense of the concrete assemblages and apparatuses that respond to this problematization of participation and organization.[3] As Gillespie notes, platforms also have edges, and finding these edges requires careful analytical work.

Wikipedia, for instance, is alternately referred to as an encyclopedia, a website, a cult, a platform, a community, a public, and a project. It is not referred to as a corporation or a non-profit organization, though it does have various members who deal with financial issues of sustainability and practical issues of organization and planning—separated out as an official foundation called Wikimedia. Clearly it possesses elements of both publics and organizations, communities and non-profits, hierarchies and networks.

It helps to make a distinction between a *Formal Social Enterprise* and an *Organized Public*. The point of this distinction is to capture, first, a simple and arbitrary distinction between formal and informal organization. On the one hand, a formal social enterprise is defined as any organization with a formal, especially a state-sanctioned legal and/or regulated existence: such as a for-profit or non-profit organization, a foundation, a university research center. Members of the organization are contractually obligated to it, and those obligations mediated by legal and technical tools like salaries and employment contracts, ID cards, offices, letterhead and email addresses, a sense of identity as an insider, a role as a manager, an employee, a consultant, a board member, an adviser, etc. Such enterprises can be organized horizontally, vertically, loosely networked, or densely and hierarchically controlled. Formal enterprises limit social access and define decision-making power. In this sense they are clearly on the "organization" side of the organization/public divide.

Opposite the formal organizations with their contracts and historically recognized modes of belonging are organized publics. Organized publics differ because belonging and membership is informal, temporary, and constituted primarily through attention. Depending on one's commitments and capacities, one could belong to several different organized publics at the same time (and, hence, there may be more or less overlap across any given set of projects, as depicted in Figure 3.1). Warner (2002) defines publics as *ad hoc* entities that come into existence only when addressed and exist only while they pay attention to that address. In his definition the form of address is classically discursive: constituted through speech and writing addressed to an imagined public that can read and respond, directly or indirectly. But that address is also technical in the sense of mediated by the forms and technologies of address and circulation. Participation in a public is at some level structured by "platforms."

Given this important structural clarification, what might the cases of the civil rights movement and Twitter in Iran look like? On the one hand, the students at the lunch counter in Greensboro, North Carolina, were very much part of an organized public: they were addressed by, and paid attention to, movement leaders, journalists, op-eds, and local discussion. They were not, at least

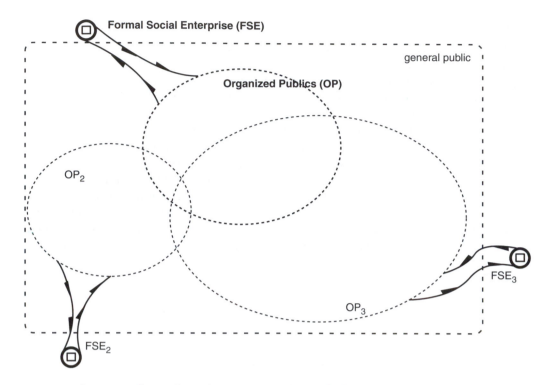

FIGURE 3.1 Structure of Formal Social Enterprises and Organized Publics

not initially, formal representatives of organizations like the National Association for the Advancement of Colored People (NAACP) or Student Nonviolent Coordinating Committee (SNCC). Indeed, one might see the history of the civil rights movement differently by using this distinction to ask how participation in the movement was structured in order to achieve participation in national politics.

In the case of Twitter in Iran, there were two different relations at stake: one was the relationship between the heterogeneous groups of public protestors and the formal organizations that tried to represent them; the other is the relationship between Twitter, Inc. and Twitter users, in Iran and elsewhere. In the first case, participation was not structured by any particular formal social enterprises—indeed, formal organizations contesting the regime are illegal in Iran, and exist primarily outside of the country. In this respect, there was perhaps very little "organization" to the public, and what little there was came through the technical affordances of Twitter, Facebook, email, cell phones, and the other local media that allow a public to loosely coordinate its actions, or prevent it. The absence of formal organizations of protest and participation are compensated with a politics of technical capacities.

In the second case, however, Twitter, Inc. more or less autocratically structures participation in Twitter. They can pull the plug if they want to, they can succumb to the pressures of national governments, they can fall victim to hackers and other direct attacks. Twitter users have very little say in how Twitter is structured, and no option for changing that other than to opt out of using it. One can imagine, then, the interlocking effects of 1) participation in the green revolution in 2009 and 2) participation in Twitter, without reducing one to the other—and both possess elements of hierarchies, networks and markets.[4]

Do organized publics and formal social enterprises include everyone? What about all the people who are neither protesters nor Twitter users? In the broadest possible sense this "General Public" cannot be said to exist as an actual entity, but only as a kind of virtual entity. If one must pay attention to become part of a public, or make a choice to become part of an organization, then the general public consists only of those people who are not making choices or paying attention. What is important about this notion is that the boundary between a general public and an organized public is porous, and the boundary between a general public and a formal enterprise is not (represented in Figure 3.1 by the path of the dashed line). To put it more precisely, organized publics become real instances of a virtual general public instantaneously: as soon as a group of individuals begins to pay attention to something, and continues so long as they interact with others who are also paying attention. This could mean watching a video online, signing up for an account, or joining protesters in the street, etc. Almost by definition, organized publics are defined such that "anyone can join"—anyone can sign up for a Facebook account; anyone can edit a Wikipedia page; anyone can shoot and upload a YouTube video; anyone can don a green armband.

By contrast, formal enterprises are not formed as instances of a general public; they are not formed by mere attention but by formal two-way recognition. Signed employment contracts, salaries, titles and roles, or other forms of official recognition are the relevant signs of participation in an enterprise, whereas attention and address are those of participation in a public. Needless to say, a select few can be members of both.

Comparing classic political participation to participation in social media or Free Software or fan fiction today reveals that there is not always a strong coupling between formal organizations and organized publics. Some publics—like civil rights protestors or Iranian protestors—are very loosely coupled, or sometimes completely unconnected, to formal organizations. But examples like social media, Free Software, or American political campaigns almost always evidence a much tighter coupling between a formal enterprise and an organized public of participants.

Resources, Tasks, and Goals: What Does Participation Do?

The *distinction* between a formal enterprise and an organized public can serve as a starting point for exploring in more detail the *relationship* between the two, and ultimately the way that relationship distributes rights, power, and resources under the label of "participation" or "democratization." For every formal enterprise and its organized public there is at least one *resource* valued by both. The term resource is deliberately vague in order to resist identifying the object of value with a technology or consumer product or service—it could just as well be knowledge, volunteer hours, or editorial decisions. It might be a resource that is transferred between an enterprise and a public (the classic model of a producer and a consumer, or a laborer and an employer) or it might be a resource that is co-produced or co-consumed by both. In any case, questions of ownership and decision-making about the resource should be at the forefront of any analysis.

It makes less sense to talk about the shared "resource" of a civil rights movement (attention? political power? critique?) than it does to speak of cases like Wikipedia or Apache Software Foundation, where the resource is a product (software in the case of Apache, collaborative articles in Wikipedia) or process ("liking" or "digging" as tools of moderation and promotion in Facebook or Digg). Whereas a civil rights public alone might not identify a concrete resource as its reason for existing (instead of goal or set of abstract values), wherever there is both a formal enterprise and an organized public, there is likely to be a concrete (and contested) resource of value for both the formal enterprise and the informal public.

Despite the fact that a great many resources are "free" in one or more senses (*gratis* and free from restrictions), they must nonetheless be actively governed to be of value. To understand the relationship between an instance of participation and a resource produced, it helps to conceive of organized action by a Formal Social Enterprise and an organized public in two ways: first, setting goals concerning the resource produced, and second, assigning specific tasks that produce the resource.

Conceiving of the goals and tasks in this way allows one to ask specific questions about each instance of participation—What is/are the resource(s)? What rights to a resource do people in a formal enterprise have vs. the rights of those in an organized public vs. those of everyone else (the general public)? Who decides goals and who has ultimate authority over a resource? Who manages tasks, assigns them, or encourages participation? How modular/granular are tasks (i.e. how small is a task and how finely divided in order to achieve something)? What is the cost of performing a task? Who can use, change, fork, or make claims about a resource? Who takes legal responsibility   for a resource? Who is the maintainer of last resort? How, for instance, is a piece of free software (governed by a copyleft license) different from a *Current TV* broadcast (owned and controlled by Current) from an iPhone app (owned by its author but controlled by Apple)? Are the resources "tethered" (controlled by Apple) or are they "generative" (allow for unconstrained re-use, remixing, or republication) (Zittrain 2008)?

Zittrain (2008) has refined this approach somewhat by distinguishing *tethered* and *generative* resources. In addition to copyleft licenses, Zittrain's distinction concerns the management of the infrastructure through which resources are available. *Generative* resources are easily available, without the permission of any FSE, for re-use, improvement, or transformation, whereas *tethered* resources are managed at the sole discretion of the FSE and require either legal or technical permission in order to be modified.

Just as we saw that there is more than one kind of participation at stake in civil rights movements (participation in the movement itself vs. participation in the process of political power), there is a difference between participation in the goals of a project, and participation in the *tasks* it sets out to perform. It is one thing to be invited to *design* a game, for instance, and quite another to be invited to *play* it. It is one thing to design a strategy for public protest, and another thing to be a participant in that designed protest. Some projects that emphasize participation blend these two activities (as in the Wikipedia "discuss" pages, which can be *de facto* sites of policy discussion) and some try to keep them separate as in the case of online gaming environments and virtual worlds.

Goals may be implicit or explicit, and tasks can be *voluntary* (self-chosen tasks that require some minimum level of conscious effort), *assigned*, or even *involuntary* (tasks that people may not know they are performing). An interesting contrast emerges between a case like the civil rights movement and a Free Software project. In the former, like most social movements, goals are explicit, frequently discussed (integration, suffrage, economic and political self-sufficiency), and often the bases of disagreements about the appropriate means (the tasks) for achieving those goals (NAACP vs. Black Power). In most Free Software projects, by contrast, goals are implicit, diffuse, and discussed much less than the practical problems of creating software (the tasks at hand). But, in both cases, the relationship between the formal enterprise and its organized public helps determine the level of involvement in both goal-setting and the execution of tasks: both theory and practice.[5]

The Macrostructure of Power

Questions about the structure of participation, or about the resources, goals, and tasks, are best directed at the internal workings of specific projects and comparison amongst them.

However, when it comes to the question of sustainability, profitability, and power, a macrostructure of relationships must also be distinguished. Because participation has been made valuable, a number of other roles emerge, specifically those of elites and clients.

On the one hand all successful projects appeal to elites of one form or another: venture capitalists, advisory boards, founders, shareholders, political allies, etc. Such elites may emerge through participation (as frequent contributors to Free Software projects or Wikipedia often do) or approached independently (beseeched in the case of venture capitalists or invited to oversee in the case of advisory boards). Participatory structures differ depending on the nature of how these elites are chosen, elected, or organically evolved. Often elites have more direct say in the governance of goals, and less interest in participation at the level of tasks.

On the other hand, *clients* form a category separate from both elites and participants. Clients are often those for whom participation is valuable but who may or may not provide structures of participation themselves: advertisers, corporations, researchers, non-profits, or governments. YouTube, for instance, has increasingly developed partnerships with clients—entertainment companies, advertisers, universities, and so on—that determine specific aspects of how uploaded videos are treated, how or if they will be promoted, branded, or categorized, and from and to whom revenue for advertising will flow. Or to take a very different example, the Linux Foundation (which now oversees the development of the Linux kernel) has clients such as Google and IBM who contribute via donations in order to support the development by programmers (participants), some of whom may well be salaried employees of those companies. Clients influence the structures of participation in ways that are different from the influence of participants themselves, or of elites. It might be said that they have a more direct access to the governance of tasks as opposed to the outcomes of those tasks.

Conclusion

Participation is a plural thing, and its relationship to power is continuously being obscured. The foregoing distinctions are avowedly abstract, but such distinctions are necessary in order to diagnose the problems of our contemporary moment. "Participating" in Facebook is not the same thing as participating in a Free Software project, to say nothing of participating in the democratic governance of a state. If there are indeed different "participatory cultures" then the work of explaining their differences must be done by thinking concretely about the practices, tools, ideologies, and technologies that make them up. Participation is about power, and, no matter how "open" a platform is, participation will reach a limit circumscribing power and its distribution. Understanding those limits requires carefully describing the structures of participation, the processes of governance and inclusion, the infrastructure of software, protocols and networks, as well as the rhetoric and expectations of individuals.

Part of this analysis is the testing of cases, and the rectification of distinctions. The civil rights movement, for instance, or the Twitter revolution provide material to think with not only in static, generalizing terms, but in specifically historical ones as well. The media situation of civil rights activists in the 1960s is in fact much different from that of the Twitter users in Iran in 2009. For one, participation has been made more tractable and concrete. Protest becomes feedback, deliberation becomes interactivity, voting becomes liking and digging. But to suggest these forms *replace* one another is to miss the ways in which they actually *supplement* each other. We proliferate ways of governing ourselves and others as we proliferate these tools, technologies, platforms, or networks—and in the process change what it means (and meant) to interact, vote, and protest. Participating in Twitter, or Facebook, or Free Software is not the same thing as participating in democracy, but it does change what democracy will become.

Notes

1 This chapter includes condensed versions of a larger text, Adam Fish, Luis F.R. Murillo, Lilly Nguyen, Aaron Panofsky and Christopher Kelty. 2011. "Birds of the Internet: A field guide to understanding action, organization, and the governance of participation," *Journal of Cultural Economy*, 4(2): 157–187.
2 Kreiss *et al.* (2011) suggest that the consensus around participatory peer production ignores the advantages conveyed by bureaucracies, and that a more careful Weberian analysis can help clarify the debate about social media.
3 On the terms *problematization*, *apparatus*, and *assemblage*, see Rabinow, 2003: 44–56.
4 Often social media are referred to as amorphous, anarchic, or self-organizing, but much research contradicts this: Free Software communities evidence clear, but highly variable, organizational structures (Weber, 2004; Feller, et al., 2005). Wikipedians have over time evolved a "hidden order" (Viégas, *et al.*, 2007) that is enforced through apprenticeship, communication of norms, and censure. FOSS projects are frequently governed by norms and moral imaginaries that are communicated horizontally amongst participants. Some projects have formalized the apprenticeship process, as in the case of the Debian New Maintainer Process studied by Coleman (2005).
5 Tasks can be further distinguished by their degree of modularity and granularity (Benkler 2006), and subsequent cost of performing the task. At one extreme of modularity and granularity are tasks whose effort is low, a simple Mechanical Turk task; at the other end are intensive and time-consuming tasks (writing a device driver for Linux, producing a documentary about the Gaza Strip for *Current TV*); there may also be room for considering the risk involved with completing a task (i.e. joining the lunch counter vs. signing the petition).

References

Benkler, Y. 2006. *The wealth of networks: How social production transforms markets and freedom*. New Haven and London: Yale University Press.
Boellstorff, Tom. 2008. *Coming of age in Second Life: An anthropologist explores the virtually human*. Princeton, NJ: Princeton University Press.
boyd, danah. 2008. *Taken out of context: American teen sociality in networked publics*. SSRN eLibrary (December 9). http://papers.ssrn.com/sol3/papers.cfm?abstract_id=1344756.
Bruns, Axel. 2008. *Blogs, Wikipedia, Second Life, and beyond: From production to produsage*. New York: Peter Lang Publishing.
Castells, Manuel. 1996. *The rise of the network society, the information age: Economy, society and culture Vol. I*. Cambridge, MA; Oxford, UK: Blackwell.
Castells, Manuel. 2001. *The Internet galaxy, reflections on the Internet, business and society*. Oxford, Oxford University Press.
Coleman, E. Gabriella. 2005. *Three ethical moments in Debian*. SSRN eLibrary (September 15). http://papers.ssrn.com/sol3/Papers.cfm?abstract_id=805287.
Feller, Joseph, Fitzgerald, Brian, Hissam, Scott, and Lakhani, Karim (eds). 2005. *Perspectives on free and open source software*. Cambridge, MA: MIT Press.
Fish, A., Murillo, L. F. R., Nguyen, L., Panofsky, A., and Kelty, C. M. 2011. "Birds of the internet: Towards a field guide to the organization and governance of participation," *Journal of Cultural Economy*, 4(2): 157–187.
Gillespie, Tarleton. 2010. "The politics of 'platforms,'" *New Media and Society*, 12(3): 347–364.
Gladwell, Malcolm. 2010. "Small change," *New Yorker*, October 4.
Jenkins, Henry. 2006. *Convergence culture: Where old and new media collide*. New York: NYU Press.
Kelty, Christopher M. 2008. *Two bits: The cultural significance of free software*. Durham, NC: Duke University Press.
Kreiss, D., Finn, M., and Turner, F. 2011. "The limits of peer production: Some reminders from Max Weber for the network society," *New Media & Society*, 13: 243–259. http://nms.sagepub.com/cgi/content/abstract/13/2/243.
Lovink, Geert and Rossiter, Ned. 2005. "Dawn of the Organized Networks," *Fibreculture Journal*, 5.
Rabinow, Paul. 2003. *Anthropos today: Reflections on modern equipment*. Princeton, NJ: Princeton University Press.

Ritzer, G. and Jurgenson, N. 2010. "Production, consumption, prosumption: The nature of capitalism in the age of the digital 'prosumer,'" *Journal of Consumer Culture*, 10(1): 13–36.

Rossiter, Ned. 2006. *Organized networks: Media theory, creative labour, new institutions*. Rotterdam: NAi Publications and Institute for Network Cultures.

Surowiecki, James. 2004. *The wisdom of crowds: Why the many are smarter than the few and how collective wisdom shapes business, economies, societies, and nations*. New York: Random House.

Tapscott, D. and Williams, A. 2006. *Wikinomics: How mass collaboration changes everything*. New York: Portfolio.

Toffler, Alvin. 1980. *The Third Wave*. New York: Bantam Books.

Varnelis, Kazys. 2008. *Networked publics*. Cambridge, MA: MIT Press.

Viégas, Fernanda, Wattenberg, Martin, and McKeon, Matthew. 2007. "The hidden order of Wikipedia. Online communities and social computing." In D. Schuler (ed.). *Online communities and social computing (HCII 2007), lecture notes in computer science*. Berlin: Springer, pp. 445–454.

Von Hippel, Eric. 2005. *Democratizing innovation*. Cambridge, MA: MIT Press.

Warner, Michael. 2002. *Publics and counterpublics*. Cambridge, MA: Zone Books.

Weber, Steven. 2004. *The success of open source*. Cambridge, MA: Harvard University Press.

Zittrain, Jonathan. 2008. *The future of the Internet and how to stop it*. New Haven: Yale University Press.

PART II

Understanding Participatory Fan Cultures

4

WIKIS AND PARTICIPATORY FANDOM

Jason Mittell

Few technological developments have had more of a visible impact on participatory culture in the 2000s than the wiki. Although the software was designed for small-scale and local uses, wikis have emerged as a major tool used by Internet users on a daily basis. From the world's most popular encyclopedia, Wikipedia, to hundreds of specialized sites serving a vast array of subcultures and groups, wikis have become one of the hallmark tools of the participatory Internet. This article will outline the development of wikis as a software platform and the cultural rise of Wikipedia before considering a range of participatory practices tied to one of the most widespread uses of wikis: as a tool for online fandom.

The Rise of the Wiki and Wikipedia

Wikis date back to the earliest years of the World Wide Web. As the web was emerging as a public platform in the early 1990s, software developer Ward Cunningham was looking for an easy-to-use tool to enable collaborative conversations about programming ideas. His solution was WikiWikiWeb, named after the Hawaiian word "wiki" meaning "quick." Launched in 1995 to facilitate discussions among programmers, Cunningham's wiki software followed basic principles that are still in use among most wikis today. A wiki is designed to be viewed in any web browser, from primitive applications of the 1990s to contemporary browsers used on mobile devices and laptops. Rather than serving as "read-only" sites requiring HTML coding to make changes, wikis function as "read/write" sites, allowing multiple editors to make changes from within their browser directly without any HTML coding. The wiki software displays content to appear like typical web pages for users accessing the site, but allows fast editing and access to revision history at the click of a button.

Cunningham designed the wiki software as an alternative to the most common online group communication tools used in the early 1990s, email listservers and Usenet bulletin boards, by organizing content around individual pages that display the most recent edited version. For programmers working on shared projects, the wiki system was an efficient way to track and discuss ongoing progress. Cunningham released his free software to create stand-alone wikis, and both Cunningham's system and alternate wiki platforms became popular tools for communities of programmers in the late 1990s, especially amongst open-source advocates who believed in making their work public and accessible to various contributors on Cunningham's own WikiWikiWeb, spinoff sites like MeatballWiki, and numerous other wikis dedicated to specific programming languages and software systems.

As is frequently the case with technologies, the intended purpose for the tool was soon eclipsed by an unanticipated use. In 2001, a team developing an online encyclopedia created a wiki to help develop content for their main site, Nupedia. Their intent with this secondary site, Wikipedia, was to serve as an open "sandbox" for editing articles to include in their more traditionally single-authored and peer-reviewed Nupedia site. However, the site was noticed by technology sites Slashdot and Kuro5hin, generating a flood of interested contributors—in its first year, Wikipedia editors had developed over 20,000 entries, compared with only twenty-four articles to success-fully pass through Nupedia's editorial process. While certainly many of the Wikipedia articles were of questionable quality, the robust results that emerged from the unintended opening up of the authorship and editing process led to the demise of Nupedia and charted a path for how wikis might be used more broadly beyond a small-scale tool for programmers.

Wikipedia was so successful that it became the prototype for the widespread use of wikis across a range of sites, and fueled the popularity of the platform for mass adoption. Shortly after launch-ing, Wikipedia's team developed a new wiki software platform to run the site, and the emerging community of Wikipedia contributors established a set of rules and guidelines to manage the site's processes and content. For many outsiders who have not actively edited a wiki, it seems counter-intuitive that a site with no top-down governance, no formal system for delegating tasks, and a crew of almost all volunteer, amateur writers and editors could create the largest encyclopedia ever made with a level of accuracy that many studies have suggested rivals or surpasses traditional encyclopedias. But by looking closely at Wikipedia's editorial model, we can better understand how wikis function as a site of participatory culture.

One important guiding principle behind Wikipedia and most other wikis is that they embrace *freedom*. When discussing software, there are two important related meanings of free: no cost and open. Wikipedia embraces both meanings, as the site is hosted by a non-profit foundation and refuses to sell advertising or charge access to its site or software, and Wikipedia is open to any user, editor, or derivative use with few limitations. The effect of these dual freedoms is that Wikipedia embraces an open-access approach to both the use and creation of its site, making the project truly dependent on participation and self-governance, rather than top-down or commercial control. Wikipedia licenses its content with a Creative Commons system that waives some of the restrictions tied to copyright, ensuring that all content is accessible, sharable, and not claimed by any individual owner. Not all wikis follow this form of complete openness, but the precedent of Wikipedia helps makes the assumed default model for wikis tend toward free and open access.

A related principle to the freedom of wikis is transparency, a facet encoded directly into wiki software itself. Most documents, whether a book or a web page, hide the work that went into their creation—you can only view a final, finished draft, with little evidence of the process behind the document's origination. Wikis make the traces of their creation visible and accessible to users. Within the Mediawiki software as well as many other wiki platforms, every page has two important linked tabs: *History* and *Talk*. The History page allows any user to view every individual edit made to the page, tracking who added what content and how the site evolved. The Talk tab hosts a conversation about the page, as editors decide on potential categories, nego-tiate over controversial edits, and consider sources. Together, every page in Wikipedia can be viewed both as a published encyclopedia entry and as part of an ongoing process of creation. For editors, this *transparency* serves as a guide to join the participatory community and facilitate collaboration.

The transparency of a wiki highlights another key facet of the format: a page is always in process, embracing *fluidity* over static form. Most print texts are published only after rounds of writing, revision, editing, and formatting, with the final version fixed as part of a permanent record. Conventional websites go through an intense development, editing, and testing process before "going live," even if they get revised eventually. But wiki pages are drafted in public— when a new event, person, or notable term emerges as a candidate for a Wikipedia page, an editor simply creates a new page, typically a short entry called a *stub*. Editors then congregate to expand and refine the page, debate its notability, or potentially to delete it altogether, all within the visible public-facing site. This process is never fully complete, as a Wikipedia page could always be refined, updated, merged with another, or deleted. Unlike print texts, Wikipedia is never fixed or static, but is always part of a fluid process of revision.

For people who have not edited a wiki, it is hard to understand how the process avoids devolving into chaos—the average Wikipedia page certainly looks like it was planned and authored by experts, not collectively built by amateurs. But Wikipedia pages are an example of an important trend of participatory culture: *emergence*. Instead of being planned and managed from above, emergent culture is a bottom-up phenomenon, coming together through the collection of small practices. Like birds flocking and ant colonies, Wikipedians organize their work without following top-down orders. Instead, they collectively decide on shared principles and goals, like style sheets, formatting norms, and guidelines for what makes a good entry, and then each editor follows his or her own interests and talents. Some editors focus on formatting, others on source citation, and others on grammar. Some have specialty topic areas they work on, while others police the site for vandalism and controversy. While pages are rarely seen as the property of any individual editor, each editor finds his or her own unique way to contribute to the site as a whole, and the entire complex system emerges out of decentralized individual participation.

The effect of accumulating the diverse participation of a wide range of encyclopedia writers and editors fits with the important concept of *collective intelligence*. Through their media analyses, Pierre Lévy and Henry Jenkins have explored how the knowledge and expertise of computer users can come together through digital tools to exceed their individualized contributions. Wikipedia might be the greatest testament to this principle, as most pages exceed the knowledge and abilities of any one editor; instead, each adds his or her own expertise to create what is arguably the most expansive and accurate compendium of information ever assembled.

The final important aspect of wikis stems from these emergent collected practices: *relative anonymity*. While most research materials like books and articles are clearly identified by their authors, and even traditional encyclopedias credit authors and editors, Wikipedia articles lack attribution. The History tab will reveal who did what, but typically there are numerous editors, each with a username or an anonymous IP address. Although some Wikipedians create elaborate profiles, complete with academic or other credentials to validate their expertise, the vast majority of editors contribute anonymously or pseudonymously with little chance of recognition from the millions of readers who consult the site on a regular basis. Entries do need to cite external sources for validity, but, within the site, expertise is tied to active participation within the Wikipedia community rather than an authorial identity—a good page is judged on its own merits, not by the credentials of who authored it. Likewise, writing an excellent entry is less of a badge of accomplishment on Wikipedia than in traditional publishing, with other participatory practices like cleaning up messy entries, adding source citations, deleting vandalism, weighing in on policies, and negotiating conflicts valued more than single authorship.

These six principles—freedom, transparency, fluidity, emergence, collective intelligence, and relative anonymity—apply to most wikis that are open to the general public. But for users familiar with Wikipedia, these are not the core principles typically associated with the site. Instead, Wikipedia's guidelines and "pillars" highlight that content needs to be presented with a neutral point of view, citing sources and avoiding original research, among other administrative policies. These are vital principles for Wikipedia, but derive more from its role as a comprehensive encyclopedia, not in its form as a wiki. Because Wikipedia has become so well known, it has come to define what a wiki is in the popular imagination. People frequently refer to looking something up on Wikipedia as "wikiing," suggesting that the wiki structure is often culturally equated with its encyclopedic function, a semantic mix-up between the *wiki-* and the *-pedia*. But the actual use of other wikis often goes beyond the encyclopedic impulse.

Fan Wikis as Participatory Culture

The wiki platform is open to a wide range of uses beyond creating an encyclopedia. Wikis can serve a small, private group, such as an internal corporate authoring tool or an academic class project. They can be used to share information to trace genealogies, like Familypedia, or to collect and disseminate secret documents, as with WikiLeaks. One of the most popular and widespread uses of wikis has been to augment fandom, especially around popular culture. Hundreds of wikis have been developed to serve as productive sites for fans to engage around objects of their affection, including television shows, video games, films, literature, comic books, sports, music, and virtually any other facet of popular culture that attracts active fans. Fan wikis provide a window into a range of participatory practices and cultural formations.

Before surveying the array of fan wikis, it's important to understand what makes a fan wiki distinct from other sites. Although it's not a firm boundary, we can best understand fan culture as existing principally in relation to another external cultural object, whether a film, sports team, or band. Other subcultural formations can coalesce around a practice (such as a knitting circle) or set of beliefs (like a Bible discussion group), but fan groups define themselves as primarily connected to the object of their fandom. This can be a slippery distinction, as we would probably not consider a general-interest book club as part of fan culture, but a reading group focusing on the *Harry Potter* series would be. The key aspect for fan culture is that participants have an emotional engagement with a shared cultural form, dedicating their time, money, and creative energies to exploring that relationship.

Fan groups create wikis to serve a wide range of practices, styles and functions for their sites. But regardless of their specific motivations, all fan wikis can be considered *paratexts*, independent cultural works that exist in relation to other texts. Most works of popular culture have officially licensed paratexts created by the media industries—a film might have trailers, tie-in merchandise like toys or T-shirts, DVD extras, sequels, and licensed media adaptations such as videogames or novelizations. Fans create their own unlicensed paratexts inspired by popular culture as well, including fan fiction, remix videos, artworks, songs, and a wide array of websites. Fan wikis, given the ease of their editing interfaces and simplicity of collaboration, have emerged as a popular platform for developing online paratexts for nearly every fan community.

Fan wikis can be used to serve a number of functions. Most fan wikis serve, at least in part, as *documentation* of their cultural object. For objects of fandom that, for lack of a better term, might be called non-fictional, like sports teams or musical acts, wikis assemble information about the real people, places, events, and other elements that capture a fan's attention. For instance, the various Beatles wikis all attempt to chronicle information about the band's songs, history, and members' personalities. However, few fan wikis can rival Wikipedia's depth and detail in chronicling information about a non-fiction topic—Wikipedia has much more information about the Beatles than any of the dedicated Beatles wikis. Such imbalances are understandable given

Wikipedia's enormous user base and well-established community and practices for documenting the real world, whether scientific discoveries or British rock bands.

The balance shifts somewhat for fictional works like films, television series, videogames, and comic books. While Wikipedia does contain entries on fictional stories, places, and characters, a key tension among Wikipedians involves the concept of *fancruft*, a derogatory term meaning overly detailed information that is seen as only relevant to the most passionate fans. Wikipedians frequently debate whether pages chronicling the fictional worlds of anime or videogames require the level of detail that some desire, often making the site inhospitable to hardcore fans of fiction in ways that it rarely is for fans of non-fictional topics. In such cases, fan wikis dedicated to documenting fictional storyworlds, as well as the real-life information about the creation of the cultural objects themselves, serve as a gathering place for fan participation. Some of the most popular fan wikis include WoWWiki (for the game franchise *Warcraft*), Wookieepedia (*Star Wars*), Memory Alpha (*Star Trek*), and wikis for Marvel and DC comics, anime series *Yu-Gi-Oh!*, *Doctor Who*, and *The Muppets*. While all of these topics have elaborate sets of pages created within Wikipedia, their stand-alone fan wikis thrive as spaces to document their fictional worlds with elaborate detail.

A contrast between wikis highlights the differing level of detail and fan participation—with the caveat that their fluidity means that these descriptions might no longer be accurate in the future. On Wookieepedia, the minor character Daultay Dofine has an independent page of 3500 words developed by more than twenty editors, chronicling his small role in *The Phantom Menace* and further development in various tie-in novels and published *Star Wars* references; the page was awarded Featured Article status in 2009, the community standard of excellence on many wikis. On Wikipedia, the Daultay Dofine page, which was never longer than 600 words and referenced only the film, was the site of a debate between users as to whether it deserves its own page or should be merged with a page that lists minor *Star Wars* characters. Eventually it was deleted, redirecting users to a list of characters, on which Dofine doesn't even appear as of September 2010. This contrast shows how dedicated *Star Wars* fans use the niche Wookieepedia to create and value content with a vast amount of detail and precision, even if the same content is viewed as fancruft within the more general Wikipedia community.

It is telling that many of the most active and extensive fan wikis focus on large-scale franchises that span multiple media and decades of cultural output. Documenting such vast narrative franchises typically requires collective intelligence, as the range of content typically exceeds any single fan's mastery. Wikis are highly effective platforms for encouraging active participation for fans to pool their expertise, but their relative anonymity does run counter to one facet of fandom: the hierarchy of status amongst collectors and experts that traditionally has been central to many fan communities. An average user of a fan wiki does not drill down into the history and discussion to identify the most trusted and accomplished expert fans, and thus some fans who are motivated by status-seeking amongst the community might prefer stand-alone authored fansites or other paratextual practices over collective wikis.

Within a fan wiki community, other hierarchies frequently emerge that do not necessarily mimic the status of fan expertise. Most wikis empower selected editors to function as System Operators (Sysops) or Administrators (Admins), roles that include expanded editing, blocking, and policy-setting functions. A wiki establishes its own policies for selecting Sysops and banning destructive users, but typically such decisions are made following collectively established policies and guidelines that value a user's contributions to maintaining order and collaboration. Once in place, Sysops help define the culture of a wiki, which can be overtly structured and hierarchical, or much more egalitarian and collective. Thus while an individual fan's expertise is rarely granted high value within a wiki community as it might be in other fan cultures, wikis do

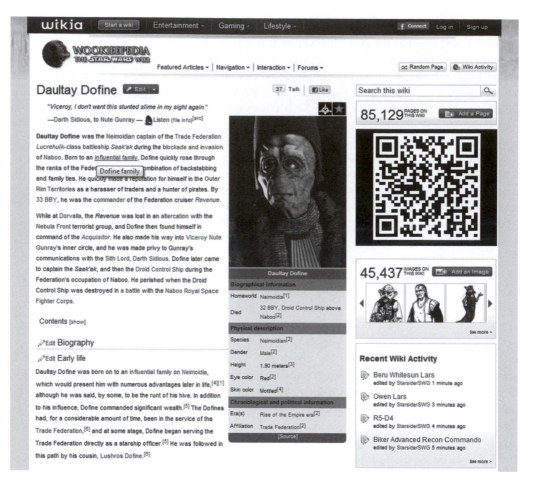

FIGURE 4.1 Unlike Wikipedia, the site Wookieepedia provides exhaustive detail about the minor character Daultay Dofine

provide validation for fans who can effectively foster consensus and collective participation rather than individual achievements.

Documentation of a cultural object is one major function of fan wikis that follows directly from precedents established by Wikipedia, but fan wikis can host a much broader range of participation and cultural production than the encyclopedic impulse. On sites focused on fictional worlds, fan wikis can serve as *alternative narratives*, retelling the canonical story of a franchise in a new form. A fan could read Wookieepedia, Lostpedia, or Memory Alpha as a retelling of the stories from their respective fictional franchises, much like annotated versions, synopses, and reference books retell classic literature and mythology. While it's hard to imagine somebody who has never watched the show reading the *Doctor Who* Wiki to retell the story, viewers certainly use wikis to fill in gaps from missed episodes and unknown transmedia extensions, or clarify narrative ambiguities and uncertainties. Such a wiki does more than just document a fiction, effectively serving as a transformed site of storytelling itself.

If many wikis focused on fictional culture retell their object's stories, videogame wikis take this impulse further by offering collectively authored walkthroughs, strategies, and guides to popular games. Such game-based wikis go beyond the documentary impulse, as the wikis become sites for conversation and collaborative strategizing for players, creating dual levels of participatory culture within both the game and the wiki. Game wikis for online games like *World of Warcraft* or *EverQuest* are particularly active as they mirror their online storyworlds with comprehensive analysis and discussion of how the games work. Many wikis, regardless of topic, extend the ludic spirit of games to the creation of the wikis themselves, as wiki systems and communities can offer "achievements" and rewards for active editors who contribute to the wiki. Such wikis map the gaming impulse of one aspect of participatory culture onto the collaborative documentation of wikis, suggesting important overlaps between cultural phenomena.

One step further away from the documentary norm is the practice of *wiki analysis*. Although Wikipedia polices its articles to exclude "original research," fan wikis often welcome research, analysis, and speculation, especially of ongoing cultural objects. Lostpedia was particularly active in this realm, providing analysis and theories for the mysteries of *Lost* as the show progressed over its run in the late 2000s. Some wikis span a broader array of cultural phenomena as an analytic object, such as the highly popular TV Tropes wiki. Starting in 2004 as a whimsical list of common conventions and clichés in fictional television, it has grown into a vast example of collaborative narratology, compiling thousands of storytelling examples and trends from a range of media. By embracing original analysis and allowing pages to grow regardless of notability or external documentation, TV Tropes provides an alternative model from Wikipedia as to how wikis can harness collective intelligence to achieve impressive results.

Although the most common and widespread uses of wikis are to create documentation and analysis, they have also been used as a tool for *collaborative creativity* of so-called "fanon," or non-canonical extensions to the original storyworld. Fan wikis certainly can embed original creative works, such as fan fiction and remix videos, that are available through other online platforms—wikis dedicated to a particular franchise often link to relevant fanon, or some wikis document the larger world of fan creativity across a range of fannish objects, such as the vast Fan Fiction Wiki. Another type of creative wiki uses the platform to collaboratively author fanon directly, creating an alternative universe of fanon to compliment the canonical source material. Often the dedicated fanon wikis for a popular franchise, like *Star Trek* and many videogames, can become as large in scope and active participation as their parallel canonical wikis. Fans often use fanon wikis as a place to create role-playing fictions, authoring narratives by each fan acting his or her part as a character within the storyworld while embracing the ludic possibility of wikis to extend the original object of their fandom.

One subset of creative wikis is particularly noteworthy, as fans embrace the wiki platform to collectively produce parody. The Uncyclopedia is a parody of Wikipedia, mocking the documentary impulse by creating a humorous encyclopedia of lies and disinformation. Another Wikipedia parody derives more directly from fandom: Wikiality: The Truthiness Encyclopedia professes to be an encyclopedia of the world as seen through the onscreen persona of Stephen Colbert from the television show *The Colbert Report*, a parody of right-wing pundits. In a 2006 episode of his show, Colbert satirically praised Wikipedia's open approach to information, coining the term "wikiality" as "a reality where, if enough people agree with a notion, it becomes the truth," and encouraged his viewers to edit Wikipedia to make it conform with his (fictional) vision of the world. After Wikipedians blocked the Colbert-inspired vandalism, fans created Wikiality.com as a site to extend Colbert's satire and create a fictional extension of the character's worldview. The effect is a work of crowd-sourced comedy, a fan-created meta-parody extending the world view of a character who himself is a satirical creation.

Whether aimed at documenting a movie franchise, extending the fictional world of a video game, or creating a parodic vision of reality as inspired by a television character, wikis have demonstrated the possibilities of collective participation to create active hubs for fan culture.

The participatory possibilities exemplified by wikis are not unique to the software platform; as new technologies develop, these examples and systems will certainly be supplanted with new facets of fan culture. However, core principles like collectivity, freedom, transparency, and emergence will certainly endure in some fashion, no matter what technologies emerge to augment and supplant wikis within the realm of participatory culture.

Further Reading

Gray, Jonathan. 2010. *Show sold separately: Promos, spoilers, and other media paratexts*. New York, NY: New York University Press.

Hunter, Rik. 2011. "Erasing 'property lines': A collaborative notion of authorship and textual ownership on a fan wiki," *Computers and Composition*. doi:10.1016/j.compcom.2010.12.004.

Jenkins, Henry. 2006. *Convergence culture: Where old and new media collide*. New York, NY: New York University Press.

Jenkins, Henry. 2007. "What Wikipedia can teach us about the new media literacies," *Journal of Media Literacy*, 54(2): 11–29.

Lévy, Pierre. 1997. *Collective intelligence: Mankind's emerging world in cyberspace*. New York, NY: Plenum Trade.

Lih, Andrew. 2009. *The Wikipedia revolution: How a bunch of nobodies created the world's greatest encyclopedia*. New York, NY: Hyperion Press.

Markman, Kris M. and Overholt, John. 2011. "Becoming 'the right people': Fan-generated knowledge building in *Mystery Science Theatre 3000*." In Robert G. Weiner (ed.). *Mystery Science Theatre 3000 and the Culture of Riffing*. Jefferson, NC: McFarland & Co., pp. 66–75.

Mittell, Jason. 2009. "Sites of participation: Wiki fandom and the case of *Lostpedia*," *Transformative Works and Cultures*. http://journal.transformativeworks.org/.

Toton, Sarah. 2008. "Cataloging knowledge: Gender, generative fandom, and the *Battlestar* wiki," *Flow*. http://flowtv.org/.

5

WHO'S STEERING THE MOTHERSHIP?

The Role of the Fanboy Auteur in Transmedia Storytelling

Suzanne Scott

If creators do not ultimately control what we take from their transmedia stories, this does not prevent them from trying to shape our interpretations.

(Henry Jenkins, 2006, p. 123)

But perhaps in a digital era, and under the rubric of new media, we are witnessing an earnest struggle to create a new variety of aura and author and to return (at least symbolically) to "older" models of creation and viewership.

(Jonathan Gray, 2010, p. 104)

Defined by Henry Jenkins (2007) as "a process where integral elements of a fiction get dispersed systematically across multiple delivery channels for the purpose of creating a unified and coordinated entertainment experience," transmedia storytelling has been celebrated by media scholars as a narrative model that promotes collaborative authorship and participatory spectatorship. But there is something paradoxical about transmedia storytelling, beginning with dual emphasis on dispersal and unification in Jenkins's definition. Transmedia stories are defined by their ability to expand: they expand and enrich a fictional universe, they expand across media platforms, and they empower an expansive fan base by promoting collective intelligence as a consumption strategy. However, transmedia storytelling is also a product of industrial consolidation and conglomeration, with the flow of content across platforms mirroring the "economic logic of a horizontally integrated entertainment industry" (Jenkins, 2006, p. 96). Transmedia stories, or at least the majority created by the mainstream media industry that I will be focusing on in this essay, produce a consolidated canon of "official" texts that frequently discourage or discredit unauthorized expansion or speculation by fans. The danger here is that, despite transmedia stories' collaborative narrative design, the media industry frequently equates fans' "participation" with their continuous consumption of texts that narratively and financially supplement a franchise.

This simultaneous textual expansion and consolidation, and the balance of artistry and industry that characterizes Hollywood's embrace of transmedia storytelling techniques, is most evident in the conflicted positioning of the author. Transmedia stories disintegrate the author figure, as artists in different media collaboratively create the transmedia text, but, in order to assure audiences that someone is overseeing the transmedia text's expansion and creating meaningful connections between texts, the author must ultimately be restored and their significance reaffirmed.

In short, the media industry's effort to create unified and coordinated entertainment experiences frequently requires the construction of a unified author figure to serve as a creative and textual coordinator. There are practical and promotional factors motivating this consolidation, but concerns arise when a unified author figure results in an attempt to unify and regulate the audience's interpretations of the text.

Despite their potential to demystify and democratize authorship and cultivate a closer relationship between producers and consumers, transmedia stories tend to reinforce the boundaries between "official" and "unauthorized" forms of narrative expansion through the construction of a single author/textual authority figure. Though digital media have allowed fans to proliferate their unofficial textual expansions and made these counter-narratives more visible, transmedia stories' renewed emphasis on authorial intent could be cynically viewed as endorsing a return to viewing the audience as "the more-or-less passive recipient of authorial meaning," in which any interpretation that deviates from the text is "viewed negatively, as a failure to successfully understand what the author was trying to say" (Jenkins, 1992, p. 25). In the case of transmedia storytelling, who is designated to speak on behalf of the text is of equal importance as what they say, resulting in a growing reliance on the authorial archetype of the "fanboy auteur," or a creator/figurehead of a transmedia franchise who attempts to navigate and break the conventional boundaries between producers and consumers. Fanboy auteurs are relatable because of their fan credentials, which are narrativized and (self) promoted as an integral part of their appeal as a transmedia interpreter for audiences. Some anecdotally suggest that their rise to professional/creator status is a product of their fan identity, while others frame their conflicted identity as an author/fan as augmenting their ability to understand what fans want, thus making them more equipped to cater to fans. Even if they do not actively self-identify as fanboys, the fanboy auteur equates his close proximity to the fans with an understanding of their textual desires and practices.

The "fanboy auteur" is only one of many authorial identities that a transmedia practitioner might adopt, several of which have been catalogued and analyzed by scholar Christy Dena (2009). Whether they characterize themselves as "super-producers," "transmedia czars," "curators," or "universe stewards," she argues that "such a practitioner needs to speak, if you like, many languages" (Dena, 2009, pp. 128–131). Specifically, the fanboy auteur's perceived ability to speak fans' "language," and his liminal positioning (his ability to present him simultaneously as one of "us" and one of "them," consumer and producer), is framed as his greatest asset, suggesting that he is an ideal interpreter between text and audience. This is not to suggest that this dual identity is a construct, or purely an industrial tool, and it isn't my intent to use the term "fanboy" pejoratively. Despite being creators of media properties, fanboy auteurs are fans, and their self-identification as fans is a large part of what makes them both likeable and powerful author(ity) figures for audiences.

While the consolidation of creative control may be necessary to ensure aesthetic consistency and narrative continuity in transmedia stories, it also needs to be viewed as an industrial strategy. We need to consider how transmedia stories make strategic use of the fanboy auteur's voice, acknowledge fans' investment in that voice, and consider how and why fans speak back. A textual authority figure that appeals to fans is better positioned to engender fans' trust, and thus has greater potential to channel fan interpretation and participation in ways that best suit the industry's financial and ideological interests. Transmedia storytelling did not create the fanboy auteur's potentially regulatory model of authorship, but it has exacerbated it by framing the word of the fanboy auteur as an essential extension of the transmedia story, or a "text" that needs to be read and analyzed in order to get the most out of a transmedia story. Just as many transmedia or complex franchises create a "bible," or a master blueprint to keep track of characters and plot lines, ultimately ensuring that "the disparate [creative] teams understand the core nature of the fictional world, which in turn facilitates new compositions that are within the logic of the fictional world" (Dena, 2009, p. 146), fanboy auteurs function as "human bibles" (Caldwell, 2008, p. 16), tasked with maintaining continuity. Consequently, though these authorial extensions (podcasts, blog posts, interviews, etc.) are not fictional contributions to the storyworld being built, they perform similar narrative work, and they reinforce the fanboy auteur as a "human bible," and the transmedia story's sole navigator and interpreter.

Though the impulse to reduce "the range of potential transmedia tongues, even as, paradoxically, we seek to grow larger and more complex fictional worlds" (Ruppel, 2010) is primarily a result of the industry's embrace of transmedia storytelling as a business model, the importance of a unified authorial "tongue" was present in Henry Jenkins's foundational work on transmedia storytelling. In "Searching for the Origami Unicorn: *The Matrix* and Transmedia Storytelling," Jenkins emphasized transmedia storytelling's potential to promote co-creation and collaborative authorship, but also acknowledged that "the most successful transmedia franchises have emerged when a single creator or creative unit maintains control" (Jenkins, 2006, p. 106). Using *The Matrix*'s Wachowski brothers as his authorial test case, Jenkins stressed that the brothers "personally wrote and directed content for the game, drafted scenarios for some of the animated shorts, and co-wrote a few of the comics" (p. 111), in addition to praising their collaboration with artists in other mediums (pp. 109–110).

Few contemporary transmedia stories benefit from the same degree of creative involvement that the Wachowski brothers had with *The Matrix*'s transmedia extensions. Many adopt the "license or subcontract and hope for the best" (p. 111) mentality that the Wachowskis, and Jenkins, rejected. In some cases, such as the critical and commercial smash *Heroes Evolutions* (a digital hub of transmedia content for the NBC series *Heroes* that included webcomics an alternate-reality game, and interactive stories), collaborating with companies that specialize in transmedia extensions can be mutually beneficial. Yet, few fans are likely to know Mark Warshaw's name, or consider him to be *Heroes'* transmedia auteur, despite the fact that he produced the content for *Heroes Evolutions*. It is unrealistic to assume that *Heroes* creator Tim Kring personally developed and signed off on every facet of each transmedia extention. It's more likely that Warshaw and his transmedia collaborators were in conversation with Kring and the *Heroes* writing team to develop meaningful connections between the television series and its transmedia extensions. Nonetheless, in interviews/commentaries Kring is presented as the face and voice of the *Heroes* transmedia franchise, and credited for its success or failure (Carr, 2010).

As this example indicates, transmedia storytelling's consolidation of authorial control may be symbolic, but the image of the author it crafts is powerful. The Wachowskis' publicized involvement with each of *The Matrix*'s transmedia extensions (videogames, animated series, etc.) canonized those texts as integral parts of the story, increasing their value for fans. The industry is understandably invested in making audiences consider all the components of their transmedia story to be required reading/viewing/playing, but the value associated with an authorial stamp of approval is also a product of fans' investment in the author. When an author is involved in (or publically approves) an extension of the transmedia story, it creates a greater emotional investment for audiences—what we might call "affective value." The creation of affective value for audiences will, theoretically, lead them to invest financially in those extensions, raising the transmedia story's commercial value. Conversely, if an author is not directly involved in (or openly criticizes) particular transmedia extensions, those extensions are more likely to fail. Addressing why a series of tie-in novels for the ABC television series *Lost* were critical and commercial failures, Ivan Askwith (2007) acknowledges that, "even if the books had been well-written, the simple fact that they were written by authors with no formal connection to the series […] made their connection to the series itself almost meaningless" (p. 127).

As the above example indicates, the transmedia author's power to demarcate primary and secondary texts, inducting some extensions of the transmedia story into the canon and excluding others, creates "'tiers' of canon [that] leads directly to tiers of perceived narrative value" (Long, 2007, p. 35) for fans. Fans themselves often replicate and reinforce these tiers. As Jason Mittell has remarked about the *Lost* wiki Lostpedia, the way that certain pages are marked creates a "clear hierarchy between creator-endorsed truth and fan-created para-truth, or perhaps truthiness, in Stephen Colbert's wiki-friendly term" (Mittell, 2009). Though Jenkins's (2007) work on trans-media storytelling emphasized that each narrative extension should be equally accessible, the industry has always been centrally concerned with creating tiers of canon, and corresponding tiers of narrative and financial value. The "mothership" has emerged as an industrial buzzword to indicate the primary text that a transmedia story is built around, typically a film or television series. It is a fitting, and appropriately geeky, metaphor: just as an alien mothership is characterized as a large spacecraft from which smaller ships are launched, the transmedia mothership views its narrative extensions (in the form of webisodes, comic books, etc.) as secondary texts. The func-tion of these secondary texts, both narratively and economically, is to bring audiences back to the mothership. As the person tasked with steering the mothership, the fanboy auteur functions in a similar manner, instructing audiences on how to best navigate this web of secondary texts while reinforcing the centrality of the mothership.

Though transmedia franchises emerge from a range of media (films, comic books, etc.), the television industry in particular has enthusiastically embraced transmedia storytelling as a narrative model, and most actively deployed the fanboy auteur as a textual navigator and interpreter. Like transmedia stories, authorship in serial television is collaborative (with its large writing staffs and rotating group of directors) and symbolically consolidated through the series' most consistent creative presence, typically the creator, producer or showrunner. We can view the television industry's adoption of transmedia storytelling techniques as the next logical step in the medium's recent trend toward narrative complexity (Mittell, 2006) and its corresponding reinvention as an "engagement medium," or "a new conceptual model of television, better suited to a multiplat-form media environment and the emerging attention and experience economies, which focuses on the development of television programs that extend beyond the television set" (Askwith, 2007, p. 3). Perhaps the reason that fanboy auteurs are most visible and vocal within the television industry is due to this embrace of narrative complexity, but Jason Mittell also notes that "part of the appeal is television's reputation as a producer's medium, where writers and creators retain control over their work more than in film's director-centered model" (Mittell, 2006, p. 31).

Just as transmedia storytelling isn't an entirely new concept (Jenkins, 2006, p. 119), the fanboy auteur isn't an entirely new authorial archetype. Through a brief overview of two prior analyses of television fanboy auteurs, we can begin to place contemporary fanboy auteurs on a continuum of authorial control and consider how transmedia storytelling increases the fanboy auteur's inter-pretive power. Transmedia storytelling has, if anything, magnified the functions of the author outlined in Henry Jenkins's discussion of Gene Roddenberry in his essay "'Infinite diversity in infinite combinations: Genre and authorship in *Star Trek*." Applying the three basic functions of the author myth outlined in Michel Foucault's 1979 essay "What is an Author?" to Roddenberry, Jenkins argued that Roddenberry's authorial presence served to classify the relationships between texts, explain textual events (or neutralize discrepancies), and to demarcate a text's value through his authorship or approval (Jenkins, 1995b, pp. 188–191). Within transmedia storytelling, these are not just the primary functions of the fanboy auteur, they are vital to the success of the transmedia story. The complexity of a transmedia story's textual network has made audiences increasingly reliant on the fanboy auteur to clarify the relationship between texts. Accordingly, the fanboy auteur's explanation of textual events is now considered integral to a comprehensive understanding of the transmedia story. And, as previously noted, his authorship or approval of each component of the transmedia story increases its affective and commercial value.

Transmedia storytelling has intensified the author's function from Roddenberry's era, and it encourages the fanboy auteur to exercise those functions in a more regulatory fashion. New media have encouraged a closer, more conversational relationship between producers and consumers, but it has also enhanced the fanboy auteur's ability to survey his audience. For example, a study of *Babylon 5* creator J. Michael Straczynski's participation in/regulation of an online fan message board from 1995 to 1996 offered an early example of a fanboy auteur's digitally enabled efforts to channel and regulate fan responses to the series. Straczynski considered himself a "navigator" rather than an "auteur" (Straczynski in Wexelblat, 2002, p. 209), but he consistently positioned himself as an auteur by "not only pointing towards the horizon; [but] claiming to have made the horizon exist" (p. 216). In this model, for the author to endorse or encourage fans' interpretations or textual production was

> tantamount to suggesting that not only are alternative interpretations of the main text possible, but that the direction and tone of the text could be determined by someone else, or that sources other than the officially sanctioned one could produce desirable material.
>
> *(p. 215)*

The narrative complexity of transmedia stories, and the difficult task of making many narrative extensions cohere and communicate, may unintentionally encourage an equally rigid view of authorship and its function.

Most contemporary fanboy auteurs are creators or producers of hyper-serialized, mythologized television series that present a natural narrative fit for transmedia extensions. Joss Whedon (*Buffy the Vampire Slayer, Angel, Firefly, Dollhouse*), Ronald D. Moore (*Battlestar Galactica*), Eric Kripke (*Supernatural*), Damon Lindelof and Carlton Cuse (*Lost*), Russell T. Davies (*Doctor Who*), and Tim Kring (*Heroes*) are all strong examples. Creators have long been referred to as "the Powers That Be" within fan communities, but this reverence is tempered by a sense of kinship and familiarity. Within fan communities, Joss Whedon is simply "Joss," Ronald D. Moore is "RDM," and Damon Lindelof and Carlton Cuse are fused into "Darlton." In all of these cases, the conflicted identity of the fanboy auteur is presented as his greatest strength, a "form of reification, in which [...] he is 'one of us,'—a fan of his own creation, and yet he is somehow special" (Wexelblat, 2002, p. 225). Borrowing a term from Jonathan Gray (2010), we could frame the fanboy auteur as an "undead author" (p. 113), or an author who understands that metaphorically "killing himself" is an ideal way to "fashion himself as 'just one of the fans,' when he is decidedly privileged in the relationship" (p. 112).

Fanboy auteurs exert this privilege through the transmedia story's promise of a more dialogic relationship between producers and consumers. As Lisa Schmidt (2010) has argued with regard to *Supernatural*'s creator Eric Kripke, the "personal and chatty" voice of fanboy auteur addresses the fan as a friend rather than a consumer. Schmidt cautions that this "is not to say that fans are in a real relationship with Kripke, but to demonstrate that the sense of intimacy between him and fans, however constructed and ultimately illusory, nevertheless has the affective and dramatic markers of a relationship." These one-sided "conversations" come in a variety of forms, from podcasts to blog entries to message board posts, in which the fanboy auteur's voice is privileged and his interpretations are posed as the "correct" reading of textual events. Jonathan Gray (2010) has argued:

> When creators try to exert control, the paratexts of interviews, podcasts, DVD bonus materials, and making-of specials are their preferred means of speaking—their textual body

and corporeal form—as they will try to use paratexts to assert authority and to maintain the role of the author.

(p. 110)

In the case of transmedia storytelling, Gray's argument can be taken one step further. Whether or not fanboy auteurs consciously use these authorial paratexts to assert their control, authorial paratexts are increasingly treated as vital transmedia extensions, both by audiences (who comb them for narrative information that will help decode the transmedia story) and by the industry (by pitching them as essential navigational tools). Thus, while fanboy auteurs might sincerely wish to establish relationships with fans through these authorial paratexts, these forms inevitably privilege the author's voice, and reaffirm his position of power in that relationship.

The weekly podcast episode commentaries released by *Battlestar Galactica*'s fanboy auteur Ronald D. Moore are a prime example. The podcasts' blend of intimacy (recorded in Moore's bedroom with "Mrs Ron," they embrace an amateur/conversational aesthetic) and authority is what makes these texts equally alluring and frustrating for fans. As Bob Rehak and I have noted (2007), Moore's podcasts frame him as

> not just an author-god, but a fan-god. […] RDM collapses the functions of author and interpreter into a single beast, and in so doing gets the final word on what a character was "really" thinking, or what "really" happened after that cutaway.

Moore's podcasts expose the danger of transmedia authors adding too much information, "preempting important lines of speculation even as [they add] information that might sustain new fantasies" (Jenkins, 2006, p. 116). These authorial commentaries/interviews/podcasts are not narrative components of the transmedia text, but they frequently fill in textual gaps and resolve ambiguities before fans are given the chance to explore them through their own speculation or textual production (Scott, 2008).

Increasingly with transmedia stories, audiences don't just "know the clues are there because the auteur has told them so" (Wexelblat, 2002, p. 215), but one of the primary functions of the fanboy auteur is to establishing "proper interpretations" of those clues, often by attempting to "hide or overpower other interpretations" (Gray, 2010, p. 89). Transmedia stories engage audiences through their exploration, and doing the textual "homework" (Jenkins, 2006, p. 94) is a large part of the fun for fans. As the voice of the transmedia auteur has become another text to be read by audiences who wish to get the full transmedia experience, fanboy auteurs are faced with a conflict. If, as in Moore's case, he speaks too frequently or adds too much textual information, he risks alienating the audience by helping them "cheat" on their transmedia homework. If they remain relatively silent, as Cuse and Lindelof attempted with *Lost*, fans will likely invest in their words even more, and analyze them more rigorously for potential clues to help them grasp the transmedia story in its entirety.

He may be infantilized in title, but the fanboy auteur's paternalistic control over the transmedia text can make him a polarizing figure for fans (Busse, 2006). When an audience is invested in a transmedia story, they tend to respond to these forms of "digitally enabled and enhanced authorial interpretation" (Pearson, 2010, p. 86) in one of two ways. Some fans adopt a "too much is never enough" view, and "revel in producer-supplied ancillary content" (p. 86). Other fans view these authorial assertions as resolving the ambiguities that make participation in transmedia stories pleasurable, arguing that interpretive power should belong to the audience (p. 85–86). These interpretive tensions between authors and audiences have been compounded by the complexity of transmedia narratives, and fans' increased dependence on the author to navigate them efficiently. While "behind the scenes" content existed well before the contemporary transmedia narratives discussed in this essay, and are also common practice for non-fiction texts, fanboy auteurs often position their paratextual explanations and interpretations of the transmedia story as a vital resource for fans to "see how the sausage is made" (Moore in Miller, 2006). Fans, in turn, make a clear distinction between wanting to know how the sausage is made and being told that there's only one correct way to consume and enjoy that sausage, and only one chef who knows the correct recipe (Scott, 2008, pp. 218–219).

Fans' complex relationship with the fanboy auteur is typically negotiated through enunciative (or conversational) forms of fan production (Fiske, 1992, p. 38), in both virtual and real space, from online message boards to fan conventions. In some cases, fans will openly question and critique the fanboy auteur's control over the transmedia narrative through their own textual production. As Gray acknowledges, in our contemporary mediascape the fanboy auteur's word can never fully "serve as gospel," because the "authors' words […] must compete with all manner of paratexts, including audience-created paratexts" (Gray, 2010, p. 110). One particularly illustrative example of such an audience-created paratext is jarrow's *Battlestar Galactica* fan vid "Tandemonium" (jarrow, 2010) set to a remix of "Momma Sed" by Puscifer. Fan vids edit video clips from a media text to a song, using the music "as an interpretive lens to help the viewer to see the source text differently" (Coppa, 2008). Francesca Coppa has characterized vids as "a visual essay that stages an argument, and thus it is more akin to arts criticism than to traditional music video" (Coppa, 2008).

"Tandemonium" takes the refrain "and they have a plan" from *Battlestar Galactica*'s opening credit sequence, and playfully reworks it to critique Moore's transmedia "plan" for the series, and his exertions of authorial control. The vid opens with a quote from Moore about how he always has to have the "last word" on what the show "is or isn't," followed by a series of shots of the show's "bible" intercut with Moore working at his computer. The vid then transitions into a series of shots from the television series, occasionally overlaid with quotes from Moore that frame his plan for the transmedia story as alternately exacting ("We're doing the show just the way I want it") and arbitrary ("I had no particular ending in mind"). A turning point in "Tandemonium" notably occurs after the lyrics "I've got something to tell you," presumably directed at Moore by the artist. As the music intensifies, so does the vid's critique of Moore's mishandling of the text. The lyrical implication that fans should "take it like a man," coupled with images of characters being brutalized and violently dispatched, could be read as a critique of Moore's aggressive exertion of textual authority, implying that fans who don't comply with Moore's views will be symbolically dispatched/dismissed. The vid's conclusive claim that "they don't have a plan," and "they never did have a plan" exposes authorial foresight as simultaneously desired and illusory, while the concept of the fanboy auteur having "the last word" is openly contested.

Tandemonium is admittedly a highly specific and poetic example of the way that fans are working through their ambivalent view of the fanboy auteur's transmediated authority. Still, through this example we can begin to see how transmedia stories intensify negotiations of authorship and textual ownership. In a conversation I had with the artist after viewing "Tandemonium," jarrow drew a parallel between creating a successful fan vid and creating a successful (trans)media text, stating, "You tell the story you're telling, but you leave enough open for viewer interpretation and exploration." While researching the vid, jarrow did read interviews and listen to Moore's podcasts, but noted that as a fan he doesn't "like to see the math," choosing to consume authorial materials only after he has "processed the whole show" (jarrow, personal interview). The growing tendency to position those interviews and podcasts as essential, rather than extraneous, components of the transmedia story, or at least central to its effective navigation, is problematic for many fans. In jarrow's own words, "the more they tell us, the less room we have to imagine and build the world for ourselves" (jarrow, personal interview). Despite the vid's critical tone, jarrow's

FIGURE 5.1 The fan video "Tandemonium" playfully critiques Ron Moore's transmedia plan for the series *Battlestar Galactica*

investment in *Battlestar Galactica*'s narrative plan, and Moore as its planner, is evident. In a post that accompanied "Tandemonium," jarrow openly acknowledged that researching and composing the vid had actually renewed his respect for Moore (jarrow, 2010).

In conclusion, Geoffrey Long (2007) has argued that stories, and transmedia stories in particular, are a carefully choreographed dance between storyteller and audience (p. 56). At the risk of overextending Long's metaphor, it is expected that transmedia storytellers will "lead" their partners in this narrative dance across media platforms. But transmedia auteurs must also remember to treat their audience as their partner and, if they aren't willing to let them lead, they should be wary of treading too frequently on their toes or interpretations. Transmedia storytelling's collaborative authorship model could "result in a demystification of the creative process, [and] a growing recognition of the communal dimensions of expression" (Jenkins, 2006, p. 179). However, if we fail to interrogate transmedia story's construction of the author, or complacently accept that "the very existence and everydayness of collaborative creation might necessitate the (artificial?) celebration of the creative sole genius, the visionary auteur, the named AUTHORity" (Busse 2007), we fail to exploit transmedia stories' potential and place limits on their power to foster participation.

Not unlike a transmedia story, this essay's discussion of the fanboy auteur and his function should be considered only one entry point to a much larger and richer topic that is ever expanding and evolving. First, this essay doesn't address how the author might function differently within transmedia franchises created by non-commercial companies, or when emerging out of media forms other than television. For example, a transmedia franchise cultivated around a comic book, a medium that is in large part defined by the unified and collaborative authorial "vision" created between a writer and an artist, would certainly complicate some of the claims in this essay. Second, at no point in this essay do I mention transmedia extensions that require a high degree of collaboration between creators and consumer, such as alternate-reality games (ARGs), which can only thrive if the puppet masters/creators and players/fans work together (McGonigal, 2007). Likewise, as creators begin to communicate directly with fans through social networking sites like Twitter with more and more frequency (McNutt, 2010), we could begin to see more explicit examples of transmedia collaboration between producers and consumers. Third, this essay doesn't address instances in which one fanboy auteur is replaced by another, such as the case with Steven Moffat supplanting Russell T. Davies as the lead writer and executive producer of *Doctor Who* in 2009. Davies and Moffat both qualify as "fanboy auteurs," but their distinct authorial identities and visions for *Doctor Who* raise a number of interesting questions about what happens when multiple fanboy auteurs become associated with one franchise, and how those multiple authorial visions might be navigated and reconciled by fans.

Finally, as the above discussion of the "fanboy" auteur and his relationship with the "mothership" indicates, the role gender plays in these constructions of authorial power deserves further consideration and discussion. For example, Derek Johnson (2007) has analyzed the fallout that occurred when fangirl auteur Marti Noxon took creative control over *Buffy the Vampire Slayer*'s sixth season in 2001. Despite the fact that she had been a consistent creative presence on the show for years, many fans sought to "delegitimize Noxon's productive authority and privileged relationship to the text" by framing her as a "pretender to the throne" that Joss Whedon would always symbolically occupy (pp. 292–293). Noxon's presence was perceived as endangering both the narrative quality and authorial continuity of the show. Though it is "unclear whether such critics were unwilling to accept a woman as Whedon's show-running successor, the female Noxon was nevertheless assigned the blame for the series' perceived dalliances in devalued, feminized storytelling forms (despite the series' prior melodramatic leanings)," (p. 292) and this tendency is something we should remain watchful of as fangirl auteurs emerge and/or take over transmedia franchises from their male counterparts.

Ultimately, at the heart of the fanboy auteur's conflicted appeal is fans' investment in who is steering the mothership and thoughtfully plotting its course across media platforms, coupled with fans' desire to question the plotted course and create their own textual detours. Thus far, most scholars have chosen to either cynically view the fanboy auteur as an industrial strategy to channel or censor audience interpretation, or optimistically embrace his potential to complicate the producer/consumer binary and create a meaningful dialogue between fans and the transmedia text. As more of a critical middle ground between these two viewpoints begins to emerge, how the fanboy auteur's identity is produced, exploited, and received, deserves further scholarly analysis before we can fully embrace transmedia storytelling's potential to create collaborative relationships not just between artists and texts, but also between auteurs and audiences.

References

Askwith, Ivan. 2007. "Television 2.0: Reconceptualizing TV as an engagement medium" (Master's Thesis). http://cms.mit.edu/research/theses/IvanAskwith2007.pdf.

Busse, Kristina. 2006. "Podcasts and the fan experience of disseminated media commentary." www.kristinabusse.com/cv/research/flow06.html.

Busse, Kristina. 2007. "Collaborative authorship, fandom and new media." http://kbusse.wordpress.com/2007/11/21/collaborative-authorship-fandom-and-new-media/.

Caldwell, John. 2008. *Production culture: Industrial reflexivity and critical practice in film and television*. London: Duke University Press

Coppa, Francesca. 2008. "Women, *Star Trek*, and the early development of fannish vidding," *Transformative Works and Cultures*, 1. http://journal.transformativeworks.org.

Austin Carr. 2010. "'*Heroes*' creator Tim Kring on his new TV series, transmedia, the future of television," *Fast Company* (July 30). www.fastcompany.com/1676076/heroes-creator-tim-kring-on-his-new-tv-series-transmedia-and-the-future-of-television, accessed 10 August 2010.

Dena, Christy. 2009. "Transmedia practice: Theorising the practice of expressing a fictional world across distinct media and environments" (Doctoral Thesis). http://dl.dropbox.com/u/30158/DENA_TransmediaPractice.pdf.

Fiske, John. 1992. "The cultural economy of fandom." In Lisa A. Lewis (ed.). *The adoring audience: Fan culture and popular media*. New York: Routledge, pp. 30–49.

Gray, Jonathan. 2010. *Show sold separately: Promos, spoilers, and other media paratexts*. New York: New York University Press.

jarrow. 2010. "New vid: Tandemonium." http://jarrow.livejournal.com/1127844.html.

jarrow. Personal interview, 25 August 2010.

Jenkins, Henry. 1992. *Textual poachers: Television fans and participatory culture*. New York: Routledge.

Jenkins, Henry. 1995. "'Infinite diversity in infinite combinations': Genre and authorship in *Star Trek*." In John Tulloch and Henry Jenkins (eds). *Science fiction audiences: Watching Doctor Who and Star Trek*. New York: Routledge, pp. 175–195.

Jenkins, Henry. 2006. *Convergence culture: Where old and new media collide*. New York: New York University Press.

Jenkins, Henry. 2007. "Transmedia storytelling 101." www.henryjenkins.org/2007/03/transmedia_storytelling_101.html.

Johnson, Derek. 2007. "Fan-tagonism: Factions, institutions, and constitutive hegemonies of fandom." In Jonathan Gray, Cornell Sandvoss, and C. Lee Harrington (eds). *Fandom: Identities and communities in a mediated world*. New York: New York University Press, pp. 285–300.

Long, Geoffrey A. 2007. "Transmedia storytelling: Business, aesthetics, and production at the Jim Henson company." http://cms.mit.edu/research/theses/GeoffreyLong2007.pdf.

McGonigal, Jane. 2007. "The puppet master problem: Design for real-world, mission-based gaming." In Pat Harrigan and Noah Wardrip-Fruin (eds). *Second person: Role-playing and story in games and playable media*. Cambridge: MIT Press, pp. 251–264.

McNutt, Myles. 2010. "Tweets of anarchy: Showrunners on Twitter." http://blog.commarts.wisc.edu/2010/09/17/tweets-of-anarchy-showrunners-on-twitter/.

Miller, Jason Lee. 2006. "Ron Moore on podcasting and *Battlestar Galactica*." www.webpronews.com/insiderreports/2006/10/05/ron-moore-on-podcasting-and-battlestar-galactica.

Mittell, Jason. 2006. "Narrative complexity in contemporary American television," *The Velvet Light Trap*, 58 (fall): 29–40.

Mittell, Jason. 2009. "Sites of participation: Wiki fandom and the case of Lostpedia," *Transformative Works and Cultures*, 3. http://journal.transformativeworks.org/.

Pearson, Roberta. 2010. "Fandom in the digital era," *Popular Communication*, 8(1) (January): 84–95.

Rehak, Bob and Scott, Suzanne. 2007. "Gender and fan culture: Round fifteen, part two." http://henryjenkins.org/2007/09/gender_and_fan_culture_round_f_4.html.

Ruppel, Marc. 2010. "(Still) waiting for the transmedia Godot." http://mediacommons.futureofthebook.org/imr/2010/07/27/still-waiting-transmedia-godot.

Schmidt, Lisa. 2010. "Monstrous melodrama: Expanding the scope of melodramatic identification to interpret negative fan responses to *Supernatural*," *Transformative Works and Cultures*, 4. http://journal.transformativeworks.org/.

Scott, Suzanne. 2008. "Authorized resistance: Is fan production frakked?" In Tiffany Potter and C.W. Marshall (eds). *Cylons in America: Critical studies in Battlestar Galactica*. New York: Continuum, pp. 210–223.

Wexelblat, Alan. 2002. "An auteur in the age of the Internet: JMS, *Babylon 5*, and the net." In Henry Jenkins, Tara McPherson, and Jane Shattuc (eds). *Hop on pop: The politics and pleasures of popular culture*. Durham: Duke University Press, pp. 209–226.

6

THE GUIDING SPIRIT AND THE POWERS THAT BE

A Response to Suzanne Scott

Henry Jenkins

> The question that Carlton [Cuse] and I get asked by far, above any other mythological question on the show is: "are you making it up as you go along?" People ask us that question, they want the answer to be "absolutely not". … However, then they also say to us: "Do you guys ever go on the boards and listen to what the fans have to say?" and they want the answer to that question to be "yes, absolutely." Now these two things are in direct opposition to each other."
>
> (Damon Lindelof, Executive Producer, *Lost*) (Jenkins, 2010)

This essay was written in response to Suzanne Scott's essay, "Who's Steering the Mothership? The Role of the Fanboy Auteur in Transmedia Storytelling." Scott's core argument has to do with the construction of the "Fanboy Auteur" as a gendered model of authorship that has claimed new visibility and authority as a consequence of the production and consumption practices I've called transmedia storytelling. Under transmedia storytelling models, bits of the story (especially background about characters, worlds, and backstory) are dispersed across media platforms with the goal that these extensions may contribute to fans' over-all appreciation and continued engagement with the franchise as a whole. In many ways, I am highly sympathetic to Scott's critique, but I also feel a desire to clarify even further the ways that authorship operates in the context of the participatory culture of fandom. Think of this essay as a friendly amendment to Scott's argument.

If the concept of transmedia auteurship had not emerged from industry discourses and practices, fans would almost certainly have invented it. As is so often the case in capitalism, it may amount to little more than the industry packaging up what fans had already created and selling it back to them. Scott describes the construction of the fanboy auteur (by definition, He) as an "industry strategy" for managing production and shaping audience expectations. This conception of the author is also a product of specific reception practices. If this emerging model of authorship constrains fans' interpretive and creative freedom, it also enables, motivates, and sustains fan productivity. I don't see storytelling as a zero-sum game where the author gains power at the expense of the audience or vice versa. Fans and auteurs were made for (and by) each other.

In the beginning, there was Gene Roddenberry. Roddenberry's authorial performance was partly the result of self-promotion (courting fans before *Star Trek* debuts through a famous World Con appearance, aligning with fans to spark the letter-writing campaign that kept the series on the air) and partly the result of fan discursive practices, emerging from fans' ability to read Roddenberry's influence off the television texts. Keep in mind that the science fiction fan world had direct contact with writers, who for the most part had emerged from their own ranks, and that comics fans had sought to discern the voice and pen of the "good duck artist" (Carl Barks) even before authors were identified by name in their comic books. Roddenberry spoke through the *Star Trek* text and he spoke to his fans about the series, inviting us to see him as its primary creator.

Through fan and industry discourse, Roddenberry was constructed as "the Great Bird of the Galaxy," a Utopian visionary and humanist philosopher, whose involvement guaranteed the integrity and significance of *Star Trek* (Jenkins, 1995a). Star Trek was "authored" television at a time when most series were still read as anonymous industrial product—not just authored by Roddenberry but also by Harlan Ellison, Theodore Sturgeon, Robert Bloch, Norman Spinrad, and other established science fiction writers whose participation was deployed to enhance the program's reputation. The myth of Roddenberry's authorship was not constructed through podcasts but through convention appearances and books like *The Making of Star Trek*. Roddenberry also sought ways to distinguish himself as "the Guiding Spirit," the auteur who actively defends and protects the creative vision that drew us to the show from "the Powers That Be" as the networks that make decisions based on ratings and other economic calculations.

We might think of the Guiding Spirit and the Powers That Be as myths about authorship that help authors and audiences negotiate the terms of their relationship with each other. The Guiding Spirit gives and the Powers That Be cancel; the Guiding Spirit imagines and the Powers That Be corrupt; the Guiding Spirit rewards and the Powers That Be punish. Not every fandom uses these same terms to describe those relationships, but most operate as if these functions were performed by different forces that, combined, shaped the production and fate of any given franchise.

The letter-writing campaign created a context where the Guiding Spirit and his fans were working together to change the minds of the Powers That Be, much as Joss Whedon has turned to fans to "pirate that puppy" when the networks refused to air an episode of *Buffy the Vampire Slayer* after Columbine. Such a model helps to manage the fan's own mix of fascination and frustration with the source material as well as our culture's difficulty in reconciling creativity and commerce.

The modern fanboy auteur has simply become more adept at playing good cop/bad cop with the audience. The fanboy auteur is the old Guiding Spirit who has stepped off Mount Olympus and walked among the fans or at least become more accessible to us via participation in online communities like "JMS" (*Babylon 5*'s J. Michael Straczynski), shared thoughts through blogs ("Joss," *Buffy*'s Whedon), podcasts ("Ron and Mrs Ron," the Moores behind *Battlestar Galactica*), and Twitter feeds (*The Sandman*'s Neil Gaiman). He is one of us, one of us, doing battle with the Powers That Be so that we can get the stories we want.

Scott is right that it is economically useful to have a figure who stitches together the diverse sites of production and reception within the transmedia franchise. The sales of *Buffy* comics increased significantly when Whedon proclaimed them the "eighth season" and, thus, part of the canon. But, at the end of the day, the Guiding Spirit only has as much moral authority over our fantasy lives as we—individually and collectively—grant him. Paradoxically, nothing destroys that moral authority like trying to exercise it over the fan in any direct or explicit manner. Fans have always shown a surprisingly high capacity to think around or through any constraints texts and producers would impose on what they can do with the characters, even to the point of wishing away whole seasons and story arcs that contradict their sense of the program's integrity.

If, as I've suggested, the transmedia franchise relies on the fan as a "hunter and gatherer" who brings the dispersed pieces together again, those pieces are still simply resources fans use to

FIGURE 6.1 Standing in front of Shuttle *Enterprise*, Gene Roddenberry and the cast of *Star Trek* meet with NASA Administrator Dr James D. Fletcher at the agency's Palmdale manufacturing facility (NASA)

construct their own fantasies. The more dispersed they are, the more the fan works to assemble them into a meaningful whole. Each piece of information added to the canon opens up new gaps, suggests new kernels, from which new lines of fan speculation and expression can spring. More information simply represents more resources for our interpretive play. Fans don't need any author's permission to do what they do with favorite programs but they often seek his blessing and often defend their activity through appeals to his creative integrity. What's striking about transmedia authorship is the push from what was an economic imperative (develop a strategy that deploys networked communications to market media content) into an aesthetic opportunity (develop a mode of storytelling that enriches the fan experience by expanding the canvas on which the story unfolds.) What distinguishes the transmedia auteur from his predecessors is his heightened awareness of the reading process, his knowledge of the cultural work that fans do to create meaning and value around the cultural shards provided by the entertainment industry. The act of dispersal represents an attempt to design a space for audience participation with the media content, albeit one, as Scott notes, that comes with a deeper understanding of some of the ways the puzzle pieces might interlock.

Some twenty years ago (Jenkins, 1995b), I was studying how the first generation of Internet fans constructed David Lynch as a particular kind of auteur to explain and justify their own intense interest in *Twin Peaks*, which in retrospect seems very much the template for contemporary cult television. *Twin Peaks* fans wanted to "crack the code" and they conceived of Lynch as the "master programmer" who left behind clues and traces to be found by the faithful. Yet, many of the fans were having a crisis of faith, fearing that there were no answers and that Lynch did not have a plan. They held their doubts at bay by reading contradictory signs and mixed signals through the image of Lynch as a trickster, misleading them so he could blow their minds with his surprise ending. The more time the fans spent trying to master *Twin Peaks'* arcane lore, the more they had to elevate Lynch onto a pedestal so they could bask in his borrowed glory.

It is easy to read this fanboy obsession as a desire to master a complex text and recover its authorized and authored meanings. But remember that the fan speculation surrounding Laura Palmer's murderer (*Twin Peaks*), the Last Cylons (*Battlestar Galactica*), or the mysteries of the Island (*Lost*) are themselves acts of fan creativity. Just as (the mostly female) fan fiction writers extend the story, (mixed-gender) participants in online discussion forums create alternative readings, and both anchor their expansions through appeal to textual evidence. These fans propose a range of diverse and competing models for what might be going on and the stories they generate are richer and more engaging than the producers can ever get on the air. Competing interpretations become competing narratives and all involved become attached to one or another of these fan narratives, often being disappointed that the serial's resolution doesn't live up to the hype. We are collectively and individually the authors of the stories we are consuming, no matter what the auteur says or, for that matter, what we say about the auteur.

Much early writing about transmedia storytelling embraced the notion of an expanded continuity—the more texts we have, the more we can "know." Continuity has long been the fanboys's creed. Yet, as Derek Johnson (2009) notes, the conditions of modern media production make it almost humanly impossible to really preserve such an elaborate continuity without contradiction. The ideal of a perfected continuity allows these fans to exert their expertise as they nitpick the aired text for its failure to live up to their idealized vision of the narrative. Ultimately, though, as these fans take pleasure in proliferating alternative speculations, they are pulled into the pleasure of multiplicity.

Fans and academics alike speculate about what sets of gendered norms and practices separates the fanboy from the fangirl (recognizing that these are cultural rather than biological distinctions). The debate between continuity and multiplicity lies at the core of the matter. Those cultural practices that originated in the sphere of female fan culture, such as fan fiction and vids, celebrate multiple, competing, and contradictory versions of the core relationships. The historically masculine fan world of the discussion forum embraces alternative ways of mapping the grand conspiracy or navigating the core mythology. The gender lines are breaking down, somewhat, in both of these spaces and so are the polarities between continuity and multiplicity.

In both cases, the fans become both the guarantors of continuity and the generators of multiplicity, but the two modes involve different degrees of closeness and loyalty to the author. One fan writer has framed the distinction as one between "affirmational" and "transformational" modes of fandom (which she also breaks down largely on gender grounds), suggesting that producers are much more comfortable interfacing with fans who embrace what they created than with fans who seek to rewrite their stories (Obsession_inc., 2009).

Scott argues in part that the stress on expanded continuity places more cards in the hands of the fanboy auteur who doles out information that he expects the audience to master. But, mastery over the program has been at the core of fan interests—masculine and feminine—for generations. Fangirls can be annoyed if "the Powers That Be" give Spock a previously unsuspected brother just as fanboys can be annoyed if they confuse red and green Kryptonite, because both still care about what makes it into the canon. Whether fan productivity is understood in terms of continuity or multiplicity, the fans count on the auteur to create the common ground from which the multiple fan interpretations and appropriations emerge.

There is a persistent fantasy that we might create a franchise where most of the core mythology comes from the fans. How could this possibly work except in the most generic terms? We can crowd source a zombie film because there are an infinite number of the undead and we all know what is going to happen next, but to achieve a story of emotional depth we need to have a shared sense of the characters and, without a founding myth and some basic ground rules, a shared mythology is going to be difficult to achieve or maintain. We can achieve consensus, at least temporarily, around Wikipedia because it has established rules of verifiability and neutrality: the collectively generated representation can be tested against published sources that becomes shared tender and common currency. By contrast, the virtual world of Second Life is, by design, incoherent, a jumble of competing fantasies, because there is no shared mythology and only technical constraints on what we can build there.

However much fandom embraces an ethos of multiplicity, the stories still rest on certain shared knowledge about who the characters are, what narrative actions matter, what the parameters of the world are. The charge of "character rape" is often the ways that the fan fiction community self-corrects its own impulses towards creative and interpretive anarchy by testing any fan creation against a shared sense, however loose, of the original characterization. This process of canonization enables fan creativity even as it also limits fan invention: we may honor these limits in the breach but at least, we all know when we are breaking the rules.

For many fans, the author represents something else—not a divine creator whom they worship and adore (or whose fire they seek to steal)—but rather a role model whose path they seek to follow. Feminists have long complained that men declared the death of the author at the very moment when women were first being taken seriously as authors. At a moment, when more and more people are gaining access to the means of cultural production and distribution, they are unlikely to dethrone the author—too many of them want to become authors, some within the commercial industry, some within the fan subculture.

The fanboy auteur represents the dungeon master made good, the guy who used to play with *Star Wars* action figures and now gets to manipulate big budget special effects. If the fanboy auteur can be self-aggrandizing, wanting to command the respect he once bestowed upon Roddenberry or Lucas, many also genuinely want to offer advice, share insights, and empower the next generation of storytellers. Such fantasies about authorship are more apt to fuel the next phase of participatory culture than to crush it. If, as Scott suggests, there is a tendency to unify the discourse around a program through the showrunner, there has also been an unprecedented degree of focus paid to the craftspeople—costume designers, art directors, special effects artists, composers—who often are guests on these same podcasts, making the production process far more transparent than ever before. All of this opens many different ways for geeks to imagine themselves as authors.

The fanboy auteur generally offers a conception that is benign, fun, playable, likable, even, lovable, when compared with historic embodiments of patriarchal authority. The fan boy auteurs have produced stories that reflect the aesthetic traditions and shared tastes of the fan communities from which they emerged and which they now seek to court. Yet, part of what gives Scott's phrase, fanboy auteur, such a sting is its association with the myth of the geek's failed masculinity (the guy who still lives in his parent's basement, doesn't take baths, and has never kissed a girl). However much respect they've gained, they are fanboys and not fanmen.

Being a fanboy auteur creates sympathy from the audience but also raises expectations; these guys can really take the heat when they cross the line from the Guiding Vision into the Powers That Be. Some (Scott, 2009, for example) are raising the legitimate concern that as the fanboy becomes the transmedia auteur, they will encode into their franchises distinctly masculine pleasures and interests to the exclusions of the female fan world's alternative traditions and norms.

After all, the fanboy auteur often speaks of creating the stories they wanted to consume as a kid and that means that they are creating shows that other boys will like to watch. Is it fair to hold the fanboy auteur accountable for the long-standing lack of diversity in the media industry, when so many of them are working hard to mentor women to break into power?

What happens when a growing number of the Guiding Spirits are fangirls? *Caprica*'s Jane Espenson, *Buffy*'s Marti Noxon, *Ghost Whisperer*'s Kim Moses, *Smallville*'s Kelly Souders, *House M.D.*'s Katie Jacobs, and *Supernatural*'s Sera Gamble are all movers and shapers of transmedia content. Some of them are protégés still finding their voices, often unfairly dismissed when they claim the same authority we easily ascribe to their male counterparts. Some are part of male/ female creative teams. Others are taking over existing series. Few are creating their own franchises—yet. But they represent a significant wave of female showrunners and will collectively change the face of genre entertainment. Are they necessarily going to be pulled into established industry conceptions of television authorship in order to prove they can be "one of the boys" or do they represent the possibility of re-imagining what cult media authorship can look like? If the fanboy auteur embodies a masculine fan culture focused on continuity, mastery and expertise, might the fan girl auteur reflect the female fan's search for community, reciprocity and multiplicity? If so, what policies should they adopt or identities should they perform? How will this figure be constructed by fans and by industry to enable a different kind of relationship with the audience?

References

Jenkins, Henry. 1995a. "'Infinite diversity in infinite combinations': Genre and authorship in *Star Trek*." In John Tulloch and Henry Jenkins (eds). *Science fiction audiences: Watching Doctor Who and Star Trek*. New York: Routledge, pp. 175–195.

Jenkins, Henry. 1995b. "'Do you enjoy making the rest of us feel stupid?': alt.tv.twinpeaks, the trickster author, and viewer mastery." In David Lavery (ed.). *Full of secrets: Critical approaches to Twin Peaks*. Detroit: Wayne State University Press, pp. 51–69.

Jenkins, Henry. 2010. "The Hollywood geek elite debates the future of television." http://henryjenkins. org/2010/06/the_hollywood_geek_elite_debat.html.

Johnson, Derek. 2009. "Franchising media worlds: Content networks and the collaborative production of culture" (Doctoral Dissertation), University of Wisconsin-Madison.

Obsession_inc. 2009. "Affirmational fandom vs. transformational fandom." http://obsession-inc.dreamwidth. org/82589.html.

Scott, Suzanne. 2009. "Repackaging fan culture: The regifting economy of ancillary content models." *Transformative Works and Cultures*, 3. http://dx.doi.org/10.3983/twc.2009.0150.

7

A LOCALIZATION SHOP'S TALE

Bringing an Independent Japanese Role-playing game to North America

Mia Consalvo

One of the keys to the global distribution of videogames is successful localization—the process of translating and adapting a game to appeal to multiple players across language barriers, different cultures, and countries and regions with conflicting laws and political stances. And just like the process of making and selling videogames, localization has evolved into a complex process undertaken by a variety of actors with different skill sets, access to materials, and approaches to carrying out the process. Localization is now done by global corporations like the developer and publisher Square Enix, by smaller companies like MangaGamer, as well as by individuals and player groups that undertake unofficial (and sometimes illegal) localizations of games that were never intended to be sold outside of their country of origin. And as part of that history, Western players have played a key role in bringing Japanese games to a wider audience, in the process convincing the industry of the demand for such products. In doing so such players have also created a form of participatory culture that has (in some cases) likewise become more sophisticated, echoing the growing commercialization of user-generated content online.

The history of game localization is therefore a mixture of both official and unofficial efforts, sometimes focused on the same games. Official localizations became standard when game companies in Japan began selling their systems and games abroad, in order to capture a wider market. Companies like Nintendo, Sega, and Capcom have been synonymous with digital games, and many of the best-selling games and game systems originated and still continue to come from Japan, such as *Super Mario Brothers*, which has sold more than 40 million copies since its release in 1985 (Steckenberg, 2007) and the *Final Fantasy* franchise, which has sold more than 85 million copies of its various games worldwide (Peckham, 2009). And all of those products needed the efforts of translators in order to make sense to players from varying backgrounds. While in the early days of videogame development there were many games that didn't leave Japan, of those that did many were instant hits, impacting the culture of the industry and popular consciousness in ways we still don't fully understand. Mario was, and still is, global.

Yet increasingly, Japanese developers and publishers have been working to re-capture the glory days of years past. Although they still control a majority of their domestic market, global sales of Japanese games have been shrinking—from as high as a 50% share of the market in 2002 to about 10% of the same in 2009—as they encounter greater competition from Western developers (Tabuchi, 2010). Indicative of this trend, at the 2010 Tokyo Game Show the head of global research and development at Capcom, Keiji Inafune, announced, "Japan is at least five years behind. … Capcom is barely keeping up … I want to study how Westerners live, and make games that appeal to them" (Tabuchi, 2010).

In response, Japanese companies have become more aggressive and experimental in their strategies. For example, Square Enix purchased the Western developer Eidos and its library of game titles, and Capcom made the decision to have Vancouver-based Blue Castle Games create the second in its series of *Dead Rising* games, in order to give the title more "western appeal" (Sheffield, 2010). And companies around the world continue to decide which games deserve global releases, which are for domestic markets only, how to develop intellectual properties that might allow for the creation of different genres of games based on the same IP but are sold in different regions, and how to successfully figure out which of these approaches is the best to take.

Such assessments are always subjective, of course, and based on hunches and guesswork as much as past sales of a genre or designer, or tie-ins to other media. While Chandler explains that, now, up to 50% of a game's revenue may come from foreign markets, it can be tricky to predict in advance just what that figure will translate to (Byte Level Research, 2010). Some companies inevitably err on the side of caution, choosing not to spend extra money on a game to translate or localize it, based on such judgments. Yet Western players of Japanese videogames aren't always content to take the word of such companies that those games are not meant for them. Like anime and manga fans, some players have hunted down such games, and either played them in the original Japanese, and/or set about figuring out how to translate and localize them for themselves and other players. Doing so often involves ROM hacking, a practice that has a rich history with fans of early Japanese videogames.

Although early fan translators likely did not self-identify as such, they could be considered a participatory culture centered on that work. As defined by Jenkins, *et al.* (2006), participatory cultures are associated with

> relatively low barriers to artistic expression and civic engagement, strong support for creating and sharing one's creations, and some type of informal mentorship. … A participatory culture is also one in which members believe their contributions matter, and feel some degree of social connection with one another (at the least they care what other people think about what they have created).
>
> *(p. 3)*

Early fan localization of Japanese videogames was often a group effort, combining the technical skills of computer hackers with the language skills of students of Japanese. Thus "hackers and translators … would work together to extract the text from the ROM and replace it with an English script" (Parkin, 2008). Additionally, "sometimes, a person adept at editing/revising is brought in to smooth the text out afterward" (Parkin, 2010). The fruits of such efforts are usually shared on aggregator web sites such as romhacking.net, which not only serves as a distribution site for hacked game files, but also as a portal for information exchange and education as well as community building and support.

One of the earliest and best-known fan translators was Clyde "Tomato" Mandelin, who now works as an official localizer for Babel Media on projects such as *Kingdom Hearts II* and Tim Burton's *The Nightmare before Christmas* (Parkin, 2010). Before working on officially approved projects, Mandelin spent time as a ROM hacker in the 1990s, helping to translate early 8-bit and 16-bit games for the Nintendo Entertainment System (NES) and Super Nintendo Entertainment System (SNES), playable after hacking via emulator systems. Before ROM hacking, English-speaking players "would have to print off hardcopy fan translations and try to follow on screen text as they played" (Parkin, 2010). Yet with ROM hacking, the translation was integrated into the game. Hackers extracted the text from a game, put it into a file for someone skilled in Japanese to translate, and then replaced that text with an English version. Such activities were particularly popular during the early and mid-1990s, when many Japanese role-playing games (JRPGs) weren't being released outside of Japan, despite increasing demand by fans. Such interest was generated by globally popular titles such as *Final Fantasy VII*, which spurred interest in older games as well as newer ones (Mackey, 2010). That demand still continues—the ROM hack for the Game Boy Advance game *Mother 3* received more than 100,000 downloads in its first week of release in fall 2010 (Parkin, 2010). Likewise, sites such as romhacking.net still release patches for retro as well as more recent Japanese games, and teams of hacker-translators continue to update, refine and release new patches for older games.

In that way players and the participatory culture that emerged from their activity have contributed to the growing globalization of the games market and games industry, as well as the media industry more generally. Such players (as localizers) make accessible games that might never appear outside of Japan, and thus contribute in ways that the official industry cannot or does not. Fans and players can take greater risks, as their work is a service atop the games themselves—they aren't responsible for the development or production of the game, merely its modification or supplementation for a different audience. In filling that gap, they also become media producers themselves, with some becoming professionals on their own, working outside established companies to pursue their interests. And that work is facilitated by the growing ease of Internet-based collaborations as well as viable markets for digital downloading, all increasingly promoted via Internet-based sites and services. And in the process, there has been an increase in professionalization and savvy on the part of fan creators, who are now helping to transform what we think of as grassroots, non-profit-centered projects into efforts that more closely resemble the commercial industry itself, on various levels.

When ROM hacking first became a popular activity, it demanded a particular level of expertise among practitioners. Unofficial game localizers have had to become adept in several areas, in order to do their work. They must have the technical skills to either ROM hack a game, or at minimum create a walkthrough file for other players to access while playing the original Japanese version. And others must be fluent in Japanese, as well as the particularities of Japanese culture, idioms and local Japanese media products, particularly if they wish to capture the complexities of the narratives in more recently released games. Such player-localizers are thus situated in a niche, between the game as originally conceived for Japanese players, and Western players who may not possess the requisite technical or language skills (or the motivation to employ them) but still wish to play Japanese games. For that larger group, fluent player-localizers fill the gap.

In doing so, those player-localizers are bridging a divide composed of various elements. At one level the divide is a language and cultural barrier—most Western players couldn't access the original version of *Final Fantasy V*, for example, because they didn't speak or read Japanese, and had to wait for the official localized version to be released in the West by Square. Additionally, Western players may not fully appreciate the influences of Japanese literature on Japanese RPGs, where stories may be structured differently, featuring seemingly unrelated side stories that are interspersed with the telling of the main tale (West, 1994). There may also be different expectations between Japanese and Western players about gameplay difficulty levels, character point of view, or other structures of gameplay that contribute to such a divide (Chandler, 2005). All such differences contribute to the potential challenges of changing games for different markets.

And for official localizations, there's also the cost of setting up and then cultivating, maintaining and possibly expanding networks for manufacturing, distribution, retail sales and marketing of those localized titles. Overall, this means a sizable divide or gap must be considered when moving out of one's home country. In such instances, player-localizers can play a valuable role—both in terms of increasing awareness of a particular game, and in generating interest in a series, genre or specific title.

Through careful organization and collaboration via the Internet, a multitude of potential models for player-translators has emerged, from the simple (technically and culturally) to the more complex. They also can comprise individuals working alone to larger production teams, with the number of people required rising with the complexity of the project:

1. *ROM Hackers*: player-translators who ROM hack a game, then release a patch for the game to be played in English.
2. *Scanlationists*: player-translators who do peripheral translations such as scanlations of strategy guides.
3. *Scriptwriters*: player-translators who play through a Japanese game, releasing full English script for the game online.
4. *Indie localizers*: player-translators who contract with small (likely other indie) Japanese developers to do licensed localization for games, releasing them in the West for a share of the revenues.

As seen, only one model works officially with Japanese developers of the game in question, and also derives revenue (whether large or small) from the project. Yet each category provides other Western players with access to games they would not otherwise be able to play.

Such activities by player-translators might initially be compared with the work of modders, who also modify existing games, adding new life or interest to a commercially released product. However, player-translators are different in a key way—modders may create new maps, items, or even build total conversions, but at their core they are adding to an already existing product, perhaps already translated and distributed globally. For player-translators, the base activity is somewhat different—the original game would remain unplayable for a particular market without that final step of translation or localization. Yet that activity by player-translators is similar to that of modders in one key regard—it too spans a range from the very professional to the very novice, dealing with core texts as well as working mainly with peripheral texts such as strategy guides and companion web sites. It's also an activity that can be encouraged by some game developers, and strongly discouraged (even prosecuted) by others. It has also become more professionalized, as player-translators are now making the leap to work for hire and founding their own companies, acknowledging the monetary value of such participatory cultures.

In engaging in such activity, players contribute to the globalization of culture, whether welcomed officially or not. Like anime fans, videogame players are working to bring a "foreign" object to a wider audience, one that doesn't have the specialized skills (or perhaps interest) to access such games in their original Japanese form.

Distribution Channels

A key way to determine the shifting of participatory cultures from fan centered to those seeking a wider audience comes from recognizing how they utilize (and/or create) distribution channels for their work. An important challenge that player-translators face is the distribution of their products, which can vary based on whether such translations are licensed or not. Player-maintained, unofficial sites such as romhacking.net may be well known within the community, but are limited in their reach and require a certain level of technical ability to take advantage of. For example, the patches released on the site are designed to be loaded into original game files via an emulation system that's running a (possibly illegal) copy of the original game on a personal computer.

Although not vigorously prosecuted, many such activities, as long as they're not for profit, have managed to keep going, albeit on the margins of game culture. In contrast, for most of their history the center of gaming activity existed via the major consoles created by companies such as Sony, Microsoft and Nintendo. Those systems were and continue to be walled gardens, until very recently only allowing the sale and play of titles via physical artifact—cartridges or CDs and DVDs that contained games that had passed stringent technical demands. Although still controlling who can release on their platforms, such systems have changed dramatically in the past five years, due to the addition of online networks that allow players to download games onto their systems, as well as additional content such as add-ons and new levels or areas to play through.

More centrally for the activities of player-translators, however, those marketplaces have also opened up to admit more indie games, and games that might appear more experimental than the typical platform games like those in the *Madden* or *Call of Duty* franchises. The opening of distribution channels such as PlayStation Network (PSN) and Xbox Live has therefore facilitated greater entry by smaller game companies into the wider marketplace, bypassing the requirements as well as production values typically associated with console gaming and creating new opportunities for a wider variety of games to centralized marketplaces, as well as increased demand for smaller, less mainstream games. That has led to wider visibility for Western-based games such as Jonathan Blow's acclaimed title *Braid*, but has also created opportunities for companies such as Rockin' Android (player-translators turned professionals), who have started the process of bringing doujin games to the PSN, with their launch of the localized versions of the *Gundemonium 2D* shooter series in mid-2010. However, with those increased opportunities for official versions of smaller games come restrictions as well. Although emulated versions of games for older consoles are fairly widely available, no emulation yet exists for the current generation of consoles, meaning that ROM hacking of games that appear on the Xbox 360 or PS3 is not (yet) possible.

But those increasing official opportunities for digital distribution, along with the affordances of participatory cultures online, have fostered conditions where player-translators can move beyond unofficial, hacked versions of games, and create licensed products that reach a wider group of players. While Rockin' Android has helped to open such marketplaces and prove that demand for smaller Japanese games is present, their emphasis on 2D shooter titles has left another gap in the market—the independent Japanese role-playing game. Produced in large numbers in Japan by equally small companies, such games have either never been exported, or struggled to find decent localization and distribution outside Japan, due to their greater narrative and cultural complexities. But that gap has started to close, filled by a pair of Western game players who decided to create their own localization company and bring such games to the west.

Localizing the Last Mile: How an Item Shop Came to North America

Recettear: An Item Shop's Tale was originally developed in 2007 by EasyGameStation, a small Japanese game developer that specializes in creating quirky RPGs. It debuted at Comiket 73, a comic market held twice a year in Tokyo that features manga, anime and videogames created independently and generally not for profit (Bunao, 2010). The game, topically a Japanese RPG, has a twist: rather than mainly play as an adventurer whose main job is to dungeon dive in search of treasure, instead the player owns the item shop that sells gear and supplies to those adventurers. As Recette, the player must pay off a large debt incurred by Recette's now missing father, which involves buying low and selling high, hiring adventurers to enter dungeons in search of loot, and strategizing how to pay off the debt, with payments that increase weekly yet with only a fixed amount of time to accomplish that goal.

In 2009 the company Carpe Fulgur acquired the rights to localize the game and distribute it digitally. The process took about eight months to complete, and the game was released on Steam and other download servers on September 10, 2010. Yet the company that did the localization, Carpe Fulgur, is only a three-person team, and the game was their first professional project.

Andrew Dice and Robin Light-Williams started Carpe Fulgur in the same year that they acquired the rights to localize *Recettear*. As their web site explains, they wanted to bring "deserving works of interactive entertainment—independently made or otherwise" from Japan to America. After securing the rights to *Recettear*, they hired an artist to help with some graphics modifications. The company officially registered in June 2010, only a few months before the release of their first game.

Like many individuals I have talked with in other contexts (Consalvo, forthcoming), Dice was an early and avid player of videogames, with favorites coming from Japanese developers such as Square. And along with that interest in games grew a fascination with the process of localizing Japanese games. He writes on his web site that he

> heard of a man named Ted Woolsey, the lead editor for (then) Squaresoft Inc., a man who took games in Japanese and did his best to make them interesting and readable in English. From the moment he heard of that job—taking a game and making it work as well as it possibly could in English—Andrew felt a calling nearly in his *bones* to pursue that path.
>
> *(Carpe Fulgur, 2010, emphasis in original)*

FIGURE 7.1 Screenshot of *Recettear: An Item Shop's Tale*

Likewise, the other co-founder shares similar passions—Light-Williams has a degree in Japanese and enjoys games as well. Both have combined their interests in Japanese culture and language with a passion for games, to create a localization company on their own. As Dice related to me, the process of gaining the contract wasn't easy—while they could easily communicate with the Japanese developers at EasyGameStation, they had to work harder to convince them of their technical ability to get the work done (personal communication, September 28, 2010).

Once they had the job, the process of localization began. Yet for Carpe Fulgur, the work of making *Recettear* presentable to Western players involved much more than basic translation. As Dice explained, they wanted to make the game accessible, keeping its special qualities, but not making it feel too "foreign" for Western players. In short, they wanted to "culturalize" the game rather than simply localize it—an approach that many professional localization companies now advocate. For example, Kate Edwards of Englobe Media and chair of the International Game Developers' Special Interest Group on localization explains that culturalization involves taking "a deeper look into a game's content choices and their geocultural risk/opportunity in local markets" (2009). As Chandler elaborates, for some games localization can involve much more than translation, and in the context of such a game

> cultural specificity is necessary to the overall look and feel of the game. These types of games present localization challenges because the localized versions need to convey the character's intent, way of talking, and interaction with the game world to a foreign audience, without removing the uniquely regional characteristics that add to the game's flavor.
>
> *(2005, p. 26)*

Dice took just such an approach with *Recettear*, which although produced by Japanese developers was situated in a "*faux*-France setting." Dice changed some of the food references that would seem incongruous with the setting—such as "characters talking about sukiyaki like it was the most common thing in the world" (personal communication). He explained that, while Japanese players might not see such food references as incompatible with the French setting, for Western players too many such references would be "immersion breaking" and would pull the player out of the experience. Overall, though, Carpe Fulgur tried to keep the experience as close to the original as possible, and made no changes to gameplay or specific mechanics. Of course to some players (and perhaps game developers) any changes to a game are unacceptable, particularly if one sees games as an artistic form, with authorial intent tied to dialogue, visuals, narrative, and other elements that could be changed. Yet Di Marco argues that

> the customization of the text can be considered appropriate only when it helps to maintain the underlying textual intention of the original source. In other words, the aim of localization is not to produce literal equivalence of the original text, but rather to create the same effect in the game experience for the player as the original text sought to create.
>
> *(2007, p. 7)*

While individual developers and localizers may vary on their stances towards localization/culturalization and stricter translations, for most commercial developers the opportunity to reach a wider audience has generally trumped the wish to remain faithful to an original that may still be incomprehensible to outsiders, even after translation.

Such practices are in line with more professional localization practices, but Carpe Fulgur also had decided to professionalize their approach to releasing and selling the game in the West.

FIGURE 7.2 Localizers modified various references when creating the *"faux*-France version" of *Recettear*

They had acquired the rights to digitally distribute the game, yet had no pre-established channels to do so, and no prior credits as localizers on which to draw for recognition. But they strategically decided not to simply post a patch file for the game on a fan site, or sell a version of the game on their web site. Instead they decided to "come out swinging as hard as we could" via the various affordances of the Internet. Dice in particular cultivated interest in the project via Western-based anime and game fan sites such as RPGamer.com and Silicon Era, releasing news about the project and giving interviews about the game's status and what the localization process entailed. He used the company's web site and Twitter account to keep interest high, and in the summer of 2010 released a free demo of the game to further stoke interest. As he explains, that demo was likely instrumental in Carpe Fulgur's eventual contract with Valve's Steam Network, which then agreed to carry the game. That exposure was huge—and guaranteed an even wider audience than they had already reached via other means. Thus Carpe Fulgur not only created a professionally localized, licensed version of a JRPG, but they also pursued digital distribution deals that ensured official, wider interest in the game.

Of course many of the actions that Dice and Carpe Fulgur took would never have been possible without the growth of multiple participatory cultures that have developed over the years—including videogame, anime and manga fan networks online, which enabled them to meet and begin their collaborations across great distances. Indeed, as of this writing Dice and Light-Williams had never met in person, although Dice had plans to move to Oregon to work more closely with his partner. Carpe Fulgur may have started as two individuals who had a great interest in Japanese interactive entertainment, but it drew on and skillfully used fan networks as well as digital distribution outlets to create a new type of product—officially licensed fan products. And, critically, they chose a game created by individuals much like themselves—a small indie company that had made a well-crafted game sold via alternative markets, never destined for triple-A status or sales. In doing so, we can see the evolution of participatory cultures, becoming more savvy and sophisticated in their responses to popular media and the growing opportunities offered by digital distribution.

Carpe Fulgur worked to overcome the divide or gap that existed between the Japanese version of *Recettear* and potential Western players of an English-language *Recettear*. In doing so their actions could be seen in another light—as overcoming a cultural "last mile." The last-mile metaphor is most often applicable to the telecommunications industry, where overcoming gaps in service usually means spanning a spatial "last mile" in coverage to scattered, remotely placed potential customers. And although the distances can often be much more than a single mile, the concept highlights the difficulties involved in the "final stage of providing connectivity" from a service provider to potential customers (Rajadhyaksha, 2009).

In studies of the last-mile issue, scholars and policy makers have emphasized that one of the most challenging elements in rolling out new technologies is traveling the final step from producer to consumer. Without the ability to span that spatial gap, all is basically for naught. However, that last mile is often quite expensive, with potential customers not easily grouped together in one easily accessible location (in game terms, not all potential players speak the same language). Historically the last-mile problem has been focused on overcoming the challenge of space, such as the dissemination of basic telephone service, where the stringing of telephone line on poles to far-flung individuals, communities or regions was difficult due to rough terrain and scattered homes. To gain access some individuals had to pay for lines to be strung in order to receive service. More recently the last-mile problem has been referenced in relation to Internet access, and high-speed broadband access in particular.

But this concept could also help to explain some of the activities of players who do the work of overcoming a different type of gap—and bridging it with a "localization last mile" of their own. Of course some games are large enough or successful enough that developers and publishers can finance the last mile on their own—there is enough history to ensure customers will want the product, as Square concluded with the *Final Fantasy* series. But in cases where the developer is unsure, or too small to undertake such projects themself, players also now step in and bridge that gap. Thus players can function as service providers, taking a product and ensuring it can reach potential consumers. And player activities have gotten more and more sophisticated over time, with that last mile now being bridged in a variety of ways, from the simple to the elegant. The actions of Carpe Fulgur demonstrate fan activities taken to the professional level— individuals who created a company, negotiated a licensing deal, and successfully localized and marketed a product from another country. Fans continue to make unlicensed, unofficial versions of games, yet they are also moving into the professional domain as well, and with them expanding our ideas about what fans can do, and how they are expanding our reach to global games and media.

Conclusions

When Carpe Fulgur released *Recettear*, they announced their hope to sell 10,000 copies of the game. That would recoup their original investment and localization costs, and give them a small cushion to fund future products. After four weeks of release, Dice announced on the company's site that they had already sold 26,000 copies of the game, far exceeding their initial hopes, and has since gone on to sell more than 100,000 copies of the game. In conversation after that, he also said that this version has outsold the original Japanese version, and the money made would pay their salaries for the next year, and then some. They entered the game in the Independent Games Festival, an annual event at the internationally known Game Developers Conference, where it was awarded Honorable Mention in the Seumas McNally Grand Prize category. In the meantime Dice and Carpe Fulgur have successfully negotiated additional localization deals, such as another agreement with EasyGameStation for their more recent title *Chantelise*. And *Recettear* continues to sell on Steam, and elsewhere.

Of course Carpe Fulgur is one company, composed of only a few individuals. But it speaks to the increasing reach of players' activities online, and how some are increasingly professionalizing, utilizing the affordances of the Internet and social media to advance their own goals as well as broaden the availability of niche media products. A small US-based company that enjoys localization worked with an equally small Japanese company to broaden its market, and expand the reach of its games. Those actions were accomplished via hard work, but also through the availability of tools only recently developed and refined—a well-known and feasible digital downloading portal, well-established fan networks, and social media that has an increasingly wide reach. Combined with a sophisticated understanding of the localization process, Carpe Fulgur bridged a localization last mile, bringing a small Japanese videogame to the Western market. Player-translators have enlarged the opportunities available to them, and added diversity to the wider market of videogames at the same time.

References

Bunao, Darryl. 2010. "*Recettear*: Hope for Japan's indie developers," *Bitmob*, September 8. www.bitmob. com/articles/recettear-a-trail-for-foreign-licenses.

Byte Level Research. 2010. "Taking video games global: An interview with Heather Chandler, author of *The Game Localization Handbook*." www.bytelevel.com/global/game_globalization.html.

Carpe Fulgur. 2010. "About Carpe Fulgur" www.carpefulgur.com/about.html.

Chandler, Heather. 2005. *The game localization handbook*. Hingham, MA: Charles River Media.

Consalvo, Mia. Forthcoming. "Cosmo-play: Japanese videogames and Western players." In David Embrick, Talmadge Wright, and Andras Lukacs (eds). *Critical social policy and video game play*. New York, NY: Lexington Books (division of Rowman & Littlefield).

Di Marco, Francesca. 2007. "Cultural localization: Orientation and disorientation in Japanese video games," *Traduccio i technologies del la informacio i la comuincacio*. www.fti.uab.cat/tradumatica/revista.

Edwards, Kate. 2009. "What is localization?" Game Developers Conference. www.gdcvault.com/play/1756/(103)-What-is-Localization.

Jenkins, Henry, Clinton, Katie, Purushotma, Ravi, Robison, Alice J., and Weigel, Margaret. 2009. *Confronting the challenges of participatory culture: Media education for the 21st century*. Chicago, IL: John D. and Catherine T. MacArthur Foundation.

Mackey, Bob. 2010. "Found in translation: How ROM hacking brought Japan-only games to a worldwide audience," 1up.com, July 10. www.1up.com/.

Parkin, Simon. 2008. "You say tomato: A pro on fan-translating Nintendo's *Mother 3*," *Gamasutra*, December 26. www.gamasutra.com/.

Peckham, Scott. 2009. "*Final Fantasy* franchise sales revealed," *PC World*, April 23. www.pcworld.com/.

Rajadhyaksha, Ashish. 2009. "Rethinking the last mile problem: A provisional definition for the cultural last mile." www.cis-india.org/research/cis-raw/histories/last-mile.

Sheffield, Brandon. 2010. "Q&A: *Dead Rising 2* and 'growing pains' for old corporate Japan," *Gamasutra*, August 2. www.gamasutra.com/.

Steckenberg, Mark. 2007. "Best-selling video games of all time," *Infoplease*. www.infoplease.com/.

Tabuchi, Hiroko. 2010. "Japanese playing a new video game: Catch-up," *New York Times*, September 20. www.nytimes.com/.

West, Neil. 1994. "Woolsey interview," *Chrono Compendium*, September. www.chronocompendium. com/.

Further Reading

Chester, Nick. 2009. "Gaijin games in Japan," *Destructoid*, March 23. www.destructoid.com/.

Fletcher, J. C. 2009. "Square Enix pulls the trigger on Chrono Trigger fan projects," *Joystiq*, May 12. www. joystiq.com/.

Nutt, Christian. 2010. "Square Enix in 2010: President Wada speaks," *Gamasutra*, July 12. www.gamasutra. com/.

RPGamer. 2010. "*Recettear: An Item Shop's Tale* interview." www.rpgamer.com/games/other/pc/recettear/recettearint.html.

PART III

Leveraging Participatory Creativity

8

COLLABORATIVE NEW MEDIA POETRY

Mixed and Remixed

Thomas Swiss and Helen Burgess

To hear the critics tell it, one problem with emergent digital literary and art forms is that they don't yet have established stars. Where's our Shakespeare of the Screen? Our Pixel Picasso? How long before we have a Digital DeMille? The assumption is that we'll have them eventually—undisputed geniuses working in what is now generally called "New Media." But behind this assumption is another assumption, one with a long, thorny history—that the "best" or "most important" art is created by an individual, a single pair of hands in the study or studio.

This chapter focuses on collaborative, new media poetry; that is, poetry in the context of networked and programmable media involving multiple "authors" working in conjunction with one another. Such projects take place, of course, within the larger context explored throughout this book: how digitality allows for and even encourages participation in the making of culture and, in this case, cultural objects. In particular, we want to talk about the way collaboration, facilitated by digital technologies, "works" in the writing and reading of new media poetry. As an example, we look at a specific digital poem, *Blind Side of a Secret*, from two different perspectives: a writer (in this case, Thom), and a reader (Helen). We ask: how does collaboration happen in the composition process? And how, in the reading process, do we account for multiple authors, including artists, poets, and software packages?

This paper is split into "voices" (Thom and Helen). But these voices, like the voices in *Blind Side of a Secret*, should be considered "mixed and remixed": in the process of writing this essay, we have mixed and remixed each other's prose to come up with a narrative that satisfies the demands of two genres: the artist's statement and the academic critique. In a fitting parallel, thus, we offer this essay as an exercise in "collaborative writing about collaborative writing."

New Media Poetry: A Collaboration Between Authors and Machines

New media poetry—composed, disseminated, and read on computers or other screens—exists in various configurations. Many of these digital "events," to borrow a term from N. Katherine Hayles, are kinetic, visual, written, and sounded, published in online journals or displayed in art exhibits and stored eventually in archives (Hayles, 2006, p. 187). Unlike mainstream print poetry, which typically assumes a bounded, coherent, and self-conscious speaker, new media literature assumes a synergy between human beings and intelligent machines. In the case of new media poetry, the work sometimes remediates procedural writing, gestural abstraction, and conceptual art, while contributing to an emergent poetics.

New forms of digital poetry, especially collaborative digital poetry, challenge already contested terms such as "poetry" and "literature," and further complicate boundaries between literary genres. New media poetry brings together writers, artists, graphic designers, sound technicians, musicians, and computer programmers. This new community constitutes a kind of artistic underground, a literary movement that alternately challenges or ignores the institutional apparatus for "traditional" or "mainstream" poetry. Yet, as new media poetry attempts to move from the margins to the mainstream, from "noise" to "music," its growing community of artists and critics—its participatory culture—represent and institutionalize this new work in time-honored ways: through its explanatory and theoretical writings; through venues such as meetings and conferences; through prizes, contests, and other public awards; and through the development of publishing outlets.

Of course the terms "mainstream" and "margin" are relational and always shifting. Indeed looking at the rhetoric of and about new media poetry as it plays out among texts, audiences, and institutions is a powerful reminder that the meaning of the term "literature" itself is always up for grabs—and that new media poetry, whatever the future might hold for it, is currently the site of many important conversations, struggles, and debates.

The Internet, of course, plays an important part in the story of collaborative new media poetry (and digital literature in general) because it increasingly connects people who share similar goals and interests, and enables writers and others to generate and disseminate ideas and creative work. It also allows for the sharing of files between artists, writers, and critics who have never met, and provides a "publication" venue for works that might never otherwise gain a wide audience. In this sense, the Internet is yet another collaborator in the composition and critical process, albeit a primarily passive one. And beyond that, we have yet another layer of invisible collaborators: the authors of software packages, who define what is technically possible in the building and dissemination of a particular poem. All of these extra voices are part of a collaborative new media poem.

Many Hands, Voices, and Drafts: Thom Writes

As a poet, I began my own collaborative, Web-based work with visual and sound artists ten years ago—with a sense that the opportunities and demands of Web-based poetry, like many other new media practices, have their roots in the shared notion of community that was integral to the development of the Internet. I was also increasingly interested in new approaches to thinking about time and the text. Many of my collaborations are embodied in Adobe Flash, a vector-based animation software, used, for example, by programmer/artist Motomichi Nakamura to create our poem *Hey Now* (2002). The collaboration had its roots in conceptual art.

Under my direction, I had two of my friends read various sections of a poem I had written titled "Hey Now." After that, Nakamura and I began experimenting with the idea of "wrapping" language. Following the ideas of Christo and Jeanne-Claude, contemporary artists well-known for wrapping artifacts, buildings, and landmarks with various materials, we were interested in what "wrapped language" might look and sound like. Christo's "The Pont Neuf Wrapped, Paris 1975–85," for example, draped the famous French bridge in fabric, and was widely regarded as a fascinating experience for its viewers because wrapping and unwrapping objects hides and then re-reveals the familiar, allowing us to see objects in a new light.

In the case of our composition, the poem is hidden and revealed by animated characters who whisper gibberish before speaking verses of a cut-up poem I wrote. From games, we developed

FIGURE 8.1 *Hey Now*, by Thomas Swiss and Motomichi Nakamura
Source: www.ibiblio.org/nmediac/heynow.html.

the notion of a pacing cartoon man on the screen, who, when clicked by the viewer/reader/user, kicks the head of a figure who whispers like an alien before launching into the next animated section of the poem. "Readers" of new media poems are often challenged to make sense of synthesis; it's an opportunity to broaden interpretations and to look critically at how language is shaped by new media.

Collaborative work redefines artistic labor in what is for me (and many of my collaborators) new and complicated ways: what is the relationship, for example, between my language and the images and sounds others create, even if under my "direction"? How do the images and sound "change" the meaning of the language (and vice versa) and in what ways can the piece be said to still be a "poem"? Collaboration allows writers and artists—like myself and those I compose with—to reconsider both our work and our identities, to literally see them anew, as we move from individual to composite subjectivity. Yet while the art world has often been open to collaborative work—in the long shadow of Duchamp's experiments with Man Ray, the shared labor of producing art in Warhol's Factory, the many hands needed to make a film—the poetry world has typically had a hard time accepting collaborative work, although our digital times and newly developing collaborative, participatory communities are changing that.

My second example is a poem titled *Blind Side of a Secret* (2007), a project that includes three finished texts. While I had a hand in all three pieces, much of the compositional labor, much of the art, fell to others. Two of my graduate students, Pam and Bastiann, read the lines of poetry I had written—Pam in English, Bas in Dutch and English. A programmer friend, John, recorded their voices, created the sound files, and mailed them along with my comments, notes, and ideas to a team of digital artists I had invited to work with me. Yoshi Sodeoka is an artist, designer, and musician based in New York City. Nils Mühlenbruch was trained as a sculptor, lives in Amsterdam, and runs a site called Drifter TV. Motomichi Nakamura lives in Brooklyn; he only uses the colors black, red, and white in both his digital work and his paintings. I've never met Yoshi or Nils or Motomichi face to face; I "met" and collaborated with them all through the Internet, and it was through this medium that we all participated in creating the poems by exchanging files, emails, web-based drafts, code, revisions, and so on.

In the collaborative spirit of this chapter, I will tell the story of *Blind Side of a Secret* by incorporating commentary by Helen Burgess, a scholar I corresponded with via email and file sharing. Here I am turning to thinking about new media poems and education. Burgess had written me out of the blue, wanting to work with and critique *Blind Side* for an article she was writing about new media poetry in general and, specifically, the three versions of "my" poem that had been published. Helen is interested in the current gap in the literature on new media poetry from an "under-the-hood" perspective. Like others teaching digital literacies, she's noticed how few critical texts provide both a reading of a digital poem as it is *presented*, and a discussion of how that work is *actually put together*, i.e. how, in the case of *Blind Side*, it is composed with participation from a number of "authors," using language, software packages, code, and multimedia files, including sound.

"Generally," Burgess writes in an unpublished paper,

> all teachers of digital works have to work with is the "finished product"—for example, I might ask students to look at a work like "Inanimate Alice," and talk about how the medium interacts with the narrative, what the color/image/navigation choices mean for the work, and so on. But what we don't have access to is the process of collaboration, the collaborators' notes and emails, and the original files that put the whole thing together mechanically.
>
> *(Burgess, 2009)*

Those files can be revealing—and helpful in teaching students both how to read and write new media poems, how to collaborate, *how to participate*, in the processes or making digital poems themselves.

Reading Many Voices: Helen Writes

Blind Side of a Secret has been "published" in three versions in an online literary journal; it has also been seen in art exhibits and shown, on French television, as a short, experimental film. Let's call these three different versions "iterations"—since "versioning" wrongly suggests a creation order, an original.

Swiss begins with phrases, lines, and fragments of his own creation and then mixes them with portions of a short story he appropriates:

> I hate secrets. No, that's a lie, and here I was hoping to tell you the truth. Start again.
>
> I hate to be on the blind side of a secret. That's more like it. Sometimes I'll be shown, let in on, something that seems a real secret to me, I'll be allowed to stand right up against it and look all I like, but I still won't understand. I might as well be staring at a length of algebra, an unknown language—it will have no meaning for me. Worse than that, I will know that it must have a meaning for somebody else. So I'm stupid. No one needs to hide this from me, it is, quite simply, beyond me. I am on the blind side.
>
> *(A. L. Kennedy,* So I Am Glad, *p. 22)*

Using this remixed text as a working script, all three iterations of *Blind Side* feature two of Swiss's students: Pam S. (who read the lines in English) and Bastiann V. (who reads the lines in English and again in his native Dutch).

Rather than muddy the waters with numbers, which are both non-descriptive and possibly suggest that one of these three is the "real" poem, I'm labeling them by the principle variable in each case, which is the collaborating artist. Thus, *Blind Side Moto* refers to the linear Flash version co-authored with Motomichi Nakamura; *Blind Side Yoshi* refers to the Quick Time version co-authored with Yoshi Sodeoka; and *Blind Side Nils* refers to the *interactive* Flash version co-authored with Nils Mühlenbrich.

Blind Side Yoshi is a QuickTime movie. Another hand in this collaboration, John B., a programmer and friend of Swiss's, sent Yoshi Sodeoka .mp3 files of two readers speaking the lines of the poem, and Sodeoka took the sound, chopped it into pieces using a program called Recycle, remixed it in Logic Studio, composed an electronic music soundtrack, and mapped the sound to visuals using a sampler and Adobe After Effects. The result is akin to a music video: it plays through from beginning to end, with visuals and aurals synchronized together.

Blind Side Moto is also a synchronized video, this time animated in Flash format. It plays through from beginning to end without requiring user input. *Blind Side Moto* is a good example of the way Flash is often used as an animation medium—it features multiple characters or cast members, each of which is tweened, and the resulting animation plays out like a movie. Flash is best known as "time-based media"; Katherine Hayles identifies, with some exceptions, a characteristic of Flash poems as "sequential with little or no interaction" (Hayles, 2008, p. 28).

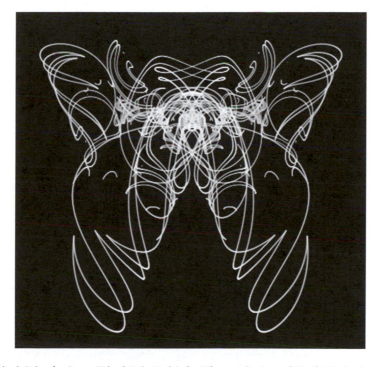

FIGURE 8.2 *Blind Side of a Secret* (*Blind Side Yoshi*), by Thomas Swiss and Yoshi Sodeoka
Source: www.hyperrhiz.net/hyperrhiz04/12-gallery/37-blind-side-of-a-secret.

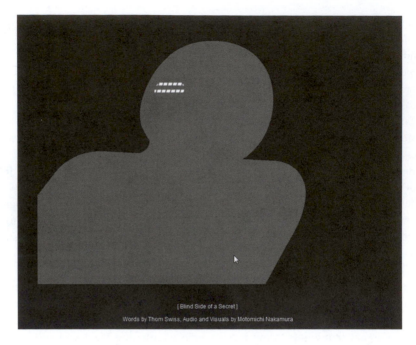

[Blind Side of a Secret]
Words by Thom Swiss, Audio and Visuals by Motomichi Nakamura

FIGURE 8.3 *Blind Side of a Secret* (*Blind Side Moto*), by Thomas Swiss and Motoko Nakamura
Source: www.hyperrhiz.net/hyperrhiz04/12-gallery/37-blind-side-of-a-secret.

Blind Side Nils, the piece I want to concentrate on, is also a Flash poem. But unlike *Moto*, the *Nils* iteration is interactive, requiring the reader to click on different sections of the movie to trigger animations and lines of the poem. Thus *Blind Side Nils* bucks the non-interactive tendency in Flash poems by being a piece that is "time based" in the sense that snippets of the poem are triggered and "play," but at the same time there is no logical ordering to the piece, and, more crucially, all the action exists on the same screen. There are no linkable, progressive lexia here, nor is there "progression" in the sense of time passing. The poem does not evolve or exhibit cumulative behavior. *Blind Side Nils* is thus unusual in the sense that it is a "time-based" poem that refuses to have any truck with time. It is a singularly self-contained piece that retains more than most poems its "object-ness."

One way to look into *Blind Side Nils* is to use three keywords adopted from the software the programmer used to create his iteration of this new media poem: trigger, layer, and module. To look at how the poem is constructed, we'll need to go into Flash and see where the trigger points are, and what is on individual layers, and how the layers are clumped into modular chunks.

When I first opened up *Blind Side Nils,* I was in for a surprise. Just from looking at the end-user version of the poem, I was pretty sure I could figure out how it was put together. The standard way to put navigation into a Flash piece is to place all the objects into layers in one timeline, place markers at various points on the timeline, and then make objects clickable so that one can jump from one part of the timeline to another. So, I was expecting to see a very long, stretched out timeline with many layers and a lot of markers to jump back and forward, like *Blind Side Moto*.

Instead, Nils has chosen to go for a much more modular approach. Each line of the poem with its corresponding animation has actually been made into a separate "movie clip," like a mini-movie. Then, all those movie clips have been placed on the stage in a single frame, all active

FIGURE 8.4 *Blind Side of a Secret* (*Blind Side Nils*), by Thomas Swiss and Nils Mühlenbruch
Source: www.hyperrhiz.net/hyperrhiz04/12-gallery/37-blind-side-of-a-secret.

and waiting to be triggered. Nils has created a nice rhetorical move in his implementation: he's layered his modules (by placing each movie clip module in a layered timeline) but also modularized his layers (because each module is made up of its own layers). This modularity is central to the reconfigurable story the poem tells: She comes home early. She sits on the edge of the bed. She tells the *story* of coming home early. She says she was driving. Is she speaking to him in bed, or is he at the doctor's overheated office? Or was it her at the doctor's office, leaving to come home early, telling the doctor the story of the sky turning red? And in the speaking, what is his, and what is hers, when the library contains unused sound files of them both reading the same lines?

Why does the way Nils has constructed the poem "under the hood" matter so much? Well, it tells me something about the way this particular collaborator approaches the poem. He doesn't see *Blind Side of a Secret* as a single narrative in time, a poem that is a river that you jump into and out of according to user clicks. This would be a kind of Formalist approach, with the "original" poem being the *fabula* and each clickable "reading" another *sjuzet*. Instead, he sees it as a completely modular grab-bag, where even the underlying structure is unordered—or rather, it is ordered spatially, not chronologically. By collapsing the timeline into modular chunks, he has *collapsed the time of the poem itself*.

Blind Side Nils suggests that new media poems possess the ability to confound the distinction between orality and literacy by confounding the distinction between space and time. The way Nils has constructed his layers of sound and image atop one another, in a single frame, belies our usual understanding (laid out by Marshall McLuhan and Walter Ong, among others) of the way space is visual, while time is oral/aural (Ong, 2002, p. 32; McLuhan, 1995, p. 300). *Blind Side Nils* incorporates both; thus, one experiences orality with the performance of each line (not because it is recorded sound, since recording in itself is a kind of transformation of sound from the oral to the written register, but because the performance is varied, responsive to audience, and made up of repeatable chunks like epithets), while at the same time one views the whole poem like a single page of text, spatially structured—what Laurie Petrou characterizes as the "simultaneous space" of concrete poetry (Petrou, 2006, p. 2). By placing all the clickable parts of the poem in a single frame, Nils has created a kind of spatial time machine.

In this iteration of *Blind Side*, the "secret" subject of the poem is paralleled by the inherently secret nature of the Flash poem (in the sense that we only ever see the "final version" as it is *played*, not as it is *constructed*). One of the conclusions we can draw from this is that it is imperative that we have access to the source files that were used to create new media poems before we can really understand them. But it's not just access that counts—it's the ability to read the source files. This is why, I think, it's crucial that readers of new media poems, students as well as critics, know how these authoring tools work, and how each authoring tool defines or constrains the composition of the work itself. Without this knowledge, we are indeed left on the blind side of a secret. As A. L. Kennedy—in the passage Swiss appropriates for his own text—writes: "I'll be allowed to stand right up against it and look all I like, but I still won't understand. … I might as well be staring at a length of algebra, an unknown language."

Conclusion: Thom and Helen Write

New forms of digital poetry, especially collaborative digital poetry, challenge already contested terms such as "poetry" and "literature," and further complicate boundaries between literary genres. Collaborative new media poetry brings together writers, artists, graphic designers, sound technicians, musicians, and computer programmers. Working together, they work *against* the worn cliché of the lone writer or artist, a cliché that still defines how we think about the production of literature and art. Collaborative digital poems invite shared participation; each contribution is meant to be as important to the process of composition as all other contributions. Contributors have equal permission to add, edit, and remove text and multimedia characteristics. The composing process is recursive, each change prompting others to make more changes. The question asked in *Blind Side of a Secret*—"What was his? What was hers?"—becomes complicated in a process where "his" and "hers" is intentionally remixed by authors, artists, and algorithmic processes.

The "authorship," in some instances, does not end with the release of a new media poem. Every "reading" of *Blind Side Nils* is a kind of remix, as the user decides where to click next, and which voice to listen to, providing yet another layer of authorship to the poem. But beyond interacting with the "finished" poem, it is a useful exercise to conduct a "deeper" reading, if one is to get a sense of the full richness and collaborative nature of a poem made up of many voices. Thus in terms of reading, teaching about, and learning from collaborative new media poems, it is important for readers to have access to the processes of collaboration, the collaborators' notes and emails, and the original files that put the pieces together mechanically. These digital files can be revealing to critics and helpful in teaching students how to read new media poems; they can also help students and others learn to participate in the collaborative processes of making digital poems themselves.

References

Burgess, Helen J. 2009. "How to read an electric poem." Unpublished conference paper. Presented at the Society for Literature, Science and the Arts, Atlanta, GA, November 2009.

Hayles, N. Katherine. 2006. "The time of digital poetry: From object to event." In A. Morris and T. Swiss (eds). *New media poetics: Contexts, technotexts, and theories.* Cambridge, MA: MIT Press, pp. 181–210.

Hayles, N. Katherine. 2008. *Electronic literature: New horizons for the literary.* Notre Dame, IN: University of Notre Dame Press.

Kennedy, A. L. 2001 [1995]. *So I Am Glad*. New York: Vintage.

McLuhan, Marshall. 1995 [1956]. "The media fit the battle of Jericho," *Explorations*, 6: 15–21. Reprinted in E. McLuhan and F. Zigrone (eds). *Essential McLuhan*. New York, NY: Basic Books.

Ong, Walter. 2002 [1982]. *Orality and literacy: The technologizing of the word*. New York: Routledge.

Petrou, Laurie. 2006. "McLuhan and concrete poetry: Sound, language and retribalization," *Canadian Journal of Media Studies*, 1(1): 1–25.

Swiss, Thomas and Mühlenbruch, Nils, 2007. *Blind side of a secret* iteration "Nils" *(Blind Side Nils)*. *Hyperrhiz: New media cultures*, 4 (winter). www.hyperrhiz.net/issue04/swiss/nils.html, accessed 29 April 2011.

Swiss, Thomas and Nakamura, Motomichi, 2002. *Hey Now. NMEDIAC*, 1(1). www.ibiblio.org/nmediac/heynow.html, accessed 29 April 2011.

Swiss, Thomas and Nakamura, Motomichi, 2007. *Blind side of a secret* iteration "Moto" (*Blind Side Moto*). *Hyperrhiz: New media cultures*, 4 (winter). www.hyperrhiz.net/issue04/swiss/moto.html, accessed 29 April 2011.

Swiss, Thomas and Sodeoka, Yoshi, 2007. *Blind side of a secret* iteration "Yoshi" (*Blind Side Yoshi*). *Hyperrhiz: New media cultures*, 4 (winter). www.hyperrhiz.net/hyperrhiz04/12-gallery/37-blind-side-of-a-secret, accessed 29 April 2011.

9

COLLABORATIVE COMICS

The Story Behind Pixton

Clive Goodinson

In late 2007, I was browsing Wikipedia, admiring its wonderfully collaborative nature. Anyone could create content and build upon or refine the contributions of others. However, as someone who loves stories and creativity, I lamented that it deals only with objective fact. Any poetic license is necessarily sifted out through peer review and consensus. What if, I thought, there were a Wikipedia for stories and other expressions of the imagination?

Then I had an "aha" moment.

I realized that the best medium in which to build a collaborative, online storytelling platform would be the highly visual and most universally loved medium of all—comics!

Born in England, I had grown up in Canada reading a lot of comics, although not in the North American tradition of superheroes. Rather I had enjoyed the wit and style of *The Beano* from Britain, *Astérix* from France, and especially *Tintin* by the Belgian, Hergé. So for me, it was natural to draw a connection between comics and storytelling.

As an expert web developer, I immediately started to envision the mechanics of a comic-making platform enabled for the social web. Anyone with an Internet connection would have ready access to the same sophisticated set of tools. Traditional, freehand drawing would be removed from the equation, enabling unprecedented collaborative possibilities. Thus, in early 2008 Pixton.com was born, a new kind of comic authored by the world.

Since then, Pixton has evolved into a thriving multilingual community, creating a shared world of digital stories and comic conversations. Authors from all walks of life come together to express themselves, to share techniques, and to create comics that entertain, inform, educate, and inspire.

The comic that follows serves a double purpose: it showcases the versatility and sophistication of Pixton's comic-making features, while illustrating the new possibilities for collaboration in an entertaining way. All the elements of Pixton comics are controlled simply and directly by clicking and dragging: fully posable characters, speech bubbles, props, backgrounds, photos, and even sounds.

Looking forward, the Pixton community will continue to inspire innovation and even more ways of reinventing comics. Hergé would be proud!

FIGURE 9.1

FIGURE 9.2

Comic © 2011 Pixton.com

PIXTON®

FIGURE 9.3

10

THE ASSAULT ON CREATIVE CULTURE

Politics of Cultural Ownership

Owen Gallagher

Introduction

Irish legend has it that in AD 561, St Colmcille, one of Ireland's best-loved patron saints, paid a visit to his old teacher, Finnian of Moville at his monastery in County Donegal. While there, he borrowed an important religious book from Finnian's collection, an illuminated manuscript similar in style to the *Book of Kells*, and produced a hand-rendered copy. When Finnian discovered that Colmcille had made this unauthorized copy, he demanded that it be handed over immediately. Colmcille refused and the case was brought to Diarmaid, the High King of Ireland, who sided with Finnian, ruling under Brehon law that 'to every cow belongs its calf, to every book, its copy'. Colmcille challenged the ruling and the dispute escalated, culminating in the Battle of Cúl Dreimne, or the 'Battle of the Books', which took place under Ben Bulben, County Sligo, in AD 561. Diarmaid's army was slaughtered and Colmcille won the day, retaining his copy of the book, which came to be known as the 'Cathach' or the 'Battler', arguably Ireland's oldest extant illuminated manuscript.

If there is any truth to this legend, it is incredible to consider that, over 1400 years later, we are still arguing over the status of cultural works as 'property' in the copyright wars, and it is with a certain sense of pride, as an Irishman whose ancestors come from County Donegal, that I take up the mantle and continue to promote the arguments allegedly put forth by Colmcille in defence of his unauthorized appropriation.

Cultural works or expressions are different from other types of possessions in that they exist primarily to communicate knowledge and ideas in one form or another, which is of benefit to society at large and, therefore, they should be copied and distributed as widely as possible. Making a copy of a book, song or movie does not use up the original, in the way that taking someone's car means that they no longer have that car. By making a copy of a cultural work, the creator still has possession of the original and the work is no worse off for having been copied, nor has its value decreased.

In this essay, I argue in favour of increased digital access to cultural works and for increased freedom to appropriate, repurpose, transform and redistribute such content. I argue that the concept of property ownership cannot be meaningfully applied to works of so-called 'intellectual property' and that this term is inappropriate and inadequate in this context. As such, I am arguing against increasing restrictions on access to digital content through legal and technical means as

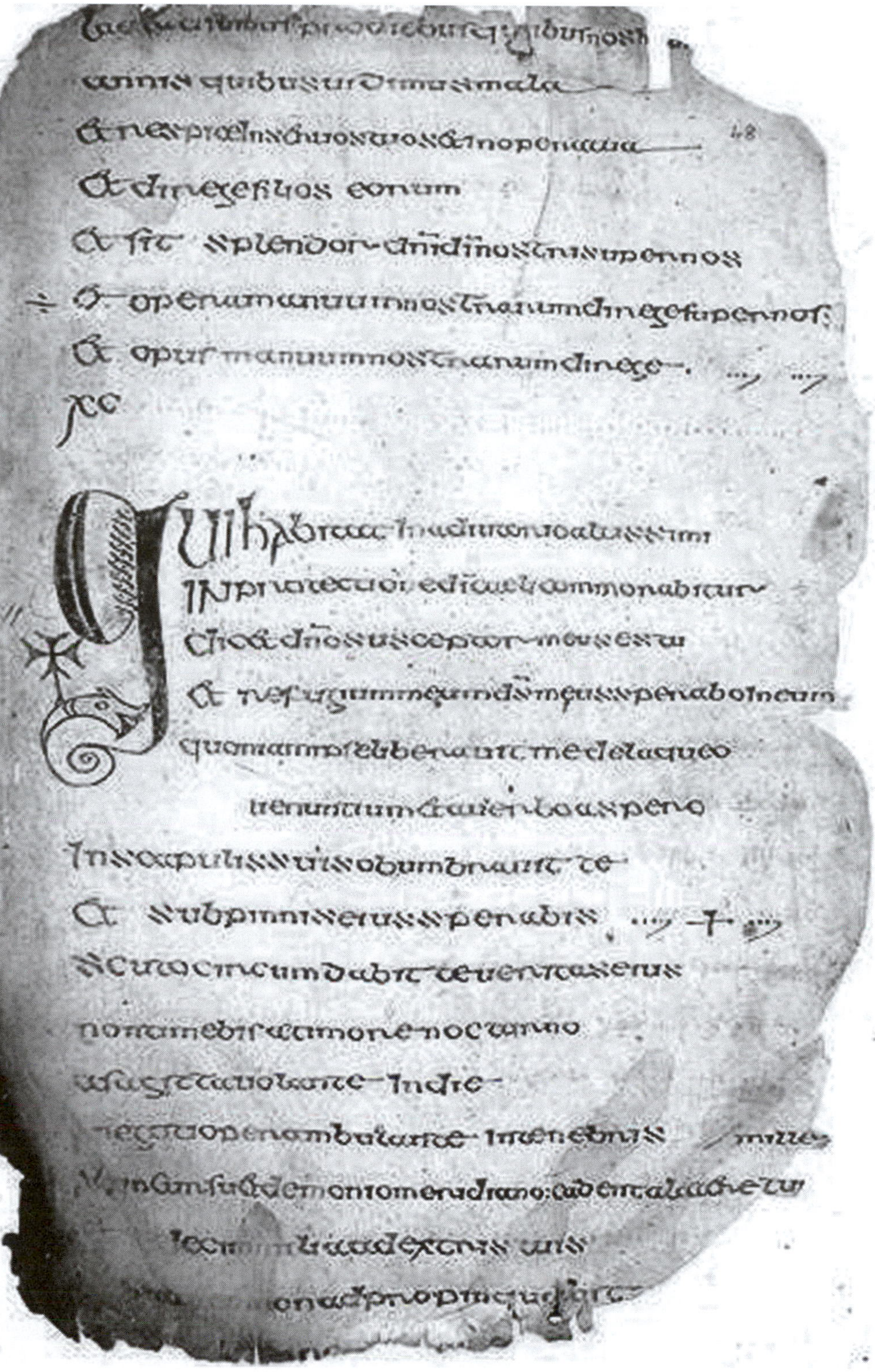

FIGURE 10.1 The Cathach

well as against increased censorship and criminalization of certain forms of 'Do it Yourself' (DIY) creativity, which rely upon the unauthorized reuse or remixing of copyrighted works.

At the heart of this debate is a struggle for power and control by a handful of multinational corporations who currently possess the copyrights to the majority of well-known songs, films and texts in the world, and who amassed incredible fortunes in the 20th century by being in a position to sell copies of these works in the form of physical media like CDs, DVDs and books. With the development of the Internet, mp3s, online video and ebooks, this outdated business model has been threatened with extinction. The existing copyright system works relatively well for controlling copies of physical media, but, once songs, movies and texts are digitized and made available via the Internet, it is effectively impossible to regulate the spread of copies, without infringing on fundamental rights to privacy and freedom of expression.

Naturally, the corporations who currently possess the majority of economically valuable copyrights, enduring unprecedented losses on their previously lucrative business model, sought to develop solutions to this perceived problem. Their first tactic was to lobby to have copyright terms extended, which they succeeded in doing, over and over again. Secondly, artificial scarcity was invoked by incorporating Digital Rights Management (DRM) and encryption technologies into digital media files, in conjunction with the development of laws, like the Digital Millennium Copyright Act (DMCA) and the European Union Copyright Directive (EUCD), which make it illegal to circumvent these digital locks.

Thirdly, they initiated an aggressive campaign of threatening lawsuits against individuals who were uploading and downloading copyrighted files to and from the Internet, ultimately leading to Draconian laws being adopted around the world, such as the UK Digital Economy Act, whereby Internet access is terminated if an individual is accused of downloading copyrighted files on three separate occasions.

Finally, and perhaps most salient to this discussion, corporations have been engaging in a form of censorship and suppression in a bid to control the use of their copyrighted content by demanding that arguably legitimate and fair uses of sampled material be taken down from video-sharing web sites without justification. They are effectively discouraging creativity and innovation by punishing artists for using the culture around them to create new cultural works.

Such measures are violations of fundamental rights to privacy and freedom of expression, and will not prevent people from downloading music and films or producing new remixes, but rather will result in the unjust criminalization of millions of people around the world.

Cultural Ownership

What is property? Property is a social convention. It is an agreed upon set of social relations between people and objects, backed up and enforced by state laws. Proponents of cultural ownership claim that cultural works like songs, films and texts are a form of property and that the person who creates the work has a natural right of ownership to that work. This is simply not the case. A song is not property. A recording of a song is not property. However, a physical CD with a recording of a song on it is property. The material object itself—the compact disc—is property, in the sense that it can be exclusively owned, but, arguably, the song and the recording of the song are not.

The three states identified in this example may be described as, 1) the immaterial idea of the work itself, 2) the recorded expression of the work and 3) the physical means of storing the recorded expression of the work. Copyright, in its current form, applies limited protection to the expression of the work, whether that is a sound recording, a notated musical composition or a lyrics sheet, in the case of songs. I propose that copyright protection does not and should not

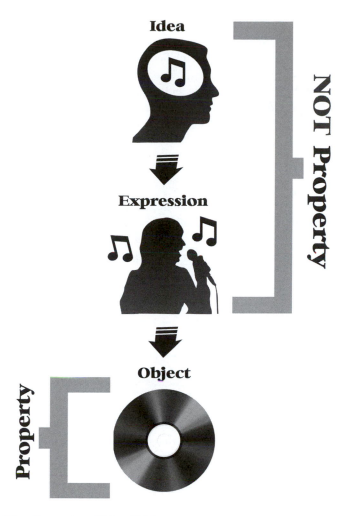

FIGURE 10.2 The Idea–Expression–Object Trichotomy

imply property ownership, but rather is a narrow set of legal protections placed upon a cultural work that is intended to protect its economic potential for a limited time and to prevent others from unfairly profiting from the author's labour.

In relatively recent history, copyright was assimilated under a nonsensical catch-all label known as 'Intellectual Property' rights, along with patents and trademarks. Intellectual property is a term that became popularized in the USA since the late 1960s, in a way that confused the meanings of copyrights, patents and trademarks, all of which are completely different sets of rights and related laws that should never have been grouped together in such a reductionist manner. The beneficiaries of this widespread confusion are the multinational media conglomerates who wish to promote the agenda that cultural works are property, which they own outright, in the same way that you may own a car.

The two widely accepted justifications for property are scarcity and effort, neither of which may be meaningfully applied to cultural works. Scarcity does not apply here because cultural works do not contain the exclusivity trait, that is, the use by one person of a song, for example, does not exclude others from using it. In relation to effort, Locke's labour theory of property states that the fruits of a person's labour are their own because they worked for it. In other words, mixing one's labour with natural resources or 'undiscovered land' creates the conditions of property ownership. Although it is clear that intellectual labour goes into the creation of cultural works, the effort justification assumes that a creator is working within a vacuum and that the intellectual products of the mind are the sole and original work of an individual. This is clearly not the case, as all cultural works necessarily draw upon those that came before them, as well as the technologies that enabled their creation and everyone and everything that has ever interacted with the creator.

Copyright

Copyright is not a natural property right. It is a limited monopoly right granted by governments. The idea that authors are entitled to be rewarded for their intellectual efforts as a natural right, let alone to a full property right in their creative output, has been repeatedly rejected by courts in numerous legal cases. In its 300 year history, copyright law has always existed to attempt to create a balance between the interests of the copyright holder and the public who would be culturally enriched by the knowledge and ideas contained in the work. The original purpose of US copyright law was to promote the progress of science and the useful arts, by securing for limited times to authors and inventors the exclusive rights to their respective writings and discoveries.

Copyright law first came into existence in England in 1710 because book publishing companies found that competing publishing companies in Ireland and Scotland were taking their authors' manuscripts, reprinting them and selling them back into the country at knockdown prices.

It was widely felt that this early example of piracy was unacceptable, so laws were drafted that provided authors with the sole right to make copies of their work for a period of fourteen years, after which the right would be relinquished, the work would enter the Public Domain and anyone would be free to make and sell copies of it. It was a very simple law, designed to enable a publishing company to enforce a monopoly on the work for a limited period of time, an economic incentive for them to continue publishing books.

With the advent of photography, cinema, radio, TV, home recording, the Internet and mobile devices, the media landscape was utterly transformed. US copyright law was extended again and again through lobbying by the film and music industries, and today lasts for the life of the author plus seventy years, or ninety-five years if the work was produced by a corporation. It changed from an opt-in system where you had to register for copyright and renew it regularly, to a system of copyright by default.

The Walt Disney Company is largely responsible for lobbying for many of the copyright term extensions that came into being in US copyright law. Coincidentally, every time Mickey Mouse was due to cross into the Public Domain, Disney successfully lobbied for a change to the law and extensions to the copyright term. The irony is that most of Disney's most successful works were based on creative works that were already in the Public Domain, such as *Snow White*, *Alice in Wonderland*, *Sleeping Beauty*, *Cinderella* and *Pinocchio*. If the creators of these works had exercised their intellectual property rights as rigidly as Disney now does today, none of these animated films would have been produced.

Disney's production of *Snow White and the Seven Dwarfs* in 1937 is the animation equivalent of putting a man on the moon, in terms of breaking new ground, implementing innovations and making history. Imagine if this, the first ever feature-length full-colour animated film had not been produced because the copyright in the *Snow White* story had been retroactively extended by the Brothers Grimm. A pivotal moment in the history and development of animation would not have occurred. How many of these pivotal moments of blinding cultural innovation are we now missing out on because of the current copyright regime?

The technology that enables the Internet and the World Wide Web is fundamentally and profoundly different from any prior media storage and information distribution system. It is a decentralized digital network, which makes it possible to produce, copy, manipulate, mass distribute and consume digital replicas of creative content at costs approaching zero.

The fundamental right within copyright law is the exclusive right to reproduce the copyrighted work. Every time you read, view, listen to, share, transform or reuse a work wrapped up in a digital media file, you are unavoidably making a digital copy of the copyrighted work in the temporary memory cache of your computer. This fact alone renders the 20th century notion of copyright obsolete. Reproduction is no longer an appropriate way to measure infringement, as, in the digital age, copying is now central to every use of a copyrighted work.

Cost of Creativity

Copyright, as a concept, could be justified at the time of its origin, because publishing companies bore significant economic costs to provide the capital required to invest in an author. Buying the equipment and materials, printing the books and distributing them to retail outlets, was an expensive business and the majority of book investments would inevitably make a loss, with the tiny minority of bestsellers making up the shortfall. But, today, an artist can produce an album, book or film using inexpensive digital equipment and software, and distribute and promote it online for free. When costs are close to zero, should it not be up to the consumers to set the price they wish to pay? Could we be seeing a return to a patronage system, similar to that which was in existence during the pre-copyright Renaissance era, when artists were patronized to finance the creation of new cultural works?

There is no question that artists should be financially compensated for their work. This is fundamental. If an author spends time and effort writing books, a musician recording albums or a film studio producing movies, they should be financially supported to the extent that they can continue to produce cultural works. In the digital age, however, the idea of selling digital copies of your work may no longer be a viable approach. Alternative revenue models are being explored and adopted. We have now evolved beyond the limited choice between patronage and copyright faced by our predecessors. Advances in technology now enable wider possibilities, such as the idea of collective patronage.

The core concept of collective patronage expands on Hyde's theories of the gift economy, in which individuals engage in gift exchange without the immediate expectation of anything in return. The idea of collective patronage envisions a self-regulated network of individuals engaging in ongoing 'gift-giving' in the form of online micro-payments, whereby the overarching goal is to provide creators of cultural works with financial support to enable them to concentrate on their art as a funded vocation.

Utilizing online distribution technologies, such as peer-to-peer (P2P) networking and secure digital payment sites like PayPal to redistribute the accumulating 'artist's fund', collective patronage offers a potentially fair, just and efficient meritocratic system that supports talented artists and combines the best of long-tail economics with open platforms, inevitably resulting in the production of more and better cultural works. The notion of the impoverished artist could be a thing of the past as the network grows and becomes a collective publisher of works, from which everyone becomes a beneficiary. We are living in a transitional period of human history, where the promise of an open, free and sustainable 'cultural industry' is just within our grasp, but where the reality is that those who have controlled the tools of production, distribution and promotion in the

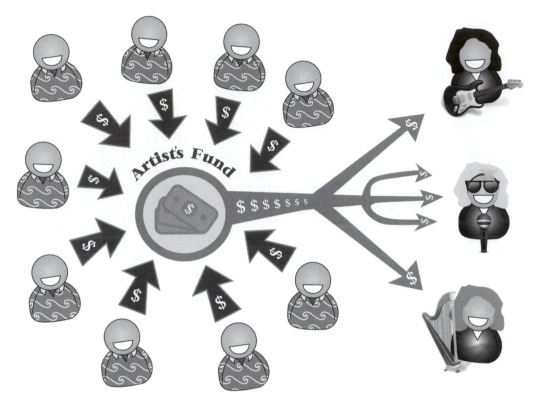

FIGURE 10.3 Collective patronage – artist's fund model

past are doing everything in their power to cling on to this control, for the sake of their own dwindling profit margins.

Political Economy

In the 20th century, record companies and movie studios played the role of typical capitalists, in the Marxist sense, retaining complete control over the 'factories' (i.e. movie and record studios), the 'machinery' and 'tools of production' (cameras, recording equipment, CD and DVD duplication machinery), the means of distribution (music stores, cinemas, movie rental stores) and promotion (print, TV and radio advertising), all of which were extremely expensive and inaccessible to the vast majority of individual artists. In 1983, there were fifty major media conglomerates in the United States, collectively controlling the bulk of significant media outlets across the globe.

By 2003, through a series of mergers and acquisitions, this number had been reduced down to five media conglomerates, who between them owned the majority of newspapers, magazines, book publishers, radio and TV stations, and movie studios of the United States. These five conglomerates were Time Warner, Bertelsmann, News Corporation, the Walt Disney Company and Viacom. By 2011, the list had expanded to include CBS and General Electric, owners of NBC.

This media cartel of extremely powerful companies regularly exercises its 'intellectual property' rights, often to the detriment of wider society. For example, Viacom initiated a lawsuit against Google-owned YouTube in 2007, claiming that the video-sharing website enabled widespread copyright infringement of their content. Three years later, the case was defeated, as it was ruled that YouTube fell within the 'safe harbour' provisions of the DMCA, meaning that, as long as they complied with takedown notices from copyright owners, they could not be held accountable for the content hosted on the site, as there is no way they could know if content is uploaded legitimately or not.

Opposition to perceived imbalances, such as copyright term extensions, unjustified takedown notices, DRM and Internet surveillance, has been significant. Organisations such as Creative Commons, the Electronic Frontier Foundation (EFF), Public Knowledge, and the Open Rights Group, among many others, represent a forward-thinking approach. A clear reflection of changing attitudes towards these issues among the European electorate saw the Swedish 'Pirate Party' acquire two seats in the 2009 European Parliament elections. The party stands for reformation of copyright law and the decriminalization of non-commercial file sharing, reduction of copyright terms and banning of DRM, the dismantling of the patent system and the ongoing protection of personal privacy in the information age. Many other country-specific Pirate Parties were established in the wake of this electoral victory.

A balance between copyright protection and freedom of expression is the prize in the copyright wars; however, extreme views on both sides do little to help attain this harmony. On a fundamental level, at both ends of the debate, greed is a motivating factor. Copyright holders campaign for greater control, increased profits and the neoliberal promise of endless growth. Their bottom line has been significantly affected by the digital revolution. On the other hand, those who expect to be able to consume music, films, books and games completely for free are also motivated by greed. Artists cannot survive without financial support in a capitalist society. A balance is required, and, unsurprisingly, it is not the extremists who are leading the charge towards achieving this elusive harmony. Those involved in the creation and nurturing of participatory cultures, such as video remixers, are leading by example.

[Re]mix

The remix was first made popular in the mainstream by DJs and hip-hop artists in the music industry who would take samples from the tracks of different artists and weave them together into a new tapestry, with the end result being something new, a transformative use of extant material. A useful parallel might be to consider the use of quotations in an academic paper. The author using the quote does not ask for permission from the original authors and uses the quotes out of their original context to support an argument or illustrate a point. Sampling and remixing takes quoting up a level and uses the materials as building blocks in the same way a collage artist might recombine cuttings from magazines, old photographs and illustrations to create something new.

One of the major issues facing those involved in unauthorized remixing is the threat of litigation by copyright holders, which effectively deters artists from freely building on the work of others, as they have always done. Remixing, as a process of creating art, is certainly not a new technique. It could arguably be dated back to Pythagoras' anagrams in the 6th century BC, when he would reorder and recombine the elements of a word, that is, the individual letters, to form a new word bearing some semiotic relation to the original—a practice that remains popular to this day. However, for much of the 20th century, audio-visual remix creativity was all but impossible for most people to produce. The equipment was simply not available or affordable to the average person. The content was not accessible. The distribution channels were reserved for those who owned the airwaves.

Essentially, the production and distribution costs associated with creating a remix were astronomically high and not economically viable. Affordable computers, digital media production

FIGURE 10.4 Screenshot from TotalRecut.com

technologies and the Internet have now removed that economic censor and so we have seen an explosion in remix creativity, clearly evident through the popularity of remix community websites like TotalRecut.com and Vidders.net.[1]

Where once, media companies produced content and audiences consumed it, today these boundaries are blurring and consumers have also become simultaneous producers of media content. Technology has transformed a one-way, top-down hierarchical system of media delivery into a multi-directional, accessible, participatory network available to anyone with a computer and an Internet connection.

Conclusion

Stifling creativity. Chilling innovation. Silencing dissidents. Suing children. These are the things that film studios, music labels and media conglomerates are coming to be associated with. By waging a 'war on piracy' they are effectively criminalizing millions of people. What our kids are doing when they download music or films from P2P networks is not wrong. It should not be illegal. If our kids are labelled as criminals for doing this, they are less likely to take the law seriously, which could lead to them ignoring other laws, eventually resulting in more serious consequences. The entire legal system is being undermined by an antiquated copyright law system that simply does not translate to the reality of online digital media.

I worry about my own children. My two daughters, aged two and four, will grow up believing that it is acceptable to break the law because everyone else is doing it. My 4-year-old loves to watch the theme tunes to her favourite Disney TV shows on YouTube. Little does she know that they have been illegally uploaded by naïve, well-meaning parents who may eventually end up being sued by Disney.

Under the current regime, media companies are suffering because their role as middlemen is under threat, now that artists can connect directly with their fans through the Web; artists lose because there is no proven model of how they are to make money from their work online and amateur creators lose because they create in defiance of copyright law, facing the possibility of being sued, just because they sampled a clip from a copyrighted movie or song to create a new remix.

These problems can largely be addressed. Media companies could relax the current regime of exercising dictatorial control over online content and begin to leverage the developing sharing economies and participatory cultures, in conjunction with their own commercial economies. They need to come to understand the distinctions between commercial competition and amateur appropriation; between creative re-purposing and piracy.

Artists need to take up the tools of production, replication, distribution, promotion, consumption and participation, and use the technologies now available to them to create and foster their own participatory cultures. New ways of making money will need to be explored when it turns out that selling the music may not be the best way to earn a living. Alternative revenue models such as collective patronage, live performance, cross-media integration, local advertising and product placement should be experimented with and thoroughly explored. And, finally, amateur remixers must continue to create, despite impending threats of legal action. Copyright law has changed drastically many times in its 300 year history and, if one thing is certain, the law is always lagging behind the technology and culture it seeks to regulate. It is only a matter of time before the laws catch up with the reality of emerging participatory cultures, and the remixers may well turn out to be the superstars of the age of digital appropriation.

I leave you with the legendary words of Colmcille, in defence of appropriation, as reiterated by Manus O'Donnell in 1532, which are perhaps more relevant today than ever before:

"I contend," said Colmcille, "that the book of Finnian is none the worse for my copying it, and it is not right that the divine words in that book should perish, or that I nor any other should be hindered from writing them or reading them or spreading them among the tribes. And further, I declare that it was right for me to copy it, seeing there was profit for me in copying this book in the form of wisdom gained, and seeing it was my desire to give the profit thereof to all peoples, with no harm therefore to Finnian, or his book."

Note

1   Total Recut is a social networking community for fans and creators of video remixes, recuts and mashups launched in 2007. www.totalrecut.com. Vidders.net is an online community of vidders, sharing and viewing fan vids. www.vidders.net.

Further Reading

Anderson, Chris. 2008. *The long tail: How endless choice is creating unlimited demand*. New York, NY: Hyperion Press.
Bagdikian, Ben. 1997. *The media monopoly*. Boston, MA: Beacon Press.
Bagdikian, Ben. 2004. *The new media monopoly*. Boston, MA: Beacon Press.
BBC News. 2010. "Q&A: The Digital Economy bill," *BBC News*, April 9. http://news.bbc.co.uk/.
"The Constitution of the United States," Article 1, Section 8, Clause 5.
DeLong, James V. 2002. *Defending intellectual property*. Washington, DC: Cato Institute.

Fisher, W. 2004. *Promises to keep: Technology, law, and the future of entertainment*. Palo Alto, CA: Stanford Press.

FreePress.net. 2011. "Media ownership chart: The big six," *FreePress.Net*, February 7. www.freepress.net/ownership/chart/main.

Gowers, A. 2006. *Gowers review of intellectual property*. London: Stationery Office.

Gu, V. 2008. "Neo-patronage: The new fan-artist connection," *The Smoke Signal*, September 15. www.thesmokesignal.org.

Hyde, Lewis. 2007. *The gift: Creativity and the artist in the modern world*. New York, NY: Vintage Press.

Jenkins, Henry. 2006. *Convergence culture: Where old and new media collide*. New York, NY: New York University Press.

Kramer, Matthew H. 2004. *John Locke and the origins of private property: Philosophical explorations of individualism, community, and equality*. Cambridge, UK: Cambridge University Press.

Kravets, D. 2009. "Pirate party wins EU Parliament seat," *Wired.Com*, June 8. www.wired.com/.

Kravets, D. 2010. "Google wins Viacom copyright lawsuit," *Wired.Com*, June 23. www.wired.com.

Kuseck, David and Leonhard, Gerd. 2005. *The future of music: Manifesto for the digital music revolution*. Boylston, MA: Berklee Press.

Lasica, J. D. 2005. *Darknet: Hollywood's war against the digital generation*. Hoboken, NJ: John Wiley & Sons Inc.

Lessig, Lawrence. 2005. *Free culture: The nature and future of creativity*. New York, NY: Penguin Group (USA).

Lessig, Lawrence. 2008. *Remix: Making art and commerce thrive in the hybrid economy*. New York, NY: Avery Publishing.

Litman, J. 2006. *Digital copyright*. Amherst, NY: Prometheus Books.

McLeod, Kembrew. 2005. *Freedom of expression: Overzealous copyright bozos and other enemies of creativity*. New York, NY: Doubleday

Martin, Scott. 2002. "The mythology of the public domain: Exploring the myths behind attacks on the duration of copyright protection," *Loyola Law Review*, 36(1): 280.

Menzies, L. 1992 [1920]. *Saint Columba of Iona*. Dublin: J. F. M. Books.

O'Kelleher, A. 1918. *Betha Colaim Chille/Life of Colmcille*. Chicago: University of Illinois Press.

Oguh, E. 2009. *John Locke and property as a human right today*. Germany: LAP Academic Publishing.

Patry, W. 2009. *Moral panics and the copyright wars*. New York, NY: Oxford University Press (USA).

Sherman, Brad. 1999. *The making of modern intellectual property law: The British experience, 1760–1911*. Cambridge, UK: Cambridge University Press.

Thierer, A. 2002. *Copy fights: The future of intellectual property in the information age*. Washington, DC: Cato Institute.

Tucker, Benjamin R. 1985. *State socialism and anarchism and other essays: Including the Attitude of Anarchism toward Industrial Combinations and Why I Am an Anarchist*. Colorado Springs, CO: Ralph Myles Publisher Inc.

PART IV
Building Cultures of Knowledge

11

THE CREATIVE CONVERSATION OF COLLECTIVE INTELLIGENCE

Pierre Lévy
Translation by Phyllis Aronoff and Howard Scott

Adopting the point of view of knowledge management, this chapter explores the creative conversation from which collective human intelligence is emerging in the new digital communication environment. The creative conversation is the fundamental engine of knowledge communities, that is, communities seen from the perspective of their cognitive functioning. The first main idea put forward in the chapter is the inseparability of collective intelligence and personal intelligence. This idea is expressed in practical terms in the dialectical interdependence of the social management and the personal management of knowledge. Secondly, I stress the growing role of the creative conversation in explicating, accumulating and organizing knowledge in the shared memories of knowledge communities.

Beyond "Collective Stupidity"

Since the publication of my book on *collective intelligence* in 1994, I have continually met with the classic (and, in my opinion, weak) objection that it is individual humans who are intelligent, while groups, more or less organized communities and, even more so, crowds are for the most part stupid. What are we talking about here? The term collective intelligence can have many different meanings, but all these meanings involve the combination of two concepts: cognition ("intelligence") and society or community ("collective"). Cognition is here, very classically, the activity of perceiving, remembering, problem solving, learning, etc. Collective intelligence refers therefore to the cognitive capacities of a society, a community or a collection of individuals. This collective cognition can be seen from the perspective of the two complementary aspects of the dialectic between individual and society. On the one hand, the individual *inherits* and benefits from the knowledge, institutions and tools accumulated by the society he or she belongs to. On the other hand, distributed processes of problem solving, decision making and knowledge accumulation *emerge* from conversations and, more generally, symbolic interactions among individuals.

With regard to inherited intelligence, it should be noted that individual cognitive capacities are almost all based on the use of tools—symbolic (languages, writing systems, various social institutions) or material (instruments of measurement, observation and calculation; vehicles and transportation networks; etc.)—that individuals have not invented themselves but that have been transmitted or taught to them by the surrounding culture. Most of the knowledge used by those who claim that intelligence is purely individual *comes to them from others*, through social institutions such as the family, the school or the media, and this knowledge could not have been accumulated and developed without long intergenerational chains of transmission.

With regard to emergent cognition, it should be noted that the most advanced contemporary societies are based on institutions whose main engine is precisely collective intelligence in the form of *well-ordered conversation*: these include democracy, the market and science.

The principles of *democracy* do not guarantee that inept or corrupt leaders will never be elected or that extremist or violent policies will never be adopted by the majority of a population. But universal suffrage, political pluralism, the balance of powers, freedom of expression for all and respect for human rights in general (and those of minorities in particular) are more conducive to civil peace and human development than dictatorships or regimes dominated by a single party or a closed group of the privileged few. In democracy, collaborative intelligence comes about, not as a result of the majority imposing its will, but rather out of the decisions of voters or the members of various parliaments after open *deliberation* during which different views can be expressed and responded to.

The existence of a *free market regulated by law* will, of course, not prevent economic crises or income inequalities. But historical experience shows that planned economies in which a small number of bureaucrats decide the orientations of production and set prices are much less efficient than market economies, in which producers and consumers as a whole contribute—imperfectly and with all the attendant distortions—to deciding prices and levels of production and consumption. Here, the creative conversation is ideally an *economic negotiation* informed by realities and respectful of laws. I note in order to avoid any misunderstanding that this perspective is obviously open to government interventions aimed at making markets more dynamic and more conducive to human development, such as through the construction of infrastructure, the creation of circumstances favourable to education and research, or the implementation of social assistance programs.

Finally, the *scientific community* is governed by principles of collective intelligence such as peer evaluation, reading and citing of colleagues, reproducibility of observations and sharing of data. All these principles prevent neither repetitive mediocrity nor errors or "false" theories. But conversation by the scientific community, conversation that is both collaborative and competitive, is obviously preferable, for the advancement of knowledge, to arguments from authority or hierarchical, dogmatic, opaque institutions with inquisitorial powers.

More recently, the success of the *open software* movement, which is based on the free collaboration of programmers worldwide, and of the multilingual online encyclopedia Wikipedia, in which authors, readers and editors exchange roles to further the dissemination of knowledge, are striking examples of the power of collective intelligence emerging from a civilized creative conversation.

Thus the facile irony about collective stupidity (which is obviously always the stupidity of "others") fails to recognize all that our individual wisdom owes to tradition and what our most powerful and most useful institutions owe to our ability to think and decide together. Need I add that my emphasis on the collective aspect of human intelligence in no way implies the abdication of critical thought or individual originality? The concept of collective intelligence for which I am arguing here is the opposite of conformism or sterile standardization. The full recognition of what we owe to the traditions or communities we are part of implies precisely the moral obligation to enrich in return the common good through original, relevant creative effort. Collective intelligence can only be productive by combining or coordinating unique elements and facilitating dialogue, and not by levelling differences or silencing dissenters. Finally—need it be repeated?—no common knowledge can be created, accumulated or transmitted without *individual* effort to learn.

Reflexive Explication and Sharing of Knowledge

Personal and Social Knowledge Management

Introduction to Knowledge Management

Most of us no longer live, as our ancestors did, in a single tribe. Contemporary social life generally has us participate in many communities, each with a different cultural tradition or knowledge ecosystem. Members of a family, speakers of a language, citizens of a city or a nation, followers of a religion, practitioners of a discipline, learners of a technique, amateurs or masters in an art, collaborators in a business or organization, fans of a TV show or a videogame, members of a thousand networks, associations or working groups, we participate in more than one cultural community. *If we look at these communities from a cognitive perspective*, they are constituted through an autopoietic process of construction, reproduction and transformation of knowledge ecosystems. These are "working" communities in the information economy or, if you will, social learning enterprises. Their creative conversations accumulate, manage and filter *memories* in which collective identities and personal identities define each other, and the capacity for thoughtful interpretation and the capacity for informed action answer each other. For each of these communities, the maintenance and use of its knowledge capital, or the management of its knowledge, is thus a major concern.

Since I am going to use the now classic term *knowledge management* (KM), I would like at the outset to prevent any misunderstandings. It is generally agreed that the only things that can be "managed" objectively and rationally are data, in particular digital data. On the other hand, it is still possible—but rather more difficult—to manage the *conditions* (financial, technical, social, emotional, etc.) of a creative conversation in which the participants will produce, discuss, explicate, filter and internalize in their practice an evolving collective memory. This second type of management is obviously much more subtle than the first, since it involves the sensitive concepts of shared views, relational familiarity, trust and incentives to creativity. Finally, actual knowledge cannot be separated from the consciousnesses in which it is reflected in the present or from the individual learning processes it starts from and returns to. This subjective dimension of knowledge obviously cannot be "managed" by some outside authority like a thing or an objective situation. It belongs to the inner world, that is, to the desire to learn and share, to individuals' work on themselves or their autonomous discipline. Having clarified these points, I will speak in familiar terms about "knowledge management," just as in general usage, people say the sun rises even though they know very well that it is the earth that revolves.

The question of knowledge management becomes more complicated when we consider the contemporary fashion of personal knowledge management (PKM).

The Cycle of Personal Knowledge Management

In the new ubiquitous digital environment—especially in social media—people are confronted with information flows so varied and abundant that they must learn to process them systematically. The complete cycle of personal knowledge management can be broken down into several distinct steps.

Attention Management

People must first learn to control their attention: they therefore have to define their interests, order their priorities, identify their areas of effective competency and determine the knowledge and know-how they wish to acquire. Once all this has been properly clarified, PKM practitioners must then strive to concentrate on their objectives without letting themselves be distracted by the multitude of information flows that cross the field of their consciousness. But this should not prevent them from remaining open or from usefully replacing their preferred objects of attention in the overall context that gives them meaning! They also have to be able to relate to people who have priorities different from theirs. The balance between openness and selectivity is a tricky exercise that must constantly be refined.

The Choice of Sources

Once we have set our priorities, we have to choose our sources of information. In contemporary social media, these sources are mainly other people. We thus need to spend time examining the information flows produced by others in order to choose those that best correspond to our objectives. We must also identify the institutions, businesses, research centres, networks and organizations of every kind that offer the information that is most relevant to us. It goes without saying that we can follow the choices made by people we trust and who share our interests, either automatically (collaborative recommendation systems are proliferating) or manually.

Collection, Filtering, Categorization and Recording of Information Flows

The information flows from all the sources identified must be aggregated or assembled in a single place so that they can be filtered in the most practical way. The collection tools can be RSS feeds from selected sites or blogs, colleagues, experts or institutions followed on Twitter or other social media, participation in online forums or various automatic alert systems. The choice of sources was the first form of filtering. But even feeds from our favourite sources have to be roughly evaluated and categorized in order to eliminate redundant information as quickly as possible. The information that has not been eliminated must then be explicitly categorized (tag, comment, source name, etc.). Tags permit flexible, emergent categorization by means of freely chosen labels (social tagging) and the formation of networks for sharing references (for example, among researchers). Generally, only categorized information will be able to be used by others sharing the short-term collective memory (e.g., Twitter or Facebook) or long-term collective memory (e.g., YouTube, Flickr, Delicious or CiteULike) where it is accumulated. It is impossible to classify without having a classification system, whether this system is implicit and unconscious or explicit and deliberately constructed. It is in our interest to make our own classification system explicit, if only to be able to perfect it and construct a more refined and effective memory.

Synthesis, Sharing and Conversation

Once the information has been filtered, categorized and recorded, we need to be able to make a critical, creative synthesis. Only by so doing can we assimilate the information and transform it into personal knowledge. This synthesis, which is as a rule periodic, can be carried out in a blog, in an article, by editing a wiki entry, in a video, through incorporation into a computer program or in any other way. The essential point is to make the synthesis public, that is, to introduce it into the open process of creative conversation of a community or network of people. The creative synthesis will be indicated in social media or disseminated through an RSS feed, or will feed an open-source collaboration process or be made accessible through search engines and reported by automatic alert or recommendation systems or through the online social activity it generates.

The synthesis will thus inevitably be exposed to criticism and comment from a community of people interested in the same subjects.

The Feedback Loop of Personal Knowledge Management

In short, we pick up information, assemble it, categorize it, filter it, synthesize it, share the synthesis with others and then repeat this cycle creatively, always keeping a critical eye on our methods and tools. In this way, we prevent the fossilization of our reflexes or blind attachment to our tools. After receiving feedback from the creative conversation, we must periodically question our priorities, redefine the context, connect to new sources and eliminate old ones, perfect our filtering and classification tools, explore new methods of synthesis, get involved in other conversations, and so on. In doing this, PKM practitioners help not only themselves but also others to whom they are connected and who are doing the same thing.

Techniques Pass, Cognitive Function Remains

We must avoid unduly reifying the tools I have mentioned, which are only those used in the most advanced practices of 2010. In fact, in a few years, they will undoubtedly be replaced by new tools, or all aspects of PKM will be brought together in technical environments unknown as I write these lines, for example, new types of browsers. In any case, the need for a personal discipline for collection, filtering and creative connection (among data, among people, and between people and data flows) will remain for a long time. Techniques pass, cognitive function remains. Without denying the importance of collective strategies and the shared visions that support them, I believe that social knowledge management should be thought of as an emergent level based on the creative conversation of many individuals' PKM. One of the most important functions of teaching, from elementary school to the different levels of university, will therefore be to encourage in students the sustainable growth of autonomous capacities in PKM. This can be done by using social media in an institutional environment that encourages collaborative learning and under the supervision of teachers that are themselves savvy in this new practical discipline. And this personal management should be conceived from the outset as the elementary process that makes possible the emergence of the distributed processes of collective intelligence, which in turn feed it.

The Role of Explication in Social Knowledge Management

Let us make an inventory of the content of the memory of a knowledge community.

It is, firstly, all the signifiers recorded and manipulated by the community: these are documents in general, texts, images, sounds, multimodal signs, software, and so on.

Secondly, we need to consider the languages or symbolic structures that organize the signifieds and make it possible to read documents: jargons, classifications, thesauruses, codes, correspondences among various systems, etc.

Thirdly, we need to add "abstract machines," ways of doing things, pragmatic rules by which documents are activated or processed, symbolic structures and relationships among people: methods, customs, know-how, and criteria and conventions of all kinds, which are often implicit. These rules include the methods of measurement, evaluation and judgment that produce the formally quantified or qualified data that are stored in the organization's memory. Only mastery of these methods makes it possible to connect the documents to their referents.

Finally, we must consider a fourth aspect of the symbolic organization of a knowledge community, which is not located at the same logical level as the others, and which ensures its self-referential looping. I am thinking here of reflexive reification, the work of self-modelling that allows the community to synthetically represent to itself its own emergent cognitive processes. We can say that one of the goals of knowledge management is to support this self-referential modelling in such a way as to encourage the improvement of the processes of collective intelligence and facilitate individuals' identification of their own roles (and those of others) in creating and maintaining the knowledge of the group they belong to.

Whether we are producing useful documents, clarifying or improving shared symbolic structures, spreading the most effective methods and practices or raising individual and collective awareness of the emergent cognition of the community, we will almost always find ourselves confronted with the problem of explicating implicit knowledge and processes.

The distinction between explicit knowledge and implicit knowledge echoes other dialectical pairs of opposites of the same type, such as objective knowledge and subjective familiarity or formal knowledge and practical competency. I suspect that the opposition between implicit knowledge and explicit knowledge reactivates in a new context the very ancient philosophical distinction between theoretical knowledge and empirical knowledge.

The explication of knowledge was particularly studied and developed by the father of contemporary knowledge management, Ikujiro Nonaka. Nonaka proposed a cyclical model of the cognitive life of organizations. According to this model, called Socialization, Externalization, Combination, Internalization (SECI), knowledge exists first of all in an implicit form in individual practices. These practices are then socialized (S) and shared informally to become incorporated into organizational cultures. The critical phase of knowledge management in organizations, according to Nonaka, is the transition from implicit knowledge to explicit knowledge (E). This externalization begins with a practice of questioning and dialogue, which can only develop in an atmosphere of trust. It consists essentially of representing in the form of written documents, software or databases the largest possible part of the informal practices and the surrounding culture. The explication of knowledge has many advantages: it makes it possible to decontextualize and thus distribute and share information on a large scale, to critically examine the state of knowledge and possibly even to automate its application. The externalization of knowledge takes the form of explicit concepts, classifications or (computer) ontologies, methodological documents, rules, algorithms or programs. Once knowledge has been formalized in concepts and rules, it can be distributed in the information system of the organization, combined (C) and applied—possibly automatically—to the data flows that indicate the internal state or environment of the organization. The personal learning effort is not forgotten, since, in the end, the results of the explication and combination phases have to be integrated or internalized (I) by the collaborators in order to be implemented, tested and perhaps transformed in practice, which will lead to a new cycle of socialization, questioning, dialogue, formalization, recombination, and so forth. The organization's knowledge is the life cycle I have broadly outlined, and not any one of its phases, artificially isolated. This model provides a general conceptual framework in which the organization can represent its own cognitive functioning to itself.

The SECI model was developed at a time when the Internet already existed but the Web was very new and social media were still unknown, except for a few pioneers of virtual communities. As I suggested above, our view of knowledge management today draws much more on collaborative learning networks using social media than on the administration of central information systems controlled by experts. We need to promote organizational cultures and technical environments conducive to transparency, flexible reorganization of skill networks and continuous collaborative creation of immediately usable knowledge. But this dialectic of socialization, explication, combination and practical integration is still relevant for understanding the sustainable functioning of a creative conversation that produces knowledge.

Dialectic of Memory and Creative Conversation

Let's elucidate now the complex relationship between shared memory and creative conversation. To start with, where does the word conversation come from? Etymological dictionaries tell us that the verb to converse originally meant "to live with or among, to keep company with." It was only in the 17th century that it acquired the meaning of talking together or exchanging ideas. However, *versare* in Latin means "to turn or return," and the prefix con- comes from the Latin *cum*, which means "with." I am therefore proposing a hypothetical first etymology according to which, in con-versation, people turn to each other and exchange the meaning of streams of discourse addressed to each other. According to my second hypothetical etymology, conversation is a process of con-version of knowledge from an implicit mode to an explicit mode and vice versa, and this reciprocal conversion is done "together" (*cum*).

The creative conversation is thus the active interface, the original environment or source of the process of individuation of the knowledge community. In the actual to virtual direction, it transforms knowledge that is implicit, opaque, immersed in action into shared memory. In the virtual to actual direction, it transforms the accumulated common memory into effective sensory-motor activity.

Although physical meetings remain essential for establishing trust, more and more conversational interactions oriented toward collaborative learning take place online, for example, through social media. Judging by my personal experience on Twitter, the most constructive exchanges consist of short messages pointing to URLs containing multimedia data. The messages categorize these data with a brief comment and/or a hashtag, a metadata label. Hashtags are used, for example, to bring together and find URLs, discussion threads or comments on a subject on specialized search engines. The now increasingly widespread experience of watches or collaborative learning using social media makes it possible to observe in action how a creative conversation constructs a common memory and is in turn constructed through the relationship to that memory. The immense flow of raw data is filtered and categorized by certain participants. Other participants confirm or dispute these categorizations, which eventually leads to discussion. The members evaluate the relevance and validity of the filtered data, reading recommendations and categorizations on the basis of their experience and their knowledge of a field of practice. If they are engaged in an active learning process, they will integrate the information received into their personal knowledge management systems, which in the end will transform their practice, and will also disseminate the information in other circles of conversation. The data are thus filtered, categorized and recategorized by a community, then found (by means of metadata) and used in practice by individuals, which changes their personal capacities to filter and categorize, and the cycle begins again. This is how a conversation engine accumulates (data) and organizes (metadata) its common memory. Through the integration of memory into practice and personal experience, creative conversation transforms data into knowledge. Symmetrically, implicit knowledge is transformed into data through blog entries, wikis and articles, and into metadata through an activity of participatory categorization.

The process of collaborative production of common memory favours individual learning in so far as the individuals involve their personal experience in the conversations (the process of explication is always instructive) and involve the results of the conversations in the reorganization of their personal experiences. Here there is no purely individual learning, since data are exchanged and pooled, the imposing of metadata in a shared memory assumes a system of metadata common to a community, and an open conversation validates the relevance of these metadata or diversifies the categorization of the data. But nor is there purely collective or only emergent learning, because the relevant filtering of data and the validity of metadata are in the end based only on experience and personal judgment.

We have seen that the creative conversation organizes the dialectic of the relations between data and metadata. At a first degree of elaboration, the data, since they are externalized and share-able, belong, of course, to explicit knowledge. But if we focus only on an analysis of digital memory, disregarding the living know-how, then the data belong rather to the implicit, opaque pole, while the metadata occupy the explicit pole that generates transparency and exchange. The explicit/implicit or virtual/actual polarity is thus more a matter of a pattern fractally repeated at various levels of analysis than of a clear and distinct separation between fields of being or knowledge. Thus, from the perspective of the constitution of common online memory, creative conversations carry out an activity of "stitching" or interfacing between the opaque actuality of data flows (digitized phenomena, including texts) and the transparent virtuality of metadata (which make it possible to organize and search for information).

What do we call the characteristic site of this creative conversation that reciprocally converts virtual and actual modes of knowledge? Nonaka proposes that it be called ba, following recent developments in philosophy in Japan. Ba is a place in the broadest sense of the word, that is, it can be material or institutional or based on a digital social medium. Its main characteristic is to enable the actual world of pragmatic action and the virtual world of discursivity to communicate within the same encompassing unit. From the point of view of social knowledge management, ba is a condition of the creative conversation that feeds the life cycle of the knowledge of a collectivity. But from the point of view of a more "emergentist" approach, we could say that ba springs from the creative conversation when a community succeeds in individuating (or in self-maintaining its process of individuation) around an activity of knowledge creation and sharing. In my view, in order to understand ba, it is best not to artificially separate the three following partial types of ba:

1. The usual physical environments: offices, classrooms, meeting places;
2. Various digital environments: certain communities are organized using Facebook, LinkedIn or Ning groups and hashtags and subscription networks on Twitter, and networks on Delicious or Diigo;
3. Occasional encounters, such as conferences, symposia and seminars.

If all these times, places and social media are used by the same network of people, they become the components of a unique ba supporting the network's knowledge creation process. It is the creative conversation and its emotional tone that will unify all the communications and meeting media in a welcoming ba, and not any specific medium or architectural element labelled "ba" that will magically create a satisfying and productive knowledge community. In short, ba is the milieu *associé*, the environment specific to the creative conversation, and it is being built as the knowledge community is individuated and its collective memory grows and is organized.

I note in conclusion that the collective individuation of a knowledge community is accompanied by processes of personal cognitive individuation on the part of its members. This personal cognitive individuation takes place horizontally, in social relationships of mutual aid, interactions among peers or relationships of users with the discussion leaders of the community. Specifically, the type of effective participation by individuals in a community (rather than their official status or place in an organizational chart) will shape their social roles as experts, discussion leaders, collaborating learners or more passive users. But personal cognitive identity is also formed vertically, in so far as, in each community, individuals occupy specific semantic places according to their areas of expertise and learning paths. These places are identified by the traces the individuals leave through their activities of construction and use of the common memory. While each knowledge community constitutes a distinct cognitive microworld, it is clear that the same areas of personal expertise will be projected differently in different communities. It should be noted in this regard that the names of users or persons often serve as markers of semantic zones. In many social media, in fact, subscription to a feed from a particular user may be interpreted as a statement of interest in the subject in which the user specializes.

In short, the creative conversation transforms implicit personal and local know-how into explicit knowledge codified in a collective memory. This construction of a common memory implies distributed work of production, filtering, categorization and evaluation of data. In its dimension of personal integration or learning, the creative conversation in turn transforms explicit knowledge into know-how applied locally in the corresponding fields of practices. This alternating cyclical transformation is coordinated in a milieu *associé*, ba, which cuts across and unites the organizational mechanisms, physical places and digital environments that support the conversation. Finally, the creative conversation is the source of personal and collective processes of cognitive individuation that determine its consistency and duration.

Further Reading

[CAS 2009] Castells Manuel, *Communication power*. Oxford University Press, USA, 2009.

[DAL 2005] Dalkir Kimiz, *Knowledge management in theory and practice*. Elsevier, NY, 2005.

[DEL 1980] Deleuze Gilles and Guattari Félix, *Mille plateaux*. Minuit, Paris, 1980/A thousand plateaux.

[HAY 1937] Hayek Friedrich, "Economics and knowledge", in *Economica* IV, new ser., 1937, pp. 33–54.

[HAY 1979] Hayek Friedrich, *Law, legislation and liberty*. 3 vols. Routledge & Kegan Paul, London, 1979.

[JEN 2006] Jenkins Henry, *Convergence culture: Where old and new media collide*. New York University Press, NY, 2006.

[LEV 1994] Lévy Pierre, *L'Intelligence collective. Pour une anthropologie du cyberespace*. La Découverte, Paris, 1994/*Collective intelligence: Mankind's emerging world in cyberspace*. Perseus Books, Cambridge, MA. 1997.

[LEV 1995] Lévy Pierre, *Qu'est-ce que le virtuel?* La Découverte, Paris, 1995/*Becoming virtual. Reality in the digital age*. Plenum Trade, New York, 1998.

[LEV 1997] Lévy Pierre, *Cyberculture*. Odile Jacob, Paris, 1997/*Cyberculture*. University of Minnesota Press, 2001.

[LEV 2000] Lévy Pierre, *World Philosophie: le marché, le cyberespace, la conscience*. Odile Jacob, Paris, 2000.

[LEV 1992] Lévy Pierre and Authier Michel (préface de Michel Serres), *Les Arbres de connaissances*. La Découverte, Paris, 1992.

[NIS 1990] Nishida K., *An inquiry into the good*. Yale University Press, New Haven, CT, 1990.

[NIS 1990] Nishida K., *Fundamental problems of philosophy: The world of action and the dialectical world*. Sophia University, Tokyo, 1970.

[NON 1998] Nonaka Ikujiro and Konno Noboru, "The concept of ba: Building foundation for knowledge creation." *California Management Review* 40(3) (spring): 40–54, 1998.

[NON 1995] Nonaka Ikujiro and Takeuchi H., *The knowledge-creating company: How Japanese companies create the dynamics of innovation*. Oxford University Press, NY, 1995.

[NON 2000] Nonaka I., Von Krogh G. and Ichijo K., *Enabling knowledge creation: how to unlock the mystery of tacit knowledge and release the power of innovation*. Oxford University Press, 2000.

[PAU 2009] Pauleen David, "Personal knowledge management: putting the 'person' back into the knowledge equation". *Online Information Review* 33(2): 221–224, 2009.

[SHIM 1995] Shimizu H., "Ba-principle: New logic for the real-time emergence of information." *Holonics* 5(1): 67–69, 1995.

[SHI 2005] Shirky Clay, "Ontology is overrated." 2005 (online).

[SHI 2008] Shirky Clay, *Here comes everybody: The power of organizing without organizations*. Penguin, 2008.

[SHI 2010] Shirky Clay, *Cognitive surplus, creativity and generosity in a connected age*. Penguin, 2010.

[SIM 1958] Simondon Gilbert, *L'individuation à la lumière des notions de forme et d'information*. Jérôme Millon, Paris, 2005 (thesis publication date: 1958).

[SUR 2004] Surowiecki James, *The wisdom of the crowds*. Random House, London, 2004.

[WEN 1998] Wenger Etienne, *Communities of practice: Learning, meaning, and identity*. Cambridge University Press, 1998.

12

BLOGGING AS A FREE FRAME OF REFERENCE

Alexander Halavais

During the first decade of the 21st century, there was an explosion in the number of people who wrote in public. Much of this was a result of the popularity of blogging, and the social media it gave birth to. In the past few years the excitement and novelty of blogging has largely given way to new technologies and new ways of interacting (cf. Zickuhr, 2010). For some, this might suggest blogging is merely a blip on the historical radar, one technology in a chain, a peculiar historical moment. But blogging is more than that. It represents a turning point in the way people think about computer networking.

It is important to mark this turning point because it tells us a great deal about what social technologies are: how they emerge from the periphery, how they are assimilated by the mainstream and how society changes itself along the way. This is not the first time we have seen the emergence of social technologies, but the breadth of this particular wave is astounding, and because of this the repercussions of blogging may be especially far reaching.

In many ways, blogging repeats a pattern of all communication technologies: pioneers experimenting in an egalitarian way, mass adoption creating and separating audiences from producers, and, finally, resistance and appropriation by those formerly known as the audience. This chapter traces out the historical antecedents to the present wave of social media, identifies the ways in which these changes are amplified in the current wave. Unlike other media, however, which were quickly stripped of the potential for free and open expression, the ideal of the blog as a free space, and of blogospheres as places of democratic engagement, has been long lived and broadly embraced. The second part of the chapter recalls the idea of a "free frame of reference," as described by the Diggers in San Francisco during the 1960s, and suggests that blogging has played a similar role in making us rethink our social order.

Déjà Vu

Many have already indicated the ways in which the web is now social. But media have been social before.

Robert Darnton (2000) describes 18th-century Paris as "an" early information society. He explores the way in which the latest news was shared informally (under the "Tree of Crakow" and similar locations) and then circulated throughout Paris by word of mouth, handwritten notes, song, and printed book. He presents this description in support of the proposition that "every age was an age of information, each in its own way," and certainly the reader is left with the impression that the informal networks of communication described are not especially unlike today's networks supported online. When we observe communication structure at these two points, separated by two centuries, we might conclude that the structure of the media environment has remained relatively stable–to borrow from a Parisian of the 19th century, that the more things change, the more they are the same.

To ignore the rise of the mass media and electronic broadcasting would be a serious oversight. Part of what makes the current media revolution so exciting is that it is at once bringing us something new and at the same time bringing us back something familiar. Of course, we could say this about all revolutions; they are always in part nostalgic. In this case, we see the resurgence of communication and conviviality after a dark period of relative passivity.

Many have set up television as emblematic of everything the collaborative, convivial web is not. Clay Shirky (2010) draws an analogy between the narcotizing dysfunction of television watching and an earlier public enthusiasm for gin and suggests that, as the era of television recedes, the audience becomes participant.

This is misleading in two ways. First, the mass media did not start with television or radio. The audience became "mass" and undifferentiated under the rise of the penny press, which sought to amass audiences for advertisers to address through systems that allowed for the same communication product to be seen by an unprecedented number of readers. Second, audiences of mass-media content have never been entirely passive and many have made use of media content in their own ways. This included the early mass newspaper that was often read and discussed in public spaces. Although it was perhaps not as visible or as widespread today, participatory culture thrived well before the web arrived, though perhaps not in ways easily visible or recorded. The roots of the new media environment run deep into the mass-media century, ready to flourish again, given the right environment.

The Mass–Demass Cycle

Associating contemporary participation with earlier eras is not merely attempting to attach a historical patina to novel practices. The last two centuries retell the same story again and again. New ways of communicating are often grasped first by the innovators and hobbyists who see little border between creating tools and creating culture around those tools. As the value, especially commercial value, of these technologies become apparent to wider groups of adopters, the structure of their use rapidly changes. Robert McChesney (1996) saw this happen with ham radio operators forced aside by commercial broadcasters and warned that the future of the Internet was likely to follow the same pattern.

He was right, to a certain extent: both blogging and the web as a whole have seen a tremendous increase in commercial traffic, with an ever-smaller number of commercial sites attracting an ever-greater amount of traffic (MacManus, 2006). It is difficult to draw a direct parallel between the broadcasting giants that came to dominate the radio airwaves and sites like Facebook and YouTube that provide an opportunity for self-expression and peer communications. This complex, simultaneously centralizing and decentralizing process is not unique to our own time. Carey (1969) identifies it as a key element in the early days of the penny press, which led to both a national media and to the development of distributed communities. Nonetheless, it would be a mistake to assume that such concentration of the most popular part of the web is without political consequence (Gillespie, 2010).

The first audiences of every new communication technology are those who create with them; not just the inventors themselves ("Watson, come here!") but the waves of early users of the technology. Ithie de Sola Pool (1984) suggests that some technologies tend toward social centralization more than others do, but the simple fact that a technology is networked rather than broadcast does not ensure its use toward democratic ends. Early developers of telephone networks—a technology that now seems "naturally" networked—flirted with the idea of making it into a broadcast medium (Morris and Ogan, 1996), but sociable uses helped to shape it into something different.

The practices of these media trace an arc. Henry Jenkins (2010) has noted the very long history of the initialism "LOL," which existed a hundred years before the first inkling of the Internet surfaced. Likewise we can trace a genealogy of writing for the web, through public letter writing, to pamphleteers employing printing technologies to spread their word, to the samizdat press encouraged by mimeograph machines, and zines supported by photocopiers. Each of these shares common strands, chief among them the ability of an individual or small group to make use of the machines—and infrastructure that they may not own—to get their own word out.

When we look at film, radio, and television, we see a similar pattern: the pioneers of the technology help to co-create it, it then comes under the control of a small number of creators who broadcast to a large audience, and, finally, it is reclaimed by that audience to put it to creative use. The printing press, for example, represented a tool that was both expensive and difficult to use, but it became more expensive and difficult to use over time, before eventually coming back to the "consumer" who was able to become a "maker." We went from block prints, to movable type, to large-scale, high-speed printers that could take up a room. But then the process reversed and printers became smaller and eventually the copy machines and laser printers were small enough, cheap enough, and easy enough to use that they fell back into the hands of a large number of people.

On each end of this historical arc, those hoping to use the technologies to their own ends often found themselves working against deep pockets and social momentum. In the early stages of a medium's popularity, experimenters who brought it about often welcomed the infusion of interest and capital that commercialization brought, but then found themselves with little voice in the direction of the technology or its content as it scaled upwards. On the trailing edge, they often find themselves vying against the giant media producers for audience and influence, always treading a fine line between resistance and co-option. Much of that later contestation happens on the Internet, where old media goes to become participatory; telegraphy becomes Twitter.

Social uses of networked computing follow a similar pattern. Licklider and Taylor's landmark 1968 article introduced the idea of the "computer as a communication device." The public was provided a window on this world with Stewart Brand's (1972) *Rolling Stone* article on the computer game *Spacewar*, which had a strong following in university computing labs. By 1974, Ted Nelson had published *Computer Lib*, which again framed the machine in a way that was opposed to the IBM vision of business computing.

The practice of social computing was emerging around the same time. The Community Memory project in Berkeley, starting in 1973, was an early forerunner of Craigslist, but many recognized the potential for what it would look like at a much grander scale (Rossman, 1975). And by this time the PLATO educational network had already been in operation for more than a decade (Smith and Sherwood, 1975). The development of Bulletin Board Systems—a kind of "call in" forum available before the internet was widespread—moved networked sociability outside of the university so that anyone with a modem and a telephone could access forums for discussion and self-expression (Glossbrenner, 1983). These social applications continued to grow into the early days of the web, spawning a range of applications with names that now seem to be relegated to historical footnotes: FidoNet, Usenet, MOOs, CU-SeeMe, and other sociable technologies. The spirit and practice of these technologies lived on in the social web.

Commercialization of the web in the 1990s led to vastly larger audiences and, while some of these newcomers found themselves drawn into online discussions, there emerged an audience of web surfers, those who read from the web but did not write to it. During the dot-com boom, users were considered customers, the source of income that would eventually justify the huge outlays of capital by investors. The idea that the web was a space for amateur producers of media seemed to be part of the history of the medium, not its future. Blogging changed that.

Sim City

The most frequently cited definitions of blogging come from Rebecca Blood's (2000) early history of the practice or from Jill Walker's (2005) definition of the genre. But blogs are nothing if not a moving target. If we look to the manifest formal nature of the page, we can come up with a set of attributes that seem common among blogs: the reverse chronological entries or the ability to leave comments, for example. But exceptions are the rule. Or you could rely on the software running the blog, but software like WordPress, an open-source blogging platform, is frequently used to support corporate sites that have nothing at all to do with blogging.

More promising, perhaps, is to look to the practices: to define "blogging" rather than "blogs." Here, too, there is some ambiguity, as there is not anything approaching a singular "blogosphere," despite the frequent use of that term and, if there is, it certainly cannot speak with a single voice. Instead there is a series of practices, often defined by the genre of blogging and by evolving norms within an amorphous community of bloggers (Bruns, 2006; Griffiths, 2004; Wei, 2004). Nardi *et al.* interviewed a small sample of 23 bloggers in 2004 and found "tremendous diversity in blog content," as well as a range of motivations and practices. But for most of what we think of as blogging, it is a vehicle for personal self-expression, for sharing ideas, but for doing so in a space that remains personalized (Blood, 2004). They may be maintained for different purposes, with different intentions, and for different audiences, but "[a]lways, they are a public face, one chosen and crafted to varying degrees, of the people who write them" (Stavros, 2004). The idea of keeping a diary is not new, but, by making it a public journal and by inviting others to comment on it, the dynamic becomes far more communal. It may be your own personal space, but it is not—generally—a private space. What makes a blog a blog is that it is shared with others and often with a public that is unknown.

If we imagine the social web to be a community, there are spaces that more clearly equate with the idea of a street corner, or with the local pub. Blogs represent the "virtual residences" of their owners. These are spaces in which the community may be invited, but, by practice and by law, they remain the property of the owners, away from the rules of the larger community (Beslay and Hakala, 2007). A person's blog is her or his castle; a place to reside, to decorate, to yearn for when away, and in some cases to pack up and leave behind.

Unlike forums, where the unity is something that users come to, join, lurk within, and eventually leave, blogospheres are made up of these personal spaces. Blogospheres emerge from an assemblage of blogs and these assemblages may fall away even when the constituent blogs remain. The permanence, ownership, and authenticity of a blog make it an important anchor for our virtual selves. We move into our blogs, decorate them, and make them a reflection of ourselves; to imitate Ralph Waldo Emerson, every spirit makes a blog.

This need to carve out a personal space was in part a reaction to the massification of the web. It is not enough to begin to contribute to the written web because it is not at all clear when I add a comment to a *New York Times* article, or a review on Amazon.com, whether I am contributing to my own exploitation. Both, after all, profit from my freely given critique. During a period of media demassification, it was important to set some clear lines marking out a personal space—even if that space is provided by Google or another massive blogging platform.

But blogs, unlike homes, are primarily public. We invite guests and hope that they engage in conversation. This bridge between the personal and the communal—between do-it-yourself and do-it-ourselves—is one that can be found across different forms of participatory culture. Creative work has to walk a line between public interaction and isolation. This is difficult enough to achieve in the physical world. In online spaces it becomes even more challenging to define where one personal territory begins and another ends.

Insofar as there emerged a culture of blogging, it was an ethics of practice. Authenticity was held up as the ideal and transparency flowed from it. Even for those who did not blog under their real name, there was an expectation that you wore your intentions on your sleeve and respected the community who visited and commented. This dedication to transparency led to other expectations, including a desire to avoid exclusion, to open up materials to the public, and to contribute to the larger community. You wanted your own space, but you also wanted to remain "loosely joined" (Weinberger, 2002) to other blogs and the people who inhabited them.

The question of "community" is as important as it is fraught with definitional issues. The term is defined and used in sometimes divergent ways. Ferdinand Tönnies (2001, orig. 1887) suggested that social organization was moving from traditional community (*Gemeinschaft*) to the more complex modern society, often found in the city (*Gesellschaft*). The social structure of the former was determined largely by tradition: you were the member of a family, a village, a tribe, or a caste without having ever chosen to become that. In the complex, urban, modern society, you were free to choose your associations, and engage in business and trade with those you might never otherwise come into contact with. The result was modern, large-scale corporations, trade unions, and voluntary organizations.

Where along this spectrum does the communal feeling of a blogosphere find itself? In some ways the blogging world represented a return to a community not just for the Internet, but for our social lives. In the 1920s, Herman Schmalenbach introduced a third category, the *Bund*, which combined the communal nature of the tribe with the voluntary nature of a modern group. David Bell (2001), among others, attempts to extend this idea to suggest something between online "community" and something more cosmopolitan. Even the idea of a *Bund*, however, connotes a closer bond among bloggers than often may exist. Instead, these assemblages seem—in their openness to the public, their authenticity, their willingness to contribute to a community through the development of standards—like the epitome of urban life. It may be for this reason that at least the more particularly public sort of blogging is often engaged in by those who live in cities (Lin and Halavais, 2006) and are disproportionately well educated (Sussman, 2009).

The emergence of blogospheres marked a turning point in the history of the web, reasserting the role of conversation to the web experience. It's not simply a matter of the "mass" versus the "post-mass" Internet, to use Lemos's (2007) terms, but rather an integration of both of these in new configurations. Indeed, blogs already occupy a middle zone between the two, and are therefore the model for these future configurations, as television, radio, print, and web finally make the long predicted technological convergence.

A Free Frame of Reference

During the late 1960s, a number of groups sought new ways of experiencing and spreading freedom. Unlike the Free Software movement, which goes to lengths to make clear the difference between "free as in beer" and "free as in speech" (Stallman, 2010), the Diggers and others saw the

The anarchists of Smith Street, feeling the heat

FIGURE 12.1 You can't steal from the "Free Store"
Source: Colin Talbot, 1970.

two as deeply intertwingled. One of their more lasting influences was one of the first "free shops," providing food, clothing, and other items for free. They named this shop the "Free Frame of Reference," and visitors passed through a large yellow picture frame when they entered the space. On occasion they gave out two-inch replicas of the frame that could be hung around the neck. The idea was to change the way the bearer thought about commodities—and much more than that, thought about the world.

It is too easy to dismiss blogging as a fad, or even as a decade-long cultural episode—the 2000s version of the "flapper." But the importance of blogging was and continues to be that it provides a free frame of reference. In the early days of public use of the Internet, the quip from A. J. Liebling was frequently applied: "Freedom of the press is guaranteed only to those who own one." Although accessing it was not always free of charge, getting something published on the web could be done with free software. Because the protocols of the web were open, anyone who took the time to learn HTML could publish. This however still represented something of a barrier. Owning a printing press is not enough; you need to be able to make one work. And particularly if you wanted to create a site that was dynamic—allowing for both frequent updating and commenting—you also had to learn a programming language. The barrier of no cost seemed suddenly to mean very little.

Luckily, as blogging became more popular, a number of hosted services and free software packages became available. If you signed up for LiveJournal, or downloaded Movable Type to install on your web host, suddenly publishing to the web became much easier. These services provided, to use Blogger.com's original motto: "Push-Button Publishing for the People." (The site, acquired by Google in 2003, has since dropped "for the People" from its slogan.)

Like stepping across a threshold, blogging provided a new frame of reference. Those who started to blog, for whatever reason, often adopted the norms and values of freedom—of thought, of opinion, of action—that came along with the blog. Politically, blogging fell across the spectrum. In the United States, the involvement of bloggers in the Howard Dean presidential campaign led to a new way of thinking about the Internet in politics and eventually influenced the election of a political newcomer, Barack Obama. The so-called "warbloggers" often took hold of their voice to speak about the invasions of Afghanistan and Iraq, and the roots of this discussion could probably find their way to the voice of the Tea Party today. In both cases, the availability of the tool shaped the way bloggers thought about the each other, the public, and their role in it.

This change in point of view provided bloggers with an independence from the mass media and from mass thought. Again, what makes blogs special is not just that they are not created by the mass-media corporations, but that they are, in many cases, personal spaces of exploration. Simply having the ability to publish as an individual is not enough to create an atmosphere of personal expression; many may continue to express themselves through the tokens of existing commercial mass culture. José Ortega y Gasset's *The Revolt of the Masses* draws a distinction between Mass Man ("self-satisfied man") and the minority of creative, thinking individuals:

> To form a minority, of whatever kind, it is necessary beforehand that each member separate himself from the multitude for special, relatively personal, reasons. Their coincidence with others who form the minority is, then, secondary, posterior to their having each adopted an attitude of singularity, and is consequently, to a large extent, a coincidence and not coinciding.
>
> *(1930, p. 9)*

We need not accept the conclusions Ortega draws from this observation to recognize that creativity requires social and cognitive space to thrive. Blogging provided that space for exposition and reflection, and importantly fused it with an ability to interact with others in an assemblage of like-minded individuals. Those who took on blogging balanced an ability to have their voice heard with an ability to easily enter into a drawn out, dispersed, conversation.

Of course, blogging did not provide this perspective to all. A certain proficiency with using computers and the Internet, along with a facility with language, both represented significant barriers to the adoption of blogging, despite the reduction in required expertise (Ratcliff, 2004). But the numbers of those who did start blogs was staggering. In 2006, the year that *Time* declared "You" as the person of the year, Pew indicated that 12 million Americans were blogging (Lenhart and Fox, 2006). The degree to which this number of bloggers is sustained is unclear and it may not—in the end—matter. Blogging has opened up the idea of presenting to a wider audience, whether that is through YouTube, Twitter, Facebook or any of the thousand other services poised to take their place. In comparison with the Diggers' Free Frame of Reference, a considerable number of people now wear a reminder that there are other ways of thinking about media and their social and political lives. That message now has spread beyond those who merely keep a blog.

The Diggers encouraged those who walked through their Free Frame of Reference to think differently about the world and the things and people in it. Peter Coyote recalls that this "forced people to improvise at the edges of their imagination in a common quest for transformation" (1999, p. 95). It would be hard to claim that blogs went nearly as far in changing the way bloggers

FIGURE 12.2 Digger poster from 1968

thought about the world. Nonetheless, most crossed into the blogging frame of reference with the intent merely to explore, or perhaps carve out a small space for self-expression. That action turned out to be radical in itself, and, particularly when these individual spaces assembled into discourse networks, the influence on the way we learn about our world was extraordinary and continues to shape a revolution in media. That revolution, in turn, is reshaping the practice of blogging.

Things Fall Apart

Blogs gave us a lot of freedom and gave it for free. In a public space of super-abundance, a new market gradually emerged: attention. This should come as no surprise; Herbert Simon noted that an abundance of information led to a poverty of attention three decades ago (1971). Very early on it became obvious that some way of filtering the blogosphere was needed. Those reading blogs began to rely on services to rank and track bloggers, reducing the messy individuality to a number of blogging stars—the "A-list" bloggers—on the top of a pyramid of what had suddenly become also-rans: those who were expressing themselves to friends and likeminded strangers on a much smaller scale.

Many of these blogs grew audiences so large that they were structurally indistinguishable from mass-media outlets. As traditional media outlets either took on blogging or changed their sites so that they were functionally similar to blogs, the line between mass and post-mass became impossibly fuzzy. If we were to pay attention to their position in the structure of hyperlinks, we might find a few that linked to no one and yet were heavily linked to by other blogs; that is, they had a mass audience. Then there were blogs that linked to other blogs in their neighborhood about as often as they themselves were linked, with many of these hyperlinks being reciprocated. Between these extremes—"stars" on one side and "friends" on the other—lies a whole range of blogs with small audiences of readers and commenters.

This lack of clear line between the "blogosphere" and the larger media environment has also led to the commodification of the process of blogging. There is still a culture of "free" among bloggers and many of the tools that are used are open source or otherwise freely made available. But there is an intense interest in blogging by marketers and others that notice influence laying un-monetized. In many cases, this interest might be seen as pernicious, particularly when it tends to undermine the ideals of transparency and authenticity that make up a large part of the culture. Nonetheless, the incorporation of microexchanges of goods means that in many cases the amounts of money are small and the scale of business maintains a craft feel.

Also worth noting is that there remains a great deal of attention mobility in the space. The earliest group blogs like Slashdot fulfilled the function of disrupting the hierarchical structure of the web, drawing massive amount of attention to lesser-known websites—often blogs (Halavais, 2001). This continues today, not only with similar community filters like Digg, StumbleUpon, Fark, and even Twitter, but also with blogs, large and small alike. As a result, there is a certain degree of felicitous instability to today's media world. The path from obscure to central has never been so potentially short.

We will not, in the foreseeable future, return a society in which the creation of public media is in the hands of the very few. Certainly, even at the height of mass media when—not so many years ago—the expectation was that we would sit comfortably and consume television programs alone, there was a great deal of what today is called "user-created media" being produced. It was not, however, widely distributed or easily discoverable. The visibility of creation today—the ability to see it if you so desire—and the appreciation and value that brings will be a difficult thing to undermine.

Statistician Corrado Gini described a measure of inequality in 1912 now referred to as the "Gini Index." It is normally used to describe relative inequality in income for various countries. A coefficient of 100 would represent a nation in which a single person received all of the nation's income and zero would mark perfect equality of income; neither extreme is likely in practice. If it were possible to measure the relationship of audience to media producer in the same way, we might see blogging as having a substantial and ongoing influence on how many people in society have the capability and motivation to create and share with their community. Equality of attention is something of an oxymoron: attention requires attenuation. But as large numbers of people have passed through the free frame of reference provided by blogging, their view of what media is and what it can be has changed for good.

References

Bell, David. 2001. *An introduction to cybercultures*. London: Routledge.

Beslay, Laurent and Hakala, Hannu. 2007. "Digital territory: Bubbles." In Paul T. Kidd (ed.). *European visions for the knowledge age*, Macclesfield, UK: Cheshire Henbury, pp. 69–78.

Blood, Rebecca. 2000. "Weblogs: a history and perspective," *Rebecca's Pocket*, 7 September. www.rebeccablood.net/essays/weblog_history.html.

Brand, Stewart. 1972. "Spacewar! Fantastic life and symbolic death among the computer bums," *Rolling Stone* (7 December). www.wheels.org/spacewar/stone/rolling_stone.html.

Bruns, Axel. 2006. *Uses of blogs*. New York: Peter Lang.

Carey, James. 1969. "The communications revolution and the professional communicator," *Sociological Review Monograph*, 13 (January): 23–38.

Coyote, Peter. 1999. *Sleeping where I fall*. Washington: Counterpoint Press.

Darnton, Robert. 2000. "Presidential address: An early information society: News and the media in eighteenth-century Paris," *The American Historical Review*, 105(1): 1–35.

Gillespie, Tarleton. 2010. "The politics of 'platforms,'" *New Media & Society*, 12(3): 347–364.

Gini, Corrado. 1912. "Variabilità e mutabilità", reprinted E. Pizetti and T. Salvermini (eds). *Memorie di metodologica statistica*. Rome: Libreria Eredi Virgilio Veschi, 1955.

Glossbrenner, Alfred. 1983. *The complete handbook of personal computer communications*. New York: St Martin's Press.

Griffiths, Mary. 2004. "e-Citizens: Blogging as democratic practice," *Electronic Journal of e-Government*, 2(3): 1–10.

Halavais, Alexander. 2001. "Slashdot: Analysis of a large-scale public conversation on the web" (Doctoral Dissertation), University of Washington School of Communications.

Jenkins, Henry. 2010. "Keynote." Digital Media and Learning Conference, May, La Jolla, California.

Lemos, André. 2007. "Cidade e mobilidade. Telefones celulares, funções pós-massivas e territórios informacionais," *Matrizes*, 1(1). www.matrizes.usp.br/ojs/index.php/matrizes/article/viewArticle/15.

Lenhart, Amanda and Fox, Susannah. 2006. "Bloggers," *Pew Internet & American Life*. http://pewinternet.org/Reports/2006/Bloggers.aspx, accessed 1 October 2010.

Licklider, J. C. R. and Taylor, Robert W. 1968. "The computer as a communication device," *Science and Technology* (April). http://citeseerx.ist.psu.edu/viewdoc/summary?doi=10.1.1.34.4812.

Lin, Jia and Halavais, Alex. 2006. "Geographical distribution of blogs in the United States," *Webology*, 3(4). www.webology.ir/2006/v3n4/a30.html.

McChesney, Robert. 1996. "The Internet and US communications policy-making in historical and critical perspective," *Journal of Communication*, 46(1): 98–124.

MacManus, Richard. 2006. "The shrinking long tail: Top 10 web domains increasing in reach," *ReadWriteWeb*. www.readwriteweb.com/archives/long_tail_shrinking.php.

Morris, Merrill and Ogan, Christine. 1996. "The Internet as mass medium," *Journal of Communication*, 46(1): 39–50.

Nardi, Bonnie A., Schiano, Diane J., Gumbrecht, Michelle, and Swartz, Luke. 2004. "Why we blog," *Communications of the ACM*, 47(12): 41–46.

Nelson, Ted. 1975. *Computer lib: You can and must understand computers now*. Sausalito: Mindful Press.

Ortega y Gasset, José. 1930. *The revolt of the masses*. Reprinted in 1950 by New American Library, New York.

Pool, Ithiel de Sola. 1984. *Technologies of freedom*. Cambridge: Belknap Press.

Ratcliff, Clancy. 2004. "'Push-button publishing for the people': The blogosphere and the public sphere," *CultureCat*. http://culturecat.net/node/402.

Rossman, Michael. "Implications of community memory," *ACM SigCas Computers and Society*, 6(4): 7–10.

Shirky, C. 2010. *Cognitive surplus: Creativity and generosity in a connected age*. New York: Penguin.

Simon, Herbert A. 1971. "Designing organizations for an information-rich world." In Martin Greenberger (ed.). *Computers, communication, and the public interest*. Baltimore: The Johns Hopkins Press, pp. 37–72.

Stallman, Richard. 2010. "Why open source misses the point of free software." www.gnu.org/philosophy/open-source-misses-the-point.html.

Stavros, the Wonderchicken, 2004. "Never mind the bollocks, here's the Wonderchicken," *Empty Bottle* (January 20). www.emptybottle.org/glass/2004/01/never_mind_the_bollocks_heres_the_wonderchicken.php.

Sussman, Matt. 2009. "Day 1: Who are the bloggers?" *State of the blogosphere* 2009. Technorati. http://technorati.com/blogging/article/day-1-who-are-the-bloggers1/.

Tönnies, Ferdinand. 2001. *Community and society*. José Harris (ed.). Cambridge: Cambridge University Press.

Walker, Jill. 2005. "Blog (weblog)," In *Routledge encyclopedia of narrative theory*, London: Routledge.

Wei, Carolyn, 2004. "Formation of norms in a blog community." In L. J. Gurak, S. Antonijevic, L. Johnson, C. Ratliff, and J. Reyman (eds). *Into the blogosphere: Rhetoric, community, and culture of weblogs*, at http://blog.lib.umn.edu/blogosphere/formation_of_norms.html.

Weinberger, David, 2002. *Small pieces loosely joined*. New York: Basic Books.

Zickuhr, Kathryn, 2010. *Generations 2010*. Pew Internet and American Life, at http://pewinternet.org/Reports/2010/Generations-2010.aspx.

13

CROWDSOURCING

A Model for Leveraging Online Communities

Daren C. Brabham

As our understanding of participatory cultures advances, there is a growing interest among practitioners and scholars in how best to take charge of the creative, productive capabilities of Internet users for specific purposes. A number of online businesses in the past decade have actively recruited individuals in online communities to design products and solve problems for them, often motivating an online community's creative output or harnessing their creative input through the format of an open challenge with various rewards. Organizations that issue specific tasks to online communities in an open-call format engage in the practice of "crowdsourcing." Crowdsourcing is a model for problem solving, not merely a model for doing business (Brabham, 2008a; Brito, 2008; Fritz *et al.*, 2009; Haklay and Weber, 2008). The crowdsourcing model is also well suited to organizations' marketing and public relations goals, as the process of managing an online community allows organizations to forge close relationships with publics and allows consumers to participate in the making of brands (Phillips and Brabham, 2011). Thus, it is important to understand how crowdsourcing works so that the collective intelligence of online communities can be leveraged in future participatory media applications for the public good. In this chapter, I further define the crowdsourcing model by putting forth a typology of crowdsourcing. Ultimately, these types may inform the design of future participatory media applications for governments, non-profits, and activists hoping to solve pressing political, social, and environmental problems.

The Basics of Crowdsourcing

Jeff Howe, a contributing editor for *Wired* magazine, coined the term "crowdsourcing" in a June 2006 article (Howe, 2006c). In a companion blog, Howe (2006a) offered the following definition of crowdsourcing:

> Simply defined, crowdsourcing represents the act of a company or institution taking a function once performed by employees and outsourcing it to an undefined (and generally large) network of people in the form of an open call. … The crucial prerequisite is the use of the open call format and the large network of potential laborers.
>
> *(para. 5)*

It is important to emphasize that this process is one that is sponsored by an organization, and that the work of the large network of people—the "crowd"—is directed or managed by this organization throughout the process. This is very different from, say, the online encyclopedia project Wikipedia, where an open space exists for individuals to work collaboratively. No one at Wikipedia, for example, issues specific tasks to the online community there and manages the creation of articles. It is a process directed and managed by others on the site. Wikipedia, then, is not crowdsourcing, but rather a different and equally important participatory culture phenomenon that Benkler (2002) calls "commons-based peer production." The same is true of open-source methods, processes most common to software production. Commons-based peer production and open–source methods share with the crowdsourcing model the notion of openness and the use of the Internet as a collaboration platform. But while these phenomena may seem quite organized and managed, they are organized from the bottom-up rather than from the top-down by a sponsoring organization issuing the task. Crowdsourcing, on the other hand, blends an open creative process with a traditional, top-down, managed process.

Crowdsourcing is necessarily dependent on the Internet. The speed, reach, anonymity, opportunity for asynchronous engagement, and ability to carry many forms of media content makes the Internet a crucial prerequisite for crowdsourcing. Certainly these processes can be taken offline with some success, but the platform of the Internet elevates the quality, amount, and pace of cooperation, coordination, and idea generation to a point that warrants its own classification. Cultures have always been participatory, long before the Internet, with roots in democratic process, collective decision making, and cooperation for survival. But participatory cultures on the Internet take on a new quality, a new scale, and new capabilities.

Furthermore, all crowdsourcing types rely on the notion of collective intelligence. Pierre Lévy (1995/1997) conceived of collective intelligence as a "form of universally distributed intelligence, constantly enhanced, coordinated in real time, and resulting in the effective mobilization of skills" (p. 13). The Internet is the technology capable of this degree of coordination of intellect, and thus, as the capabilities of the Internet grow, so do the possibilities for leveraging this intellect. Given the will to act, problem solving with collective intelligence and networks can be scaled-up to address even global concerns (Ignatius, 2001).

Finally, all individuals engaged in a crowdsourcing application, or any aspect of participatory culture, are in some way motivated to participate. This may seem obvious, but understanding how and why individuals participate in crowdsourcing applications is necessary to design effective problem-solving applications going forward. A number of interviews and surveys have been conducted at various crowdsourcing sites, with each study asking individuals in those crowds to explain why they participate (Brabham, 2008b, 2010a, 2010b; Lakhani *et al.*, 2007; Lietsala and Joutsen, 2007). These studies indicate that there are many common reasons why people participate, both intrinsic and extrinsic, but there is no single motivator that applies to all crowdsourcing applications. For instance, the opportunity to develop one's creative skills, build a portfolio for future employment, and challenge oneself to solve a difficult problem are motivators that emerge among several crowdsourcing cases, but some crowds are driven by financial gain and do not mention these motivators. Drawing from these existing studies, some motivations for individuals in crowds that emerge across more than one case include:

- the desire to earn money;
- to develop one's creative skills;
- to network with other creative professionals;
- to build a portfolio for future employment;
- to challenge oneself to solve a tough problem;
- to socialize and make friends;
- to pass the time when bored;

- to contribute to a large project of common interest;
- to share with others; and
- to have fun.

In regards to motivations, then, crowdsourcing is not that different of a phenomenon from other forms of participatory culture, such as blogging (e.g. Liu *et al.*, 2007), creating open-source software (e.g. Bonaccorsi and Rossi, 2004; Hars and Ou, 2002; Hertel *et al.*, 2003; Lakhani and Wolf, 2005), posting videos to YouTube (e.g. Huberman *et al.*, 2009), contributing to Wikipedia (e.g. Nov, 2007), or tagging content at Flickr (e.g. Nov *et al.*, 2008). Generally speaking, members of a participatory culture, including crowds, "believe their contributions matter and feel some degree of social connection with one another" (Jenkins, 2006, p. 3).

Toward a Typology of Crowdsourcing Applications

Some of the notable case studies of crowdsourcing help illustrate how the model functions in four different approaches and how the model resembles a problem-solving process. There are four dominant crowdsourcing types: the knowledge discovery and management approach, the broadcast search approach, the peer-vetted creative production approach, and distributed human intelligence tasking (see Table 13.1).

TABLE 13.1 A Crowdsourcing Typology

Type	How it works	Kinds of problems	Examples
Knowledge Discovery and Management	Organization tasks crowd with finding and collecting information into a common location and format	Ideal for information gathering, organization, and reporting problems, such as the creation of collective resources	Peer-to-Patent *peertopatent.org* SeeClickFix *seeclickfix.com*
Broadcast Search	Organization tasks crowd with solving empirical problems	Ideal for ideation problems with empirically provable solutions, such as scientific problems	InnoCentive *innocentive.com* Goldcorp Challenge *Defunct*
Peer-Vetted Creative Production	Organization tasks crowd with creating and selecting creative ideas	Ideal for ideation problems where solutions are matters of taste or market support, such as design or aesthetic problems	Threadless *threadless.com* Doritos Crash the Super Bowl Contest *crashthesuperbowl.com* Next Stop Design *nextstopdesign.com*
Distributed Human Intelligence Tasking	Organization tasks crowd with analyzing large amounts of information	Ideal for large-scale data analysis where human intelligence is more efficient or effective than computer analysis	Amazon Mechanical Turk *mturk.com* Subvert and Profit *subvertandprofit.com*

The Knowledge Discovery and Management Approach

In the knowledge discovery and management approach, online communities are challenged to uncover existing knowledge in the network, thus amplifying the discovery capabilities of an organization with limited resources. The assumption is that a wealth of disorganized knowledge exists "out there," and a top-down, managed process can efficiently disperse a large online community of individuals to find specific knowledge and collect it in specific ways in a common repository. This crowdsourcing type most closely resembles commons-based peer production, such as at Wikipedia, except with one crucial difference: a sponsoring organization determines exactly what information is sought, for what purpose, and how that information is to be assembled. In this approach, the more users there are and the more involved they are, the better the system functions, a fact that could very well be applied to most participatory culture phenomena.

The Peer-to-Patent Community Patent Review project is an exemplar of the knowledge discovery and management approach to crowdsourcing (Noveck, 2006). Peer-to-Patent was a pilot project from 2007 to 2009 between New York Law School and the US Patent and Trademark Office (USPTO), with support from a number of major corporate patent holders. In the Peer-to-Patent project, the USPTO siphoned off a small number of patent applications it received to an online community. Working for no monetary reward, this online community of more than 2000 reviewed applications for evidence of "prior art." Prior art is any evidence that a similar invention already exists that would negate the originality of a patent application. These findings were then routed back to the USPTO. Overburdened and backlogged with patent applications, the USPTO then used these findings to help determine whether new patents should be awarded.

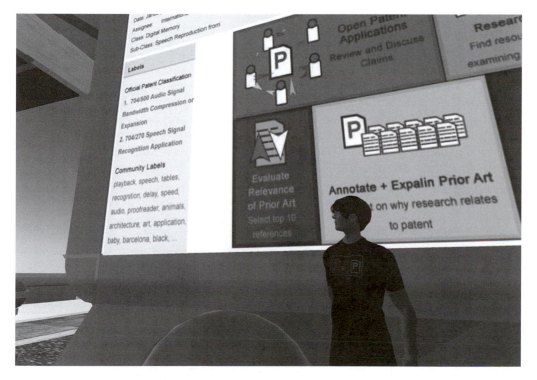

FIGURE 13.1 The Peer-to-Patent project was supplemented with a virtual auditorium in Second Life
Note: auditorium created by David McDonough and Metaversatility, Inc., 2007.

Another example of the knowledge discovery and management approach is SeeClickFix. SeeClickFix is a web site that allows people to report non-emergency problems in their local community, either by using the SeeClickFix web site or a free mobile phone application. These problems include potholes, graffiti, malfunctioning traffic signals, obstructed wheelchair access ramps on sidewalks, and other issues of public safety and disrepair. City governments, as well as journalists, use SeeClickFix as an intelligence-gathering mechanism to better understand issues facing a community and to better allocate resources to fix the problems. According to a SeeClickFix spokesperson, "on average, more than 40 percent of issues reported on the site get resolved" (Smith, 2010, para. 13).

The Broadcast Search Approach

Broadcast search approaches to crowdsourcing are oriented towards finding the single specialist with time on his or her hands, probably outside the direct field of expertise of the problem, who is capable of adapting previous work to produce a solution. In theory, the wider the net cast by the crowdsourcing organization, the more likely the company will turn up the "needle in the haystack," that one person who knows the answer. The broadcast search approach is appropriate for problems where a provable, empirically "right" answer exists, but that answer is simply not yet known by an organization. Broadcasting the problem in an open way online draws in potential solutions. Scientific problems, such as developing new chemicals and materials or locating resources for mining using geophysical data, are best suited to the broadcast search approach. In the broadcast search approach, monetary rewards are common for individuals in the crowd who provide a solution to a challenge, though financial incentive is not the only motivation for these crowds to participate in these arrangements.

InnoCentive, founded in 2002, focuses on providing research and development solutions for a broad range of topic areas, from biomedical and big pharmaceutical concerns to engineering and computer science topics. An exemplar of the broadcast search approach, InnoCentive boasts a community of dozens of client companies, called "Seekers," and an online community of 165,000 "Solvers." Seeker companies issue difficult scientific challenges to the Solver community, with cash awards ranging from US$5000 to US$1 million. According to Lakhani *et al.* (2007), "[s]olution requirements for the problems are either 'reduction to practice' (RTP) submissions, i.e., requiring experimentally validated solutions, such as actual chemical or biological agents or experimental protocols, or 'paper' submissions, i.e., rationalized theoretical solutions codified through writing" (p. 5). Submitted solutions are never seen by other Solvers; only Seekers pour over submissions. Solvers with winning solutions are awarded the cash bounties in exchange for the Seeker company taking ownership of the intellectual property, and InnoCentive receives a fee from the Seeker company for listing the challenge and facilitating the process.

The problem set in broadcast search approaches consists of difficult, if well defined and scoped, scientific and engineering challenges. Lakhani *et al.* (2007) conducted a statistical analysis of the InnoCentive service between 2001 and 2006. They found that the Solver community was able to solve 29% of the problems the Seekers—all large companies with internal labs and researchers—posted after they were unable to solve these problems internally. Moreover, the results found a positive correlation between the distance the Solver was from the field in which the problem was presented and the likelihood of creating a successful solution. That is, Solvers on the margins of a disciplinary domain—outsiders to a given problem's domain of specialty—performed better in solving the problem.

The Goldcorp Challenge was a similar broadcast search crowdsourcing case (Tischler, 2007). Goldcorp, a Canadian gold-mining company, developed the Challenge in March 2000.

According to a company press release, "participants from around the world were encouraged to examine the geologic data [from Goldcorp's newly acquired Red Lake Mine in Ontario] and submit proposals identifying potential targets where the next six million ounces of gold will be found" ("Goldcorp," 2001, para. 6). By offering more than US$500,000 in prize money to 25 top finalists who identified the most gold deposits, Goldcorp attracted "more than 475,000 hits" to the Challenge's web site and "more than 1400 online prospectors from fifty-one countries registered as Challenge participants" ("Goldcorp," 2001, para. 6). The numerous solutions from the crowd confirmed many of Goldcorp's suspected deposits and identified several new ones, 110 deposits in all.

The Peer-Vetted Creative Production Approach

The logic of the peer-vetted creative production approach is that, by opening up the creative phase of a designed product to a potentially vast network of Internet users, some superior ideas will exist among the flood of submissions. Further still, the peer vetting process will simultaneously identify the best ideas and collapse the market research process into an instance of firm–consumer co-creation. It is a system where a "good" solution is also the popular solution that the market will support. Peer-vetted creative production is appropriate, then, for problem solving concerning matters of taste and user preference, such as aesthetic and design problems.

Howe (2006b) calls Threadless one of the exemplar cases of crowdsourcing: "pure, unadulterated (and scalable) crowdsourcing." Based in Chicago and formed in late 2000, Threadless is the flagship property of parent company skinnyCorp, whose motto is "skinnyCorp creates communities" (skinnyCorp, n.d.). Threadless is an online clothing company, and as of June 2006, Threadless was "selling 60,000 t-shirts a month, [had] a profit margin of 35 per cent [*sic*] and [was] on track to gross [US]$18 million in 2006," all with "fewer than 20 employees" (Howe, 2006b, para. 1).

At Threadless, the ongoing challenge to the registered members of the online community is to design and select silk-screen T-shirts. Members can download T-shirt design templates and color palettes for desktop graphics software packages, such as Adobe Illustrator, and create T-shirt design ideas. They then upload the designs to a gallery on the Threadless web site, where the submissions remain in a contest for a week. Members vote on designs in the gallery during this time on a five-point rating scale. At the end of the week, the highest rated designs are finalist candidates for printing, and the Threadless staff chooses about five designs to mass produce each week. These "t-shirts are then produced in short production runs and sold on the site," back to members in the online community (as well as to unregistered visitors to the site) through a typical online storefront (Fletcher, 2006, p. 6). Threadless awards winning designers US$2000 in cash and US$500 in Threadless gift certificates in exchange for their intellectual property.

User-generated advertising contests, such as the Doritos Crash the Super Bowl Contest, are also examples of the peer-vetted creative production approach (Brabham, 2009), as are participatory design contests, such as Next Stop Design (Brabham *et al.*, 2010). Next Stop Design was an effort in 2009–2010 to crowdsource public participation for transit planning beginning with a competition to design a better bus stop shelter. The project, funded by the US Federal Transit Administration, allowed participants to upload bus stop shelter designs to a gallery on the Next Stop Design web site, and then to rate the designs of peers in the gallery. The three designs with the highest average score at the close of the four-month competition were declared the winners. Without any monetary incentive or promise to actually construct the winning designs, nearly 3200 registered users submitted 260 bus stop shelter designs in the competition.

Distributed Human Intelligence Tasking

Different still from the previous cases is the distributed human intelligence tasking approach to crowdsourcing. This is an appropriate approach for crowdsourcing when a corpus of data is known and the problem is not to produce designs, find information, or develop solutions. Rather, it is appropriate when the problem itself involves processing data. It is similar to the concept of large-scale distributed computing projects, such as SETI@home and Rosetta@home, except replacing spare computing cycles with humans engaged in short cycles of labor. Large data problems are decomposed into small tasks requiring human intelligence, and individuals in the crowd are compensated for processing the bits of data. Because this crowdsourcing approach is certainly the least creative and intellectually demanding for individuals in the crowd, monetary compensation is a common motivator for participation.

The most notable example of the distributed human intelligence tasking approach is Amazon Mechanical Turk (Barr and Cabrera, 2006). At Mechanical Turk, "Requesters" can use the site to coordinate a series of simple tasks they need accomplished by humans, tasks that computers cannot easily do, such as accurately tagging the content of images on the Internet for a search engine. Individuals in the Mechanical Turk community, known as "Turkers," can then sign up to accomplish a series of these "human intelligence tasks" (HITs) for very small monetary rewards paid by the Requester. Mechanical Turk essentially coordinates large-scale collections of simple tasks requiring human intelligence.

This kind of distributed human intelligence tasking can be seen in other cases. For example, Subvert and Profit uses this format to coordinate the gaming of social media sites such as Digg and StumbleUpon (Powazek, 2007). Confidential clients pay Subvert and Profit to distribute rating tasks for certain stories and web sites to a crowd of registered users, who can each make small amounts of money for performing the tasks. Calling their product "social media optimization," Subvert and Profit claims to have placed thousands of content items on the front pages of high-traffic sites like Digg, resulting in millions of views for paid items. On its site, the company estimates its method is "30 to 100 times more cost effective than conventional Internet advertising" ("FAQ," n.d.).

Limitations of Crowdsourcing

There are a number of potential issues surrounding the crowdsourcing model that are worth exploring. First, for crowdsourcing to be successful, it must rely on a robust, active, motivated crowd. Though much research has been done about online communities, there is still no coherent set of best practices for organizations hoping to build and sustain these kinds of online communities. We know that a good deal of time and attention must be paid by an organization to grow an online community, we know these communities need to be motivated to participate, and we know that crowds can turn on an organization in ways that damage a brand's reputation (e.g. Bosman, 2006), but our understanding of fickle online communities is still quite undeveloped. Online community management will likely become an important sub-field of public relations and marketing as more organizations integrate crowds into their operations in coming years.

Second, crowdsourcing requires a great deal of transparency and trust on the part of an organization. To open a challenge to an online community requires an organization to specify the parameters of a given problem, which may require the organization to expose its proprietary data, its inner workings, or its anxieties and weaknesses. To leverage the power of crowds, organizations must surrender a bit of their own power by letting online communities become meaningful stakeholders. Not all organizations or industries are willing and able to do this.

Third, crowdsourcing applications can be manipulated and gamed just like any other aspect of participatory culture. The success of a company like Subvert and Profit, for instance, casts doubt on the organic, democratic virtues of so-called peer-recommended news aggregation sites such as Digg. Competitions, especially those in the peer-vetted creative production vein, can be flooded with fraudulent votes or phony accounts. Essentially, one cannot claim that a crowdsourcing application is completely "of the people, by the people," as surely some people exert additional influence through subversive means in these applications. Crowdsourcing should never be claimed as a complete replacement for more secure, regulated forms, especially if crowdsourcing is used in government affairs.

Issues of cheating aside, there is a fourth limitation in claiming that a crowdsourcing process resulted in something that "the people" wanted. This limitation concerns representation. Since crowdsourcing occurs on the Internet, and since Internet access is lower among the economically disadvantaged and racial and ethnic minorities, we can never fully claim a design that wins in a crowdsourcing competition is what is wanted by all. In fact, making this claim works to mask critical conversations about technology access and democratic participation in these crowdsourcing forms. If crowds are relatively homogenous and elite in their makeup, then crowdsourcing applications may work to reproduce the hegemonic values of those in power through a kind of aesthetic tyranny of the majority. We must take great care in the ways we talk about crowdsourcing's virtues.

Lastly, there is a valid complaint that crowdsourcing is exploitive. Compared to the profits Threadless makes on the sale of its crowd-made products, for instance, the prize money earned by winning designers is quite small. And even very large cash prizes at InnoCentive for successful Solvers likely result in enormous profits for the scientific companies who secure the intellectual property rights to an invention. These industry shifts brought on by crowdsourcing and other participatory media processes have also driven down the prices graphic designers and other creative professionals were once able to command for their work. Crowdsourcing, then, may well favor the crowdsourcing organization at the expense of the individual laborer in the crowd.

Conclusion

Crowdsourcing is one specific form of participatory social media, part of a greater media landscape that includes open-source production, commons-based peer production, blogging, video-posting and photo-sharing sites, massively multiplayer online games, and other forms. Unlike these forms it is unique, however, in that it involves an organization–user relationship whereby the organization executes a top-down, managed process that seeks the bottom-up, open, creative input of users in an online community. Because an organization issues specific tasks to an open community and manages the process, crowdsourcing can leverage the power of crowds to tackle specific challenges in specified formats and on planned schedules. Thus this element of management is what makes crowdsourcing different, productive, and full of potential to do good.

Each of these various crowdsourcing types—knowledge discovery and management, broadcast search, peer-vetted creative production, and distributed human intelligence tasking—can be employed in specific contexts to accomplish certain goals. Depending on the nature of a problem, the type of input needed from a crowd, and understanding what motivates these crowds to participate in a specific task environment, any number of new media tools could be designed to meet the needs of an organization in search of a solution to a problem. And why not design these tools to serve the public good, rather than focus entirely on for-profit applications? Why not draw upon this typology of crowdsourcing applications to make governance more efficient and inclusive, to search for difficult scientific solutions, to craft better public policy, or to otherwise leverage the collective intelligence of online communities to improve the human condition? By opening up the problem-solving process and managing the input of crowds to address focused needs, crowdsourcing could be used to improve public participation in the crafting of government policies, injecting more of the voice of the people in democratic processes. Or crowdsourcing could be used to innovate cleaner forms of energy or develop better medicines and cures for diseases. Or perhaps crowdsourcing can facilitate public art projects, redesign public transit systems, and help government agencies collect data or enforce compliance with laws in a community. Crowdsourcing may very well be a model for solving the world's most challenging problems, channeling the energies of participatory cultures for a greater purpose.

References

Barr, Jeff and Cabrera, Luis Felipe. 2006. "AI gets a brain: New technology allows software to tap real human intelligence," *ACM Queue*, 4(4): 24–29.

Benkler, Yochai. 2002. "Coase's penguin, or, Linux and the nature of the firm," *Yale Law Journal*, 112(3): 369–446.

Bonaccorsi, Andrea and Rossi, Cristina. 2004. "Altruistic individuals, selfish firms? The structure of motivation in open source software," *First Monday*, 9(1). www.firstmonday.org/htbin/cgiwrap/bin/ojs/index.php/fm/article/view/1113/1033.

Bosman, Julie. 2006. "Chevy tries a write-your-own-ad approach, and the potshots fly," *New York Times* (4 April). www.nytimes.com/2006/04/04/business/media/04adco.html.

Brabham, Daren C. 2008a. "Crowdsourcing as a model for problem solving: an introduction and cases," *Convergence: The International Journal of Research into New Media Technologies*, 14(1): 75–90.

Brabham, Daren C. 2008b. "Moving the crowd at iStockphoto: The composition of the crowd and motivations for participation in a crowdsourcing application," *First Monday*, 13(6). www.uic.edu/htbin/cgiwrap/bin/ojs/index.php/fm/article/view/2159/1969.

Brabham, Daren C. 2009. "Crowdsourced advertising: How we outperform Madison Avenue," *Flow: A Critical Forum on Television and Media Culture*, 9(10). http://flowtv.org.

Brabham, Daren C. 2010a. "Crowdsourcing as a model for problem solving: Leveraging the collective intelligence of online communities for public good" (Unpublished Doctoral Thesis), University of Utah.

Brabham, Daren C. 2010b. "Moving the crowd at Threadless: Motivations for participation in a crowdsourcing application," *Information, Communication & Society*, 13(8): 1122–1145.

Brabham, Daren C., Sanchez, Thomas W., and Bartholomew, Keith. 2010. "Crowdsourcing public participation in transit planning: Preliminary results from the next stop design case." Paper presented at the annual meeting of the Transportation Research Board of the National Academies, Washington, DC.

Brito, Jerry. 2008. "Hack, mash, & peer: Crowdsourcing government transparency," *The Columbia Science and Technology Law Review*, 9: 119–157.

"FAQ." n.d. *Subvert and Profit*. http://subvertandprofit.com/content/faq.

Fletcher, Adam. 2006. "Do consumers want to design unique products on the Internet? A study of the online virtual community of Threadless.com and their attitudes to mass customisation, mass production and collaborative design" (Unpublished Bachelor's Thesis), Nottingham Trent University, UK.

Fritz, Steffen, McCallum, Ian, Schill, Christian, Perger, Christoph, Grillmayer, Roland, Achard, Frédéric, Kraxner, Florian, and Obersteiner, Michael. 2009. "Geo-Wiki.org: The use of crowdsourcing to improve global land cover," *Remote Sensing*, 1(3): 345–354.

"Goldcorp Challenge Winners!" 2001. The Goldcorp Challenge. www.goldcorpchallenge.com/challenge1/winnerslist/challeng2.pdf.

Haklay, Mordechai (Muki) and Weber, Patrick. 2008. "OpenStreetMap: User-generated Street Maps," *IEEE Pervasive Computing*, 7(4): 12–18.

Hars, Alexander and Ou, Shaosong. 2002. "Working for free? Motivations for participating in open source projects," *International Journal of Electronic Commerce*, 6(3): 25–39.

Hertel, Guido, Niedner, Sven, and Hermann, Stefanie. 2003. "Motivation of software developers in the open source projects: An Internet-based survey of contributors to the Linux Kernel," *Research Policy*, 32(7): 1159–1177.

Howe, Jeff. 2006a. "Crowdsourcing: A definition," *Crowdsourcing: Tracking the rise of the amateur* (Weblog, 2 June). http://crowdsourcing.typepad.com/cs/2006/06/crowdsourcing_a.html.

Howe, Jeff. 2006b. "Pure, unadulterated (and scalable) crowdsourcing," *Crowdsourcing: Tracking the rise of the amateur* (Weblog, 15 June). http://crowdsourcing.typepad.com/cs/2006/06/pure_unadultera.html.

Howe, Jeff. 2006c. "The rise of crowdsourcing," *Wired*, 14(6) (June). www.wired.com/wired/archive/14.06/crowds.html.

Huberman, Bernardo A., Romero, Daniel M., and Wu, Fang. 2009. "Crowdsourcing, attention and productivity," *Journal of Information Science*, 35(6): 758–765.

Ignatius, David. 2001. "Try a network approach to global problem-solving," *International Herald Tribune* (29 January). www.iht.com/.

Jenkins, Henry, Clinton, Katie, Purushotma, Ravi, Robison, Alice J., and Weigel, Margaret. 2009. *Confronting the challenges of participatory culture: Media education for the 21st century*. Chicago, IL: John D. and Catherine T. MacArthur Foundation.

Lakhani, Karim R., Jeppesen, Lars Bo, Lohse, Peter A., and Panetta, Jill A. 2007. "The value of openness in scientific problem solving," *Harvard Business School Working Paper*, number 07-050. www.hbs.edu/research/pdf/07-050.pdf.

Lakhani, Karim R. and Wolf, Robert G. 2005. "Why hackers do what they do: Understanding motivation and effort in free/open source software projects," In Joseph Feller, Brian Fitzgerald, Scott A. Hissam, and Karim R. Lakhani (eds). *Perspectives on free and open source software*. Cambridge, MA: MIT Press, pp. 3–22.

Lévy, Pierre, 1997. *Collective intelligence: Mankind's emerging world in cyberspace* (trans. Robert Bononno). New York: Plenum (original work published 1995).

Lietsala, Katri and Joutsen, Atte. 2007. "Hang-a-rounds and true believers: A case analysis of the roles and motivational factors of the *Star Wreck* fans," In Artur Lugmayr, Katri Lietsala, and Jan Kallenbach (eds). *MindTrek 2007 Conference Proceedings*. Tampere, Finland: Tampere University of Technology, pp. 25–30.

Liu, Su-Houn, Liao, Hsiu-Li, and Zeng, Yuan-Tai. 2007. "Why people blog: An expectancy theory analysis," *Issues in Information Systems*, 8(2): 232–237.

Nov, Oded. 2007. "What motivates Wikipedians?" *Communications of the ACM*, 50(11): 60–64.

Nov, Oded, Naaman, Mor, and Ye, Chen. 2008. "What drives content tagging: The case of photos on Flickr." In Margaret Burnett, Maria Francesca Costabile, Tiziana Catarci, Boris de Ruyter, Desney Tan, Mary Czerwinski, and Arnie Lund (eds). *Proceedings of the 26th Annual SIGCHI Conference on Human Factors in Computing Systems*. New York: Association for Computing Machinery, pp. 1097–1100.

Noveck, Beth Simone. 2006. "Peer to patent: Collective intelligence, open review, and patent reform," *Harvard Journal of Law & Technology*, 20(1): 123–262.

Phillips, Laurie and Brabham, Daren C. 2011. "How today's digital landscape redefines the notion of control in public relations." Paper presented at the 14th annual International Public Relations Research Conference, Coral Gables, FL.

Powazek, Derek. 2007. "Exploring the dark side of crowdsourcing," *Wired* (11 July). www.wired.com/techbiz/media/news/2007/07/tricksters.

skinnyCorp. n.d. www.skinnycorp.com, accessed 15 September 2010.

Smith, Abbe. 2010. "SeeClickFix celebrates 50G issues reported," *New Haven Register* (7 August). www.nhregister.com/articles/2010/08/07/news/aa3_neseeclickfix080710.txt.

Tischler, Linda. 2007. "He struck gold on the Net (really)," *Fast Company* (19 December). www.fastcompany.com/magazine/59/mcewen.html.

14

HOW PARTICLE PHYSICISTS CONSTRUCTED THE WORLD'S LARGEST GRID

A Case Study in Participatory Cultures

Sarah Pearce and Will Venters

Particle physics is the study of the fundamental building blocks of the universe, the things from which everything is made. In order to understand the structure of matter, physicists must collide sub-atomic particles at higher and higher energies, using ever-larger particle accelerators. By studying the minute debris from these collisions, they gain an insight into the quarks, leptons and bosons that comprise the alphabet of matter.

Currently the most powerful collider is the Large Hadron Collider (LHC) at CERN, the European particle physics laboratory. For this chapter we discuss the development and use of a global grid computing infrastructure by UK particle physicists to allow them to analyse the data emerging from the LHC. In doing this we have conflated many conversations between the authors into a dialogue reflecting our interests.

The scene in which this dialogue takes place is in the early evening in a pub near a UK university where GridPP has recently finished one of its meetings. Sarah Pearce, who works for GridPP, is discussing the project over a pint of beer with Will Venters, a lecturer in information systems at the London School of Economics who has begun studying how particle physicists are building their grid.

The Participatory Culture of Particle Physics

WILL: I guess some would say that particle physicists, particularly experimental particle physicists, are the epitome of a participatory culture! Whereas academics are often stereo-typed as lone thinkers you come together in global collaborations of thousands, and produce tools and techniques to support such collaboration. In fact, you were once described by a sociologist as "Communitarian" [Knorr-Cetina, 1999]. What makes you such a participatory culture?

SARAH: There are certainly some similarities between living in a commune and working in particle physics. We are committed to pooling our individual work to achieve a shared goal, and this shared goal defines and shapes individuals' practices. We are definitely a big commu-nity—the experiments we have built at the LHC at CERN have thousands of physicists working at hundreds of institutions. But our community began small—with desktop particle accelerators designed, built and run by one university [Gallison, 1997]. Because of the scale of particle physics experiments now, no one can afford to work alone; we have to collaborate, and our individual goals rely on the whole endeavour working. We now move from one large project to the next and this global collaborative way of organisation and management is ingrained from the earliest days of a student's PhD. Our experimental collaborations don't typically have leaders who can individually force things to be done—it's about enabling and encouraging people who share a common goal and common attitude. Although there's a spokesperson who is the leader of the collaboration, decisions are taken more by committee and consensus than by decree from the top [Zheng *et al.*, in press].

WILL: So communication is vital—perhaps that is why Tim Berners-Lee came up with the idea of the Web at CERN?

SARAH: Yes: he saw that physicists across CERN needed a way to share their information, and in 1989 the first proposal for the Web was the result [Gillies and Cailliau, 2000]. It probably also helped that CERN and particle physics tends to be at the cutting edge of computing.

WILL: Why is that?

SARAH: Because we produce so much data! Look at the LHC in Geneva—it's been called the 'big bang' machine because it accelerates protons to nearly the speed of light in a circular tunnel 27 km long, and then collides them together to recreate conditions as they were in the early universe, immediately after the big bang. The only way we can look at these collisions is through four large detectors the size of cathedrals, ATLAS, CMS, LHCb and ALICE, which produce a vast amount of data. By analysing huge numbers of these collisions, we can look for signs of fundamental particles and so work out what matter is made of. One of the LHC's main aims is to find the Higgs boson, which could explain why particles have mass.

FIGURE 14.1 Aerial view of CERN with LHC ring marked
Source: courtesy of CERN.

WILL: You say vast amounts of data—but what are we talking about here?

SARAH: Each of the four experiments produces massive streams of data. Once it's been through initial processing, there will be around 15 million gigabytes of data from the LHC every year—that's a DVD worth of data every 5 seconds, which needs to be shared between thousands of researchers at hundreds of universities around the world. *The Economist* estimated this as 1% of all global information production a few years ago [*The Economist*, 2004].

Grid Computing for the LHC

WILL: So how are you going to process that data from the new LHC—what computing facility will you use?

SARAH: Around ten years ago, particle physicists looked for the best way to deal with this, and decided to use a new concept called grid computing.

WILL: A grid is a network of computers, a bit like the Web. …

SARAH: Yes, but it's more than that. When you use the Web, you mainly use it to get and share information. The latest articles in your field, headline news, what your friends were doing last night. But the grid lets you take things further—it allows you to share resources such as storage and CPU power in addition to information. For example, you can run your own programs on computers on the grid, meaning that the vast amounts of processing power from machines around the globe are available to you as though they were inside your local PC. This is particularly useful if you need to run millions of simulations of particle physics collisions, or analyse the data from the LHC.

WILL: So you built a grid for the LHC then?

SARAH: Yes, in collaboration with scientists across Europe, the US and worldwide. Our grid now has 150,000 computers at 600 sites in sixty-two countries. Most of these are at research centres and universities.

WILL: But why? Why not just buy a supercomputer, or lots of supercomputers, and put them at CERN?

SARAH: You're back to our participatory culture again. It would certainly have been possible to store all the LHC data at CERN, and build a massive computing centre there. But that could have been difficult politically—why would a university in Finland, say, be interested in paying for computers at CERN? Whereas by building a grid, the university in Finland pays for the computers on their own campus. These resources are under the university's control, and they can be used by other scientists at the university as well as particle physicists. Essentially the grid allows us to turn local university resources into a shared resource for all.

WILL: Like a commune shares everything!

SARAH: Yes—but this isn't altruism—we all gain. If each university kept their own resources to themselves and local particle physicist researchers used that …

WILL: … like traditional batch processing in other sciences where you submit your computing job to a local computer system and wait for the result …

SARAH: … but then you miss out on the greater economy of scale available by sharing. Grid computing is an analogy to the electricity grid because it provides computing power on demand like electricity [Foster and Kesselman, 1999]. And like electricity it can handle peaks and troughs in demand and supply because all the resources and demands are pooled. The grid is run by "middleware", which is essentially the operating system for the grid. It links the hardware resources together and makes them transparently available to users. When you submit a job, the grid middleware looks at what sites are already busy, and sends your job where it will be run most quickly. So with a grid, you don't need to wait for your local cluster to be free before your computing job runs—and because grid sites are spread at hundreds of institutes around the world, there's a better chance that you'll get quick access to the resources you need.

WILL: Back to your commune—everyone puts their food in the pot and everyone shares the soup! But what links all these computers together—how do they collaborate?

SARAH: There are several layers to a grid. The most fundamental of these is probably the network: a means of connecting the computers together. In the UK, GridPP runs over the standard academic network, but we also have dedicated high-speed connections between some sites—for example we have two 10 gigabits per second dedicated lines from CERN to the Rutherford Appleton Laboratory. The next layer is the hardware: clusters of hundreds or thousands of computers and storage elements. We don't typically use PCs that you might have on your desk, because that's not the cheapest type of hardware for us to run—rather, we have racks of processors set up in machine rooms that need high levels of air-conditioning because of the heat the computers produce. These are connected by very high-speed local networks to large amounts of storage, on disk or tape.

WILL: So all this is as well as the middleware?

SARAH: The middleware is the next layer, which deals with making the grid work: distributing researchers' jobs, arranging storage, monitoring how the grid is running, and managing security issues such as authentication and authorisation. Then finally, on top of that, we have the applications layer. This is the layer that users interact with, and covers software from all the disciplines that use the grid—particle physics, chemistry, biological sciences, even archaeology and linguistics. It enables users to submit their programs to the grid, extract data from it and monitor the progress of their computations.

WILL: So you can share this grid with others—very communal? I thought this grid was for particle physicists—after all, the impetus behind it came from the LHC.

SARAH: Certainly particle physics was the driving force in creating this grid, but one of grid computing's great advantages is that the hardware can be shared. The particle physics grid has tens of thousands of computers, but they don't all run particle physics all the time. You can compare it to Amazon, whose computer centre is very busy in the lead-up to Christmas but quieter at other times. Particle physicists run a lot of programs just before conferences, for example, trying to get their papers ready in time, so the grid might be full then. But at other times there can be some spare capacity. And because of the grid's architecture, it's easy for researchers from other disciplines to use that spare capacity. The grid we helped develop has had 170 research communities use it [EGEE, 2010]. Apart from particle physics, the main users were from areas such as computational chemistry, earth sciences and astronomy. But a range of more unlikely disciplines has also run computations on the grid, including archaeology, finance and civil protection. One of the most interesting uses of the grid has been an Italian project which recreated the sound of the epigonion, a harp-like ancient Greek musical instrument [ASTRA]. Using data collected by archaeologists, engineers and historians, the project was able to model what the epigonion would have sounded like, playing the result on an electronic keyboard. They have since extended this to other ancient instruments, creating a "lost sounds orchestra".

WILL: That's fascinating but can you give me an example of what other sciences are using your grid for?

SARAH: Biomedical scientists used over 7 million computer hours on the grid in 2009. One of the earliest uses of the grid for biomedicine was in drug discovery, which employs computer models to predict molecules that might be useful in the fight against certain diseases. Researchers in France and Taiwan identified promising candidates for drugs against avian flu

FIGURE 14.2 Looking down ATLAS along the beam path
Source: courtesy of CERN.

and malaria. In this way, the number of molecules that needs to be tested in the lab can be reduced, speeding up the process and reducing its cost.

WILL: Your grid sounds like it has similarities with SETI@home where people volunteer their computers to search for ET.

SARAH: Volunteer computing does have similarities with the grid, and we even have a similar project called LHC@home. As with the grid, in volunteer computing the hardware is distributed and not owned by the project, which makes serendipitous use of your computer when you're not using it. The key difference though is the software. For SETI@home the project has a very firm control over what's run on volunteer computers—which is essential because you wouldn't want just anybody running something on your PC.

WILL: Yes, but you allow users to run their own jobs and software on your grid. Surely you can't trust them all that much even if you are communitarian! How do you manage that? How do you stop someone using the grid for nefarious purposes or just over-using it?

SARAH: We make sure we know exactly who has access to the grid by giving them a digital certificate to identify themselves—essentially a digital passport for the grid. To apply for this passport involves registering at a certificate authority with some identity document—a real passport for instance. Once we know exactly who the person is they must join a Virtual Organisation or VO, which we use to manage users on the grid. Each of the main research communities has their own VO—the ATLAS experiment for example—and individual grid sites can then decide which VO to support. Sites can contact your VO if you do something wrong—bringing a site to its knees either accidentally or deliberately. At this point your digital certificate can be immediately revoked, or your local administrator can help ensure you fix the problem.

WILL: Have you had any security incidents?

SARAH: One or two minor ones with no damage done. Security is taken very seriously and we can respond to security issues very quickly.

Building the Grid

WILL: How did particle physicists go about building this infrastructure—did you contract an IT company to help build it?

SARAH: No—we formed a collaboration to build it ourselves. When we started in 2001, only some of the fundamental software tools existed. As such we had to build it ourselves and our natural way of working is to collaborate—so we developed a collaboration of physicists and computer experts. Researchers at CERN worked with the UK and other countries to get the grid project off the ground [CERN Council, 2001]. In the UK, our collaboration was based at twenty universities and research institutes, and paid for by government research funding. We called ourselves GridPP. The UK was a driving force behind the development of the grid for particle physics: in GridPP's first phase, it funded CERN to help kick-start the project that's now known as the Worldwide LHC Computing Grid (WLCG). WLGC is now the world's largest grid, and amalgamates regional grids from the USA [Pordes *et al.*, 2008], Scandinavia [Eerola *et al.*, 2003] and Europe.

WILL: How has GridPP changed over these past nearly ten years?

SARAH: The first phase aimed to establish a prototype grid, so a great deal of the project's effort in those days was focused on software development: writing the middleware that would run the grid. By the end of GridPP's first phase in 2004, there was a test grid running across seventy-eight sites worldwide, with 6000 computers. The UK was the largest contributor to this, with 1000 computers at twelve sites [GridPP, 2004].

WILL: The next phase of GridPP was called "From prototype to production"—what does that mean?

SARAH: In 2004, the grid was still a prototype: the middleware wasn't terribly reliable, sites tended to go on and off the grid. Although scientists were using the grid, it was quite sporadic and temperamental. So GridPP2 aimed to build a "production" grid—that is, one that was large scale, stable and easy to use. We achieved the first two of these, at least!

WILL: So GridPP2 involved expanding the grid to more sites and more computers?

SARAH: And making the grid more stable. By this phase of the project, we were beginning to be less focused on writing the middleware. There was still software development going on but the core of how the grid would work was established. Our key challenge in this phase was to quickly ramp up the number of computers and the amount of storage at GridPP sites ready for the demands of the LHC, while working out how to run a "production grid": a stable, reliable infrastructure physicists could actually use.

WILL: You're currently in GridPP3—with the strapline "From production to exploitation". What's the aim of this part of the project?

SARAH: GridPP3 is the culmination of the first two parts of the project: the LHC has switched on, data is flowing and we're using the grid to analyse it. So this part of the project is focused on making sure the grid works for LHC data—that all the preparation we've done in GridPP1 and GridPP2 has paid off.

WILL: Has the grid been working well with real LHC data?

SARAH: It's been very successful so far—having an extra year because of the LHC's launch problems also helped to ensure we were ready. Towards the end of GridPP2 and at the start of GridPP3, we were part of end-to-end tests of the grid run by WLCG, so we were quietly confident that the grid would work when data came [Britton *et al.*, 2009; Coles, 2008]. However, things have probably gone better than expected. The LHC isn't yet at its full luminosity though, so data rates will increase, and that's when the grid will really be tested.

WILL: Has GridPP been involved in the first discoveries that are starting to come from the LHC?

SARAH: GridPP provided more than 10% of the LHC's computing in the last quarter of 2010, so it's a good bet that any LHC paper will include some computing run on our grid. As well as managing the grid, many of GridPP's staff members are also deeply involved in the LHC experiments and the physics they are producing.

Organising GridPP's Effort

WILL: Running a production grid must involve more than just collaborating—there must be some management and control to ensure stability.

SARAH: Yes—like any project we need some oversight and direction. GridPP is run by a Project Management Board (PMB), which meets weekly and includes representatives from each of the main LHC experiments as well as experts on specific areas such as security or networking. That's overseen by a Collaboration Board, which only meets a couple of times a year but includes the particle physics group leaders from each of the sites. Although the vision is set by the Project Leader, decisions are taken collectively through discussion and consensus. We don't manage members of the collaboration too closely: they're given a degree of latitude to meet their goals whatever way they see best and it's more carrot than stick.

WILL: So your project staff are free to work on what they want?

SARAH: Not exactly—there is a framework of milestones and metrics that are reviewed every quarter, and people work in their areas of expertise. But we recognise that there's no point in management watching over someone's shoulder—team members are generally at the cutting edge, and know more than we do about their area. Also, the project managers don't have line management of GridPP's staff, who are employed by individual institutions. It's more a question of setting the general structure within a longer-term strategic view, and fire-fighting when things go wrong. We keep a close eye on indicative figures from the sites, for example availability, the amount of CPU and storage they contribute, how many jobs were run on their infrastructure. The PMB hears weekly reports from the experiments, the Tier-1 and the Production Manager, so if there's anything wrong we usually know about it quickly.

WILL: Such loose management is perhaps fine for individuals who are dedicated to the LHC, but what about the institutions providing hardware and staff time? You must have contracts for those services?

SARAH: Not contracts, but there is a Memorandum of Understanding with each site that sets out what levels of service and resources we expect. That's not really relied upon as a method of enforcement through, more as a means of ensuring the university has a clear understanding of what GridPP needs. The grid is generally very open: we welcome new sites that want to join the grid; they just need to run the middleware and make sure they meet our security requirements.

WILL: With all those university IT departments hosting the grid, some must be better than others. Without a contract how do you ensure you get what you want from them—they might not be as collaborative as you are?

SARAH: It's difficult but money helps. In practice, if sites don't deliver as we expect, that feeds through into the next round of funding. We fund staff at most of our sites, and also pay for hardware. Importantly, the amount of hardware and staffing allocated to a site depends on its performance during the previous phases of the project, so we hope it's a virtuous circle, where the good sites get better and are able to supply more resources. It also allows small sites that perform well to get bigger. Having said that, some individual sites on the grid have set up a charging system within their university where their computing cluster is provided centrally, and GridPP just buys time on it for the jobs it runs on the grid, rather than paying for hardware.

WILL: Is contracting for a service centrally like this easier?

SARAH: Generally no, although it can work. It's often difficult to persuade central computing services at the university to install the right software and provide the necessary service levels for running the grid. We've found it works best if GridPP also pays for staff time at the university to help manage the computers directly, and then uses competition for funding to improve quality.

WILL: Do you use competition in managing any other parts of the project?

SARAH: Yes, among those writing software. Although there is coordination of this work from WLCG, there's also a degree of competition, so that several groups might write, for example, monitoring software that allows you to check how the grid is working. Over time, grid sites will adopt the version of the monitoring software that they feel works best, and eventually one version might become the *de facto* standard. So it's more a 'survival of the fittest' approach, with less effective software being left behind.

WILL: Doesn't that lead to a lot of repetition, with different groups doing the same thing?

SARAH: It does, but it also seems to work. Particle physicists democratise innovation [von Hippel, 2005] in their field—they don't just do what they're told. If there's something that doesn't work how they want, they're likely to write their own version. Ultimately this encourages excellence and does not trap the project into sub-optimal products. That said we do see some loss of morale amongst those whose software is rejected. They tend to be quite dedicated to the cause of particle physics though, so typically just move on to the next set of software being developed.

Collaborating across Europe

WILL: While GridPP and particle physicists have been developing this grid, have they been working with other grid projects?

SARAH: We have collaborated closely with, and relied upon, other projects in Europe and worldwide. Initially the European Commission funded a project called the European Data Grid, in which WLCG and GridPP were closely involved, and which drew heavily on WLCG expertise. This was later replaced by "Enabling Grids for E-sciencE" (EGEE) [Jones, 2005] whose main aim, apart from coordinating a permanent, reliable grid infrastructure across Europe, was to encourage scientists from disciplines other than particle physics to use the emerging grid. GridPP, the UK particle physics grid, contributed its infrastructure to EGEE as part of the worldwide grid—as did other grids in countries across Europe and elsewhere. EGEE needed to demonstrate that the grid was useful for scientists of all types, not just particle physicists, and was instrumental in getting the sciences we discussed before to use the grid.

WILL: All these European projects—that can't bode well for a sustainable future—what happens when the projects run out?!

SARAH: The EGEE project has been replaced by a new model called the European Grid Infrastructure (EGI). EGI's aim is to be a long-term structure for grid computing in Europe, which won't depend on year-by-year project funding.

WILL: So EGI will run the European Grid infrastructure?

SARAH: It coordinates the grids from different countries and regions, similar to the way networks in each country are coordinated at the European level. Each area is expected to have a National Grid Infrastructure (NGI) that meets central standards and contributes to running the grid as a whole. In the UK, our NGI will be a partnership between GridPP and the National Grid Service, which provides grid computing for other disciplines.

Infrastructure for Collaborating

WILL: With all this collaboration—between projects, sites, experiments and people—communication must be really important.

SARAH: It is. We put a great deal of effort into ensuring GridPP works as a functioning team. As well as weekly PMB meetings by phone, there are weekly technical meetings to discuss more specific issues with sites or software. We meet as a whole collaboration twice a year, and we also hold face-to-face meetings of the PMB to tackle issues that require more discussion. In addition, there's a User Board that meetings quarterly, for input from the experiments—it's particularly useful to hear from the smaller experiments, who aren't represented on the PMB. Although we have an extensive structure of Boards and meetings, these are really just a way of ensuring communication, rather than a top-down way of managing the project. We like to think we're a very open project, and that any individual can easily make their voice heard through our collaboration meetings or by coming directly to the project management.

WILL: Presumably you also use electronic communication—having invented the Web?!

SARAH: All the time. We have a very extensive web site, which includes a wiki and blogs covering much of the operations work and regular news items. There's a general mailing list, and several more focused mailing lists for specific issues. But although we do send and receive a huge amount of email, I'd say our most useful communication tool is the phone conference.

WILL: That doesn't sound terribly high-tech: do you also use more complex collaboration tools?

SARAH: Not really. We did use video conferences, but found they weren't really reliable enough so reverted to the phone. But crucially we all know each other very well: some of the PMB members have been working together since they were PhD students, and they're now professors. So we can communicate effectively without the visual clues that a video conference adds. We find that using simple tools, but using them often, builds a very strong, trusting collaboration.

WILL: What about more informal communication?

SARAH: I think that's fundamental to the collaboration. We all get on very well together, and that's reinforced by long sessions in the pub after meetings. Actually, it's in the pub after collaboration meetings or PMB meetings that many of the more difficult issues for the collaboration get sorted out because ideas can be explored in a less formal context, and certainly that's where the long-term future is planned. Discussions in the pub are brainstorming sessions: less structured than a meeting, with fewer time constraints, they allow us to get into the strategy of what we're doing.

WILL: So this type of discussion, in a pub after a collaboration meeting, is what drives the project?

SARAH: Exactly.

References

ASTRA. www.astraproject.org/index.html, accessed 6 October 2010.

Britton, D. *et al.* 2009. "GridPP—The UK grid for particle physics", *Proceedings of the UK e-Science All Hands Meeting 2008*, Edinburgh, UK, *Phil Trans R Soc A*, 367: 2447–2457

CERN Council. 2001. "Proposal for building the LHC computing environment at CERN", CERN/2379/Rev

Coles, J., 2008. "Grid computing for UK particle physics", *Proceedings of the UK e-Science All Hands Meeting 2007*, Nottingham, UK, *J Phys: Conf Ser*, 119 052011.

The Economist. 2004. "One grid to rule them all", *The Economist*, 372: 74.

Eerola, P. *et al.*, 2003. "The NorduGrid production grid infrastructure, status and plans", *Proceedings of Fourth IEEE International Workshop on Grid Computing*. Phoenix, Arizona, pp. 158–165.

EGEE. 2010. "EGEE leaves a lasting legacy for the future." http://press.eu-egee.org/index.php?id=294, accessed 6 October 2010.

Foster, Ian and Kesselman, Carl. 1999. *The grid: blueprint for a new computing infrastructure.* San Francisco: Morgan Kaufmann.

Gallison, P. 1997. *Image and logic.* Chicago: University of Chicago.

Gillies, James and Cailliau, Robert. 2000. *How the web was born: The story of the world wide web.* New York: Oxford University Press.

GridPP. 2004. "GridPP at the All Hands Meeting." www.gridpp.ac.uk/news/?p=259, accessed 10 October 2010.

Jones, B. 2005. "'An overview of the EGEE project.' Peer-to-peer, grid, and service orientation in digital library architectures", *Lecture Notes in Computer Science, no. 3664*. Berlin, Germany: Springer, pp. 1–8.

Knorr-Cetina, K. 1999. *Epistemic cultures: How the sciences make knowledge.* Cambridge, MA: Harvard University Press.

Pordes, R., *et al.* 2008. "The open science grid status and architecture", *Proceedings of the International Conference on Computing in High Energy and Nuclear Physics 2007*, Mumbai, India, *J Phys Conf Ser* 119(5): 052028.

von Hippel, E. 2005. *Democratizing innovation.* Cambridge, MA, MIT Press.

Zheng, Y., *et al.* 2011. "Collective agility, paradox and organizational improvisation: the development of a particle physics grid", *Information Systems Journal* 21(4):303–333.

PART V

Fostering Participatory Civic Cultures

15

RESTRUCTURING CIVIC ENGAGEMENT

Meaningful Choice and Game Design Thinking

Benjamin Stokes[1]

The digital world brings new questions to the design of civic life. We are redesigning some of the structures of civic contribution—from how to volunteer time, to how we advocate for change, fundraise, and learn from one another. In this chapter, I argue that we must look beyond the red herring of new civic tools, and borrow a broader systems approach from the analytic frameworks of game design. This is quite different from the recent hype to "gamify" civic action with points and scout-like reward badges.[2] Instead, I propose to ask how game-like *thinking* can shift civic design and strategy, especially around meaningful choice.

This essay is grounded in my experience as a practitioner, in addition to the scholarly literature. I have gone through a journey which informs this analysis: after prototyping civic activities including games, I worked in the policy world of foundation funding. In what follows I weave practitioner insights with theory, partly to synthesize across the silos of technical code, participatory culture, and civic impact.

Which Civic Engagement?

This is an exciting time to analyze and design civic media. Technology aside, the very definition of "civic engagement" is broadening, and the term is simultaneously becoming more popular among funders, schools and government (Levine, 2007). Credit for this expansion goes in part to scholars of participatory culture, including several authors of this book. Traditionally, civic analysis focused on political acts like voting and joining civic organizations. But scholars of participatory culture have helped pull the civic into an analysis of everyday life. Participatory culture itself may depend on low barriers to civic engagement, according to the definitions of Jenkins *et al.* (2007).

Simultaneously, the field of political science is beginning to question its traditional definitions of civic engagement to account for more "global citizens" and transnational activism. In the education sector, there is new momentum to recognize "moral citizenship" (e.g. Haste and Hogan, 2006). And the spectrum of civic acts is also broadening, such as adding to boycotting the act of the buy-cott (to reward good companies, instead of simply punishing the bad; e.g. see Stolle *et al.*, 2005).

Such broadening of civic analysis, of also makes our analytic tools less precise.[3] It is harder than ever to compare any two people, and say which is the more civically engaged. Clearly this blur makes life difficult for those who evaluate the impact of civic media. Most importantly for this paper, it also raises a profound design challenge: how do we imagine civic activities online, if our conceptual models are simultaneously in flux? My practitioner training would suggest that we temporarily set aside normative model debates, and consider everyday life choices.

Toward "Meaningful Choice"

For better and worse, our time can be subdivided across more causes and civic modalities than ever before. The problem is particularly poignant online, where the civic palette now ranges from tracking international micro-credit loans, to online mentoring for youth activists. More tools means greater civic choice, but that is not necessarily a good thing.

Expanding choice makes it harder to know which choices are most important. Psychological studies of satisfaction have shown that an expansion of choice can actually undermine happiness (Schwartz *et al.*, 2002). The initial decision can seem simple (e.g. "I want to donate to fight poverty in India"), but when that decision also necessitates selecting between twenty possible non-profits, the burden of maximizing impact shifts to the individual participant. How many of us have the time to fully investigate each choice? As a society, we cannot simply design *more* civic tools, without offering participants more *meaningful* choices.

Meaningful choice is at the center of a new discipline: game design. This will sound strange to new ears, who have primarily encountered the discourse of games in popular culture debates, and heard games lumped with television as diversions that distract from civic life.[4] Even those who have seen so-called "games for change" may not have recognized the paradigmatic utility of game design thinking.

This cognitive mode is hidden by analyses of games which are blindly focused on content. Content myopia is even worse with so-called serious games, which largely seek to distribute or teach civic messages (Raphael *et al.*, 2009). Focusing on messages and content delivery misses the distinctive power of games to create meaning through real-time play. Games do not play themselves—they demand participation to unfold. This is an important historical shift. For the first time, we can create media that offer participants meaningful choice, iterative improvement and immediate feedback.

Game Design as Disciplinary Thinking

I am not arguing here for games as a metaphor, but as a distinct and increasingly useful kind of *disciplinary thinking*. Design itself is often mistakenly assumed to mean "graphic design" (perhaps because the value of graphic design is so immediate, and because skillful designers remain rare). In fact, design thinking is broader, and represents a methodology for creative problem-solving, one that is simultaneously systematic and strategic (Erlhoff and Marshall, 2008). Such multi-purpose design thinking is already applied across fields and disciplines, from business management to urban planning. In this paper, I am focused on a subset: the kind of design thinking that emerges from game design, which centers on interactivity and participant choice.

Game design thinking is particularly coherent for evolutionary reasons: game design is incredibly difficult and most games fail. Over time, game professionals iteratively developed their own particular set of analytic questions. Specifically, the discipline of game design has oriented to the delicate balance of *engagement* that makes or breaks a game: if it is too difficult, players quit in frustration; too easy, and players quit because it is boring.

My question is whether such game design thinking has implications for civic engagement.[5] I propose the answer is a resounding yes, and, more specifically, that game design thinking offers a useful mode of strategic planning for policy makers, civic funders and non-profit executives. In particular, game design thinking can be a kind of methodology for problem-solving engagement through meaningful choice.

Below I introduce two very different innovations in civic media. One emerges from an actual game, while the other focuses on the transfer of traditional volunteering into an online service.

Looking for Choice—from Fundraising to Teaching

To understand game design thinking, it helps to begin with a game. In 2004, I was on a team that built a "real life" fundraising challenge to extend a civic videogame, *Peter Packet* (for a brief case study, see Stokes, 2010). Among other things, *Peter Packet* aimed to teach youth about extreme poverty in Haiti, India, and Mexico. Yet our design focus was not on the game. Instead, we asked: what happens *after* and *around* their initial engagement?

We brainstormed. We were tempted initially by the tired strategy of offering content—a "toolkit" containing narratives of injustice, tips on reaching large audiences, and directions for collecting funds and signatures. These dissemination-oriented approaches can be powerful, but are often only accessible to the already committed organizers. So we considered: is it possible to design meaningful civic choices that extend the design approach of the game?

The result was a 10-day civic experiment featuring the same animated characters from the game (see Figure 15.1). We offered participants two actions: recruit others to learn about poverty by trying the game, and recruit others to donate for the specific projects described in the game. Although this was a fundraising challenge on the surface, participants were more significantly

FIGURE 15.1 Screen shot from the *Peter Packet* Challenge

contributing their voice, since both recruiting options required the player to advocate via email or in person. We set point values to match this civic mode: 2 points for recruiting another participant, and 5 points for the more difficult challenge of securing a donation of any amount.

Such points provided feedback to participants that their actions were valued fairly: although poor families might make smaller dollar donations, the point structure rewarded them equally—affirming that their advocacy contribution was in securing participation, not in having rich friends. Like all meaningful choices, the options were greatly reduced—participants could not change which actions received more points, nor could they introduce new actions. Yet all participants could see the total money the group had collectively raised. The combination of collective feedback about their impact along with individual points for participation was powerful, according to exit interviews we conducted with a handful of the participants. One 12-year-old described her parallel motivations: "every day … I went to check my points and the total money for poverty."

Points provide a powerful demonstration of how game design structures choice. First, points declare a limited zone of action (since only recognized actions can receive points), and in so doing they limit the scope of civic engagement. This is both frustrating and what makes their orienting mechanism so powerful. With *Peter Packet*, the point system prioritized engagement over the amount of funds raised, and thus enacted a functional definition of civic engagement. Second, point systems are subjective—there is no "right" way to determine the point values. Of course, prioritization is at the heart of all value systems, but points are insistently quantitative.

Quantifying civic values is a radical shift for most non-profits, which tend to traffic in rhetorical definitions of civic engagement. In my time co-directing a national industry group for civic games called Games for Change,[6] I repeatedly witnessed how the process of game design was transformative for non-profit staff. In particular, ranking different civic actions quantitatively was painfully difficult. Why? I assert that the valuation process of assigning points directly parallels the transformative process of strategic planning, with all the associated politics and judgment calls. For traditional civic strategists, assigning points remains highly unusual.

The lens of game design can also help online civics to become more conversational. By this, I mean to support the kind of conversations that take place so naturally offline at events like repainting a local school, or during walk-a-thon fundraisers. Such conversations are invaluable. Through conversation, we develop the social ties to sustain participation. Through conversation, we reflect and build the skills and identities to become more effective in civic life. What does this look like?

In the *Peter Packet Challenge*, we turned the methods of game design toward the goal of increasing conversation. Our breakthrough came in realizing that "functional" messages could also embed conversation catalysts. Here is how it worked: youth used the system to recruit participation from both other youth and adults by email (see Figure 15.2). These recruiting emails are co-authored by the *Peter Packet* system, which embeds some additional text for recipients. When contacting adults—perhaps a relative or teacher—the system not only gives donation details, but also prompts the adult to start a reflective conversation offline with the sender (e.g. asking why they want to fight poverty, and why they are competing for points). The challenge thereby invites an offline conversation in the participant's existing social network, providing a prompt for civic deliberation in everyday life.

Currently, many social networking web sites and civic systems send notification emails, e.g. "Your friend has accepted your request." Yet designers often fail to recognize the potential for turning these small moments of interaction into a conversation. Game design thinking pushes us to move beyond "notifying" our participants, which is typically an endpoint, and instead

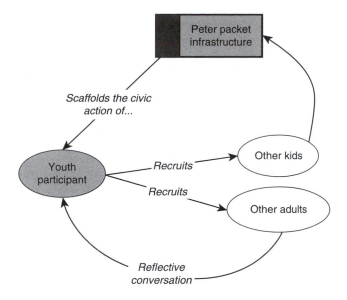

FIGURE 15.2 Actions available in the *Peter Packet* Challenge

to demand that we give feedback to drive further participation. "Friend" notifications are particularly powerful design spaces because we can embed reflection and spark conversation inside existing social relationships—which is where more substantial behavior change often occurs.

Contrasting Case: Online Volunteering

Since my claim is not about games *per se*, but meaningful choice and game design thinking, it is vital to consider a case without a hint of games. So as counterpoint, consider the United Nations' "Online Volunteering" service in its formative years *circa* 2003. Volunteering is a powerful example because it grounds digital uncertainties in a cornerstone of civic contribution, i.e. giving labor and time. Volunteering is also noteworthy as one of the few areas of civic growth that almost everyone agrees on (Levine, 2007), and today more than 25 percent of Americans volunteer with organizations annually (Bureau of Labor Statistics, 2010). In this example of migration into online spaces, we will see the emerging parallels with game design thinking.

The Online Volunteering service first appeared in 1999, as a joint project of the United Nations Volunteers (UNV) and technology giant Cisco Systems. It was the first global effort to match the skills of people who could work from home to international organizations in poor countries. For example, a bilingual volunteer in Alaska might translate a South African organization's brochure into a funding proposal, to help raise money to fight HIV/AIDS. By 2003, more than 10 thousand hopeful volunteers had registered, and requests for their time had come in from nearly 300 non-profits in sixty countries (Dhebar and Stokes, 2008). At face value, this was a civic marketplace to coordinate the exchange of volunteer time.

The service worked very well for some online volunteers. In 2003, I interviewed dozens of both volunteers and host organizations from around the world, randomly chosen based on their levels of participation with the service (ibid.). Volunteers reported great satisfaction when they felt their contributions were valued. In fact, we were surprised to discover that many volunteers were willing to significantly delay volunteering in order to appropriately determine the value of their work.

They actually requested that more organizations refuse to place volunteers until they had completed "trial work," such as re-translating an old document before being invited to translate the new brochure.

Although our analysis did not approach the Online Volunteering service from the perspective of participatory culture—the framing of Jenkins *et al.* only emerged years later—the parallel of "appropriately valuing contributions" maps neatly onto Jenkins's definitions of participatory culture. In fact, there are broad similarities between Jenkins's criteria for participatory culture and online volunteering: strong support for sharing, low barriers to engagement, and some form of social connection. The primary divergence in volunteer communities is the greater role for institutional management (like non-profits and schools), whereas participatory cultures are more autonomous with less formal mentorship between newcomers and experts.

Curiously, as volunteering moves online, the parallel to participatory culture may be increasingly necessary. Our research found that only a small percentage of online volunteers went on to complete a second assignment. In fact, retention was probably the greatest shortcoming of the service. The cause? Interviews indicated frequent shortcomings among host organizations in volunteer management.

We found that preexisting managerial deficiencies seemed aggravated online, especially around basic communication and feedback. Volunteers reported being upset with a troublingly common occurrence: organizations appeared to forget about them, as if they were simply a project buried on a busy desk—treatment that would be culturally unacceptable when volunteering face to face. Yet we can also sympathize with host organizations, as they simultaneously struggle to manage staff in the physical world and provide services on shoestring non-profit budgets.

For game design, some amount of uncertain tension between the needs of volunteers and hosts is actually a good thing. Games take as a prerequisite some unpredictability; solved problems do not invite play. By contrast, hard problems can be incredibly compelling—but only if our effort feels productive. We need the feedback loops that give us clues to improve performance, and to remind us of our goals. Thus the tensions in volunteering described above can be healthy; they only become problematic if there is insufficient opportunity to improve.

Game design thinking is an unusual methodology for analyzing volunteer management. More traditional best practices would simply critique the performance of the manager. Now, with digital services, we need methods to also critique the volunteering service—not as a "tool," but as a structure of participation. In this case, we have been applying a touch of game design thinking to re-articulate the management problem in terms of the feedback loops given to staff and volunteers.

Managers can only make meaningful choices if they know when volunteers are feeling neglected, and whether volunteers are clueless about details like the size of the organization.[7] (Surprisingly, volunteers we interviewed often had no idea whether the organization had a staff of ten, or closer to 1000.) Game designers call these important cues "state information," and believe that omitting them is not only unfair, but also a failure of the design process. Good management training is difficult, and for too many volunteers in our interviews it was hit or miss. One solution is to demand more of our civic services online, to approach them as structures of participation rather than simply tools, and to optimize them with the analytics of game design.

Lessons from Game Design

Again, I am not talking about building actual games—which are an ancient form, with a long history offline in education, military strategy, business planning, economics, etc. Rather, my focus is on applying the thinking of game design to civic engagement. This is increasingly possible as game design itself becomes better theorized, but also as the professional practices of game design become more coherent.

Game design is taught increasingly in professional programs at universities that draw from departments as diverse as computer science and film studies, engineering, and social psychology. All of us use design thinking to some extent,[8] but the practice of game design in particular is increasingly recognized as a specialized one, with the potential for increasingly refined methods and expert skills.

Here are the three components of game design thinking, borrowed from curricula taught increasingly in game design schools, which I think have the greatest value for civic engagement:

1. Meaningful Choice

As a method of engagement, meaningful choice is focused on presenting carefully optimized problems for participants to problem-solve. In the civic domain, people themselves are part of the fabric (Light and Miskelly, 2009), and so the most meaningful choices and feedback loops are often social. Curiously, the choice to be part of something bigger than ourselves is both an attribute of civic life, and a reason people play games (McGonigal, 2011).

2. Play

Play is how humans develop mental models, test hypotheses, and even build social ties.[9] Here it is important to shift from a narrow focus on play as "fun," and instead to consider "engagement," because play for serious players is constantly testing their limits—whether in chess or athletics—which is not light fun, but rather an engagement that is constant and compelling. Designing to encourage productive failure is counter-intuitive, but central to the craft of master game designers like Will Wright (e.g. see interview in Crecente, 2009).

3. Iteration to Build Coherence

Probably the most overlooked component of games, iteration is the secret *how* for designing interactivity; this is how games achieve their profoundly challenging integration of storytelling, experience, engineering, and visual aesthetics. There are no formulas for problems at this level of complexity. While iteration is also mirrored in the obsessive editing of film and poetry, for game design, the iteration is about shaping *choice* by optimizing the delicate feedback loops that guide participants—ensuring that just the right kind of information arrives at the right time. These cycles of performance help players develop new identities and even new worldviews (Squire, 2006).

The resulting discipline—game design thinking—is a particular cognitive approach for problem-solving. It has distinctive perspectives, interpretations, heuristics, and predictive models. For hard problems, it is unlikely that any one cognitive approach alone can provide solutions, but a diversity of cognitive frameworks might (Page, 2008). Game designers are not replacements for non-profit management—they are members of the team, and desperately need other perspectives too (in particular, I have met very few game designers with anything beyond a very rudimentary understanding of social change strategy).

As a society, we need the right kind of cognitive diversity to design the next generation of online civic experiences—largely because the underlying societal problems are profoundly difficult—from urban redevelopment policy, to climate change and public education priorities. Design failure can come from both ends: experts on a social issue far too often override good design with literal solutions; conversely, designers often fail to select game mechanics that fully embody deep models of social change. Teams can better navigate such conflict by more formally recognizing game design as a disciplinary orientation, not just a technical skill set. Yet we also need to develop more deliberate design processes that rotate attention not just between power stakeholders, but between cognitive perspectives that include game design thinking.

Strangely Akin to Strategic Planning

Beyond the outcomes, the process of game design can itself be transformative. I saw this repeatedly in my years organizing the field of civic games—whether the result was a finished game or not. In particular, non-profits described the process as surprising. Game design seemed to force an unusually systemic reflection on an organization's goals. Unlike the work with games in Entertainment Education (e.g. see Wang and Singhal, 2009), which tends to focus on raising awareness or motivating beliefs, games can also be about offering your audience a useful problem—not for solving, but for the experience of tackling that problem. Initially, many organizations fall victim to the temptation of offering their values as the "right solution"—but such games are rarely playful or able to retain participation.

Facing this dilemma, organizations must reflect on how to recombine their content, reward structures, and choices with a new goal: to make their values emerge as natural consequences of problem-solving. Of course, traditional community organizing also revolves around problem-solving, by listening to communities and empowering them to act. For the first time, civic media can begin to communicate this experientially: training communities to spread feedback loops to experience their perspective, not just their voices. Such efforts are inherently imperfect, but over time may become preferred strategies for communicating worldviews through interactivity.

Opening Designs across Civic Platforms

Funders play a critical role in encouraging platforms to open for cross-campaign engagement, and more creative structures of participation. As the *Peter Packet Challenge* demonstrated, it is increasingly possible to remix the experience of basic civic acts like fundraising. Yet this is only possible when visual interfaces can be created with some autonomy from the underlying databases that track donations and petition signatures. Few non-profits open their databases to third parties, effectively excluding remix over the civic experience. This barrier is significant, and deserves attention at the level of sectoral strategy. In particular, funders can encourage broader thinking in their grantees. Allowing for modifications to the experience ("modding" in the language of games) can allow various participatory cultures to each make the experience more meaningful, according to their distinct values. For some civic actions online, there may even be an ethical imperative to leave open some of the content framing and experience for remix.

All Together Now

Incorporating game design thinking demands an unusually systemic approach to civic engagement. It begins by appropriately valuing participants' contributions. As seen with online volunteering, the formal contribution might quietly rely on an obscured civic mode: what seems like the giving of time (volunteering) can depend on sharing organizational knowledge (teaching). In the case of the *Peter Packet Challenge*, contributing funds (donating) can demand that participants use their voices to recruit others' participation (advocacy). If Jenkins is right that participatory cultures thrive on valuing members' contributions, then designers must also seek to maximize meaningful choice for the civic modes that matter most to participants.

In this article, I have particularly discussed two kinds of iteration on meaningful choice. The first is about process: how designers integrate the multiple dimensions of civic engagement (from aesthetic, to technical, to ensuring political impact). Second, iteration is also a goal for the product: to keep participants returning for meaningful choices and problem-solving. Compared with traditional civic strategies for online "retention," iteration shifts our attention to the feedback loops we provide participants. Such loops are how participants learn to improve their strategies, and optimize their civic skills—and this learning process is itself engaging.

Game design thinking can be helpful if it injects more strategic and system-based planning into the development of civic media platforms. Especially if this design process is participatory, odds increase for more equitable design goals and outcomes. The inherent focus on meaningful choice will also be helpful, pushing designers to go beyond what is "good for" disadvantaged populations, and toward designing experiences that are meaningful in the terms expressed by communities themselves. Funders and policy makers can multiply these opportunities by pushing civic services to open their tools, and allow others to remix the feedback loops for everyday civic life.

The quality of a democracy can be proxied to the meaningful choices it offers participants. For an increasingly digital world, we may need the practice and cognitive perspective of game design to redesign civic engagement.

Notes

1   The author expresses his gratitude to Henry Jenkins' Civic Paths research group and to Tracy Fullerton, both at the University of Southern California, for their formative discussions and feedback on drafts of this paper. Similar thanks are due to Katharine Foo.
2   As a bellwether of this trend, the Serious Games summit at the largest annual gathering of game developers dedicated one of its two days to investigating the rising trend of "gamification"—or the "sometimes questionable process of building game-like incentives into non-game applications, to address issues like productivity, health, marketing, and so forth" (Serious Games Summit at GDC, 2011).
3   Peter Levine insightfully observes that the term "civic engagement" thus becomes a Rorschach blot of "benign connotations" (2007, p. 1).
4   In fact, the only nationally representative survey to investigate correlations between game play and civic behavior found no broad connections (Kahne et al., 2008). Furthermore, they found that more social games were connected to more civic behavior than single-player games; i.e. what matters is the type of game played, not the fact that the media is in game form.
5   Note that this goes beyond treating games as "third spaces" (Steinkuehler and Williams, 2006) – an approach that does advance social science research by legitimizing and reframing the study of digital worlds, but is perhaps less useful for rethinking current civic activities.
6   More information on Games for Change's history in the emerging practice of making civic videogames is available in the "Games for Change" entry on Wikipedia.
7   Besides being demoralizing, such weak organizational culture is known to decrease employee coordination, social glue, and sense-making (Ojo, 2009).
8   In an everyday sense, design thinking is the "liberal art of technological culture" (Buchanan, 1992, p. 5). Our modern lives give us many choices, and we design how they fit together—we each can design how we will communicate with our friends online, where we will post our digital pictures, how we construct our digital identities. The proliferation of choice in modern life increases the importance of design as both a literacy and a practice for all citizens.
9   It is no coincidence that Putnam's influential book Bowling Alone addressed civic engagement around a sport league (2001).

References

Buchanan, R. 1992. "Wicked problems in design thinking," *Design Issues*, 8(2): 5–21.
Bureau of Labor Statistics. 2010. *Volunteering in the United States—2009*. US Department of Labor. www.bls.gov/news.release/pdf/volun.pdf.
Crecente, B. 2009. "Maria Montessori: The 138-year-old inspiration behind *Spore*." *Kotaku*, 29 April. kotaku.com/#!5164248/maria-montessori-the-138+year+old-inspiration-behind-spore.

Dhebar, B. B. and Stokes, B. 2008. "A nonprofit manager's guide to online volunteering," *Nonprofit Management and Leadership*, 18(4): 497–506.

Erlhoff, M. and Marshall, T. 2008. *Design dictionary: Perspectives on design terminology*. Basel, Switzerland: Birkhauser Basel.

Haste, H. and Hogan, A. 2006. "Beyond conventional civic participation, beyond the moral-political divide: young people and contemporary debates about citizenship," *Journal of Moral Education*, 35(4): 473–493.

Jenkins, H., Clinton, K., Purushotma, R., Robison, A. J., and Weigel, M. 2009. *Confronting the challenges of participatory culture: Media education for the 21st century*. Chicago, IL: John D. and Catherine T. MacArthur Foundation.

Kahne, J., Middaugh, E., and Evans, C. 2008. *The civic potential of video games*. Chicago, IL: The John D. and Catherine T. MacArthur Foundation. www.civicsurvey.org/White_paper_link_text.pdf.

Levine, P. 2007. *The future of democracy: Developing the next generation of American citizens*. Lebanon, NH: Tufts University Press.

Light, A. and Miskelly, C. 2009. "Brokering between heads and hearts: An analysis of designing for social change." Presented at the Undisciplined! Design Research Society Conference of 2008, Sheffield, UK.

McGonigal, J. 2011. *Reality is broken: Why games make us better and how they can change the world*. New York: Penguin.

Ojo, O., 2009. "Impact assessment of corporate culture on employee job performance," *Business Intelligence Journal*, 2(2): 388–397.

Page, S. E. 2008. *The difference: How the power of diversity creates better groups, firms, schools, and societies*. Princeton, NJ: Princeton University Press.

Putnam, R. D. 2001. *Bowling alone: The collapse and revival of American community*. New York: Simon & Schuster.

Raphael, C., Bachen, C., Lynn, K., Baldwin-Philippi, J., and McKee, K. A. 2009. "Games for civic learning: A conceptual framework and agenda for research and design," *Games and Culture*, 5(2): 199–235. doi:10.1177/1555412009354728.

Schwartz, B., Ward, A., Monterosso, J., Lyubomirsky, S., White, K., and Lehman, D. R. 2002. "Maximizing versus satisficing: Happiness is a matter of choice," *Journal of Personality and Social Psychology*, 83(5): 1178–1197.

Serious Game Summit at GDC, 2011, March 14. from www.gdconf.com/conference/sgs.htm006C, retrieved 15 March 2011.

Squire, K. 2006. "From content to context: Videogames as designed experience," *Educational Researcher*, 35(8): 19–29. doi:10.3102/0013189X035008019.

Steinkuehler, C. A. and Williams, D. 2006. "Where everybody knows your (screen) name: Online games as 'third places,'" *Journal of Computer-Mediated Communication*, 11(4): 885–909.

Stokes, B., 2010. "*Peter Packet* challenge: Featuring a videogame, corporate partnership trade-offs, and pre-teen activists." In *From participatory culture to public participation* (1st edn). USC Annenberg, Los Angeles, CA: Civic Engagement Research Group. sites.google.com/site/participatorydemocracyproject/case-studies/peter-packet.

Stolle, D., Hooghe, M., and Micheletti, M. 2005. "Politics in the supermarket: Political consumerism as a form of political participation," *International Political Science Review/Revue internationale de science politique*, 26(3): 245.

Wang, H. and Singhal, A. 2009. "Entertainment-education through digital games." In *Serious games: Mechanisms and effects*. New York: Routledge, pp. 260–90.

16

THE FUTURE OF PARTICIPATORY BUDGETING

Political Participation and Practicable Policy

Rolf Luehrs and John Heaven

1. Introduction

The British public was disgusted by the MPs' expenses affair in 2009 when Members of Parliament (MPs) were found to have used their parliamentary expenses to pay for items trivial (such as bath plugs), more significant (second homes) and obscure (duck houses). An unwritten rule appeared to have established itself amongst MPs whereby they were able to make up for, in their opinion, relatively low salaries by making spurious expenses claims.

Why did MPs feel the need to keep the true level of their remuneration from the prying gaze of the public? One possible answer is that expectations of what MPs should get in return for their work were unrealistic, and that it would have been politically unfeasible to increase MPs' salaries to fairly reflect their actual work. Keeping this information secret reinforced expectations that MPs were prepared to work for a salary much lower than what they might expect in an equivalent job with similar hours, and the public was happy to go on making demands of MPs without discussing what they ought to be paid.

When a national newspaper, the *Daily Telegraph*, uncovered the extent of expenses claims the red mist of public disgust took weeks to clear. Having thought they knew what their representatives were getting paid, the public was shocked to find that they had been misled. Any MP who tried to explain that second homes were necessary for MPs who travelled to Westminster from constituencies far afield had little prospect of winning public sympathy.

We argue that in an age of increasing transparency, as the public is let ever further into the workings of government, they may be disappointed to find that their demands and expectations are not met. But in order to make positive change, citizens will need to understand the reality of how policy is made, including an appreciation of what can be achieved with limited resources. This will not only lead to policy-makers changing their ways, but also to citizens who will learn not just to make demands but to prioritise and justify them in financial terms.

This conversation between public servants and the public about what should, and can, be achieved with limited resources must eventually be part of every participatory process if citizens are to have a serious impact on politics. In short, citizens will learn to "get real," and participatory budgeting will change from a standalone consultation exercise to a built-in "reality check" in every participation exercise. We look forward to a future where public servants do not automatically defend their decisions at all costs, but feel a duty to explain to citizens why they make the decisions they do.

We will set the scene by describing how more transparency (2.1), greater expectations on the part of citizens (2.2), and cuts due to the financial crisis (2.3), will make a change in the terms on which citizens and public officials interact essential. We will then discuss participatory budgeting and electronic participatory budgeting (ePB), including some case studies from Germany that show the flexibility of the participatory budgeting concept. Finally, we will set out a vision for the future of participatory budgeting that will address the three issues we identify at the outset.

2 The Current Situation

2.1 A New Age of Transparency

According to a saying often attributed to Germany's first Chancellor, Otto von Bismarck, "Laws are like sausages—it is best not to see them being made."

These days, we are seeing increasing levels of government transparency, partly thanks to the Internet's ability to proliferate huge amounts of information with equipment that is available to almost everyone. In some cases, this is initiated by governments themselves: the US website data.gov, where government datasets are released for all to see, was followed by the UK version, data.gov.uk. A whole host of other government organisations are opening their data, which is undoubtedly a victory for movements like the Sunlight Foundation, which argue "sunlight is the best disinfectant" (Sunlight Foundation, 2007).

But whether they like it or not, governments are being forced to become more transparent by outside forces: WikiLeaks' release of hundreds of thousands of documents about the wars in Afghanistan and Iraq shone a light on areas of the conflicts that the government would prefer to keep secret; the German project "Offener Haushalt" took government budget data by scraping it from government websites and made it accessible to the public at large. TheyWorkForYou.com, a project by the UK organisation MySociety that publishes information about MPs' attendance of parliamentary debates and voting records, has been followed by similar websites in Germany and Italy.

It is not hard to see the appeal of transparency: just as these days consumers want to know how their sausages are made—from the welfare of the pigs to the number of additives that are used in the recipe—they want to know how their laws are made. It would have come as no surprise to Bismarck that they are, in both cases, often disgusted with what they find.

Alluring as transparency is, it does have its problems. It has quickly become apparent that open data do not enable each and every citizen to shine a light inside government and see what is happening. Rather, most people rely on others to help them interpret data, for example through online visualisation tools. This means that the creators of these tools can put a particular slant on the results that they yield. In fact, you might argue that it is impossible not to put a slant on these results. Online data visualisation applications help non-experts make sense of large sets of data; but it is clear that without a basic understanding of statistics and a healthy scepticism of an intermediary's agenda, citizens are liable to manipulation or can simply make false assumptions about the meaning of data.

In an interview with Paul Miller (Miller, 2010), Richard Stirling of the UK Cabinet Office, responsible for data.gov.uk, addressed this issue by describing efforts to contextualise datasets by adding accompanying information. This is an example of how increasing transparency puts the onus on government officials to provide contextual information that increases citizens' understanding of the background to their decisions. In the case of open data, it will be necessary to develop programmes to increase data literacy amongst the public.

Transparency can have unintended societal consequences: Michael Grimes cites the planned Mapumental website (which is still in private Beta), which will allow people to find areas to buy houses that fit their budget, amongst other things. Grimes noted that this may be societally detrimental if it leads to residents grouping according to salaries, but does not criticise Mapumental. Instead, it is everybody's duty to consider how technology can have unintended societal effects:

> [W]hose job is it to encourage users of [tools like Mapumental] to engage critically, rather than just use them to assert their rights, hold people to account, or provide excuses for not addressing an issue? Unfortunately it's not as easy as allocating "the job" to someone or to a group of people. It's rather down to all of us using those tools—members of the public and decision-makers alike—to do so with a keenness for rigorous, informed and effective debate.
>
> *(Grimes, 2010)*

In his provocatively-titled paper "Against Transparency," Lawrence Lessig (2009) argues that transparency can have negative consequences if citizens make judgements without being in possession of comprehensive information, or taking the time to find out. He ultimately concludes that the trend towards transparency will continue regardless, but that the negative effects should not be forgotten.

We have seen that transparency can result in disgust when expectations are not met, frustration if citizens make unsound judgements because they are unable to view the information they have access to in the right context, and can even have detrimental societal impacts if citizens are unable to think for themselves about the consequences of transparency.

In the following section, we will present a similar argument that stems from another recent development in the relationship between citizen and state: namely, the expectations that citizens now have as customers. We will argue that citizens increasingly expect to be treated as customers, and are acquiring the tools to make demands of government more effectively; as they do so, they need to be aware that there are limitations to what can be delivered.

2.2 Demanding "Customers"

Government bodies increasingly view citizens as customers and new channels empower these customers to make demands of government agencies. Sites like FixMyStreet.com make it easy to report issues such as potholes and broken street lights. Technically advanced customer relations management systems, online customer portals and hotlines allow citizens to report issues and find information in a similar way to a customer. Even the name of the website TheyWorkForYou.com suggests that politicians provide services in return for payment. Patient Opinion (patientopinion.org.uk) allows patients to say what they think about the services they receive from doctors, choosing a doctor or hospital according to the reviews that others have given them. Online petitioning systems allow citizens to mobilise behind one demand.

These developments are rightly hailed as an improvement of opportunities for citizens to engage with public representatives and a breakthrough in so-called "citizen-led service design." But if the future of political participation is simply about making it easier for citizens to demand their issues be addressed with little regard for necessary resources or possible consequences, then it will ultimately lead to frustration amongst citizens. For their part, public officials will face unmanageable mountains of complaints and requests, and will revert to a decide–announce–defend mode of operation instead of collaboration.

To ensure that their interaction with government is productive and fruitful, citizens need to prioritise their concerns. To do so, they require access to the information that officials possess and an understanding of the context in which they operate. As argued in the previous section, the onus is on officials to aid this understanding by providing contextual information.

As we have shown, public understanding of the conditions in which policy-makers operate is not only crucial to avoid disappointment when the public is allowed to see what happens inside government, but it is also crucial if a new culture of citizen involvement is to bring about truly inclusive governance that produces feasible policy with foreseeable outcomes.

2.3 Financial Crisis: Public Budgets Cut

Across Europe, public budgets have been cut in response to the financial crisis. In October 2010, the UK Chancellor announced widespread cuts in his Comprehensive Spending Review. Although in real terms public spending will be cut by 3 percent over the next four years, the impact on particular departments will be felt much more heavily due to others (such as the health service) being protected. Central government payments to local government, for example, will be cut by 27 percent; the Home Office and Ministry of Justice will each face cuts of 25 percent. A total of 500,000 public sector jobs are expected to be cut and a similar number of private sector jobs are expected to follow (*The Economist*, 2010).

Ernst & Young (Ernst & Young, 2010) surveyed 300 heads of finance in German local authorities about public finance over the coming years. The report found that many local authorities are expecting increasing costs and reduced income to result in a reduction in funding. In France, the raising of the retirement age has led to street protests and direct action including the blocking of oil refineries. Greece is facing a raft of strict austerity measures to avoid economic meltdown, and Spain implemented a programme of cuts to avoid a similar plight.

With these cuts in place, it is clear that the public sector will have to become a lot smarter in conducting its business if it is to avoid cutting services. Having said that, whereas doing more with less is often possible—especially where citizens are given the chance to express their needs and ideas—it is important for citizens to accept that sometimes you simply have to do less with less. As we show later, participatory budgeting is, and will continue to be, an important catalyst in both of these areas: it can harness the public's ingenuity and local knowledge in proposing more efficient ways of working, and it can identify areas where cuts would be less painful and thereby increase public acceptance of them.

3 Participatory Budgeting

In this section, we will give a short description of where participatory budgeting originated, and how far it has come since it was first deployed in Brazil. An important step in this development was the recent exercises in Internet-based participatory budgeting (electronic PB, or ePB). Finally, we will return to the issues we identified in section 2—transparency, budgeting literacy, and realistic expectations—to see where participatory budgeting will help to address them.

3.1 What is Participatory Budgeting?

Whether online or offline, Participatory Budgeting can take many forms. Participants can be involved in passing a budget by:

- commenting on proposals
- creating their own proposals

- setting an entire budget by making adjustments to the various budget headings
- voting for projects to be funded by a dedicated budget
- publicly deliberating on priorities for a dedicated budget
- suggesting ways that money can be saved
- suggesting reprioritisation of money to suit citizens' needs and wishes.

The origin of participatory budgeting can be traced back to Porto Alegre in Brazil. In the 1980s, the newly elected mayor wanted to give added legitimacy to the budget-making process against a backdrop of widespread corruption and clientelism. Strikingly, the project managed to reverse the trend of declining political participation, and included a high proportion of people on lower incomes in the budgeting process. In addition, the average income of the participants was lower than that of the population as a whole. By the end of the nineties, 8.4 percent of residents in Porto Alegre claimed to have taken part in participatory budgeting. Participatory budgeting has since spread across Brazil and beyond.

Participatory budgeting is a flexible concept: when Ruth Jackson, from the UK's Participatory Budgeting Unit, reflected on her experience at a conference in Germany she concluded that the meaning of participatory budgeting there and in other countries is different from in the UK (Jackson, 2010). Indeed, whereas the continuing participatory budgeting programme in Porto Alegre has successfully shifted priorities towards poorer neighbourhoods and is a complex process of deliberation, electing delegates and prioritising demands, participatory budgeting in Europe is increasingly conducted in the context of saving money in order to cut state deficits. For example, the German city of Solingen invited citizens to give their views on measures for cutting their deficit and avoiding having to pass an emergency budget under supervision of the federal government. The London Borough of Redbridge is conducting an online participatory budgeting exercise in which participants are asked to make GBP 25m in savings, must balance the budget, and are limited to a maximum Council Tax increase of 5 percent. The ePB tool they developed has since been adopted nationwide, made available to all English and Welsh local authorities for free by the Improvement and Development Agency (IDeA, 2010).

There is evidence that participatory budgeting can help to increase public acceptance of reductions in services where cuts need to be made, and also make the public more willing to accept tax rises. Further, more effective targeting of services to meet citizens' needs (and withdrawing services that are not so popular) can ensure that money is spent more efficiently and in a way that optimises citizen satisfaction. Finally, harnessing the creativity and local knowledge of citizens (many of whom are also public servants) can only increase the quality of service provision. In a recent paper making the case for more democratic participation, the Democratic Society cited a participatory budgeting exercise conducted in Leicestershire where the ultimate result was a willingness to make cuts in areas with far larger budget cuts than before the exercise; the results were summed up as follows:

> [W]ith the right tools, intensive information-based democratic engagement could allow councils to, in Richelieu's metaphor, pluck more feathers with less squawking.
>
> *(Zacharzewski, 2010)*

This has certainly been borne out in the German experience: Paul Witt, Professor at the Kehl University of Public Administration, said: "You can achieve a lot by inviting citizens to engage. You can ask them for saving suggestions, as Freiburg and Bonn did. You can teach them to argue from a finance point of view" (Hannemann, 2009).

Participatory budgeting exercises like Hamburg's (see 3.3 below), where citizens could propose changes to the budget but had to compensate increases in one budget heading with cuts in another, or Redbridge's limitation of Council Tax rises to 5 percent, illustrate Witt's point.

We have already seen that participatory budgeting is a concept that has been adapted to suit the conditions where it is being carried out and the purpose to which it is being put. It is also flexible enough to be implemented entirely or partly online. As we will demonstrate in the following section, online tools can make the process more accessible and interactive, as well as communicating the parameters within which citizens' suggestions can have real influence.

3.2 Doing Participatory Budgeting Online

It would be a mistake to see ePB as a tool in itself. In fact, many of the tools that are commonplace in Internet-based citizen engagement projects are apt to be applied to participatory budgeting: looking at the list of ways that citizens can engage in participatory budgeting in the previous subsection (3.1), it is easy to see where online voting, discussion forums, commenting, and interactive budget sliders can be used alongside one another.

Combinations of tools are limited only by the imagination, and it is commonplace to combine online and offline elements. The most important offline part of a participatory budgeting exercise is publicity: without drawing people's attention to the participatory budgeting process, it will not be possible to attract a satisfactory level of participation. The German city of Freiburg (see 3.3.2) provides an example of ePB that is strongly integrated with an offline approach, where a large publicity campaign encouraged citizens to have their say in a participatory budgeting exercise that combined online interaction with physical events.

The advantages of using online tools for participatory budgeting are:

- *Cost-effectiveness*. Where the primary aim of a participatory budgeting exercise is to make cuts in public spending, it makes sense to deliver the participatory budget itself as cost-effectively as possible, as it may be difficult to justify spending money on what some may criticise as a "nice to have" rather than an essential.
- *Convenience*. Citizens can take part at the time and place of their choice (providing they have access to an Internet-enabled device). In a direct comparison between two participatory budgeting exercises conducted in Belo Horizonte, Brazil, Tiago Peixoto noted that the participation in the online exercise was higher than the offline one. An important caveat is that the two exercises were running in parallel and Peixoto stated that there were important differences between the two. Nevertheless, the existence of the online element appears to have led to "unprecedented levels of participation" (Peixato, 2010).
- *Aggregated results*. Where interactive sliders allow participants to adjust budget headings according to their preferences, you can easily find out what citizens think by glancing at figures representing the average increases or cuts that people suggested. Paul Johnston argues that aggregation is a way of ensuring results that are of use to policy-makers, and hence have more influence (Johnston, 2010).
- *Clearly presented, interactive information*. This was demonstrated by the German project "Offener Haushalt" (http://bund.offenerhaushalt.de), which collated data on the federal budget and visualised it in a simple form. Anyone could then view the budget, consisting of a rectangle divided into smaller rectangles whose area was proportional to the size of the budget heading. Clicking on one of these blocks broke that individual budget heading down into its sub-headings, and so on.
- *A central point of information*. Catering to Internet users is growing in importance: in Germany, a study found that over 68 percent of the population had used the Internet within the past

four weeks (ARD & ZDF, 2010), and in the UK the number of adults with access to broadband Internet was 71 percent in the first quarter of 2010 (Ofcom, 2010). In the whole EU, 60 percent of people use the Internet at least once per week (Eurostat, 2010).

3.3 Examples from Germany

Here we present three participatory budgeting exercises from Germany, two of which were based on the DEMOS methodology. For more examples of German ePB exercises, see our article on the Pan-European eParticipation Network (PEP-NET) blog (Luehrs, 2009) or the online case study map created by Tiago Peixoto, an excellent resource for information on international participatory budgeting case studies. The link to this map is in the references.

The DEMOS methodology comprises three phases: The first phase is a moderated discussion. The issues that are raised here are identified and discussed in greater detail in the second phase. Finally, in the third phase the discussion is summarised and participants are invited to edit the summaries using a wiki (an online document that any participant is able to amend). Across all phases, there are live chats with important figures such as politicians and participants can add ideas to a list and rate those that others have submitted.

Where interactive "budget sliders"—which allow participants to increase or reduce individual budget headings—are used in DEMOS participatory budgeting exercises, participants are prompted to give justifications for their decisions. These decisions and justifications then feed into the discussion.

3.3.1 Hamburg ePB exercises, 2006 and 2009: Mid-term Budget Planning with Real-Life Budget Information

In 2006, the Hamburg State Parliament called upon all citizens of Hamburg to discuss the budget and submit suggestions online. Due to their satisfaction with levels and quality of participation in the first exercise, it was repeated in 2009. A unique aspect of this ePB was that the budget in question was for the years 2016 to 2020. This allowed participants to have more influence because budgets are set far in advance.

Another unique aspect was the use of a budget calculator, which allowed participants to make changes to individual budget headings by moving interactive sliders. With discussions, interviews with experts, live discussions with members of the Hamburg State Parliament and idea lists that allowed participants to rate others' ideas and submit their own, the project used a blend of social media tools to create a lively and varied discussion.

The marketing campaign was an important part of the project and was based on three pillars: press relations, online marketing and social media marketing through channels such as Facebook, Twitter and StudiVZ, a German social network. In the second exercise, hard-to-reach groups were encouraged to take part by providing an offline questionnaire that was integrated into the process.

In the Hamburg example, 50,000 citizens visited the website during the consultation and 3500 of them registered to use it, 2138 people submitted their own budgets, and 38 wiki documents with budget concepts were created collaboratively.

3.3.2 Freiburg: ePB with Gender Impact Assessment

The Freiburg ePB exercise also allowed participants to suggest adjustments to the existing budget using interactive sliders. Unlike the Hamburg exercise, this ePB emphasized the consequences of budget decisions from women's point of view, summed up by the slogan "Chances = Equality." This project was part of a larger campaign, also comprising offline elements such as representative surveys and physical events.

The level of participation amongst women was especially pleasing, with almost 39 percent of participants being female. This compares with 15 percent for the Hamburg ePB exercise. In Freiburg, 1863 people registered to use the website and 914 people used the interactive sliders to create budgets of their own, 757 people provided written justifications for their spending decisions and 22 wiki documents with budget concepts were collaboratively written.

3.3.3 Cologne: Your City, Your Money

In 2008, Cologne invited its citizens to take part in planning the budget. In a measure of the first exercise's success, it was repeated in 2009.

Cologne concentrated on a few selected budget headings: in 2008, streets, pathways, squares, green spaces and sport; in 2009, schools and education, and environmental protection. Before the first exercise, the city committed itself to considering the top 100 proposals selected by participants. Uniquely, the process was closely integrated into the local authority's organisational structure by mapping the consultation procedure to form a workflow. Conducting the preparation, execution and analysis of the consultation in as systematic and regimented a manner as possible enabled some types of suggestions to be routed to the appropriate officials automatically and their responses to be published on the website through the same channel.

A comprehensive publicity campaign, for example sending invitations to a large number of households, led to an impressive level of participation. In 2009, around 10,000 Cologne citizens actively participated in the ePB exercise, submitting 1254 ideas.

3.4 Where Will Participatory Budgeting Go from Here?

Thus far, we have presented a policy context of increased transparency in the public sector, high citizen expectations, and tightening of resources due to public spending cuts. As citizens are increasingly able to look at the inner workings of government, they are likely to be disappointed when their high expectations are not met. New forms of participation, especially conducted using the Internet, allow citizens to change what they find for the better; but for this to happen it is important that they make suggestions that are based on sound judgement and can be put into practice. Perhaps the most important consideration that citizens should take into account is available resources, requiring them to develop what we will term "budgetary literacy."

Evidence from the Democratic Society's white paper (Zacharzewski, 2010) and from Paul Witt (above, Hannemann, 2009) suggest that participatory budgeting can help citizens develop this budgetary literacy. By interacting with the information made available to them and being subjected to some of the conditions that policy-makers make, such as having to return a balanced budget (in the Hamburg example), or only being able to raise Council Tax by a limited amount (as in Redbridge's "YouChoose" exercise), ePB becomes a learning exercise. By getting hands-on experience of what it is like to work under these restrictions, citizens can develop exactly the kind of appreciation of the policy context that we described at various points in this paper.

But is there a place for participatory budgeting in the future? We have already shown that participatory budgeting is a flexible concept, having evolved from an innovative offline process that enabled underrepresented groups to exercise much greater influence over local budgets and reduce corruption and clientelism, to one that is often conducted using a blend of online and offline elements and is aimed at addressing the impact of financial cutbacks by harnessing the creativity of citizens, educating them about budgeting, and increasing acceptance of cutbacks through involving them in the process. There is nothing to suggest that participatory budgeting cannot continue to evolve. But how might it look?

As it stands, participatory budgeting is a discrete exercise that is operated as a participatory intervention in its own right. We believe that, in the future, participatory budgeting will have to be integrated into all forms of public discourse as citizens realise that money is an important limiter on what they can realistically expect from their governments. With the help of public officials, citizens will have to "get real" about what they demand, and participatory budgeting will be the "reality check" that will ultimately force us to think carefully about what we ask for and prioritise our demands. This will require a culture change within government and society at large. Otherwise we risk an increasingly frustrated public with unprecedented levels of political disillusionment and a defensive, secretive public sector.

4 Conclusion

They say money makes the world go round, and the public sector is no exception. Whereas, in our private lives, most of us accept that our possibilities are limited by the means at our disposal, the same does not always go for our expectations of public services. We expect potholes to be fixed without delay—without understanding that it would be far more expensive to fix issues on demand rather than in regular sweeps—and complain that too much of our hard-earned money is taken away from us only to be wasted on frivolous undertakings that don't make a difference anyway.

It would be naïve to expect online tools alone to lead to a radically higher quality of public participation, or for consensus to emerge through online political engagement. But it is fair to say that modern participatory budgeting can help ensure that increasing transparency and citizens' willingness to make ever more exacting demands of public servants do not cause a divide between citizens and their representatives, but rather a mutual understanding and ethos of cooperation in addressing the issues that our societies face.

This will take place in the context of limited resources, especially over the next several years, and citizens will need to work within this and other limitations (or work to abolish them) if they want to set their public representatives achievable, affordable tasks with positive and foreseeable outcomes.

The onus is on public servants to arm citizens with the contextual information about the limits that they are subject to, but active citizens will need to develop a new set of skills. Participatory budgeting can help citizens develop possibly the most important skill in this set, budgetary literacy. Bringing money into the equation focuses the debate on prioritising tasks and making compromises. Maybe I could wait a month for that pothole to be repaired if I knew that the money saved could be spent on recycling my rubbish.

References

ARD & ZDF. 2010. "ARD & ZDF Onlinestudie." www.ard-zdf-onlinestudie.de/index.php?id=onlinenutzung, accessed 28 October 2010.

The Economist. 2010. "Day of the long knives." www.economist.com/node/17316567/, accessed 28 October 2010.

Ernst & Young. 2010. "Kommunen in der finanzkrise: Status quo und handlungsoptionen." www.ey.com/Publication/vwLUAssets/Ernst_and_Young_Kommunenstudie_2010/$FILE/EY%20Kommunenstudie%202010.pdf, accessed 28 October 2010.

Eurostat. 2010. http://appsso.eurostat.ec.europa.eu/nui/show.do?dataset=isoc_ci_ifp_fu&lang=de, accessed 28 October 2010.

FixMyStreet. 2010. www.fixmystreet.com, accessed 28 October 2010.

Grimes, M. 2010. "Using the internet for effective citizenship." http://savvycitizens.bcs.org/citizenship/using-the-internet-for-effective-citizenship, accessed 28 October 2010.

Hannemann, M. 2009. "Nicht nur grund zur Freude," *Brand Eins*. www.brandeins.de/archiv/magazin/stadt/artikel/nicht-nur-grund-zur-freude.html, accessed 28 October 2010.

IDeA. 2010. "YouChoose: participatory budgeting tool." www.idea.gov.uk/idk/core/page.do?pageId=22436695, accessed 28 October 2010.

Jackson, Ruth. 2010. "What is PB really?" www.participatorybudgeting.org.uk/blog/archive/2010/02/19/different-types-of-pb...what-is-pb-really-by-ruth-jackson, accessed 28 October 2010.

Johnston, P. 2010. "Transforming government's policy-making processes: Why encouraging more and easier citizen input into policy-making is not enough," *JeDEM*, 2(2): 162–169. www.jedem.org/article/view/43/44, accessed 28 October 2010.

Lessig, L. 2009. "Against transparency: The perils of openness in government." In: J. Gøtze & C. B. Pederson (eds). *State of the eUnion: Government 2.0 and onwards*. 21gov.net, pp. 173–193.

Luehrs, R. 2009. "Participatory budgeting in Germany." http://pep-net.eu/blog/2009/10/20/e-participatory-budgeting-in-germany/, accessed 28 October 2010.

Miller, P. 2010. "Talking with Richard Stirling about progress with data.gov.uk." http://cloudofdata.com/2010/07/talking-with-richard-stirling-about-progress-with-data-gov-uk/, accessed 28 October 2010.

Ofcom Quick Facts. http://media.ofcom.org.uk/facts/, accessed 28 October 2010.

Offener Haushalt. http://bund.offenerhaushalt.de/, accessed 28 October 2010.

Patient Opinion. 2010. www.patientopinion.org.uk, accessed 28 October 2010.

Peixato, T. 2009. "Beyond theory: e-Participatory budgeting and its promises for eParticipation," *European Journal of ePractice*, 7(March): 1–9. http://api.ning.com/files/7YjIWhOFjmQljjnvaU1DuOyB24Bq-IPpHzu8oLvR00BEB8PhGdyyMHEQ-THuxATXanbzSOgGSrR6h7WMgFrKsnHUNmJTCjtwF/epb.pdf, accessed 28 October 2010.

Peixato, T. 2010. "Participatory budgeting map." http://maps.google.de/maps/ms?ie=UTF8&hl=de&msa=0&msid=11482483520400710569.00045675b996d14eb6c3a&ll=7.013668,28.125&spn=156.732916,96.679687&z=2, accessed 28 October 2010.

Sunlight Foundation. 2007. "Sunlight is the best disinfectant." http://sunlightfoundation.com/presscenter/articles/2007/01/11/sunlight-is-the-best-disinfectant/, accessed 28 October 2010.

Zacharzewski, A. 2010. "Democracy pays: How democratic engagement can cut the cost of government," *Democratic Society*. www.demsoc.org/static/Financial-Case-white-paper.pdf, accessed 28 October 2010.

17

PARTICIPATORY DEMOCRACY

Dieter Fuchs

Introduction

The term "participatory democracy" has manifold meanings in political science. An overview of different definitions and approaches is given in several publications (cf. Held, 2006; Hilmer, 2010). This contribution doesn't intend to add another one. The aim is to develop a systematic concept of participatory democracy with a definition as narrow and precise as possible. This way, it can gain analytical usefulness and be clearly differentiated from other concepts of democracy. This is how I will proceed. Participatory democracy is conceived as a primary subtype of democracy. Therefore, the first necessary step is a definition of democracy as the basic concept. The second step is a definition of participatory democracy and a distinction of it from representative democracy. In a third step, different subtypes of participatory democracy are specified, which could be realized under conditions of modern societies. In doing so, special attention will be paid to deliberative democracy.

Strategy of the Concept Analysis

My strategy of analysis orientates itself on studies that conceptualize democracy hierarchically (Collier and Levitsky, 1997; Goertz, 2006). The highest hierarchical level is a general definition of democracy, which is referred to as a "root concept" by Collier and Levitsky (1997, p. 436) and as a "basic concept" by Goertz (2006, p. 6). Based on this "basic concept" different types of democracy can be differentiated. The two primary subtypes of democracy are participatory democracy and representative democracy.

As participatory democracy is regarded as a primary subtype of democracy, at first democracy as the basic concept has to be defined. The problem is that there is a multitude of definitions that differ from each other considerably. It is an "essentially contested concept" (Gallie, 1956) and "correspondingly one finds endless disputes over appropriate meaning and definition" (Collier and Levitsky, 1997, p. 433). From my point of view there are two strategies to get a relatively binding definition: 1) by orientating oneself on a "representative set of definitions" (Sartori, 1984, p. 41)—definitions from prominent and acknowledged authors, and 2) by considering the two basic forms of democracy that actually existed—ancient Athenian direct democracy or modern-era representative democracy. This way, a definition without any reference to reality is avoided and the probability of filling the terms with arbitrary meaning is reduced.

Conceptual Analysis of Democracy

The meaning of the concept of *democracy* can again be outlined in a hierarchical structure (Munck and Verkuilen, 2002). This structure contains three levels, which are: 1) the concept, 2) its attributes, and 3) on the lowest level, the components of attributes (cf. Figure 17.1).

Almost all definitions of democracy tie in with the etymological origin of the word *demokratía*. This approach allows not only a first grasp at the meaning but it also references the first democracy that developed in history and still influences the idea of democracy to this day—ancient Athenian democracy. Sartori explains,

> Etymological democracy is democracy conceived in the original, literal meaning of the term. Thus the etymological definition of democracy is, very simply, that democracy is the rule or power of the people. This is an appropriate start. Not only do words have a history but, invariably, a very telling history. [...] The original meaning is never a fancy or fanciful meaning.
>
> *(1987, p. 21)*

This idea of democracy, which is based on the etymology of *demokratía*, is shared by several authors. However, it is cast in various translations: government by the people (Cohen, 1971, p. 3; Pennock, 1979, p. 6), rule by the people (Dahl, 1999, p. 20), self-government (Przeworski, 2010, p. 1) and collective self-rule (Warren, 2003, p. 247). In this chapter, then, democracy will be termed *government by the people*. This definition contains two attributes, namely *government* and *people*. What is the meaning of both of these attributes?

In the two basic forms of democracy that have existed so far—Athenian direct democracy and modern-era representative democracy—*governing means the regulation of the people's common affairs through decisions that bind all the people* (see Bobbio, 1987). Or, to put it differently, the realisation of collective goals through collectively binding decisions. Therefore, the two components of the attribute government are *common affairs* and *collectively binding decisions*.

If one takes the meaning of government by the people seriously, then an idea that is frequently connected to the term democracy has to be eliminated. Several authors consider self-government to be the self-determination of the *demos* to decide upon their own life situation (amongst others Held, 1995; Scharpf, 1999). This understanding neither aligns to the literal sense nor to the reality of Athenian or modern representative democracy. By understanding self-government as

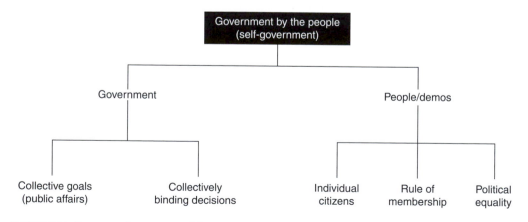

FIGURE 17.1 Conceptual structure of democracy

self-determination, democracy is reduced to a means to an end and, furthermore, it is joined to a claim that is hardly accomplishable. Already in Antiquity, affairs of the private households (*oikoi*)—and with it the individual's immediate life situation—were exempt from political decisions. Particularly in modern complex societies, the immediate life situation is shaped by several functionally differentiated subsystems of which the political system is only one part.

The attribute *people* can also be defined in such a way that it applies to both Athenian and modern democracy. Such a definition contains three components: Firstly, the people consist of *individual members* of a societal community, who possess political rights. Secondly, there is a *membership rule* that determines who is part of the group and who is not. Thirdly, all members enjoy the same political rights and their ballots are equal in all political decisions. The latter two criteria can be subsumed as *political equality*.

With these three components and on a certain level of abstraction, the people of Athens as well as of modern democracy can be defined. However, there is a major difference when it comes to the specification of the membership rule. The Athenian democracy only accepted male Athenians to be their *demos*. According to Pericles' civil liberties act (451/0 BC), another condition was that the parents also had to be Athenian. Women, foreigners (*metics*) and slaves were barred from the *demos*. A considerable change of meaning has taken place in regard to this membership rule in modern times. This can be seen, for example, in Dahl's inclusion criterion (Dahl, 1998, p. 78, 86), which defines the *demos* as *all* adults living permanently on the territory of a democracy and having equal political rights.

This shift raises additional, important questions.

> But, what could it mean that 'the people governs itself'? Note that "the people" always appears in this phrase in the singular, as *le peuple, el pueblo, das Volk, lud*, and so on. "We, the people" is a single entity. This people in the singular is the only authority that can enact laws to which it would be subject.
>
> *(Przeworski, 2010, p. 19)*

Habermas (2001) postulates the existence of a clearly defined "self" that can be assigned collectively binding decisions as a prerequisite for democracy. The question is how this single entity can arise without giving up the basic postulate that the *demos*'s constitutive element is individuals. This paradox of simultaneity of entity and individuality can only be solved—and from a historical perspective has been solved—if the individuals who formally belong to the *demos* also subjectively count themselves as part of the *demos* and identify with it. The "we" therefore is a we-feeling or a feeling of belonging together that is based on perceived common ground. Examples are a common language, shared values and common history. By adding this subjective feature, demos *can be defined as a group of individuals who consider themselves to be a collective in which every individual shares equal political rights with equal voting power.*

Conceptual Analysis of Participatory Democracy

According to Held (2006, p. 4) participatory democracy besides representative democracy is one of the "broad types" into which all models of democracy can be subdivided. The specific difference between the participatory and the representative mode is that, in the former, citizens are *directly* involved in political decisions whilst, in the latter, they are *indirectly* involved through representatives elected by the people. There is an extensive consensus within democratic theory in regard to this simple differentiation (amongst others Barber, 1984; Sartori, 1987; Dahl, 1989; Hilmer, 2010; Przeworski, 2010). The adjectives "direct" and "participatory" are used almost synonymously: "Participatory democracy [...] denotes the form [of democracy] in which the people literally rule themselves, directly and participatorily" (Barber, 1995, p. 921). In the same text but a few lines later, Barber offers an even more precise definition:

> To its advocates, however, participatory democracy involves extensive and active engagement of citizens in the self-governing process; it means government not just for but by and of the people. From this perspective, direct or participatory democracy is democracy itself, properly understood.
>
> *(1995, p. 921)*

It is still too imprecise to define participatory democracy as the citizen's direct participation in decisions over public affairs, at least if participatory democracy is understood as a subtype of democracy that differs systematically from representative democracy. In order to attain a sharper definition, two questions need to be raised: First, in how many political decisions do citizens have to participate? And, second, how many citizens need to participate so as to comply with the term of participatory democracy? For example, it is hardly plausible to designate a democracy as participatory if only few decisions—possibly just a single one—are made by the people. The problem is exacerbated if only a small minority of citizens make the single or limited decisions.

To describe the amount and kind of activity required for a participatory democracy, Barber speaks of "extensive participation" and Hilmer (2010, p. 1) uses the word "maximum," writing that "Participatory democracy theory envisions the maximum participation of citizens in their self-governance." However, what is "extensive," what is "maximum"?

In order not to give it a more or less arbitrary meaning, I return to ancient Athenian democracy, which is generally considered to be a real-world model for participatory democracy. The institutional core of Athenian democracy is the meeting of the *demos* (*ecclesia*), which is where all the *polis*'s affairs are discussed and decided upon. All Athenians have access to this assembly as well as equal rights to participate in discussions and equal voting power. Not all Athenians could always take part in the assembly. However, the number frequently reached about 6000 or more out of 35,000 citizens. It is important to know that the assembly attendees were put on the same level as the entire *demos*. Several circumstances added to the perceived identity of assembly attendees and the *demos* as a whole. Apart from the high percentage of attendees, there were also manifold ways of direct cooperation among Athenian citizens that were constantly carried out in different institutions such as the Council of 500, the courts of law, and other institutions on the local level.

On the basis of the reality of Athenian democracy and by acuminating preceding definitions, the following definition of participatory democracy arises: *Participatory democracy is a primary subtype of democracy in which all public affairs are regulated through the counselling and decision-making of the entire* demos. *All citizens share equal power in counselling and decision-making.*

The described and defined participatory democracy has a double character. First, it actually existed (namely in ancient Athens). Second, it is even nowadays taken as a normative model by many authors. The problem is that it isn't possible any more in this pure form due to the changed scale (territorial state, audience of millions) and the social complexity of the modern era. But there are theoretical concepts and at least one current real-world example that a participatory democracy is also possible in a modified form in a modern society. These are described below as the three subtypes of participatory democracy: "strong democracy," the "deliberative democracy," and the "semi-direct democracy" in Switzerland.

Subtypes of Participatory Democracy

The most important criterion for differentiation between participatory democracy and representative democracy consists is in the way citizens are involved in political decisions. In a representative democracy this only takes place indirectly via elected representatives, while in a participatory democracy citizens are directly involved. The subtypes of participatory democracy have to keep the criterion of direct participation but at the same time they have to be appropriate for the conditions in modern societies. Barber (1984) specifies a type of democracy, which he calls "strong democracy" (see Figure 17.2) and which meets both aspects. While he understands participatory democracy as a form of government in which all of the people govern themselves in all public matters all of the time (Barber, 1995, p. 921), he defines strong democracy as "a form of government in which all of the people govern themselves in at least some public matters at least some of the time" (Barber, 1984, p. xiv).

The question of how many public matters have to be decided by direct participation of the citizens and how many citizens have to participate at all in order to be a participatory democracy, however, isn't answered by Barber.

In his book Barber (1984, Ch. 10) makes suggestions about "Institutionalizing Strong Democracy in the Modern World." Essential elements in these "strong democracies" include referenda and initiatives as well as other institutional avenues for participation, such as for neighbourhood assemblies and electronic balloting. Barber emphasizes that, for "strong democracy" to occur, multiple avenues of citizen participation must be implemented at the same time.

In comparison with strong democracy, the direct participation of citizens in political decisions in the so-called semi-direct democracy of Switzerland rests (at least on the national level) solely on referenda and initiatives. Most political decisions in Switzerland, however, are made by the elected representatives in representative organs. Therefore, Switzerland represents a hybrid type of democracy that contains elements of both participatory and representative democracy. In the typology of Figure 17.2 it is considered a subtype of participatory democracy as the possibility and reality of referenda and initiatives in Switzerland change the character of the political decision-making and politics in general (Kriesi, 2005; Kriesi and Trechsel, 2008).

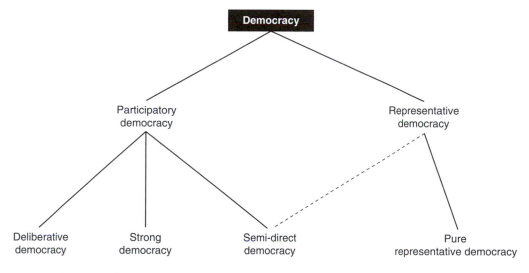

FIGURE 17.2 Types of democracy

The third subtype of participatory democracy in Figure 17.2 is "deliberative democracy." Deliberative democracy is the most prominent normative model discussed as the alternative or complement to representative democracy. Bohman (1998), slightly effusively, speaks of "the coming age of deliberative democracy." There's a multitude of variants of deliberative democracy but central ideas can be identified that are shared by all, namely, that citizens have to be directly involved in political decisions. However, the crucial point for them is that a debate must precede the decisions of the citizens and this debate must meet special requirements—those of "deliberation."

The central idea of all deliberations is that, via a regulated exchange of arguments for different positions on a controversial issue, consent can be achieved that the participants can agree with for good reasons (Cohen, 1989; Bohman, 1996; Habermas, 1996; Dryzeck, 2000; Gutman and Thompson, 2004).

Different desirable outcomes are connected with the concept of the citizens' deliberation. First it is assumed that, through the opinion-forming process that is based on the exchange of arguments, the quality of the participants' political preferences improve and consequently the quality of the decisions also improve (Estlund, 2001; Chambers, 2004). Furthermore it is assumed that the deliberative participation of citizens increases the legitimacy of the political decisions and ultimately of the regime. A long list of desirable outcomes, which are linked to deliberative processes, is provided by Mutz (2008, p. 536).

Currently, there is much disagreement about whether deliberation is possible in practice and whether it can generate the desired outcomes. The empirical results are quite different and some come to critical findings concerning assumptions of the theory of deliberative democracy (Delli-Carpini et al., 2004; Steiner et al., 2004; Fishkin and Luskin, 2005; Mutz, 2008; Thompson, 2008; Bächtiger et al., 2010). Thus, the debate isn't over yet.

The citizen's participation in political decisions is an essential feature of democracy. According to empirical studies (Cain et al., 2003), this normative demand has grown stronger towards a real demand due to social processes of change such as an increase in the average educational level, the amount of information a citizen can access, as well as a fundamental change of values. The result is a growing scepticism toward politicians, parties and institutions of representative democracy. Thereupon follows secondly an increase in participation in unconventional forms of political actions. Cain et al. (2003, p. 2) draw the following conclusion: "These trends suggest that the public's preferred mode of democratic-decision making is moving toward new forms of more direct involvement in the political process." As a consequence of the people's new demands, most representative democracies carry out institutional reforms, for instance introducing or expanding referenda and initiatives, or creating new information opportunities and governmental policies as well as citizens' and advisory boards dealing with administrative decisions (Cain et al., 2003, p. 16). To what extent these developments mean a transformation from representative democracy to a form of participatory democracy is still an open question that can only be answered by the further development of these sub-forms of participatory democracy.

References

Bächtiger, A., Niemeyer, S., Neblo, M., Steenbergen, M.R., and Steiner, J. 2010. "Symposium: Toward more realistic models of deliberative democracy. Disentangling diversity in deliberative democracy: Competing theories, theory blind spots and complementarities," *The Journal of Political Philosophy*, 18(1): 32–63.

Barber, B.R. 1984. *Strong democracy. Participatory politics for a new age*. Berkeley, LA and London: University of California Press.

Barber, B.R. 1995. "Participatory democracy." In S. M. Lipset (ed.). *The encyclopedia of democracy*. London: Routledge, pp. 921–924.

Bobbio, N. 1987. *The Future of Democracy*. Minneapolis: University of Minnesota Press.

Bohman, J. 1996. *Public deliberation. Pluralism, complexity and democracy*. Cambridge and London: MIT Press.

Bohman, J. 1998. "Survey article: The coming of age of deliberative democracy," *The Journal of Political Philosophy*, 6(4): 400–425.

Cain, B. E., Dalton, Russell J., and Scarrow, Susan E. (eds). 2003. *Democracy transformed? Expanding political opportunities in advanced industrial democracies*. Oxford and New York: Oxford University Press.

Chambers, S. 2004. "Behind closed doors: Publicity, secrecy, and the quality of deliberation," *The Journal of Political Philosophy*, 12(4): 389–410.

Cohen, C. 1971. *Democracy*. New York: The Free Press.

Cohen, J. 1989. "Deliberation and democratic legitimacy." In A. Hamlin and P. Petit (eds). *The good polity*. Oxford: Blackwell, pp. 17–34.

Collier, D. and Levitsky, S. 1997. "Democracy with adjectives. Conceptual innovation in comparative research," *World Politics*, 49: 430–451.

Dahl, R.A. 1989. *Democracy and its critics*. New Haven and London: Yale University Press.

Dahl, R.A. 1998. *On democracy*. New Haven and London: Yale University Press.

Dahl, R.A. 1999. "Can international organizations be democratic? A skeptic's view." In Ian Shapiro and Casiano Hacker-Cordon (eds). *Democracy's edges*. Cambridge: Cambridge University Press, pp. 19–36.

Delli-Carpini, M.X., Cook, F.L., and Lawrence, L.R. 2004. "Public deliberation, discursive participation and citizen engagement: A review of the empirical literature," *Annual Review of Political Science*, 7: 315–344.

Dryzeck, J. S. 2000. *Deliberative democracy and beyond. Liberals, critics, contestations*. Oxford and New York: Oxford University Press.

Estlund, D. 2001. "Political quality." In D. Estlund (ed.). *Democracy*. Oxford: Wiley-Blackwell, pp. 175–212.

Fishkin, J. S. and Luskin, R. C. 2005. "Experimenting with a democratic ideal: Deliberative polling and public opinion," *Acta Politica*, 40: 284–298.

Gallie, W. B. 1956. "Essentially contested concepts," *Proceedings of the Aristotelian Society*, 56: 167–198.

Goertz, G. 2006. *Social science concepts. A user's guide*. New Jersey: Princeton University Press.

Gutman, A. and Thompson, D. F. 2004. *Why deliberative democracy?* Princeton, NJ: Princeton University Press.

Habermas, J. 1996. *Between facts and norms. Contributions to a discourse theory of law and democracy*. Cambridge: Polity Press.

Habermas, J. 2001. *The postnational constellation. Political essays*. Cambridge: Polity Press.

Held, D. 1995. *Democracy and the global order. From the modern state to cosmopolitan governance*. Stanford: Stanford University Press.

Held, D. 2006. *Models of democracy*. Cambridge and Malden: Polity Press.

Hilmer, J. D. 2010. "The state of *participatory* democratic theory," *New Political Science*, 32(1): 43–63.

Kriesi, H. 2005. *Direct democratic choice. The Swiss experience*. Oxford: Lexington Books.

Kriesi, H. and Trechsel, A. H. 2008. *The politics of Switzerland. Continuity and change in a consensus democracy*. Cambridge: Cambridge University Press.

Munck, G. L. and Verkuilen, J. 2002. "Conceptualizing and measuring democracy: Evaluating alternative indices," *Comparative Political Studies* 35: 5–34.

Mutz, D. C. 2008. "Is deliberative democracy a falsifiable theory?" *Annual Review of Political Science*, 11: 521–538.

Pennock, R. J. 1979. *Democratic political theory*. Princeton, NJ: Princeton University Press.

Przeworski, A. 2010. *Democracy and the limits of self-government*. New York: Cambridge University Press.

Sartori, G. 1984. *Social science concepts. A systematic analysis*. Beverly Hills: Sage Publications.

Sartori, G. 1987. *The theory of democracy revisited. Part one: The contemporary debate*. Chatham: Chatham House Publishers.

Sartori, G. 1987. *The theory of democracy revisited. Part two: The classical issues*. Chatham: Chatham House Publishers.

Scharpf, F. 1999. *Governing in Europe? Effective and democratic?* Oxford and New York: Oxford University Press.

Steiner, J., Bächtiger, A., Spörndli, M. and Steenbergen, M.R. 2004. *Deliberative politics in action: Crossnational study of parliamentary debates*. Cambridge: Cambridge University Press.

Thompson, D. F. 2008. "Deliberative democratic theory and empirical political science," *Annual Review of Political Science*, 11: 497–520.

Warren, M. 2003. "A second transformation of democracy?" In Bruce E. Cain, Russell J. Dalton, and Susan E. Scarrow (eds). *Democracy transformed? Expanding political opportunities in advanced industrial democracies*. Oxford and New York: Oxford University Press, pp. 223–249.

18

CULTURES OF PARTICIPATION IN SOCIAL MOVEMENTS

Donatella della Porta and Alice Mattoni

Introduction

Mainstream definitions of democracy stress its representative character: the institutional rules to elect representatives are considered as the main indicator for the presence or absence of democracy. From the normative point of view, this means that accountability is considered as mainly linked to electoral practices. In existing democracies, however, this type of accountability is challenged by a decline in electoral participation and, more generally, conventional forms of political participation (such as membership in political parties). Consequently, there is an increasing mistrust, not in democracy as a principle, but in the functioning of democratically representative institutions. Additionally, transformations in media systems have been said to reduce the possibilities for citizens to hold their elected officials accountable, as commercialization of media foments a personalization and spectacularization of politics.

In part as a reaction to these perceived challenges to representative democratic institutions, alternative conceptions of democracy have emerged and re-emerged. As Pierre Rosanvallon has observed in his recent publication on *Counterdemocracy*,

> the idea of popular sovereignty found historical expression in two different ways. The first was the right to vote, the right of citizens to choose their own leaders. This was the most direct expression of the democratic principle. But the power to vote periodically and thus bestow legitimacy to an elected government is almost always accompanied by a wish to exercise a more permanent form of control over the government thus elected.
>
> *(2006, p. 12)*

As he notes, in the historical evolution of democracy, near to the growth of institutions of electoral accountability, there has been the consolidation of a circuit of oversight anchored outside of state institutions. In fact, the understanding of democratic experiences requires the consideration of the "functions and dysfunctions" of electoral representative institutions and the organization of distrust.

In what follows, we will discuss how social movements have nurtured visions of "another democracy," stressing its participatory quality. We shall add, however, that the meaning of participation changed in place and time, so that we can single out different cultures (plural) of participation. In particular, contemporary social movements' participatory visions have been linked to deliberative ones, with a new emphasis on consensus building. The stress on dialogue makes conceptions and practices of communication all the more important. Different cultures of participation are also at work with regard to the use of media in the social movement milieu, both with regard to interpersonal and intergroup communicative practices to organize mobilizations and to the development of media practices oriented towards the creation of alternative media.

Participatory Practices in Social Movements

While in representative conceptions of democracy social movements remain at the margin, they acquire instead a central position in participatory conceptions. In the debate on transformations in democracy, social movements appear to play a potentially crucial role. Recognizing the democratic potential of mistrust means, in fact, to push forward the reflections of the democratic role played by non-institutional actors in the political system. Recent research on political participation noted that, while some more conventional forms of participation are declining, protest forms are instead increasingly used. Citizens vote less, but are not less interested or less knowledgeable about politics. And if some traditional types of associations are less and less popular, others (social movement organizations and/or civil society organizations) are growing in resources, legitimacy and members. They are in fact considered as most relevant for conceptions of democracy in which society has a voice. Collective sentiments are articulated, judgments on government and its actions are constructed, and counter-knowledge (or counter-expertise) is formulated and demands are issued (Rosanvallon, 2006, 20).

Not by chance, social movements, especially of the left, challenged representative conceptions of democracy, promoting different democratic qualities. In their "metapolitical critique" these movements suggest an alternative conception of politics itself (Offe, 1985). In this sense, they kept alive in their theorization and practices

> an ancient element of democratic theory that calls for an organisation of collective decision making referred to in varying ways as classical, populist, communitarian, strong, grass-roots, or direct democracy against a democratic practice in contemporary democracies labelled as realist, liberal, elite, republican, or representative democracy.
>
> *(Kitschelt, 1993, p. 15)*

From a diachronic (or historical) perspective, it is possible to see different cultures of participation and conceptions of democracies. As it emerged, the labour movement did not limit itself to the promotion of social rights, but also proposed and practiced alternative democratic values (della Porta, forthcoming; Sewell, 1980; Thompson, 1991). While in liberal conceptions of democracy, political rights were essentially individual ones, the labour movement supported the right of association as a collective right (Bendix, 1964). In addition, the labour unions joined forces with other movements (such as the Chartists in Great Britain) in order to extend electoral participation, pushing for universal suffrage. Beyond democratic claims addressed to political institutions, the labour movement also at times experimented with organizational models that went beyond representation. Direct forms of democracy were kept alive and re-emerged in periodic surges of internal criticism against internal bureaucratization. Grassroots organizing based on equal participation primarily developed during cycles of protest. The reading societies and other associations linked to the labour movement worked as spaces of debates, contributing to the development of alternative publics.

When the New Left emerged in the 1960s, a main criticism addressed the institutionalization of the Old Left, with a call for a renewed vision of participatory democracy. The anti-authoritarian frame, typical of the student movement, promoted claims of self-management and democracy from below. At least since the 1960s, social movements have in fact criticized delegation as well as oligarchic and centralized power, legitimating instead forms of direct participation and grassroots, horizontal, egalitarian organizational models. These claims became central in the so-called new social movements: the women's movement introduced the consideration of the personal as political, organizing in consciousness-raising groups; the peace movement developed affinity groups; the environmental movements pushed for grassroots organizing.

Transnational Social Movements and Cultures of Participation

These historically rooted cultures of participation survived within various social movement organizations, contributing to contemporary debates on democracy. Contemporary movements are now blending these core values with an emerging interest in deliberative democracy. Deliberative democracy refers to the decisional processes that occur under conditions of equality, inclusiveness and transparency, and where communicative process based on reason (the strength of a good argument) are able to transform individual preferences, leading to decisions oriented to the public good (della Porta, 2005). Recent movements, especially the Global Justice Movement (GJM), have emphasized consensus building as a main democratic quality. They put an emphasis on preference (trans)formation with an orientation to the definition of the public good, stressing argumentation and dialogue. Participation has in fact maintained a relevant, though plural, meaning for the organizations belonging to the GJM (della Porta, 2009b, 2009c). Its nature as "movements of movements" is reflected in the presence of a plurality of conceptions and practices of democracy.

In particular, participation acquires different meanings in different movement areas. In the organizations rooted in the Old Left, participation and delegation are seen as highly compatible, and the stress on participation appears as a recovery of original values of democratic centralism. For the New Left groups, the emphasis is on direct democracy and self-organization, while new social movement organizations stress the prefigurative role of participation as a "school of democracy." Finally, searching for coherence between their criticism of existing democratic institutions and their internal practices, the organizations emerged with the GJM's elaborate counter-models that combine concrete proposals of reform with a utopian aspect (Reiter, 2009).

Even if rooted in different cultures of participation, most of the organizations studied in the DEMOS (Democracy in Europe and Mobilization of Society) project—which examined activist groups using a web-based platform to increase participation between citizens and government officials (della Porta, 2009b)—show an increasing attention to the discursive quality of democracy. Here there is an emphasis on four elements that are usually stressed in normative theory on deliberative democracy: the transformation of preferences, the orientation to the public good, the use of arguments, and the development of consensus. Sometimes explicitly (with references to the concept of deliberative democracy), more often not, the organizations of the GJM adopt deliberative norms. First of all, they stress that there are no easy solutions to complex social problems, or ones derived from big ideologies. Many conflicts must be approached by reliance on the potential for mutual understanding that might develop in an open, high-quality debate. The notion of a common good is often recalled (e.g. water as a common good) as is democracy as a common good, which is constructed through communication, exchanging ideas, knowledge sharing. The value of discussion among "free and equal" citizens is mirrored in the positive emphasis on diversity and inclusion, but also in the attention paid to the development of structured arenas for the exchange of ideas, with the experimentation of some rules that should allow for horizontal flows of communication and reciprocal listening.

Consensus is mentioned by half of the organizations analysed in the DEMOS research as a general value, as well as an organizational principle in internal decision-making. In fact, even though social movement organizations have stressed conflict as a dynamic element in society, more and more they tend to balance it with a commitment to different values, such as dialogue and mutual understanding. Consensus is presented as an alternative to majoritarian decision-making, which is accused of repressing and/or alienating minorities. Consensual decision-making, instead, increases the awareness of collective contribution to decisions. In addition, the dialogue between different points of views would help "working on what unites," constructing a shared vision while respecting diversity.

Cultures of participation based upon consensus building spread transnationally, in particular thanks to the symbolic impact and concrete networks built around the Zapatistas experience and the following adoption of consensual principles and practices in the Social Forum process. Dedicated publications, workshops and training courses helped the diffusion of consensual practices and the principle of consensus in the movement.

Here as well, however, we have to note the multiple meanings attached to consensus as a special quality of cultures of participation. In particular, when coupled with an assembly, horizontal tradition, the consensual decision-making is perceived as a way to reach a collective agreement that reflects a strong communitarian identity. This vision, particularly widespread among small and often local groups within the autonomous tradition, resonates with an anti-authoritarian emphasis and an egalitarian view. In these cultures, group life assumes a prefigurative value. An alternative, and more pragmatic, view is spread in the new (even transnational) networks. Here, consensual decision-making is accompanied especially by an emphasis on diversity and the need to respect it, but also improve mutual understanding through good communication (della Porta, 2009a).

Within this general attention to the participatory and deliberative qualities, visions and practices of democracy in the GJM vary. Debates tend to develop on the intrinsic democratic qualities of participation and deliberation. First, participatory conceptions that stress inclusiveness of equals (high participation) are contrasted with those based upon the delegation of power to representatives (low participation). In this sense, there is a continued presence of direct forms of democracy that puts a strong emphasis on the assembly, but also on processes of institutionalization of social movement organizations (often stressed in social movement research in the last two decades) that have spread a principle of delegation of power. A second dimension refers to the prevalence of majoritarian decision-making based upon vote versus public discussion, the common good, rational arguments, and transformation of preferences. The traditional use of the vote as a decision-making mechanism even within the assembly organizational model has been challenged by the emerging emphasis on values and practices that stress good communication. If all these diversities created tensions inside the GJM, they however also made possible a cross-fertilization between different models: the development of new forms, such as modern networks, but also a transformation of already existing groups. Communication has been seen as fundamental in order to keep diverse actors together.

Communicative Practices and Cultures of Participation

In the previous section, we illustrated the existence of different cultures of participation and conceptions of democracy in social movements, in the past and in the present. Whether individual activists or activist groups, social movement actors experiment with different democratic practices to make ordinary and extraordinary decisions about themselves and their actions in the political realm. As underlined above, good communication is particularly relevant in order to sustain and practice effective forms of participatory democracy based on the transformation of preferences and the development of consensus. Communicative mechanisms have a great importance in the construction of relations within and beyond the social movement milieu (Mische, 2008). Communicative practices are essential in the achievement of satisfactory instances of participatory and deliberative democracy within social movement networks. In settings like assemblies and preparatory meetings for subsequent collective actions, activists participate to deliberative processes according to a model of synchronous participation. They engage in face-to-face interactions that are spatially and temporally situated. The co-presence of activists that participate in the discussion is essential to reach common decisions. This is true in local affinity groups as well as in transnational social movement networks.

Communicative practices, however, may be also sustained through media, technological supports enabling the exchange of information between individuals and groups of individuals. Depending on the culture of participation at stake, media may be used in different ways to sustain communicative practices. In the case of transnational social movements, where preparatory meetings and assemblies are particularly important to organize mobilization, media may be used to involve lay citizens. Individual activists and activist groups employ media—from leaflets to radios, from mobile phones to mailing lists—to inform people within and beyond the social movement milieu about the organization of a public assembly where lay citizens, together with activists, are called to take decisions about future collective actions. In this regard, media are employed to enhance and expand participation of activists and potential activists to those moments of deliberation in which social movement actors experiment with new forms of democracy. In this sense, the media sustain future forms of *synchronous participation* revolving around face-to-face communication. However, these moments of synchronous participation do not always take place. The rising of information and communication technologies (ICTs) and, in particular, the spread of portable and personal digital devices such as mobile phones have sustained, in some cases, the emergence of more immediate forms of collective action. A relevant example in this direction is the demonstration in Spain after the terrorist attacks in March 2004 when the use of brief text messages calling for protest in the street spread quickly amongst the citizens of Madrid, resulting in a public demonstration of 20,000 people in the streets of the capital city (Sampedro, 2005). In this specific case, there were no collective moments of discussion and deliberation where social movement actors prepared mobilizations, planned protest strategies, or constructed common claims. The participation in the demonstration followed a different pattern in which the time for collective organization and the space for political reflection basically shrunk in the immediacy of mobile text messages. This specific media, therefore, promoted massive participation in a demonstration that was mostly based on an individualized culture of participation. Similar observations may arise when considering the employment of "social networking sites" (boyd and Ellison, 2007), such as Facebook, that seem to enhance a strong politics of the self in which a culture of political participation based on "mutual individualism" prevails (Barassi and Fenton, 2010).

Individual activists and activist groups taking part in local, national and transnational social movement networks also employ media to engage in processes of *asynchronous participation* sustained through ICTs and, in particular, Internet applications or web platforms. Mailing lists, for instance, can be seen as means of discussion allowing for a many-to-many model of communication similar to the ones that characterize public assemblies and preparatory meetings. Asynchronous participation based on computer-mediated communication intertwines with synchronous participation based on face-to face interactions in these movements, as it has been shown in the case of the transnational Euro Mayday Parade network against precarity—the lack of access to steady employment (Mattoni, 2008)—and for the European Social Forum (Kavada, 2005). In the European Social Forum, the one-to-one model of communication behind email exchanges among individual activists, the one-to-many model of communication behind informational websites set up by activist groups, and the many-to-many model of communication behind mailing lists involving an entire community of individual activists and activist groups intertwined and recombined according to different articulations (Kavada, 2005). Similarly, organization of the Euro Mayday Parade, a transnational parade against precarity occurring since 2004, was sustained by a network of activist groups rooted in different European countries, through online and offline communication. The online and offline environments were not mutually exclusive for the organization of the demonstration. Rather, deliberative processes took part both online, through the mailing list, and offline, through preparatory meetings. The offline preparatory meetings agendas were set collectively online through the mailing list, where discussions to organize the parade continued even after preparatory meetings ended (Mattoni, 2008). Also at the analytical level, the online and offline realms were not in opposition in that they were part of a continuum that activists experienced in its totality and complexity when involved in this unconventional form of political participation.[1]

Activist Media Practices and Cultures of Participation

Along with communicative practices, social movement actors also engage in creation of their own media, usually labeled alternative (Atton, 2002; Couldry & Curran, 2003a), radical (Downing, 1984), autonomous (Langlois & Dubois, 2005) or community (Hackett, 2007) media, with each term highlighting some specific aspects of them.[2] The production of alternative media outlets and the creation of alternative technological infrastructures are deeply linked to the social movement milieu. Political participation, here, acquires a specific meaning in that it is oriented in the production and diffusion of alternative and radical media cultures in societies. Far from being merely oriented towards the creation of content and infrastructures, this specific set of "activist media practices" (Mattoni, 2012) is inherently political. Indeed, these media create spaces that oppose the dominant cultures in a direct manner and, hence, challenge mainstream and mass media power that have the monopoly over the naming of realities (Couldry & Curran, 2003b).

These various activist media practices oriented towards the creation of alternative media share many features. They also differ in many respects. For instance, they may involve different creation and distribution technologies, from pieces of papers for leaflets to internet infrastructures to set up and develop an informational web site. Therefore, they also change according to the technological availability of a certain moment in time and space (McCurdy & Feigenbaum, 2010). Activist media practices may also be based on and hence mobilize different cultures of participation. Alternative media, indeed, may be radical with regard to processes that lead to their production and to the very form that they take as final products (Atton, 2002). Three dimensions of media practices, and their related axes, are relevant to understand and categorize cultures of participation through alternative media: collectiveness, openness, and possession.

The *degree of collectiveness* in the creation of alternative media outlets and technological infrastructures is the first axis. At one end of the axis there are those activist media practices that involve the collective production of alternative media outlets. The creation and production of electronic media in Latin America (Rodriguez, 2001), Telestreet in Italy (Ardizzoni, 2010; Berardi *et al.*, 2003) or grassroots street newspapers in North America (Howley, 2005) all involve a group of individuals, either activists or non-activists, who make decisions collectively. In this regard, the creation of alternative media outlets and alternative media texts, like radio broadcasts or newspaper articles, also contribute to the empowerment of people participating in such processes.

Individuals involved in the production of alternative media outlets and texts regain their voice in societies, speak for themselves and do not delegate their narratives to any external media professional (Rodriguez, 2001). In doing so, these individuals change the way in which they think about themselves and undertake a process of subjectivity empowerment and citizenship enactment.[3] At the other end of the axis, there are media practices that involve individual participation in the creation of alternative media outlets and texts. Blogs, for instance, are usually, though not always, managed by individuals and not by groups of individuals. In this case, the individual writing online engages in the production of "challenging codes" (Melucci, 1996) that oppose the dominant system of meanings. His or her alternative media texts could be easily accessed, reproduced, circulated, and even debated online and offline. In this way, the alternative media text may become part of discussions in the general public sphere and hence gain a certain degree of collectiveness. During the Second Persian Gulf War, for instance, the famous blogger Salam Pax wrote reports on his daily life in Baghdad and offered an alternative point of view on war narratives proposed by Western media corporations. Soon his blog became known worldwide, and his posts spread in through a variety of media outlets. From his home in the bombed Baghdad, therefore, Salam Pax was part of a collective debate on a global scale. But he conceived and wrote his posts alone. This example shows that what changes most in the creation of these alternative media texts, such as post in blogs, is the communicative act behind their creation, which is individual and not collective, experienced alone and not shared with others.

The *degree of openness* of participation in the making of alternative media outlets and alternative media text is the second axis. In this case, at one end of the axis there are those alternative media outlets that are easily accessible and, as such, can be considered open to a variety of contributions. At the other of the axis, there are those alternative media outlets that tend to revolve around a small, closely knit group of activists. In the Italian mobilizations against precarity, two different models of participation have been observed in the creation of alternative media outlets and texts that could be put at the two opposite end of this axis (Mattoni, 2009). On the one hand, there are the activists who considered it more fruitful to develop a communication tool available to everyone, not only as media audiences but also as media producers. Indymedia Italy was based on an open-publishing system that granted the anonymity of those who wished to publish articles, comments and other contributions. Participation in the newsmaking process, therefore, rendered Indymedia Italy and similar Independent Media Centres in other parts of the world a medium in which activist and non-activists engage in direct democratic practices (Coyer, 2005). On the other hand, there are the activists who preferred to create their own communication tool with which to organize participation in protest events and offer their own particular political analysis. The informational website Global Project, for instance, was organized through informal groups of activists who acted as decentralized local newsrooms sending their contributions to the website. While in Indymedia Italy comments were admitted, anonymous and unmoderated, the Global Project website did not provide for comments.

The *degree of possession* of the media outlet and/or technological infrastructure is the third axis. At one end of this axis there are individual activists or activist groups that use media outlets not situated in the social movement milieu. Although activists and non-activists participate either individually or collectively in the production of alternative media content, they do not own or control the media outlet. An example, here, is individual activists and activist groups who decide to use, for strategic and tactical reasons, already existing applications such as Facebook and YouTube. In other words, social movement actors are actively involved in "mainstreaming the alternative" media content (Askanius & Gustafsson, 2009). For instance, in recent mobilizations against the financial cuts to the public education system in Italy many unconventional political actors established their presence in social networking sites (Caruso *et al.*, 2010). Since social movement actors do not control these web applications, they have to adapt to the technological constraints and aesthetic appearance set by the owner of the platform. Moreover, in employing these applications they implicitly accept control over content they produce when uploading alternative content. At the other end of the axis, there are individual activists and activist groups that decide to employ alternative media outlets and technological infrastructures that could be positioned within social movement milieu. Indeed, sometimes social movement actors also participate in the production of the technological infrastructure hosting alternative media content and develop "communicative emancipatory practices" (Milan, 2009). A relevant example in this direction are Independent Media Centers, a "new genre of do-it-yourself media" (Kidd, 2010) first created during the November 1999 protest against the World Trade Organization in Seattle and then spreading across the world.

Conclusions

In the social sciences, the recent focus on democratic qualities points to tensions between different democratic values and goals. Various definitions of democracy can, in fact, be counterposed with each linked to specific values. Representative democracy resonates with terms such as efficiency, delegation, individual, majoritarian, vote, institutions, procedures, instrumentality, singular, professionalism. Participatory "counter-democracy" privileges inclusion, direct exercise of power, associative practices, discursive deliberation, the society, the process, the normative, plurality, the lay citizens. If the historical evolution of representative democracy has privileged some of these values, the renewal of democracy should bring about a re-evaluation and adaptations of elements that (such as control, participation, deliberation) were well present in the "ancient" conceptions of democracy. Old or new (or even newest), the different elements of what Rosanvallon (2006, p. 16) defined as counter-democracy "do not represent the contrary of democracy, but instead the form of democracy that contrasts the other, the democracy of indirect powers that are disseminated in the social body, the democracy of the organized defiance face to the electoral legitimacy." Marginal actors in representative democracy, social movements acquire instead more and more relevance in (participatory) conceptions of counter-democracy, as they contribute to the creation of critical public spheres (e.g. Cohen, 1989; Dryzek, 2000; Young, 2003) or, more in general terms, enclaves free from institutional power (Mansbridge, 1996).

Social movements have historically promoted and kept alive cultures of participation in at least two ways. On the one hand, they experiment with democracy in its internal practices; on the other, they develop proposals for a democratic reform of institutions at different levels. In this way, they emphasize some democratic qualities that are less and less present in, and cherished by, contemporary institutions. As we observed, however, even within social movements conceptions of participation vary. In recent periods, participation has been bridged with deliberation. With a positive value given to the networking of diversity, the Global Justice Movement conceives of participation as a continuous dialogue oriented to the definition of public goods (democracy being one of them). In these emerging cultures of participation a particular emphasis is put on good communication.

Communicative mechanisms and practices amongst social movement actors are indeed important in the making of democracy within the social movement milieu. In order to set the ground for mobilization, individual activists and activist groups engage in preparatory meetings and assemblies where participation is essential to take collective decisions about how, why and when to act. During these essential moments synchronous communicative practices take place. Through the use of media technologies, collective discussions and confrontation also take place according to asynchronous communicative practices. However, the latter do not replace the former.

Rather, social movement actors tend to rely on both synchronous and asynchronous participation. Innovations in the media environment, like the one produced by the rise of ICTs, may actually support new forms of political participation based on the individual level of immediate commitment and engagement in public protests, rather than on the collective level of preparatory meetings and assemblies to prepare mobilization. The qualities of informal political participation in an era of digital and portable media are hence changing and deserve further research.

Social movement actors also engage in the creation of their own media. Like interpersonal and intergroup communicative practices, activist media practices oriented towards the creation of alternative media are linked with and at the same time sustain different cultures of participation. Three axes seem to be particularly useful to understand this linkage: 1) the degree of collectiveness in the creation of alternative media content and infrastructures, 2) the degree of openness in the making of alternative media content, and 3) the degree of possession of the infrastructures on which the alternative media outlet or content is originally published. Combining the three dimensions, we can analytically single out alternative media based on different cultures of participation. On one hand, there are alternative media messages spread through outlets that are open, based on collective participation and rooted in autonomous technological infrastructures. On the other hand, there are alternative media messages spread through outlets that are closed, based on individual participation, and rooted in commercial, technological infrastructures. In the middle, there are multiple combinations that render even more plural the meaning of culture of participation when addressing activist media practices in contemporary societies.

Notes

1   Although this is not the focus on this chapter, it has to be mentioned that specific forms of political participation taking place in the online realm have also developed in the recent past. For a discussion on this issue see Jordan (2002), Jordan and Taylor (2004) and Costanza-Chock (2003).
2   For a comprehensive discussion on different types and model of alternative media outlets see Hadl (2007) and Atton (2007).
3   For this reason, Clemencia Rodriguez suggests to call these media outlets "citizen media" (Rodriguez, 2001).

References

Ardizzoni, M. 2010. "Neighborhood television channels in Italy: The case of Telestreet." In M. Ardizzoni and C. Ferrari (eds). *Beyond monopoly: Globalization and contemporary Italian media*. Lanham: Lexington Books, pp. 171–184.

Askanius, T. and Gustafsson, N. 2009. "Mainstreaming the alternative: Changing media strategies of protest movements," II Global Conference on Shaping Europe in a Globalized World? Protest Movements and the Rise of a Transnational Civil Society. Zurich.

Atton, C. 2002. *Alternative media*. London: Sage.

Atton, C. 2007. "Current issues in alternative media research," *Sociological Compass*, 1(1): 17–27.

Barassi, V. and Fenton, N. 2010. "Alternative media and social networking sites: The politics of individuation and political participation," Communication and Citizenship—IAMCR Conference, Braga, Portugal.

Bendix, R. 1964. *Nation building and citizenship*. New York: Wiley & Sons.

Berardi, F., Jacquemet, M., and Vitali, G. 2003. *Telestreet. Macchina immaginativa non omologata*. Milano: Baldini Castoldi Dalai.

boyd, M. D. and Ellison, B. N. 2007. "Social network sites: Definition, history, and scholarship," *Journal of Computer-Mediated Communication*, 13(1): 210–230.

Caruso, L., Giorgi, A., Mattoni, A., and Piazza, G. (eds). 2010. *Alla ricerca dell'onda. I nuovi conflitti dell'istruzione superiore*. Milano: Franco Angeli.

Cohen, J. 1989. "Deliberation and democratic legitimacy." In A. Hamlin and P. Pettit (eds). *The good polity*. Oxford: Blackwell, pp. 17–34.

Costanza-Chock, S. 2003. "Mapping the repertoire of electronic contention." In A. Opel and D. Pompper (eds). *Representing resistance: Media, civil disobedience and the Global Justice Movement*. Westport, CT: Praeger, pp. 173–191.

Couldry, N. and Curran, J. 2003a. *Contesting media power: Alternative media in a networked world*. Lanham, MD: Rowman & Littlefield.

Couldry, N. and Curran, J., 2003b. "The paradox of media power." In N. Couldry and J. Curran (eds). *Contesting media power: Alternative media in a networked world*. Lanham, MD: Rowman & Littlefield, pp. 3–15.

Coyer, K., 2005. "If it leads it bleeds: The participatory newsmaking of the independent media centre." In W. De Jong, M. Shaw, and N. Stammers (eds). *Global activism, global media*. London: Pluto Press, pp. 165–178.

della Porta, D. 2005. "Making the polis: Social forums and democracy in the global justice movements," *Mobilization*, 10(1): 73–94.

della Porta, D. 2009a. "Consensus in movement." In D. della Porta (ed.). *Democracy in social movements*. London: Palgrave, pp. 73–99.

della Porta, D. (ed.). 2009b. *Another Europe*. London: Routledge.

della Porta, D. (ed.). 2009c. *Democracy in social movements*. London: Palgrave.

della Porta, D. Forthcoming. "I movimenti sociali e la democraciza." In A. Pizzorno (ed). *Lo Stato democratico*. Milano: Feltrinelli.

Downing, J. 1984. *Radical media. The political experience of alternative communication*. Boston, MA: South End Press.

Dryzek, J. S. 2000. *Deliberative democracy and beyond*. New York: Oxford University Press.

Hackett, M. 2007. "Community radio and television." In *Encyclopedia of activism and social justice*. London: Sage.

Hadl, G. 2007. "'Community media'? 'Alternative media'? Unpacking approaches to media by, for and of the people," *Papers in International and Global Communication*, 7.

Howley, K. 2005. *Community media: People, places, and communication technologies*. Cambridge: Cambridge University Press.

Jordan, T. 2002. *Activism! Direct action, hacktivism and the future of society*. London: Reaktion Books.

Jordan, T. and Taylor, P. A. 2004. *Hacktivism and cyberwars*. London: Routledge.

Kavada, A. 2005. "Exploring the role of the internet in the 'movement for alternative globalization': The case of the Paris 2003 European Social Forum," *Westminster Papers in Communication and Culture*, 1.

Kidd, D. 2010. "Whistling into the typhoon: A radical inquiry into autonomous media." In C. Hughes (ed). *In the middle of a whirlwind*. Oakland: AK Press, pp. 199–210.

Kitschelt, H. 1993. "Social movements, political parties, and democratic theory," *The Annals of The AAPSS*, 528: 13–29.

Langlois, A. and Dubois, F. (eds). 2005. *Autonomous media: activating resistance and dissent*. Montreal: Cumulus Press.

McCurdy, P. and Feigenbaum, A. 2010. "From Greenham to Gleneagles: Analyzing the media strategies of pre and post-Internet social movements," MeCCSA Conference, London School of Economics.

Mansbridge, J. 1996. "Using power/fighting power: The polity." In S. Benhabib (ed.). *Democracy and difference: Contesting the boundaries of the political*. Princeton: Princeton University Press, pp. 46–66.

Mattoni, A. 2008. "Organisation, mobilisation and identity: National and transnational grassroots campaigns between face-to-face and computer-mediated-communication." In S. Baringhorst, V. Kneip, and J. Niesyto (eds). *Political campaigning on the web*. Bielefeld: transcript, pp. 201–232.

Mattoni, A. 2012. *Media practices and protests politics. How precarious workers mobilise*. Farnham, England; Burlington, VT: Ashgate.

Melucci, A. 1996. *Challenging codes: Collective action in the information age*. Cambridge: Cambridge University Press.

Milan, S. 2009. "Stealing the fire. A study of emancipatory practices in the field of communication," Social and Political Sciences (PhD Dissertation). Florence, European University Institute.

Mische, A. 2008. *Partisan publics. Communication and contention across Brazilian youth activist networks.* Princeton: Princeton University Press.

Offe, C. 1985. "New social movements: Challenging the boundaries of institutional politics," *Social Research*, 52: 817.

Reiter, H. 2009. "Participatory traditions in the Global Justice Movement." In D. della Porta (ed.). *Democracy in social movements*. London: Palgrave, pp. 44–72.

Rodriguez, C. 2001. *Fissures in the mediascape. An international study of citizens' media.* Cresskill, NJ: Hampton Press.

Rosanvallon, P. 2006. *La Contre-démocratie. La politique a l'age de la defiance.* Paris: Seuil.

Sampedro, V. B. (ed.). 2005. *13-M. Multitudes on line.* Madrid: Los Libros de la Catarata.

Sewell, W. H. J. 1980. *Work and revolution in France. The language of labour from the old regime to 1848.* Cambridge: Cambridge University Press.

Thompson, E. P. 1991. *The making of the English working class.* London: Penguin Books.

Young, I. M. 2003. "Activist challenges to deliberative democracy." In J. S. Fishkin and P. Laslett (eds). *Debating deliberative democracy*. Malden, MA: Blackwell, pp. 102–120.

PART VI

Encouraging Participatory Activism

19

FROM CULTURES OF PARTICIPATION TO THE RISE OF CRISIS MAPPING IN A NETWORKED WORLD

Sophia B. Liu and Jen Ziemke

> The spread of information networks is forming a new nervous system for our planet. When something happens in Haiti or Hunan, the rest of us learn about it in real time—from real people. And we can respond in real time as well. Americans eager to help in the aftermath of a disaster and the girl trapped in the supermarket are connected in ways that were not even imagined a year ago, even a generation ago. That same principle applies to almost all of humanity today. As we sit here, any of you—or maybe more likely, any of our children—can take out the tools that many carry every day and transmit this discussion to billions across the world.
>
> (Secretary of State Hillary Rodham Clinton, January 21, 2010)

Secretary Clinton's timely comments mark the beginning of an exciting new epoch, an era in which public participation at a global level occurs *en masse* and in real time. In one case, an individual caught underneath the rubble after an earthquake in Port-au-Prince uses her phone to send an SOS via a text message. One thousand miles away, an office worker logs on during her lunch break to translate SOS texts from Haitian Creole, her native language, into English. In another city, students far from the disaster stay up all night reading these translated real-time texts. When the students are not able to identify the street name or neighborhood on any current map of Haiti, the Haitian diaspora again shares its local knowledge, improving existing maps as well as helping to identify the trapped person's location. Still others, far from the scene of the emergency, work from home combing the web and social media services like Facebook and Twitter to find and share contextual, up-to-the-minute information about the emergency as quickly as possible to those on the other side of the globe. A group of students uses this information to create geo-referenced, real-time situation reports. This global, emergent collaboration offers emergency responders the best, most comprehensive source of contextual information currently available about the area in crisis. Translated and geo-referenced SMS texts connect emergency responders to survivors on the ground. The information that emerges from this collaboration helps save lives.

All along this chain of emergency communication, people from all walks of life with different kinds of knowledge, from different locations, and with different backgrounds and affiliations offer remote assistance in service to strangers trapped in an emergency situation. This participation intimately binds both local and remote participants together, unified by a common cause to help those in need.

The academic, military, policy, and humanitarian aid communities now recognize that individual voices, when aggregated, serve as a promising new source of hyper-local, real-time, news. Learning how to channel, visualize, and analyze this "crowdsourced" crisis information for effective humanitarian response is one of the goals of emergent volunteer networks like the Crisis Mappers Network and Crisis Commons. The Crisis Mappers Network was created in October 2009 in response to growing interest in Crisis Mapping, a new interdisciplinary endeavor. Together, these networks are taking a cue from the example set by the crowd itself of adopting the crowd's seeming urge to share and be open. Both individually and as part of a network, people are now newly empowered to participate in ways that connect all of us to the human experience. We have adopted new habits and are developing new norms of sharing in order to affect positive, meaningful change, especially during calamitous times. We make use of new technologies, but the technologies themselves are not responsible for this generosity: such sharing emerges from the human spirit. However, technologies can ably empower many of us to do what we have always longed to do, which is to help those in need.

An Emerging Culture of Participation

A global, participatory culture is quickly developing because of both the rapid rise of information and communication technologies (ICTs) like the Internet and increasingly powerful mobile devices as well as an emerging ethos of participation. But the mere expansion of ICT technologies alone cannot explain the remarkable emergence of such participation. In fact, participatory culture is as much a function of the *design* of these technologies themselves as anything else. We argue that *how we design our computing technologies will determine what kind of experience and interaction we will have*.

New rituals of participation have emerged in an era of nearly ubiquitous ICTs. As consumers of information transform themselves into active *participants* in the production process, a more decentralized, socially distributed form of interaction has developed. Fischer defines a "culture of participation" as a culture where "people are provided with the means to participate actively in personally meaningful activities" (2009, p. 1). Thus, cultures of participation are no longer just consumed by all but also produced by all in order to contribute to social well-being. Wessels (2010) explains through a socio-cultural perspective that in the Internet era "social relations have become increasingly 'virtualized' … to provide a basis for new forms of community, a revival of democratic citizenship" (p. 165), which has led to an increase in democratic participation, a revival of freedom of speech, and the provision of free information and communication channels. Ultimately, the values of free and open communication were inherently designed into the development of the Internet and the resulting World Wide Web.

Participatory technology like Web 2.0 and social media speaks to the shift towards designing web-based applications that support the participatory, "read–write" web. O'Reilly (2005) initially explained Web 2.0 as web applications that allow users to contribute their own data, which improves when more people use it, that consume and remix data from multiple sources, and that create network effects through an "architecture of participation." Social media is ultimately about facilitating online conversations and sharing information by remotely participating, thus allowing a global network to form. Although this participatory form of computing may seem recent, it was futurists like Ted Nelson (1987) who began envisioning this intellectual and social revolution of having access to the panoply of thought and knowledge, which we now get from the web, in his book *Computer Lib*. Nelson further states that it is how we design our computing technologies that will determine what kind of experience and interaction we will have. In the next section, we explain how the design of web-based Geographic Information Systems (GIS) are facilitating new forms of participation through spatial communication.

Participatory Forms of Mapping

The pervasive use of participatory mapping technologies has led to the rise of the neogeography movement and subsequently facilitated the emergence of Crisis Mapping as a new endeavor for interdisciplinary collaboration. The term *neogeography* refers to geographic tools and techniques that go beyond traditional GIS. It is a term that Dangermond (1995), Monmonier (1998), and Krygier (1999) hoped for more than a decade ago, urging that next-generation GIS should be more interactive and accessible to citizens in order to foster public participation and collaboration around geographic information. Turner (2006) explains that neogeography is about "people using and creating their own maps, on their own terms by combining elements of an existing toolset" (p. 3). Goodchild (2009) also explains that neogeography is also about "blurring the distinctions between producer, communicator and consumer of geographic information" (p. 82), thus allowing other non-professionals to become a part of the mapping process.

The Geospatial Web has in large part facilitated a much wider use of geospatial data than in the past. Ultimately, maps can be used as a visual communication tool and to prompt decision-making (Kraak, 2001, p. 12), since it is geographically contextualized information. Many Internet mapping services, like Google Maps and OpenStreetMap, are facilitating new forms of participatory mapping. Subsequently, Google Earth was dubbed "the People's GIS" by AECNews.com. This is also an accurate way of describing map mashups as well.

Mashups are web applications that typically use openly published Application Programming Interfaces (APIs) to access, extract, and recombine data feeds from multiple sources into a single integrated application. Hackley *et al.* (2008) explain this phenomenon as a shift towards "an inter-networked, participatory model where users also collaboratively create, share and mash-up data" in ways that make information more accessible to the general public (p. 2033). In the crisis domain, mapping has always been crucial for emergency management; however, it is no longer just created and used by GIS professionals and formal responders but also by members of the public during crises.

Crisis Mapping as an Emerging Interdisciplinary Endeavor

Mapping crisis information is not entirely new; yet, over the past five years, we have seen an increase in real-time mapping activities in response to recent disasters by emerging crisis-related technology communities. Clearly, the rise of neogeography and participatory journalism as outlined above helped launch Crisis Mapping as a new arena for collaboration and research.

The Crisis Mappers Network is an engaged interdisciplinary forum of people from the government, the technology industry, academia, humanitarian and human rights organizations, and news agencies. They are united by their common interest in leveraging ICTs to help visualize, understand, and respond to crisis events of all kinds. *Crisis Mappers* create visual representations of the discrete, individual crisis events that, when aggregated together, make a crisis map. The best crisis maps are compelling, multi-layered interfaces that offer a window into the situation on the ground. End users have at their fingertips a wide range of analytic tools to help make sense of these crisis maps. Finally, crisis maps are used by the community and emergency responders to help save lives and coordinate relief efforts.

The value of looking at participatory cultures during crises is in part because these are inherently participatory environments. Disaster researchers have long documented how citizens from the affected population, community-based organizations and emergent groups near the impact zone of a disaster self-organize to address unmet needs during crisis situations through improvisation (Fischer, 1998; Tierney *et al.*, 2001). Therefore, we must not forget that, when a crisis affects a community, members of the public are often the true first responders who self-organize to provide critical rescue assistance, relief resources, and information to the general public. It is during times of crisis when we see ways in which people innovatively adapt to adversity, especially in the information age.

With the pervasive use of ICTs during crises, we are witnessing the emergence of virtual disaster volunteer communities. Nourbakhsh *et al.* (2006) foresaw this "emergence of a new breed of volunteers—online data managers" facilitating a "web-based community approach to disaster operations" (p. 787). There is an increasing need to map these data to gain better situational awareness. In the following section, we provide recent examples of Crisis Mapping in action.

Ushahidi: A First-Generation Crisis Mapping Platform

Since its early deployment in Kenya in 2007, the very successful Ushahidi instance has been used to help keep governments and their constituents accountable during elections. Organizations have deployed instances of Ushahidi to help track possible fraud, intimidation, vote tampering, and violence in places like Kenya, India, Burundi, Colombia, Namibia, Lebanon, Togo, Mexico, Ethiopia, Sudan, Philippines, Mozambique, and Guinea. Other groups have used the platform to monitor harassment of racial minorities, or to track acts of violence of all kinds in places like South Africa, New Mexico (US), Atlanta (US), and the Democratic Republic of Congo. Recently, Crisis Maps of demonstrations in repressive regimes have emerged in 2011 in places like Egypt, Tunisia, Libya, Sudan, and Algeria. The platform has also been notably used in 2010 to track incidents of crises emerging from natural and technological hazards, such as the earthquakes in Haiti and Chile in 2010, the 2010 oil spill in the Gulf of Mexico, and the 2010 floods in Pakistan, to name a few.

Most notably, the Haiti–Ushahidi (see Figure 19.1) deployment demonstrated, for the first time, the real potential of Crisis Mapping to affect change and facilitate humanitarian response on the ground in near real time. Many actors were involved in the Haiti–Ushahidi deployment of 2010, including a team of students at the Fletcher School of Tufts University as well as many other individuals working from around the world. An SMS-based system was set up, Project 4636, allowing free text-messaging to anyone inside Haiti with a mobile phone. Volunteers worked around the clock and in several time zones on various tasks: translating texts from Creole to English, surfing the web, processing incoming SMS messages, creating incident reports, and carefully geolocating each incident. The result was a publicly accessible map that became an important resource for the Joint Task Force Command Center, the US State Department, the Red Cross, the UN Foundation, the International Medical Corps, the Clinton Foundation, and other emergency responder organizations. Eventually, as trapped and urgent messages abated, the entire project was turned over to the Haitian people themselves to facilitate recovery and development efforts.

For the Chile–Ushahidi deployment, several factors contributed to its success. Media monitoring and crisis mapping activities were modeled largely after the Haiti-Ushahidi instance developed barely a month before. Free cloud computing tools (i.e. Google Groups, Google Docs and Forms, and Skype Public Chat) were used along with Facebook Groups and Events to facilitate

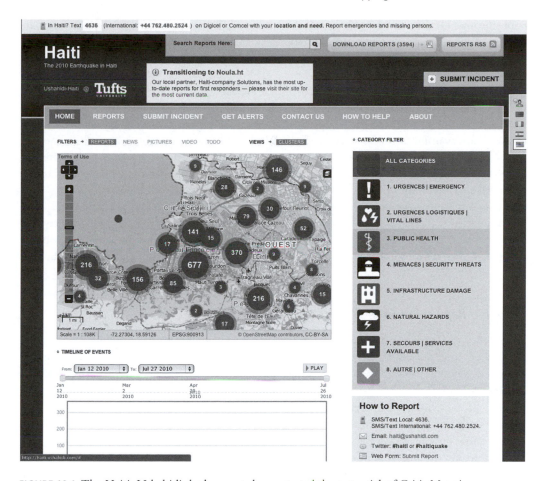

FIGURE 19.1 The Haiti–Ushahidi deployment demonstrated the potential of Crisis Mapping

the distributed coordination efforts for Ushahidi Haiti and Chile. These social networking tools have become pivotal for building bridges between many stakeholders, which ultimately helped support participatory Crisis Mapping.

CrisisCommons: CrisisCamps and Humanitarian OpenStreetMap (HOT)

CrisisCommons, founded in March 2009 at a Government 2.0 Camp, is a global network of citizen volunteers, emergency management organizations, international humanitarian relief agencies, and people representing non-profits and the private sector. Their vision is to create and sustain a culture of information-sharing to improve emergency management and humanitarian activities. Their core values are independence, openness, sharing, and connecting different stakeholders within their global network of volunteers.

In response to the January 12, 2010 Haiti earthquake, over forty-five CrisisCamps—BarCamp or participant-driven events intended to unite the global network of technology volunteers in local public spaces and collaborate on technology projects that would help people in crisis—were set up for Haiti in six different countries with around 1500 participants in total. One of the projects that the participants worked on was providing surge capacity for an open-source mapping effort through OpenStreetMap. OpenStreetMap relies on the donation of high-resolution satellite imagery and a volunteer workforce to generate a free and editable wiki map of the world. Volunteers from CrisisCamp and others around the world worked on the OpenStreetMap project to help create a new basemap of Port-au-Prince. The *OpenStreetMap – Project Haiti* Vimeo video is a timelapse visualization of the edits made to the Haiti map, which provides a visual depiction of the immediate response to mapping Haiti just thirteen days after the earthquake struck. The Haitian government sent a direct request for these maps since they were praised as the most up-to-date maps available at the time. As such, the WorldBank and OpenStreetMap in collaboration with CrisisCommons deployed a team to Haiti on February 9, 2010 to deliver these maps on hard drives to the Haitian government. Additionally, the Haiti–Ushahidi deployment switched to the OpenStreetMap version of Haiti, since it was more complete than Google Maps.

CrisisCommons volunteers are not just coders or programmers but also geospatial specialists, social media users, everyday Internet users, and just people willing to donate their time to help during a crisis. With their motto as "Think locally, act globally, build locally," these distributed volunteers are drawn together by a call to service to help during any type of crisis anywhere in the world.

Mapping Repopulation Indicators for New Orleans

In response to Hurricane Katrina in 2005, the Greater New Orleans Community Data Center (GNOCDC.org) created the *Repopulation Indicators for New Orleans* map (see Figure 19.2). Often described as going "beyond the typical Google mashup," this map visualizes "patterns of density and repopulation across New Orleans, as well as block-by-block within neighborhoods" using the ratio of households who received postal mail recently to households who received postal mail pre-Katrina. The purpose of this map mashup is to generate repopulation patterns in order to visually show how many people have returned since the 2005 Hurricanes Katrina and Rita.

What makes this map mashup participatory is in part due to how it was designed and also how the local community has used it. With a usability expert on this team, participatory design (Greenbaum and Kyng, 1991) approaches were employed. First, they used their existing "Ask Allison" feature on their GNOCDC website to determine the value of repopulation data (e.g. businesses could make investment decisions and human service agencies could decide how to allocate scarce resources). Then, they explored different sources of population data and found that the United States Postal Service (USPS) data would be the best fit for indicating repopulation information. After they incorporated the 3,000+ requests received from the Ask Allison system to inform the design of their map mashup, they then conducted usability testing in the Lower Ninth Ward to address any user interface design issues when the map was viewed on residences' own computers. This was critical for understanding the size of computer screens people generally used and the context in which these maps would be used.

As a Community Data Center, they provide reliable, targeted data to help leaders create positive change in their community. Here are a few examples of how the Repopulation Indicators map was used by the local community. The Lower Ninth Ward used it to deploy their volunteers on projects focused on rebuilding homes. A grocery store chain used it to plan the development of new stores. An interesting use of the service occurred when two different stakeholders used the same repopulation data against each other to describe the impact of building a hospital. A university planning team used the data to promote the proposed medical center, whereas, a neighborhood association in the area used the data to show the possible displacement of many active households and the destruction of historic sites due to the proposed construction of the center. This example shows that the interpretation of the information in the map can lead to

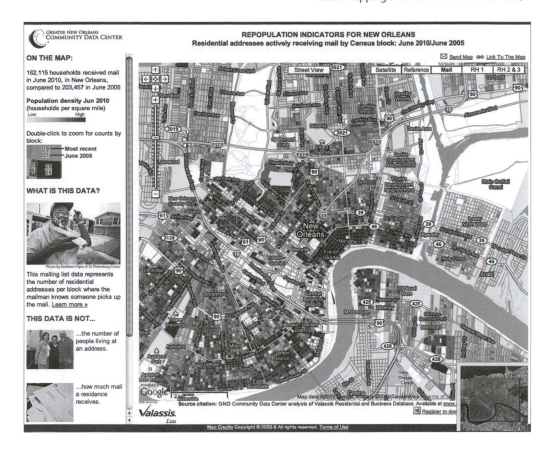

FIGURE 19.2 Population indicators for New Orleans crisis map

conflicting uses. Ultimately, the success of the Repopulation map was how it was developed through a participatory design process and how it helped to facilitate discussions of rebuilding efforts between multiple stakeholders.

Google My Maps Mashups for Wildfires

The first significant use of Google My Maps for a crisis after launching in April 2007 was for the October 2007 Southern California wildfires. KPBS San Diego and LATimes.com were the first two news organization to notably create Google My Maps and annotate information about the wildfires (i.e. the location of the fires, containment percentages, destroyed or damaged structures, evacuation information, etc.). These publicly accessible online maps were particularly useful for people outside of the impact zone to remotely monitor the wildfire to see if their loved ones' homes were directly affected. This kind of location-specific crisis information is often difficult to obtain from afar, since it may be difficult to access local news channels, and news anchors do not routinely provide real-time information for all affected areas of a crisis. Additionally, Google My Maps allow users to zoom in and out to geobrowse any location to obtain detailed crisis information on a particular location of interest.

For the 2009 Los Angeles Fires, Rong-Gong Lin II, a *Los Angeles Times* staff writer, created another Google My Maps (see Figure 19.3; Lin 2009) after having experience creating one for the

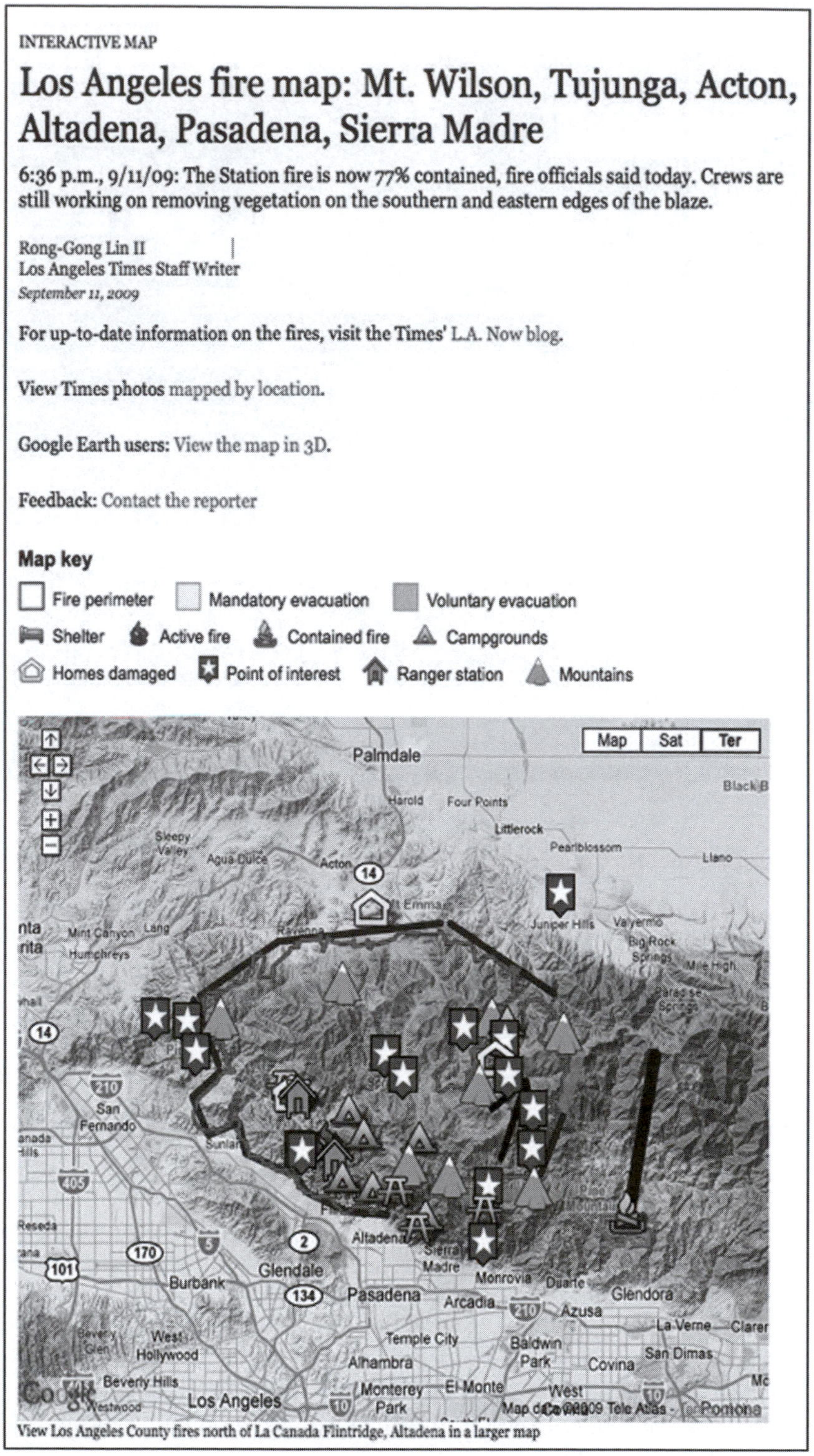

INTERACTIVE MAP

Los Angeles fire map: Mt. Wilson, Tujunga, Acton, Altadena, Pasadena, Sierra Madre

6:36 p.m., 9/11/09: The Station fire is now 77% contained, fire officials said today. Crews are still working on removing vegetation on the southern and eastern edges of the blaze.

Rong-Gong Lin II
Los Angeles Times Staff Writer
September 11, 2009

For up-to-date information on the fires, visit the Times' L.A. Now blog.

View Times photos mapped by location.

Google Earth users: View the map in 3D.

Feedback: Contact the reporter

Map key

☐ Fire perimeter   ☐ Mandatory evacuation   ▨ Voluntary evacuation

▧ Shelter   ♨ Active fire   ♨ Contained fire   △ Campgrounds

⌂ Homes damaged   ⚑ Point of interest   ⌂ Ranger station   △ Mountains

View Los Angeles County fires north of La Canada Flintridge, Altadena in a larger map

FIGURE 19.3 2009 Los Angeles fire maps using Google mapping tools

2007 wildfires. He explains how the advantage of using a map interface to communicate crisis information is that it provides a "better sense of scale" and it is the "fastest way to communicate" news about a wildfire, a natural hazard phenomenon that changes rather quickly. One important addition that Lin made for the 2009 map is the addition of the following line in the LATimes.com news article: "Feedback: Contact the Reporter," which is a link to an online comment form within the LATimes.com site that immediately sends a message to Lin. He recounts how helpful this and the comment feature within Google Maps were because "getting real-time feedback made the map better and easier to understand." More specifically, he viewed these two-way communication features as a way to "get tips for reporting," which ultimately compelled reporters in the field to search for information based on requests from members of the public. For example, he received feedback about notable sites (e.g. well-known café, etc.) that had not been updated yet but were heavily discussed by members of the public. He also received comments suggesting corrections to make the map more accurate (e.g., moving icons or showing active fire fronts and not just fire boundaries).

Lin goes on to explain how maps are a "powerful way of illustrating news stories … that you would not be able to show through text alone" because "when you map things out, you can definitely see trends that were not there before … [and] it helps give me the sense of what the story is." Maps often are a better and faster way to communicate information about certain kinds of location-specific news events, such as wildfires. The value of creating annotated maps like Google My Maps is that it allows us the ability to see geographic trends that we would not have otherwise noticed as easily when linearly listed in a text-based format, such as in news articles.

Crisis Mapping in a Networked World

Indeed, the very motivation for the entire crisis mapping effort is to effect change and to provide situational awareness for affected populations. The case studies of crisis mapping in action presented above are but a few examples of the crisis mapping history that has emerged from our networked world. It was these many early crisis mappers who saw before the rest of us that a participatory revolution was coming and it was to occur through a mapping interface. In this final section, we specifically discuss how one crisis mapping community has emerged and become officially established through online networking technologies.

Crisis Mappers Net

In October 2009, the Harvard Humanitarian Initiative and John Carroll University convened the first International Conference on Crisis Mapping (ICCM). The conference brought together scholars and practitioners across business, industry, military, government, and non-profit NGOs working in this arena.

The Crisis Mappers Network was launched at the end of the first conference using a customizable platform for creating online social networks (Figure 19.4). The network sustained the enthusiasm from this highly successful conference. This group of over 1000 participants from fifty countries remained in contact largely via a Google Group over the course of the year (Figure 19.5).

Members of the Crisis Mappers Network met their first test of this new relationship and commitment in the hours and days after the devastating earthquake that hit Haiti in January 2010. How could the Crisis Mappers group work together to help facilitate effective humanitarian response? Did our mobilization matter? Would it help save lives? The answer was that Crisis Mappers worked together and for long hours to meet this challenge. People began posting

Crisis Mappers Net
THE INTERNATIONAL NETWORK OF CRISIS MAPPERS

Follow us on Twitter

 **Harvard Humanitarian Initiative**

Many thanks to the Harvard Humanitarian Initiative, for supporting the network, conference series & website!

■ THE CRISIS MAPPERS NETWORK

[Scroll down for info on the 2011 Crisis Mappers Conference]

Crisis Mappers leverage mobile & web-based applications, participatory maps & crowdsourced event data, aerial & satellite imagery, geospatial platforms, visual analytics, and computational & statistical models to power effective early warning for rapid response to complex humanitarian emergencies.

The **International Network of Crisis Mappers** is the largest and most active international community of experts, practitioners, policymakers, technologists, researchers, journalists, scholars, hackers and skilled volunteers engaged at the intersection between humanitarian crises, technology and crisis mapping. The Crisis Mappers Network was launched by 100 Crisis Mappers at the first International Conference on Crisis Mapping in 2009. This website has since been accessed from 191 different countries. As the world's premier crisis mapping hub, the Network catalyzes communication and collaboration between and among crisis mappers with the purpose of advancing the study and application of crisis mapping worldwide.

FIGURE 19.4 In October 2011, Crisis Mappers Net connected 2858 participants from 129 countries

FIGURE 19.5 Crisis Mappers network member map

messages asking and offering help, which included anything from technical minutiae, to the status of key roads and bridges, to "I have grain to distribute from a nearby warehouse but need to locate fuel to get it to those most in need," and they immediately received assistance through the Crisis Mappers Network. Working in close collaboration with other networks like CrowdFlower and Mission 4636, the Crisis Mappers Network collectively helped save lives by continuously updating our collective understanding of what was taking place on the ground in near real time, thereby improving situational awareness and effective response.

Recent discussions on the Crisis Mappers Google Group indicate that the only way to continue to move forward and to revolutionize the network boils down to this: Share as much as you can, until it hurts. We learned this idea from the norms embedded by the crowd itself and its emergent participatory culture. Like individuals from other volunteer networks and their counterparts "on the ground," individuals in the Crisis Mappers network also embodied the same ethos. They have already shown an incredible willingness to share, even when it might result in personal sacrifices and hurt chances for promotion, credit, tenure, and the like. Ultimately, we agree that we have a collective responsibility to do our part to help improve our systems and workflow, enhance effective communication, and cope with a variety of ethical, security, and privacy challenges. These efforts to enhance collaboration and accountability are more important than our institutional and personal differences, inter and intra-agency competitions, and other politics within our respected professional communities.

Conclusion

It is our belief that the so-called "expert networks" work best when emulating the crowd's best practices, and in conjunction with affected populations. Crisis mapping is only one part of an emergent global participatory culture in which everyone contributes his or her own localized or specific knowledge to the global commons. However, like all participatory endeavors, crisis mapping is and will always be subject to abuse. Peaceful protesters may use platforms and social networks to help organize their campaigns while their opponents could potentially sift through available information in order to thwart their plans and identify, repress, and imprison them. Repressive regimes may also engage in the deceptive use of participatory technology in an attempt to squash their opponents. Spam is also becoming an unwieldy issue in open platforms that require additional effort to detect and mitigate rumors. Finding the signal within the noise is an ongoing problem when opening the floodgates of information. Additionally, validating user-generated content will always be an issue as well. Each deployment of a crisis map is very different and each carries with it attendant risks and a new set of ethical, security, political, and moral concerns that should always be considered before proceeding.

That said, however, we must not be quick to discard a useful tool because it can be misused. After all, throughout human history, certain individuals have used whatever medium they had available at the time to record, perpetuate, or further their malicious behavior. The maliciousness is not the fault of the medium. One cannot blame the microphone, the printing press, the video camera, or the Internet itself for the behavior of specific individuals using these tools. However, the community needs to continue to engage in ongoing conversations about the many serious issues related to privacy, security, ethics, norms, and responsibilities in order to facilitate meaningful projects and purposeful collaboration around crisis mapping.

Nothing concentrates the mind like a crisis. Crises facilitate cross-cutting collaboration between tireless individuals who offer their expertise, skills, and time to the group. Behind each crisis mapping deployment are thousands of emails and tens of thousands of lines of text from multiple Skype chats. Mappers share virtual laughs, tears, and high-fives of encouragement with one another, in a high-stress, real-time environment. These new friendships and synergistic partnerships often abide even after the crisis fades. Synergistic new projects emerge that otherwise would have never coalesced. These new partnerships accelerate the pace of change across a vast number of issue-areas, and their cumulative effect is immeasurable. The relationships themselves end up contributing the most meaningful, lasting value in a changing world.

References

Clinton, Hillary Rodham. 2010. "Remarks on internet freedom." Washington, DC: *The Newseum*. January 21, 2010. www.state.gov/secretary/rm/2010/01/135519.htm.

Dangermond, Jack. 1995. "Public data access: Another side of GIS data sharing." In H. J. Onsrud and G. Rushton (eds). *Sharing geographic information*. New Brunswick, NJ: Center for Urban Policy Research, pp. 331–339.

Fischer, Gerhard. 2009. "Cultures of participation and social computing: Rethinking and reinventing learning and education." In *Proceedings of the International Conference on Advanced Learning Technologies (ICALT)*, Riga, Latvia: IEEE Press, pp. 1–5.

Fischer, Henry W. III. 1998. *Response to disaster: Fact versus fiction and perpetuation* (2nd edn). New York, NY: University Press of America.

Goodchild, Michael. 2009. "Neogeography and the nature of geographic expertise," *Journal of Location Based Services*, 3(2): 82–96.

Greenbaum, Joan M. and Kyng, Morten. 1991. *Design at work*. Hillsdale, NJ: Erlbaum.

Hakley, Muki, Singleton, Alex, and Parker, Chris. 2008. "Web mapping 2.0: The Neogeography of the geoweb," *Geography Compass*, 2(6): 2011–2039.

Kraak, Menno-Jan. 2001. "Trends in cartography." In M.-J. Kraak and A. Brown (eds). *Web cartography: Developments and prospects*. London: Taylor & Francis, pp. 9–19.

Krygier, John. 1999. "World wide web mapping and GIS: An application for public participation," *Cartographic Perspectives*, 33: 66–67.

Lin, Rong-Gong II. 2009. "Los Angeles fire map: Mt. Wilson, Tujunga, Acton, Altadena, Pasadena, Sierra Madre," *Los Angeles Times*, September 11, 2009. www.latimes.com/news/local/la-me-la-fire-map-html,0,7464337.htmlstory.

Monmonier, Mark. 1998. "The three R's of GIs-based site selection: Representation, resistance and ridicule." In: D. R. Fraser Taylor (ed.). *Policy issues in modern cartography, modern cartography volume three*. Oxford: Elsevier Science Ltd, pp. 233–247.

Nelson, Ted, 1987 [1974]. *Dream machine/Computer lib*. Chicago, IL: Theodor Nelson.

Nourbakhsh, Illah, Sargent, Randy, Wright, Anne, Cramer, Kathryn, McClendon, Brian, and Jones, Michael. 2006. "Mapping disaster zones," *Nature*, 439: 787–788.

O'Reilly, Tim. 2005. "Web 2.0 compact definition: Trying again." 2006-10-01. O'Reilly Radar. http://radar.oreilly.com/archives/2005/10/web-20-compact-definition.html, accessed 29 October 2008.

Tierney, Kathleen J., Lindell, Michael K., and Perry, Ronald W. 2001. *Facing the unexpected: Disaster preparedness and response in the United States*. Washington, DC: John Henry Press.

Turner, Andrew. 2006. *Introduction to neogeography*. Sebastopol, CA: O'Reilly Media Inc.

Wessels, Bridgette. 2010. *Understanding the Internet: A socio-cultural perspective*. New York, NY: Palgrave Macmillan.

20

DIGITAL ACTIVISM IN AUTHORITARIAN COUNTRIES

David M. Faris and Patrick Meier

1. Introduction

Wael Abbas is a journalist. But he is also the creator of a well-known web site called Misr Digital (Misr means Egypt in Arabic), which offers a critical take on political events in Egypt, with a particular focus on human rights. Because of the activities of this web site, Abbas is not known primarily as a journalist, but rather as a practitioner of digital activism—and quite a successful one at that, perhaps best known for his role in exposing police torture in Egypt. For years he ran what amounted to a tiny, one-man press room out of his parents' house off the El-Demerdash stop on the Cairo Metro, his bedroom crammed with computer gear, stacks of papers, and camera equipment, where his phone buzzed every other minute with news from fellow activists. Abbas undertakes this craft at great risk to his personal safety, because, unlike young activists in democratic settings, his activism is aimed squarely at the transgressions of Egypt's authoritarian government. The country was governed under a state of emergency for nearly 30 years between 1981 and 2011, and periodic local, parliamentary and presidential elections were not considered democratic. Furthermore, the government and its security services not only heavily curtailed political rights, but they also placed serious restrictions on journalists (Freedom House, 2010). For activists like Abbas, this meant that not only might his actions fail to ignite the passions of his fellow Egyptians, they might also land him in jail—a place where the torture he has so ably written about might be used against him. Yet in spite of these risks, digital activists like Wael Abbas were instrumental in the protest wave that swept the Arab World—which remains the most repressive region in the world—in early 2011 and forced the government of Hosni Mubarak out of power. The ways in which new digital technologies allow activists like Abbas to challenge repressive states like Egypt is the focus of this chapter.

The past several years have witnessed several events that observers have hailed as the coming of a new digital politics in authoritarian countries. In 2009, Iranians used the microblogging service Twitter both to organize and coordinate massive demonstrations against a fraudulent presidential election. The protesters in Iran were violently repressed, leading many to dismiss the potential of digital activism in authoritarian countries (Morozov, 2010). But, in 2011, hundreds of thousands of Egyptians responded to a call to protest disseminated by two prominent groups that unquestionably began on Facebook, and, several weeks later, the thirty-year tyranny of Hosni Mubarak was history. Meanwhile, protests in other states, like Bahrain, were unsuccessful in changing the government. But, regardless of outcomes, digital technologies clearly enable rapid, many-to-many communication that can be deployed tactically in moments of crisis. But these and other forms of digital participation—Facebook groups, blogs, and text-messaging, just to name a few—offer more than just a new tool in the tactical array of activists; rather they may fundamentally alter certain types of interaction between authoritarian governments and their opponents. They also, perhaps most importantly, provide individuals with avenues to participate in public life, a venue that is mostly closed to most citizens in these kinds of environments. While levels of repression vary from regime to regime, all authoritarian regimes feature restrictions on civil and political rights that have the effect of making individuals powerless to affect change, advocate for causes, or make themselves part of political and social processes.

It is best to conceptualize digital tools not as a series of separate (and fleeting) applications, but rather as *social media networks* (Faris, 2010). Digital tools that operate through social media networks can be characterized by the following criteria—First, they operate through an individual's social network. Information travels through social media networks via friends and friends-of-friends. Second, social media networks function at very small costs to the user, typically paying for the underlying utility itself rather than the tool. For instance, the costs of using social networking sites are included in the cost of the digital device and access to the Internet. Social media networks are further characterized by multiple channels of access—in other words, they can be accessed on cell phones, computers, laptops, or any other digital device. An increasingly integrated information ecosystem is developing. Social media networks are also easy to use—they require no specialized

FIGURE 20.1 Iranian protesters congregate in Tehran for a silent demonstration (June 16, 2009)
Source: image courtesy of Milad Avazbeigi.

technical knowledge beyond basic computer literacy and feature platforms that can be mastered in minutes.

2. Digital Activism and the Collective Action Problem

Organizing coordinated dissent, protest, or direct action in authoritarian countries is a collective action problem—a dilemma of persuading individuals to contribute to the production of a public good (in this case a more democratic order) from which they cannot reasonably be excluded even if they do not participate themselves. Mancur Olson was the first to theorize that individuals will be reluctant to contribute to shared undertakings because of the costs—both direct and opportunity—of participation itself (Olson, 1965). Typically this problem has been solved by large organizations that can bring the resources to bear on problems of collective action—whether that is interest group organizations like the Sierra Club, or entities like political parties. Such groups can employ selective incentives to help individuals overcome their natural inclination to "free-ride" on the work of others. The trouble is that these large organizations come with huge price tags—offices, administrators, taxes, and more. Such organizations are particularly easy targets for repression in authoritarian countries.

How do social media networks help solve these problems? Bimber, Flanagin, and Stohl argue that three basic functions are requisite to all collective action: 1) a means of identifying people with relevant, potential interests in the public good; 2) a means of communicating messages commonly perceivable among them; and 3) a means of coordinating, integrating, or synchronizing their contributions (2005, p. 374).

Social media networks give organizers of collective action tools that were the means "to communicate in coordination with others in ways that until recently were feasible almost exclusively for formal organizations" (Bimber *et al.* 2005, p. 375). Scholars therefore argue that digital activism is challenging the older, large-scale modes of organization. Karpf, for instance, contrasts low-cost organizations like MoveOn and Democracy for America with older models and finds that the former are increasingly effective organizations that tap into the potential for new media forms to raise money, connect interested and likeminded individuals, and organize quick action (Karpf, 2009). However, in authoritarian contexts, even mobile, low-cost organizations have to contend with state interference, and may or may not be permitted to operate. Rights organizations with substantial online presences, like Egyptian Initiative for Personal Rights, have both struggled to continue organizing and acting in the face of official repression. The Hisham Mubarak Law Centre, for instance, has been the subject of attempts to close down its website, while Gamal Eid, the director of the Arab Network for Human Rights Information, was tried for defamation based on a blog entry (Protection Online, 2010). Under such conditions, it has been typically the tactical applications of digital activism that have drawn the most attention and users.

Digital activism undertaken via social media networks directly impacts the costs of connecting diffuse actors with common interests (Shirky, 2008; Diamond, 2010). Digital tools have the capability of lowering the costs of group-formation, group-joining, and information-sharing to nearly nothing. Social media networks also make it easier for members of such groups to agree upon ideas and courses of action, and dividing the labor accordingly. By lowering the cost of contribution, they make it more likely that individuals will participate in one of the many ways afforded by the technologies themselves. The ability of organizers to reduce these previously fixed organizing costs has a direct result on the calculus of the collective action problem itself—although, in non-democratic regimes, organizers must also overcome the not-inconsequential costs of repression. Short of lowering repressive costs on the activist side, organizers of collective action must rely on changes in the state's willingness or capacity to use repression to enforce order (Wickham, 2002).

3. Tactical Coordination

Mobile technologies have the effect of streamlining the tactical organization of dissent. Instead of printing flyers, leaflets, and calls to action, and then having to organize and execute meetings in physical spaces, the Internet makes it possible to take all of these actions electronically, in theory. Avoiding public planning may also reduce the repressive costs to organizers of group action by making it less likely that individual activists will be arrested for commonplace activist activities. By lowering those participatory costs, digital tools make fence-sitters more likely to get involved. Second, digital tools make it easier to coordinate. The instantaneity of communications conducted electronically, as well as the ability to conduct many-to-many communications, means that many more people can be reached in a much shorter period of time—making it possible to adjust plans on the go. Advanced "scouts" can be sent to potential sites of activism, where they can report back to group leaders about police or military presence. Both during and after collective actions, these tactical mobile technologies can also be used to contact families, lawyers, and international organizations about the disappearance of activists into state gulags. The timely dissemination of this information in some locales can be the difference between a brief detention and a weeks-long odyssey into the bowels of authoritarian repressive systems.

The greatest barrier to group action in repressive countries is not just the collective action problem, but also the additional repressive challenges faced in these contexts by anyone seeking to organize and act collectively. Even in contexts where the majority of citizens would like to see and even participate in change, individuals are afraid to participate because of the potential physical or emotional costs to themselves. In authoritarian countries this problem is compounded by the absence of available information about the intentions of individuals in our social networks. If we see those friends and neighbors supporting collective action, we are more likely to support and participate in that action ourselves. This revelation of preferences involves crossing the boundary between public and private realms (Bimber *et al.* 2005, p. 377). Timur Kuran, for example, argues that very small changes in individual support for a regime can cause a cascade effect, as more and more individuals' revolutionary thresholds are crossed. External shocks, such as an external patron declaring its intention not to use force to prop up the status quo, can affect these thresholds, in so far as they affect individual calculations for supporting the opposition, or by reducing the potential costs of revolutionary action (1991). Changes in those thresholds are particularly important because, under conditions of authoritarianism, material, interest-based calculations will rarely lead individuals to participate—organizers must provide the mobilizing rationale, the "frames" that "motivate and legitimate" collective action (Snow and Benford, 1988)—to convince individuals to engage in fundamentally risky behavior like protests.

By exponentially increasing the speed and depth of information (including processes of framing), digital activism can help instigate what are known as informational cascades—widespread changes in the attitudes and behavior of individuals. Bikhchandani *et al.* defined informational cascades as occurring when "it is optimal for an individual, having observed the actions of those ahead of him, to follow the behavior of the preceding individual without regard to his own information" (1992, p. 994). Online social networks facilitate the exchange of formerly private information about political preferences—information that is known to individuals themselves but unknown to others—which in turn makes political or informational cascades more likely. Cascades are situations in which there is a widespread and sudden change in collective attitudes, beliefs, or behavior. The widespread use of social media makes it easy for individuals to share these political preferences with one another, and therefore can have the effect, under certain circumstances, of reducing revolutionary thresholds. While authoritarian regimes have extensively monitored social media networks (and sometimes shut them off outright, as Egypt did on January 28, 2011), they have very rarely been able to shut down the information-transmission process at the heart of those networks. Under certain circumstances, the cascades triggered by this activity might lead to rapid and spontaneous collective action of the sort that generates large protest movements and in some circumstances brings down governments. And while social media networks are vulnerable to shutdown, in many circumstances the critical framing and organizing processes have already taken place by the time authoritarian elites realize there is a crisis. Thus by the time the Egyptian state shut off the Internet three days after the protests of January 25, 2011, a critical mass had already taken to the streets, and no longer needed social media networks to sustain their challenge to the regime. Activists noted that the shutdown actually backfired on the regime by driving people into the streets to seek the latest news.

Reducing costs also means making the tools easy to use for non-tech-savvy individuals. While running and hosting a web page was probably beyond the skill set of the average computer user in the 1990s, the tools of social media networks are accessible to anyone with basic computer literacy. You can set up a blog in a matter of minutes with nothing more than an Internet connection, and creating a Twitter account takes moments. The interfaces for these tools are simple, straightforward, and easy-to-navigate. As the Egyptian activist Hossam El-Hamalawy argues, "We are not IT savvy. It's true that these web 2.0 tools are increasingly becoming very easy to use, designed for the average user. I don't possess 1/10th of the IT knowledge that others have."[1] The particular platform or application used is less important than the general principle—simple, creative tools designed to help ordinary individuals produce media content, organize groups, and execute actions. The increasing density of networks making use of these technologies is a self-reinforcing process that increases the utility of these networks. Reed's Law argues that, in a "many-to-many, group-forming network, which allows network members to form and maintain communicating groups," the value of that network increases exponentially with the number of users (Reed, 2001, pp. 2–3). As the number of users of social media networks has increased in even relatively low-connectivity authoritarian societies like Egypt and Tunisia, the disruptive potential of digital activism has risen accordingly.

Castells (2007) phrases it somewhat differently, referring to the process as "the rise of self-communication" (p. 246). Rather than serving as passive recipients of information in newspapers, or, at best, as letter-writers or the lucky chosen few of the call-in satellite talk shows, the Internet turns citizens into co-producers and mediators of information. This is not exactly a new point. The difference-in-kind is that, while the state may still arrest individual writers or block web sites, with digital activism it is harder to shut down pathways of dissent—in other words you can arrest a blogger or disrupt a social media web site, but chances are that someone is still writing and distributing information about something the state would like to quash. Digital media tools, in the hands of ordinary citizens, also make it possible for citizens to document and challenge rights abuses by the state, by capturing images and videos of transgressions.

4. Digital Activism and Information Aggregation

In theory, digital tools have the potential to invert surveillance, and to make agents of the state the ones who are undergoing surveillance. The term "sousveillance" was coined by Steve Mann to describe the "ability of people to access and collect data about their surveillance and to neutralize surveillance" (Mann *et al.*, 2003). But it is quite rare for the surveilled to quite literally invert their own surveillance by monitoring the surveiller. According to the theory, it is the very act of making the watcher aware of being watched that neutralizes the surveillance. Sousveillance is thus "self-empowerment in opposition to modern technologies of surveillance" (Mann *et al.*, 2003). Foucault's original formulation of the Panopticon itself noted that it was designed to ensure in the watched "a state of conscious and permanent visibility that assures the automatic functioning of power" (Foucault 1977, p. 201, quoted in Mann *et al.*, 2003). A constantly surveilled citizenry complies even without constant enforcement from authority. Likewise, in theory, state agents subject to the possibility (if not always the reality) of sousveillance may begin to behave in ways more congruent with human rights norms.

An everyday form of sousveillance has evolved in common parlance, in which citizens turn their digital cameras and cell phone video recorders on agents of authoritarian regimes during contingent moments of crisis or contention. Whatever it is called, this form of sousveillance is less about challenging surveillance *per se*, and more about undermining narrative control. In practice, it has typically taken the form of filming or photographing human rights abuses by police and security forces at protests, demonstrations, or even during routine police actions. Such videos, photographs, and first-hand accounts have played critical roles in disseminating information about events in Iran during the unrest following fraudulent elections in 2009, and in Egypt during the street protests that ultimately forced Hosni Mubarak from power. Sousveillance is designed both to make powerful actors aware that they are being watched, and also to reach local, national, and international audiences with documentary evidence of the activities of those same actors. In the "generalized sousveillance society," it is individuals who now possess the power to collect and distribute information (Ganascia, 2010).

Of course, repressive regimes are not powerless in the face of digital activism. In the lead up to Egypt's parliamentary elections in the fall of 2010, the government closely monitored the use of the Ushahidi platform to independently observe the elections. Ushahidi is an African-based non-profit technology company that develops free and open-source software for live mapping—the platform crowdsources information by integrating SMS, Twitter, Facebook and other applications. The Ushahidi platform has been used to monitor elections in Kenya, the Sudan, Lebanon, and Afghanistan amongst other countries. In the fall of 2010, Mubarak prevented official international election groups from monitoring the elections. In collaboration with Freedom House, an Egyptian human rights group therefore launched a project called U-Shahid (you "witness"), which used the Ushahidi platform to monitor the Egyptian elections. Egyptian security services found out about the project very early on, before it was even made public. They tapped the phones and intercepted emails of those involved in the project and called the director in for questioning. They then detained two members of the staff for several days, regularly followed staff and prevented an employee of Freedom House to enter the country. Interestingly, however, the project was allowed to continue and proved to be one of the most successful applications of the Ushahidi platform for citizen-based election observation. The Egyptian group running the project was able to document 2700 individual reports of election violations, including hundreds of pictures and videos documenting the election irregularities. Perhaps surprisingly, this project spawned several copycats in the lead up to the election, with four additional Ushahidi platforms popping up, including one run by the Muslim Brotherhood.

Perhaps the Egyptian group got lucky. Not so in neighboring Sudan. Following the spectacular fall of Ben Ali in Tunisia and Mubarak in Egypt, Sudanese protestors in Khartoum were eager to replicate this success in the Sudan. Just a few days after the January 25 march in Egypt, a Sudanese Facebook group appeared calling for protests in Khartoum on January 30. Thousands of activists in the Sudan and elsewhere joined the Facebook group. On the day, those in Khartoum headed to the location specified on Facebook and were promptly arrested, beaten, and tortured. It turns out the Facebook group in question was set up by the Sudanese government as a trap

(Meier, 2009). Repressive regimes are not getting dumber; they are becoming more sophisticated in leveraging social media networks to further their own ends.

The Sudanese activists ran into what Dan Schultz and Andreas Jungherr have called "The Trough of Disillusionment" in the hype cycle of any new technology or application (2010, p. 35). They argue that "Those who joined with unrealistic expectations will leave with numerous complaints." While digital activism offers new avenues for participation in authoritarian societies, it also creates new ways to get arrested and puts pressure on states to respond in kind and to protect their entrenched interests. In sum, it is important to remember that the application of technology can be used for both good and ill. Repressive regimes have never stood idly by when their powers have been challenged throughout history. They too can leverage technologies to repress, survey, and censor.

Yet repressive regimes are more centralized and hierarchical organizations than civil society networks. Decision-making structures in the former are more rigid since only a very small elite can make decisions. This means that repressive regimes are large bureaucracies that do not adapt or innovate rapidly relative to more hybrid and decentralized organizations like civil society networks. Learning and adaptation are key to surviving rapidly changing environments. In sum, while the new possibilities afforded by new digital technologies are an important part of the equation, knowing how to use and adapt these technologies, integrate them tactically and strategically, and learn quickly are important factors that will determine the future of the cat-and-mouse game between repressive regimes and popular resistance movements.

But just because regimes are less nimble does not make them powerless. In fact, the Egyptian government, recognizing the power that Wael Abbas has accumulated through his digital empire, tried him in absentia in early 2010 on the mysterious charges of selling communications devices without a license. The embattled Abbas, however, has continued writing and creating Twitter posts for his legion of followers. More importantly, other digital activists organizing under the same set of demands and principles put out the call for protests on January 25, 2011—protests that eventually succeeded in toppling the dictatorship of Hosni Mubarak. Because of successes like those that can be claimed by digital activists in Egypt and elsewhere, the coming years are likely to see more vigorous and coordinated state responses to digital activism—from trials and prison terms to sophisticated surveillance tactics and partnerships with the private sector designed to interfere with free expression. However, as Tom Glaisyer has argued, "to date, digital activism has not been completely eliminated in any state where it has been able to gain a foothold (2010, p. 97). Even with arrests and repression taken into consideration, digital tools have opened up stable avenues of expression and dissent in many authoritarian countries, which might have unpredictable effects on future politics (Faris, 2010).

Case Heaven, Data Hell

For all of the rich cases, stories, and anecdotes collected by scholars, journalists, and practitioners over the past ten years, we still lack the kind of data that might help us make more rigorous predictions and come to more complete understandings of how digital activism in repressive environments works. Scholars lacking datasets are forced either to use indicators that at best measure secondary effects (like World Bank indicators) or to reason from single cases. The lack of mixed methods research in the study of digital activism is perhaps the biggest handicap that the field faces (Meier, 2009).

Many of the debates in the field of digital activism are based on strings of anecdotes. Some rigorous qualitative case studies do exist but their cumulative impact on our understanding of the dynamics of digital activism is limited. These case studies use different methodologies and focus on different questions and time periods. The limited empirical research that does is largely limited to highly aggregated proxy indicators. This means that the study of digital activism is easily hijacked by debates based purely on the biased use of anecdotes. The lack of data-driven analysis also means that perceptions of digital activism are based on the outcomes of a small number of spectacular cases, like Iran's Green Revolution. That the activists were unable to dislodge the entrenched Iranian state from power does not mean that their efforts were meaningless or that digital activist networks should be abandoned.

The field of conflict analysis had similar origins. But some important data development since the 1990s has enabled political scientists to go beyond vague statements on the causes of conflict to more empirically grounded statements. This was only possible when mixed-methods research was an option thanks to the availability of datasets on conflict event data. Comparable datasets on digital activism and repression are needed if the study of digital activism is to mature and inform both practice and policy. This is why the recent initiative by the Meta-Activism-Project (MAP) is an important milestone in the field. MAP is a non-traditional think tank that promotes empirical, data-driven research to better understand the impact of digital networks on social power. The ultimate goal of MAP is to make digital activism a more effective means of achieving a transparent, democratic, and participatory global society. To this end, MAP launched the Global Digital Activism Data Set (GDADS) in response to Patrick Meier's call for more data-driven research (Meier, 2009). The dataset initiative represents the first serious attempt to "quantitatively study digital activism as a global phenomenon. It is an all-volunteer project to create an open case study database under a Creative Commons license that will be accessible to scholars and activists around the world." The dataset currently includes over 1000 cases, which are being coded and analyzed using an innovative coding framework specifically designed for the study of digital activism.

Conclusion

This chapter has sought to outline the opportunities and challenges of digital activism in repressive environments. Individuals are becoming increasingly empowered thanks to new social media networks. To be sure, digital technologies clearly enable rapid, many-to-many communication that can be deployed tactically in moments of crisis. But these and other forms of digital participation—Facebook groups, blogs, and text-messaging, just to name a few—offer more than just a new tool in the tactical array of activists; rather they may fundamentally alter certain types of interaction between authoritarian governments and their opponents. This necessarily changes the dynamics of state–society relations. These new technologies are dramatically reducing the costs of communication, greatly facilitating recruitment and group formation, and thus influencing the calculus of collective action. That said, repressive regimes are becoming increasingly savvy in their ability to manage the impact of the information revolution. And, of course, these regimes also have recourse to their monopoly of violence. We have argued that digital activists in Egypt and elsewhere are increasingly turning to sousveillance in order to push back against the power of the state and thereby create more transparency. The ability to organize, innovate tactically, and adapt rapidly is key in digital activism. It remains to be seen whether repressive regimes can alter their hierarchical organizational structure to make more effective use of changing technologies or whether this pressure to adapt will force authoritarian states to become more democratic over time.

Note

1   From an interview I conducted with El-Hamalawy in Cairo, Egypt, May 27, 2009.

References

Bikhchandani, Sushi, Hirshleifer, David, and Welch, Ivo. 1992. "A theory of fads, fashion, custom and cultural change as informational cascades," *Journal of Political Economy*, 100(5): 991–1026.

Bimber, Bruce, Flanagin, Andrew J., and Stohl, Cynthia. 2005. "Reconceptualizing collective action in the contemporary media environment," *Communication Theory* 15(4) (November): 365–388.

Castells, Manuel. 2007. "Communication, power and counter-power in the network society," *International Journal of Communication*, 1: 238–266.

Diamond, Larry. 2010. "Liberation technology," *Journal of Democracy* 21(3) (July): 69–83.

Faris, David. 2010. "Mediating tyranny: Reimagining authoritarian media systems in the digital age." Paper presented at the American Political Science Association Conference in Washington, DC. September 2–5, 2010.

Freedom House. "Egypt." *Freedom in the World 2010*. www.freedomhouse.org/template.cfm?page=22&year=2010&country=7816

Protection Online. 2010. "Gamal Eid, Ahmed Seif El Islam Hamad and Amr Gharbeia, human rights activists and blogger respectively: to be tried before a criminal court." Protection Online. July 20, 2010. www.protectionline.org/Gamal-Eid-Ahmed-Seif-El-Islam.html

Ganascia, Jean-Gabriel. 2010. "The generalized sousveillance society," *Social Science Information*, 49: 489–507.

Glaisyer, Tom. 2010. "Political factors: Digital activism in closed and open societies." In Mary Joyce (ed.). *Digital activism decoded. The new mechanics of change*. New York, NY, and Amsterdam, the Netherlands: International Debate Education Association, pp. 85–98.

Karpf, Dave. 2009. "Unexpected transformations: The Internet's effects on political associations in America" (PhD Dissertation), University of Pennsylvania.

Kuran, Timur. 1991. "Now out of never: The element of surprise in the East European revolution of 1989," *World Politics*, 44(1): 7–48.

Mann, Steve, Nolan, Jerry, and Wellman, Barry. 2003. "Sousveillance: Inventing and using wearable computing devices for data collection in surveillance environments," *Surveillance and Society* 1(3): 331–355.

Meier, Patrick. 2009. "The impact of the information revolution on protest frequency in repressive contexts." Paper presented at the 50th International Studies Association Conference in New York City, February 15–17, 2009.

Morozov, Evgeny. 2011. *The net delusion: The dark side of internet freedom*. New York, NY: PublicAffairs.

Olson, Mancur. 1965. *The logic of collective action*. Cambridge, MA: Harvard University Press.

Reed, David P. 2001. "The law of the pack," *Harvard Business Review* (February): 2–3.

Schultz, Dan and Jungherr, Andreas. 2010. "Applications: Picking the right one in a transient world." In Mary Joyce (ed.). *Digital activism decoded: The new mechanics of change*. International Debate Education Association, pp. 33–46.

Shirky, Clay. *Here comes everybody: The power of organizing without organizations*. New York, NY: Penguin Press, 2008.

Snow, David A. and Benford. Robert D. 1988. "Ideology, frame resonance and participant mobilization," *International Social Movement Research*, 1: 197–219.

Wickham, Carrie Rosefsky. *Mobilizing Islam: Religion, activism and political change in Egypt*. New York: Columbia University Press, 2002.

21

ACTIVISM ON THE GROUND

Habitat for Humanity

Cynthia Hawkins

Possibly one of the biggest misconceptions about Habitat for Humanity is that it's a charitable organization gifting homes to families in need. It's far more accurate to say that Habitat for Humanity depends upon participatory culture to help keep the cost of building a home low enough as to be affordable for qualifying homeowners. Participants, including the new homeowners themselves, volunteers, and a support staff from the Habitat organization, work together to build a house from the ground up and ready it for occupancy.

When I set out to explore in more detail the nature of participatory culture as it pertains to Habitat for Humanity, I asked Vice President of Development and Communications for Habitat For Humanity San Antonio, Stephanie Wiese for two things: the opportunity to interview a pair of willing homeowners who were on the verge of completing their house and a first-hand look at what they and the other volunteers do on site. Wiese sent me a map, a list of build dates, and a time when I could meet Wiese at the build so that she could introduce me to homeowners to interview.

From the moment I made my way up the new neighborhood street crisscrossed by volunteers in matching shirts and shook Antoinette and Henry's hands, the homeowners at the center of the narrative that follows, I knew I'd be laying sod with my notepad in my back pocket. Participatory culture, especially one that's galvanized for a good cause, is infectious. So I asked my questions as we worked and paused now and then in the shade of the eaves or by the curbside table lined with water bottles to write down the answers.

What I discovered in the process was that Antoinette, Henry, and the volunteers seemed more comfortable in an environment that was less of an interview and more of the sort of conversation that takes place every day on the site. I might have been the only one preparing a story that day, but I wasn't the only one asking questions. Many of the volunteers asked each other about their lives, their work, and their reasons for volunteering. They asked questions of Henry and Antoinette about the home and their plans, and Antoinette and Henry likewise wanted to know more about this fresh batch of volunteers who'd shown up to assist them that day. This too is part of participatory culture, that sense of community and connection developing over the course of the project. It was one of the most organic interviews I'd ever conducted. No prepared questions. No back and forth over a recorder. Just some friendly conversation, a lot of sod, a little cake, and this story:

August 7, 2010

Antoinette and Henry picked the color themselves. Lemon yellow. White trim. The siding echoes the vast line of the horizon. The broad even blue of the sky reflects across each window. When I imagine their paint brushes trailing across the trim around the doors, I imagine their work in reverse from the paint to the siding to the insulation to the framework to the concrete slab they must have stood on in wonder back in March. It is August, the hottest month of summer thus far, the temperature even this early in the morning poised to reach one hundred degrees.

"That was really hard to do, that siding," Henry says.

"Oh, it wasn't that bad," a volunteer with his name, Doug, on masking tape peeling off his shirt adds with a smile. Turns out it wasn't this house Doug had nailed siding on. It was another on the same block. Habitat for Humanity of San Antonio in Texas facilitates the building of whole neighborhoods at a time, expanding into its grid of new streets until it becomes a completed little community of people who've all worked to build their own homes, of neighbors who've grown to know each other with hammers in their hands. In 2010, Habitat for Humanity of San Antonio will have built fifty-four homes. Previous to this, 628 homes have been built since their inception. It wasn't this house Doug hung the siding on he realizes in a squint at the yellow color, but he assures me as he pulls his T-shirt collar up to catch the sweat on his chin it's all the same work. He takes up the wheelbarrow handles and moves past us.

"But that's done, and all we have left, really, is the grass," Henry says.

Antoinette rakes rocks across the dirt and into a pile in a corner where the fence and the house butt against each other. In a small eddy of dust, she nudges the pile in tighter and explains how she wishes she could show me the inside, complete with the exception of a few last-minute details, but it's locked. She and Henry will get their keys, she says, when construction is complete and they sign the papers at closing. "I can't wait," she says with a broad smile. "Sometimes it seems like it's gone by fast, and then sometimes it seems like forever." After dragging one last small chunk of concrete across the dirt, she straightens and asks, "Where'd the wheelbarrow go?"

★ ★ ★

As a young married couple, Antoinette and Henry have split time living together at their respective parents' homes, one then the next, while looking for an affordable place of their own. Antoinette works the early morning shift at a membership warehouse store. Henry sells tickets at an area tourist attraction. It was while he was at a job-training center, entertaining thoughts of moving on to a different line of work, that he spotted a flyer for Habitat for Humanity of San Antonio.

"It's unbelievable," Antoinette says, "how expensive homes are. Even really small ones. There was just no way until we heard about this."

Habitat for Humanity of San Antonio's president at the time of this interview, Dennis Bechhold, likes to say that the Habitat model isn't a charitable handout, but rather a "hand up." After meeting certain requirements, including having at least three years' verifiable income and the ability to make a feasible down-payment, homeowners invest a minimum of 300 hours of hands-on work on their own homes, assisted by volunteers.

"We finance the homes ourselves," Bechhold explained to me. "We have a twenty year, 0% interest mortgage. The average payment, including taxes and insurance, is under $400 per month. The principle that we collect is put back into the program."

"We applied, and they accepted us," Antoinette says with her brows raised, her breath held for just a second, and on the exhale she adds with a glance at the charming yellow home that had only months ago seemed impossibly out of reach, "and here we are."

★ ★ ★

A square of grass in my hands, thumbs rubbing its cool underside of damp dirt, I carry it with a sag in the middle as if it were some kind of opened, oversized compendium from a library stand. I drop it at my toes with a slap of sound, a waft of dry earth, and give it a nudge against the adjacent square. Each time my fingers instinctively press into the grass to give the square a gentle tap before I step out of the way of the volunteer waiting behind me with her own bowed swath of sod. This does nothing, this tap, but I do it anyway as if this gesture will secure its destiny to grow lush underfoot and be mowed again and again, and slowly rise from the indentations of footfalls. Without direction or discussion we've fallen into a pattern together, moving in a line past the wheelbarrow and down the last barren strip of dirt, dropping our squares one after the next, filling in our path.

After I dust my hands of the last square I carried, I move around the side of the house to the front. I'd left my water bottle on a table set up at the curb. A six-foot-five man in a floppy hat, casting an impressive shadow, had loaned me a red Sharpie with which to scrawl my name on the bottle. It had just enough ink left for the first three letters, but I kept going, tracing through the bottle's fresh perspiration. In less than an hour it has gone as warm as tap water, half of my name sliding off. The plastic pops in my hands, shimmers in the full sun, as I drink and admire the house's cheery façade.

Down the street: tables at the ends of driveways, clusters of volunteers, hard hats and hammers, water coolers and Dixie cups and bottles, machinery with dirt packed in the treads. In a squint you might mistake this for a festival in the making. Everyone's laughing. Laughing or smiling. A rivulet of water carries a dead, dried leaf around my shoe sole in the gutter. The front lawn is finished. A woman with canvas slacks bagging around her sneakers angles a garden hose over the solid green. When the wheelbarrow, full of sod once more, makes its way from the palette of sod in front to the back, I follow it along with the straggle of other volunteers, all of us quickly falling in line again.

"Have you gotten to know many of the volunteers?" I ask Antoinette.

"Not really," she says. "They're not always the same volunteers."

Habitat for Humanity of San Antonio hosts an average of 10,000 volunteers per year on their build sites doing a variety of work from hammering to landscaping to providing lunches. Sometimes they arrive in groups with matching shirts and hats. Sometimes they arrive on their own accord. But they all arrive under the guidance of a detailed, hand-drawn, and copied map of otherwise unmapped streets newly carved into what had been an unused field littered with broken bottles and tires. Now signs point the way for volunteers to park on one of the last empty lots. If it looks like a festival in the making, it feels like one as well, a parade of volunteers making their way on fresh asphalt to a check-in table in the shade of an awning, everything orchestrated for ease.

Antoinette tells me how the volunteers often rotate from one house to another on different days. This surprises me because all morning I'd assumed the volunteers knew each other, and Antoinette and Henry, very well. They converse easily. They laugh at each other's jokes. They offer knowing nods. And I'd also thought the woman in overalls and the kerchief tying her hair back, the one ahead of me in the line, was a veteran volunteer. As I followed her with my square, I'd said, "So you've been doing this awhile."

"All morning," she answered.

"I mean, volunteering for Habitat."

"Oh! No," she breathed, dropping her square in the dirt. "This is my first day."

I think it was something about the way she didn't give the grass a gingerly tap or perhaps the way she moved, chin-tucked, with purpose that made me think she was as an old pro.

"Do you work with landscaping or construction for a living?" I asked.

"No," she laughed. "I work for an investment firm. I've never done anything quite like this before. But I've always wanted to. I've always wanted to volunteer here. I was just waiting for a free weekend."

Maybe Antoinette will never see the overalls woman again, but that square of grass under the kitchen window that she scooted into place will forever be here. That one and every fifth square around the tool shed and down the north side of the house and one right by the patio.

Bechhold noted that this is one of the extraordinary things about Habitat. "They're working with and getting to know people they might never know otherwise," he said, adding that in many cases some volunteers "stay in contact with the families."

Once the backyard has a double-rowed border of solid grass, our group proceeds in a checkerboard pattern of dirt and sod. When we're halfway through, the oversized man in the floppy hat peers over the chain-link fence from the neighbor's and says, "Looking good. Except, well … you all laid it side-by-side instead of end-to-end." The volunteers around me stop and assess the checkerboard pattern, bringing shirt hems to their glistening faces, brows furrowing under sunglasses.

"Oh no," someone whispers. "Do we take it up and do it all over again?"

"Isn't it just like the yard over there?" another offers.

After some mumbling discussion, someone passes word back. "He's just kidding."

"Wait." A volunteer, under a shelter of hands over his eyes, peers at the oversized man next door. "You were kidding?"

"Ah!" The man laughs. "Now you're getting to know me!"

"What did he say?" A woman in a white tank top asks. "Do we have to do it over?"

"He says he was just kidding," was the answer.

After a long pause, the woman in white twists her ball cap on her head, grabs some sod, and smiles in a lopsided grin that lingers.

★ ★ ★

Henry and Antoinette press into the sliver of shadow under the eaves, the tips of their muddied sneakers still in the full sun, one row of fresh sod bristling around their toes. I join them, my back against the siding. We're waiting for the wheelbarrow to come around again. The frame of another house goes up in the adjacent lot, a grid of two-by-fours dissecting the cloudless sky, a symphony of hammer thwacks punctuating a mock property dispute.

"You better get your shovel back inside your fence line!"

"What. This fence line here? Or is it here?"

If it weren't for the laughter ricocheting off the concrete slab under the rubber feet of ladders they would have fooled me.

"Are they still at it?" one volunteer asks me.

"Sounds like it," I answer.

She laughs, shakes her head, and makes way for the wheelbarrow coming through.

"That was you not too long ago," I say to Antoinette with a nod toward the beginnings of the house next door.

Antoinette's eyes grow big. "I can't believe it," she says. "I can't believe we did that."

Antoinette and Henry have full-time jobs. When their shifts end, they come here to build their house. They've had many long days, she tells me.

"Did you ever stop back then and think, 'What have I gotten myself into?'"

She laughs. "Oh, yes. Especially the first day. It was rough."

"It was a lot harder than I thought," Henry adds. "I could barely drive the nails all the way in at first."

"But it got better every day," Antoinette says.

"It got better. We got used to it," Henry says.

"And it must have helped when you saw the volunteers showing up to work with you," I add.

"Thank God for them," Antoinette nods.

It has been a dizzying spectacle, one she's enjoyed, she tells me, meeting people, talking to the press, shaking hands with the mayor on the local nightly news. "I didn't know they were recording me right then," she laughs. "I thought it was practice or something and that they'd record the real thing later. I can't watch it, but my sister has it on tape!"

I try to imagine Henry and Antoinette after all the hard work, after all the excitement subsides and they find themselves in their quiet living room or kitchen, looking out the windows at this same backyard, empty of the rest of us. The house leader comes over to ask where they might like to set up a picnic table and chairs when they move in. If they can point out such a spot, he'll make sure to fill this area in all the way, he explains. Though it's hard for me to imagine what comes next for Henry and Antoinette, Antoinette wastes no time raising a finger toward an area diagonal from the back step. "That's where we'll sit," she says in response. The house leader nods his approval.

We step into the sun again and join the line of volunteers at the wheelbarrow. One by one, we take our turns lifting a square of grass by grabbing either side, letting the middle sag, and one after the next we drop the square on a barren patch of dirt.

★ ★ ★

August 20, 2010

Bits of grass stick to the sweat down my 2-year-old daughter's legs as she sits in the shadow of the family clustered under an umbrella. She empties my tote-bag on the lawn of a Habitat home completed maybe a year ago. A sippy cup. A string of beads. The folded map of this neighborhood. My cell phone. She squashes it to her cheek and says, "Hello?" My 9-year-old daughter picks up the map and fans herself. "Where are the people you met?" she asks me, and I nod toward Antoinette and Henry in line. Behind us, behind the fence, two small dogs wear a narrow tread in the backyard, nose at patches of grass, and curl up in the shade of a picnic table. In front of us, on the other side of the street, a Habitat for Humanity San Antonio board member explains the significance of the Bibles and the toolkits he's about to hand out as a gift to the new home owners, assembled at the end of the stage, ready to receive them along with a certificate honoring their accomplishments.

One week after the sod was laid in Henry and Antoinette's lawn, they stand with their hands crossed and wait for their turn—Antoinette in a dress, Henry in slacks and shoes that catch the glint of the sun. When their names are called, Antoinette steps to the microphone and unfolds a piece of paper shaking in her fingers. She'd told me the day we'd carried squares of sod side by side that she was nervous about this very moment.

This is one of the only house dedications Bechhold as president has had to miss since he began working at Habitat nine years ago, though celebrations like this are his favorite part of the job. "This is a time that we recognize the families for their hard work," he explained to me, "dedicate their new home, and bless them as they start on a new phase of their lives."

He likes to tell the story at the dedications of a transition his family once made from Arkansas to Texas.

FIGURE 21.1 During the past thirty-five years, Habitat for Humanity has built more than 400,000 affordable homes
Source: Cynthia Hawkins

"A lot of things had happened in our lives over those years in Arkansas," he'll say at dedications, "and as we were leaving the house for the very last time, my wife was the last person out of the house. She said that as she took that doorknob in her hand, all of the memories we shared there came flooding back to her. She says that even now she can close her eyes and feel the doorknob in her hand and experience those same memories. I know as our Habitat families come to their new home for the very first time and take the doorknob in their hand and, with each turn, witness that impossible dream become a reality, that, just like my wife, they'll never forget that moment."

In the pause just before Antoinette starts to speak, I realize the hammers have fallen silent. All of the volunteers are here, clustered in the street around the stage. Antoinette begins by thanking them, and as she attempts to express what this day means to her she stops mid-sentence, swallows, and dots the corner of an eye with her curled finger. Henry takes the paper, squints at it, tries to find the spot where she'd left off. When he doesn't do it justice quickly enough, they both laugh as Antoinette fans her hand for the paper to be passed back to her.

"That's them?" my daughter asks me in a whisper as the little one sprawls out flat in the grass at my feet and the small crowd claps at the end of Antoinette's speech.

"That's them."

After one last prayer and round of applause, Antoinette and Henry invite us to join them around the corner at the little yellow house with its white porch rails tied with balloons. My daughters sit on the porch under the front windows and share the large piece of cake Antoinette's family give them. The little one, cross-legged and ruddy-cheeked, waits for her turn with the fork. The older one holds the plate. The balloons bump together in the breeze. A line of well-wishers snake past us to shake Antoinette and Henry's hands in congratulations and move on to the next open house. You can still see the seams between the individual squares of sod on the lawn, but one of these days it'll all come together and the seams will be gone. The hammers strike up their even rhythms again at the other end of the street.

PART VII

Rethinking Education in the Age of Participatory Culture

22

PARTICIPATIVE PEDAGOGY FOR A LITERACY OF LITERACIES

Howard Rheingold[1]

People act and learn together for a rich mixture of reasons. The current story that most of us tell ourselves about how humans get things done is focused on the well-known flavors of self-interest, which make for great drama—survival, power, wealth, sex, glory. People also do things together for fun, for the love of a challenge, and because we sometimes enjoy working together to make something beneficial to everybody. If I had to reduce the essence of *Homo sapiens* to five words, "people do complicated things together" would do. Online social networks can be powerful amplifiers of collective action precisely because they augment and extend the power of ever-complexifying human sociality. To be sure, gossip, conflict, slander, fraud, greed, and bigotry are part of human sociality, and those parts of human behavior can be amplified, too. But altruism, fun, community, and curiosity are also parts of human sociality—and I propose that the Web is an existence proof that these capabilities can be amplified, as well. Indeed, our species' social inventiveness is central to what it is to be human. The parts of the human brain that evolved most recently, and which are connected to what we consider to be our "higher" faculties of reason and forethought, are also essential to social life. The neural information-processing required for recognizing people, remembering their reputations, learning the rituals that remove boundaries of mistrust and bind groups together, from bands to communities to civilizations, may have been enabled by (and may have driven the rapid evolution of) that uniquely human brain structure, the neocortex (Dunbar, 1993).

But I didn't start out by thinking about the evolutionary dynamics of sociality and the amplification of collective action. I started out by experiencing the new ways of being that Internet social media have made possible. To me, direct experience of what I later came to call virtual communities (Rheingold, 2000) preceded theories about the ways people do things together online. In the 1980s, I was part of what we called "the Electronic Networking Association," a small group of enthusiasts who thought that sending black and white text to BBSs with 1200 baud modems was fun.

By the early 1990s I had begun to branch out from BBSs and the WELL to make connections in many different parts of the world. The fun of talking, planning, debating, and helping each other online came before the notion that our tiny subculture might grow into a worldwide, many-to-many, multimedia network of a billion people. We started to dream about future cyber-social possibilities only after personally experiencing something new, moving, and authentic in our webs of budding friendship and collaboration. In recent years, cyberculture studies has grown into a discipline—more properly, an interdiscipline involving sociologists, anthropologists, historians, psychologists, economists, programmers, and political scientists. Back when people online argued in 1200 baud text about whether one could properly call what we were doing a form of community, there was no body of empirical evidence to serve as a foundation for scientific argument—all theory was anecdotal. By now, however, there is plenty of data.

One particularly useful affordance of online sociality is that a great deal of public behavior is recorded and structured in a way that makes it suitable for systematic study. One effect of the digital Panopticon is the loss of privacy and the threat of tyrannical social control; another effect is a rich body of data about online behavior. Every one of Wikipedia's millions of edits, and all the discussion and talk pages associated with those edits, is available for inspection—along with billions of Usenet messages. Patterns are beginning to emerge. We're beginning to know something about what works and what doesn't work with people online, and why.

Does knowing something about the way technical architecture influences behavior mean that we can put that knowledge to use? Now that we are beginning to learn a little about the specific socio-technical affordances of online social networks, is it possible to derive a normative design? How should designers think about the principles of beneficial social software? Can inhumane or dehumanizing effects of digital socializing be mitigated or eliminated by better media design? In what ways does the design of social media enable or prevent heartfelt *communitas*, organized collective action, social capital, cultural and economic production? I've continued to make a direct experience of my life online because online media made it possible to connect with people who shared my interests, even if I had never heard of them before, even if they lived on the other side of the world. But in parallel with my direct experience of the blogosphere, vlogosphere, twitterverse, and other realms of digital discourse, I've continued to track new research and theory about what cyberculture might mean and the ways in which online communication media influence are shaped by social forces.

The Values of Volunteers

One of the first questions that arose from my earliest experiences online was the question of why people in online communities should spend so much time answering each other's questions, solving each other's problems, without financial compensation. I first encountered Yochai Benkler in pursuit of my curiosity about the reason people would work together with strangers, without pay, to create something nobody owns—free and open-source software. First in "Coase's penguin" (2002), and then in *The Wealth of Networks* (2006), Benkler contributed to important theoretical foundations for a new way of thinking about online activity—"commons-based peer production," technically made possible by a billion PCs and Internet connections—as a new form of organizing economic production, together with the market and the firm. If Benkler is right, the new story about how humans get things done includes an important corollary—if tools like the PC and the Internet make it easy enough, people are willing to work together for non-market incentives to create software, encyclopedias and archives of public-domain literature.

While the old story (Olson, 1971) is that people are highly unlikely to cooperate with strangers to voluntarily create public goods, the new story seems to be that people will indeed create significant common value voluntarily, if it is easy enough for anybody to add what they want, whenever they want to add it ("self-election"). There is plenty of evidence to support the hypothesis that what used to be considered altruism is now a byproduct of daily life online. So much of what we take for granted as part of daily life online, from the BIND software that makes domain names work, to the Apache webserver that powers a sizable chunk of the world's websites, to the cheap Linux servers that Google stacks into its global datacloud, was created by volunteers who gave their creations away to make possible something larger—the Web as we know it.

To some degree, the explosion of creativity that followed the debut of the Web in 1993 was made possible by deliberate design decisions on the part of the Internet's architects—the end-to-end principle, built into the TCP/IP protocols that make the Internet possible, which deliberately decentralizes the power to innovate, to build something new and even more powerful on what already exists. Is it possible to understand exactly what it is about the web that makes Wikipedia, Linux, FightAIDS@Home, the Gutenberg Project, and Creative Commons possible? And, if so, can this theoretical knowledge be put to practical use? I am struck by a phrase of Benkler's from his essay in this book: "We must now turn our attention to building systems that support human sociality." That sounds right. But how would it be done? It's easy to say and not as easy to see the ways in which social codes and power structures mold the design of communication media.

A Participative Pedagogy

To accomplish this attention-turning, we must develop a participative pedagogy, assisted by digital media and networked publics, which focuses on catalyzing, inspiring, nourishing, facilitating, and guiding literacies essential to individual and collective life in the 21st century. Literacies are where the human brain, human sociality, and communication technologies meet. We're accustomed to thinking about the tangible parts of communication media—the devices and networks—but the less visible social practices and social affordances, from the alphabet to TCP/IP, are where human social genius can meet the augmenting power of technological networks. Literacy is the most important method *Homo sapiens* has used to introduce systems and tools to other humans, to train each other to partake of and contribute to culture, and to humanize the use of instruments that might otherwise enable commodification, mechanization and dehumanization. By literacy, I mean, following on Neil Postman and others, the set of skills that enable individuals to encode and decode knowledge and power via speech, writing, printing, and collective action, and which, when learned, introduce the individual to a community.

Literacy links technology and sociality. The alphabet did not cause the Roman Empire, but made it possible. Printing did not cause democracy or science, but literate populations, enabled by the printing press, devised systems for citizen governance and collective knowledge creation. The Internet did not cause open-source production, Wikipedia or emergent collective responses to natural disasters, but it made it possible for people to act together in new ways, with people they weren't able to organize action with before, in places and at paces for which collective action had never been possible. Literacies are the prerequisite for the human agency that used alphabets, presses, and digital networks to create wealth, alleviate suffering, and invent new institutions. If the humans currently alive are to take advantage of digital technologies to address the most severe problems that face our species and the biosphere, computers, telephones and digital networks are not enough. We need new literacies around participatory media, the dynamics of cooperation and collective action, the effective deployment of attention and the relatively rational and critical discourse necessary for a healthy public sphere.

Media Literacies

In "Using participatory media and public voice to encourage civic engagement," I wrote:

> If print culture shaped the environment in which the Enlightenment blossomed and set the scene for the Industrial Revolution, participatory media might similarly shape the cognitive

and social environments in which twenty first century life will take place (a shift in the way our culture operates). For this reason, participatory media literacy is not another subject to be shoehorned into the curriculum as job training for knowledge workers.

(Rheingold, 2008, pp. 99–100)

Participatory media include (but aren't limited to) blogs, wikis, RSS, tagging and social book-marking, music-photo-video sharing, mashups, podcasts, digital storytelling, virtual communities, social network services, virtual environments, and videoblogs. These distinctly different media share three common, interrelated characteristics:

Many-to-many media now make it possible for every person connected to the network to broadcast as well as receive text, images, audio, video, software, data, discussions, transactions, computations, tags or links to and from every other person. The asymmetry between broadcaster and audience that was dictated by the structure of pre-digital technologies has changed radically. This is a technical-structural characteristic.

Participatory media are social media whose value and power derives from the active participation of many people. Value derives not just from the size of the audience, but from their power to link to each other, to form a public as well as a market. This is a psychological and social characteristic.

Social networks, when amplified by information and communication networks, enable broader, faster, and lower-cost coordination of activities. This is an economic and political characteristic.

Like the early days of print, radio, and television, the present structure of the participatory media regime—the political, economic, social, and cultural institutions that constrain and empower the way the new medium can be used, and which impose structures on flows of information and capital—is still unsettled. As legislative and regulatory battles, business competi-tion, and social institutions vie to control the new regime, a potentially decisive and presently unknown variable is the degree and kind of public participation. Because the unique power of the new media regime is precisely its participatory potential, the number of people who participate in using it during its formative years, and the skill with which they attempt to take advantage of this potential, is particularly salient (Rheingold, 2008).

I believe that a participatory culture in which most of the population see themselves as creators as well as consumers of culture is far more likely to generate freedom and wealth for more people than one in which a small portion of the population produces culture that the majority passively consume. The technological infrastructure for participatory media has grown rapidly, piggyback-ing on Moore's Law, globalization, the telecom bubble, and the innovations of Swiss physicists and computer science students. Increasingly, access to that infrastructure—the ability to upload a Macaca video or uncover a threat to democracy—has become economically accessible. Literacy—access to the codes and communities of vernacular video, microblogging, social bookmarking, wiki collaboration—is what is required to use that infrastructure to create a participatory culture. A population with broadband infrastructure and ubiquitous computing could be a captive audi-ence for a cultural monopoly, given enough bad laws and judicial rulings. A population that knows what to do with the tools at hand stands a better chance of resisting enclosure. The more people who know how to use participatory media to learn, inform, persuade, investigate, reveal, advocate, and organize, the more likely the future infosphere will allow, enable, and encourage liberty and participation. Such literacy can only make action possible, however—it is not in the technology, or even in the knowledge of how to use it, but in the ways people use knowledge and technology to create wealth, secure freedom, resist tyranny.

Note

1   This essay was originally published in Joi Ito's (2008) anthology *Freesouls: Captured and Released*. It has been modified for inclusion in this book.

References

Benkler, Yochai. 2002. "Coase's penguin, or Linux and the nature of the firm," *Yale Law Journal*, 112(3): 369–446.

Benkler, Yochai. 2006. *The wealth of networks: How social production transforms markets and freedom*. New Haven, CT: Yale University Press.

Benkler, Yochai. 2008. "Complexity and humanity." In Joi Ito (ed.). *Freesouls: Captured and released*. http:// freesouls.cc/essays/06-yochai-benkler-complexity-and-humanity.html.

Dunbar, R. I. M. 1993. "Coevolution of neocortical size, group size and language in humans," *Behavioral and Brain Sciences*, 16(4): 681–735.

Olson, Mancur. 1971. *The logic of collective action: Public goods and the theory of groups*. Cambridge, MA: Harvard University Press.

Rheingold, Howard. 2000. *The virtual community: Homesteading on the electronic frontier*. www.rheingold.com/ vc/book/.

Rheingold, Howard. 2008. "Using participatory media and public voice to encourage civic engagement." In W. Lance Bennett (ed.). *Civic life online: Learning how digital media can engage youth*. The John D. and Catherine T. MacArthur Foundation Series on Digital Media and Learning. Cambridge, MA: The MIT Press, pp. 97–118. doi: 10.1162/dmal.9780262524827.097.

23

LEVERAGING DIGITAL MEDIA TO CREATE A PARTICIPATORY LEARNING CULTURE AMONG INCARCERATED YOUTH

Barry Joseph and Kelly Czarnecki

Few would differ with the notion that all youth deserve a good education. This chapter will speak about one innovative attempt to improve the education of two groups of youth, within youth jails, through the innovative application of digital media. Are there concerns or questions already forming in you mind? If so, good, as this report is less about what we did than about the questions we too had to face, how we worked through them, and how the lessons learnt might inform others similarly engaged. Before we describe the project and what we faced, we will first introduce you to the theoretical questions underlying our efforts, the unique form this report will take, and the broader initiative that framed this one project.

In October 2006, Henry Jenkins and colleagues helped shed light on the new hidden curriculum, powered by the informal use of digital media, creating a new divide between youth prepared with the skills required to succeed in the new century and those being left behind. The report *Confronting the Challenges of Participatory Culture: Media Education for the 21st Century* defined a participatory culture as one in which there are "relatively low barriers to artistic expression and civic engagement, strong support for creating and sharing one's creations, and some type of informal mentorship whereby what is known by the most experienced is passed along to novices" (Jenkins *et al.*, 2009, p. 3). A new gap was emerging, Jenkins argued: the participation gap.

Five years later, we are no longer just focusing on questions pertaining to digital media access (e.g. the digital divide) but, increasingly, inequalities in access to opportunities for participating in cultures supporting the development of these new competencies and social skills (e.g. the participation gap). Jenkins and colleagues look to afterschool programs and informal learning communities to take the lead transforming educational practices to support participatory cultural practices, given their ability to change in contrast with the resistance often found within formalized learning environments. As a participatory culture shifts the focus from one of individual expression to one of community involvement, the development of these new literacies "involve social skills developed through collaboration and networking" (Jenkins *et al.*, 2009, p. 4). Collaboration is as much a valuable tool utilized within participatory culture as a desired educational outcome. The Partnership for 21st Century Skills, for example, defines collaboration as working effectively and respectfully with diverse teams, exercising flexibility and willingness to make compromises to accomplish a common goal, and assuming shared responsibility for collaborative work while valuing individual contributions.

Allan Collins and Richard Halverson's book *Rethinking Education in the Age of Technology* offers one framework for developing such participatory cultures within afterschool programs. Within their list of the enhancements digital media offers for educating learners are "multimedia," "publication," and "reflection." In short, digital media provides learners with new ways to express themselves (multimedia), share that expression with real audiences and demonstrate their learning in legitimate contexts outside the classroom (publication), and engage in meaningful reflection built into the learning environment (reflection). The Partnership for 21st Century Skills takes a similar approach, promoting youth to develop the ability to create media products which demonstrate their understanding and ability to use "the most appropriate media creation tools, characteristics and conventions."

Afterschool programs can combine these two—collaboration and self-expression—to develop a participatory culture. Furthermore, the transition from the privacy of the program's learning environment to a public collaboration and sharing of youth media creates new challenges and opportunities crucial for youth to learn to navigate. Jenkins and colleagues refer to this as the Ethics Challenge, resulting from "the breakdown of traditional forms of professional training and socialization that might prepare young people for their increasingly public roles as media makers and community participants" (Jenkins *et al.*, 2009, p. 3). Howard Gardner's GoodPlay Project at Harvard focused on digital media and ethics, valuing two key related literacies—privacy and participation—which arise as youth increasingly interact in public online spaces. Developing literacies related to privacy and participation requires learning "the meaning of responsible conduct and citizenship in online communities." So, developing educational programs that leverage digital media to engage youth in collaborative and self-expressive media practices provide opportunities to develop ethical behaviors fit for our new digital age.

But what happens when the youth in question have been judged by society to be lacking in ethical behavior, to, in fact, be incarcerated in youth jails due to crimes committed? How can a participatory culture be created within an institution where self-expression is discouraged, where the idea of collaborating with adults and fellow incarcerated youth in other jails challenges key assumptions and structural components of the institution's culture and practices? The following worked examples will explore how one collaboration, within and among youth at two youth jails, sought to create a participatory culture while negotiating the edge point where the potential of digital media and learning ran into conflict with existing cultural practices and norms.

Worked examples are a new approach to scholarship pertaining to digital media and learning practices. The practice is best articulated by James Paul Gee in his March 2010 report for the MacArthur Foundation, *New Digital Media and Learning as an Emerging Area and "Worked Examples" as One Way Forward*. Those engaged with building the emerging fields of Digital Media and Learning (DML)

> would publicly display their methods of valuing and thinking about a specific problem, proposing them as examples of "good work" in order to engender debate about what such work in DML might come to look like and what shape the area itself might take. The goal would not be for the proposed approach to become the accepted one but for it to become fodder for new work and collaboration.
>
> *(http://tinyurl.com/workedexamplesreport)*

As such, these are not case studies, *per se*, describing something the authors did that others should copy. Rather, they are more concerned with explaining why the authors did what they did, rather than how, and what they had to negotiate to get there.

Finally, before learning more about the actual project and getting into the details of the worked examples, some context might prove useful to understand why certain program decisions were made. This work with incarcerated youth was performed not in isolation but within a broader collection of innovative digital media programs, called the Edge Project, coordinated by Global Kids, Inc. Global Kids is a New York City-based educational non-profit that supports urban youth to become global citizens, community leaders, and successful students. The Edge Project was a Global Kids initiative funded by the MacArthur Foundation with the goal of expanding the capacity of civic and cultural institutions to use new media as innovative educational platforms that engage youth in learning and promote youth civic participation. More specifically, the Edge Project is interested in civic and cultural institutions bringing cutting-edge digital media into their youth educational programs. It is equally interested in where this type of programming—due to technology, its pedagogical implications, or both—is a disruptive force challenging the educators and/or the institution to work on the edge of their comfort level. There is a balancing act they must undertake, being receptive to how new media challenges their current educational culture and practice while, in turn, challenging the educational potential of new media through interacting with that very culture and practice. At the end of the day, Global Kids seeks to better understand the following questions: How do institutions find their balance working on this edge? And do different types of institutions respond in different ways?

To be clear, those speaking about innovative practices often use the term "edge" in a different way, as if contrasting, say, the center of power and those outside it, as in John Hagel and John Seely Brown's assertion: "To transform the core, start at the edge." We mean something else. Picture the edge of a knife, sharply dividing two things inextricably linked. Better yet, picture the edge where the ocean (the vast potential of digital media for learning) washes up on the beach (the hard but ever shifting cultural practices and norms of institutions), an edge that is never the same from one moment to the next but is continually in play as forces press from either side. We are cognizant, as well, of Clayton Christianson's work on innovation, such as his book *Disrupting Class*, which contrasts "sustaining innovations," which build on existing innovations to meet the needs of current markets, with "disruptive innovations," which create new markets and redefine the measure of success. The Edge Project leans towards the latter, attempting to introduce "disruptive innovations" into civic and cultural institutions.

While there is a wide range of new media practice within civic and cultural institutions, the Edge Project deliberately selected a common set of criteria for its programs to distinguish it from other initiatives and contextualize its findings. The primary sites of learning were not online but in person, facilitated by an adult within the institutions. The programs were all informed by youth development and youth media pedagogies. Finally, the program designs were focused less on scale and breadth and more on innovation and depth, with the understanding that developing good theory through iterative practice is just the first step towards scalable designs.

The Edge Project explored these questions over two years (2009–2011) through a series of short-term educational projects developed and implemented in partnership with a variety of national civic and cultural institutions that are exemplars within their communities of practice. These demonstration projects were designed to challenge institutions to incorporate one specific form of digital media into their ongoing youth programs and to do so in a way that builds upon the organization's existing strengths and interests. In addition, the program designs were geared to address the specific needs of the organization and its constituencies, and to highlight how the organization serves as a leader within its professional networks, whose work in this area can provide a model from which others can learn. The projects all aimed to conclude with at least one worked example, such as this, to explore how each went to their "edge" to support learning through digital media.

The first Edge Project was named uCreate.

1. uCreate: Working on the Digital Edge with Incarcerated Youth

uCreate was the first completed Edge Project and took place within two jail facilities in the US. While most states have separate juvenile detention and adult jails, North Carolina treats sixteen- and seventeen-years-olds as adults within the judicial system. Therefore, they can be held within adult jails for pre-trial detention but are housed in separate youthful offender sections. In Madison, Wisconsin, however, youth sixteen and younger are held in separate facilities and treated as minors.

Libraries and library services offered at juvenile detention centers, jails, or prisons serve some of the same purposes as public libraries do in our communities. Empowering people through access to information, whether it be fiction, law books, videos, or audiobooks, is a key goal of the library. Advancing knowledge and expanding minds through resources that people might not otherwise be exposed to in their schools or at home is another important mission of many libraries. Most public libraries also provide technology access, whether it is through videogaming, robotics, Internet, or movie creation. Libraries serving the incarcerated population also help to give people something productive and meaningful to do with their time.

While public libraries can help towards keeping many people off the streets, especially teens, by offering afterschool activities, jail and prison libraries can provide materials that bring people's minds to a place other than their current situation, which may help ease stress, boredom, and pressure. As one participant in the uCreate program wrote, "Well i really like what we are doing its a chance to get out of the cell block" (KB, February 18, 2010).

In development from November 2009 through January 2010, uCreate ran for six weeks between February and March 2010. Young adult males, ages sixteen to nineteen, met twice a week, from 9 a.m. to 11 a.m., within their facilities. Global Kids, centered in New York City, had a collaborative history with the Charlotte Mecklenburg Library in Charlotte, North Carolina, which, in turn, had collaborated with the library staff within a local facility, Jail North. For over a year, the three partners had used the virtual world of Teen Second Life, in a project funded by the Robert Wood Johnson Foundation, to support youth in Jail North to develop social entrepreneurial skills.

When Global Kids approached the librarians about a follow-up project, they recommended the project expand to include the Madison Public Library in Madison, Wisconsin, who shared a similar relationship with their local youth jail, the Dane County Jail. With the second jail on board, it became clear that the program could leverage collaboration as both a powerful incentive for participation and a key component of the intended educational outcome. Efforts to bring in other jail systems, however, fell short. For example, while numerous individuals throughout the New York City juvenile justice system expressed great interest—from the youth jail on Riker's Island to staff at half-way houses—policies that prevent youth from accessing the Internet or even computers, under any circumstance, made their "edge" impossible to work around.

In the end, there were seven youth aged eighteen and nineteen in the uCreate program at Jail North. At the end of the six weeks, that number dropped to three (some due to losing interest in the program, taking a work study class that conflicted with the time of uCreate, or being sent to another jail during the program). At the Dane County Jail, there were three youth ages sixteen and eighteen, and all three stayed the length of the program.

The plan was always to work with incarcerated youth to develop their digital media skills in order to tell personal stories about critical choices they have faced. The specific educational objectives, the required digital media to meet them, and the exact nature of how youth would collaborate within and amongst the jails to bring a participatory culture into the jail library, however, was an evolving conversation that took many turns and changed many times in the lead up to, and even during, the program. Through weekly phone conferences and the use of Google docs, the curriculum was jointly created, and helped bring the theme and focus together along with what software, hardware, and other resources would be used to accomplish each task. In addition, the curriculum was flexible enough that the facilitators at each site were able to modify the workshops to meet the needs of their site, either in advance or during the program.

The use of digital media typically involves sharing, collaborating, and expressing oneself publicly. Because of the constraints in place at the jail facilities, this wasn't always possible. However, we were often able to navigate around those boundaries and modify the program so that it would fit the needs of the jail and allow the participants to still use various digital media.

It was anticipated that most, though not all, of the participants in uCreate would return to the community after serving their sentence.

The following three worked examples will each highlight one form of youth media produced in the program, define the edge points that emerged as pedagogies and practices came into conflict, and explore how those points were negotiated. These edge points tended to form around two sets of forces, the specifics of which will be detailed within the examples.

In general, however, one set of forces encouraged the use of digital media for learning. These included pedagogies and cultures found within public libraries, youth media practices, and Global Kids, which, in a general sense, aims to empower youth through the critical consumption of digital media and its production. The second set of forces constrained the use of digital media for learning. These included the jail's need to maintain control over the lives of the inmates within their care, the youth's needs to successfully navigate the judicial system, and the youth's needs to not create a digital trail that would unintentionally follow them, and potentially harm them, later in their lives. This conflict should not be viewed as a description of a good side versus a bad, of progressive versus regressive forces. Rather, this is simply a description of the interplay of a variety of institutions and its players, each trying to meet their own desires and objectives, and what happens when digital media and learning gets caught up within its web.

2. Worked Example: Synchronous vs. Asynchronous Collaboration—Virtual Worlds and Voicethreads

The original plan for uCreate was to bring the youth together in a common third space, a virtual world, to leverage their unique abilities to offer embodied experiences and bring people together from remote locations. We envisioned giving the youth the skills they needed to build in collaboration their own virtual world, populate it with thematically related digital media they would produce in the program, then, once they left, open it up to the public to experience, their offering to the world. We soon encountered two obstacles, each, with its own resolution, shaping the rest of the project.

First was the question of whether the youth from the two sites should be allowed to be in the world at the same time. Concern was raised about live interaction amongst the youth. Within such an open environment, might the conversations go every which way, leaving the facilitators unable to moderate it quickly enough? And how could the schedules be coordinated, especially given the time zone difference of one hour? Given time, this might have all been resolved—for example, the conversation topics might need additional structure—but we just agreed to have the youth represent themselves through their creations, to be left for the other group to visit on their own.

As a result, moving forward, the collaboration and communication between the jails would be limited to asynchronous means, as you will see. At first, this seemed to be a poor use of the affordances of virtual worlds. However, that concern was rendered moot with the second obstacle: the virtual world unexpectedly announced, the week before Christmas and three weeks before the launch of uCreate, that they were closed for business.

That was one edge we couldn't cross. As a result, the outline of the program was restructured to use a range of social media tools, whose companies we further gambled would last until the end of the project, and link them together to create one larger project. In the end, this was in good alignment with our switch to asynchronous collaboration, as many of the tools that would be used afforded such opportunities, such as the first project, Learning Ecology Maps shared through VoiceThread.

Learning Ecology Maps are a practice developed by Global Kids through work with their own youth. It emerges from the recognition that digital media is challenging what learning looks like, when it happens, where and with whom. Take Tashawna for example, a Global Kids youth leader in New York City. Tashawna is a high school senior in Brooklyn, New York. In the morning she leaves home for school listening to her MP3s, texting her friends about meeting up after school at Global Kids, where she participates in a theater program, or FIERCE, the community center for Lesbian, Gay, Bisexual and Transgendered youth. On the weekend she'll go to church and, on any given day, visit MySpace and Facebook as often as she can. While she misses television and movies, she says she just can't find the time.

This describes what we can call Tashawna's distributed learning network, the most important places in her life where learning occurs. Not just at home, school and church but also through digital media, like MP3s, SMS, and social networks, and at youth-serving institutions, like Global Kids and FIERCE. Some are places that require her presence, like school, while others are self-directed, like MySpace. But the learning she gathers across the nodes in her network are preparing her to succeed in ways no one node could do on its own.

And Tashawna is not alone. In part due to the changes in education, in part due to the affects of digital media, youth have a wide array of options for learning knowledge and developing skills. But how many youth feel in charge of their networks, or are even aware they exist as an interconnected whole? How do they learn to synthesize what they learn and communicate it to future employers and college admission staff who won't learn of their strengths on most school transcripts?

The Learning Ecology Maps are a step in the direction of supporting youth to visualize their distributed learning network, develop language to talk about it, and increase their ability to intentionally structure and navigate their way around it. To create the maps, youth are asked to list all of the places in their lives where they learn. It is left to the youth to determine how to define "places" and "learn." After an iterative process in which youth share drafts of their list and eventual maps, a final map is produced, such as Tashawna's below:

Once the map is created, that is just the beginning. Youth are then asked to discuss and annotate their maps, to provide a tour, as it were. As the youth could not communicate synchronously between the jails, an asynchronous solution was found with VoiceThread. VoiceThread is a free, easy to use, online social media tool that affords the ability to link together digital media assets in an online presentation and offer guided text or voice narration. Finally, these maps were designed to be used as the foundation for the program so that at the end of the six weeks they could discuss how they incorporated what, how, and where they learned about digital media into their maps. The maps were also used as reflection tools throughout the six weeks when they focused on their critical choices throughout their lives.

Within the VoiceThread, the text narration read as such:

> This is my learning map and I'm going to try to explain it to you. Well first, if you can't tell what that figure standing in the middle is, thats my attempt to draw a brain. And if you have any questions as to what he's doing or what he's holding, then the answer is simple as well. The brain is fishing for knowlegde with a passion as guess you could say by the expression on his face.

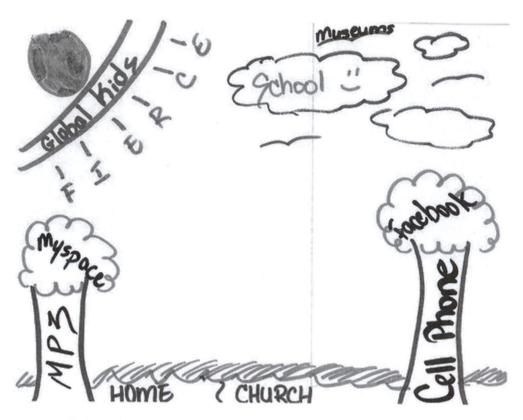

FIGURE 23.1 Tashawna's Learning Ecology Map describes the most important places in her life where learning occurs

The images at the top of the picture are the tree most used and most effective ways that I learn. The T.V. repesents the things i learn from watching the news, history channel, natgeo, discoverychannel, C-SPAN, and CNN. OH, and include ESPN as well, i'm a real sports junkie. The T.V comes first not because it's the most important, but because it's the one that I seen every day. No matter what I'm looking at the new at least once a day.

Image number two is a book, an encyclopedia to be more specific. It's second only because I dont always get a chance to the paper or abook but now that I think about it I also read when I watch T.V. Hmm, well I did make that realization until now, thats another good reason I'm explaining this to you. So I would definetly say reading is my most important method learn, and I'm sure many would agree when I say it's probably in every bodies top three. If you think about it we all read something every day even if its not in abook or paper, there's commercials T.V. wich consit of deals and prices ussually ignorantly hyperbolized.

Amongst other things, it is worth noting how through the very act of presenting his map, through teaching another how to view it, he has a moment of realization (about his multitasking books with television) that is then encoded into the presentation itself: "well I did [not] make that realization until now, thats another good reason I'm explaining this to you." He is aware that he is "explaining it," in part, so that he can make "realizations."

The use of VoiceThreads to share their maps forced us to address three different edge points.

Edge Point 1: Barriers to Collaboration

Viewers of a VoiceThread are offered multiple ways to annotate each segment of the presentation with text and even voice, allowing the youth the opportunity to comment and question each other's presentation, to turn an activity focused on self-expression into an opportunity to collaborate. Throughout the project we found that monitoring the guys while they were leaving comments was helpful, otherwise they typically seemed to say something inappropriate (i.e. 'trash talking') or would leave a one-line phrase such as "that's cool, man." It wasn't that these comments were necessarily inappropriate because we were in a jail, it was more that we were trying to further develop how they could look at the media and respond to it. We would not only monitor, but also give them prompts such as: What do you like about it? What do you have a question about? They often verbally articulated within the classroom their first reaction to the project in greater detail than they would in an audio or text comment. As the comments became more of a dialogue, the youth learnt how to make more appropriate comments.

Being able to comment through digital media forced uCreate to work on the edge as the ability to collaborate within a jail environment is severely curtailed, even more so with the outside world or into another jail. For example, talking in the hallways is not allowed in order to minimize any fights that might break out if someone says something that might upset another. If the guys are in a classroom such as the library, they are not allowed to look out the windows into the hallway where others might be passing by. They need special permission to work on a project together outside of the classroom. This is often difficult. Permission might be granted at one level of authority yet, due to a lapse of communication, never get approved at the next level.

Comments on each other's projects were not only provided by the youth but by the facilitators as well. Global Kids staff, for example, viewed the VoiceThread entries and responded via text or audio. The staff chose to use real photos of themselves for their representation, unlike the youth who used the letters of their initials or screen name initials. This real-life element actually made some of the youth comment that they wanted to carry on a conversation directly with the Global Kids staff, to get to know them better. While this was a natural response in a social interaction, the jail could not permit incarcerated youth to enjoy unmoderated, open-ended conversations with people physically outside the system, even designated educators. As such, VoiceThread's limited comment capabilities forced the youth's conversation with Global Kids staff to be confined to details about their projects while excluding a lot of open-ended, personal dialogue.

At the end of the day, the educational forces pushing collaboration successfully used VoiceThread as a communications device that could function within the required strictures of the jail and its need for isolation.

Edge Point 2: Informal Learning vs. Formal Learning

uCreate was unusual for most if not all of the youth in the program in how it situated digital media production within an educational setting. When it comes to digital media, they usually experienced it, before their incarceration, as largely youth- and interest-driven. They used it because they wanted to use it, not because someone told them they had to.

uCreate was a far cry from their educational experiences as well, both inside and outside the jail. In a GED class offered within the institution, we often observe youth learning to "game the system," doing the work to meet not their own expectations but those of the teacher and program. They will ask questions like, "How many pages do you want me to write?" and "Tell me what I need to know to pass the test."

As a result, uCreate forced its participants, on one hand, to sacrifice the freedom they were used to with digital media while, on the other hand, affording them opportunities for personal expression rarely experienced within traditional educational programs. So while we had to restrict youth's access to the full learning potential of digital media, we also had to empower them to use the resources we were making available. Throughout the design and implementation process, we tried to be very aware of how we would present the information to the participants so that their project wasn't the result of what they thought we wanted to hear. Since the use of digital media was in a pretty controlled environment, and, thus, somewhat artificial in terms of how they might use it at home or a public library space, they might naturally have felt that we were looking for a certain product or response. We wanted to steer clear of them feeling like they had to give us a "right" answer, as well as "us" being perceived as the teacher and them as the student. Rather, we tried to foster a more natural response in using the technology as if they were in an unregulated environment.

We did this by giving them broad instructions for their activity and supporting them to apply the lessons in the best ways they saw fit. We showed them a previously created learning map, for example, but then encouraged them to complete their own. If they expressed interest in responding in an unanticipated manner, such as through the video response to GK described below, we could support them to do so. We also tried to create an atmosphere where they didn't feel like they were being negatively judged or graded and offered opportunity to display their developing skills and knowledge. The participants at Jail North, for example, were encouraged to informally present their work to one another, providing feedback while gaining confidence in their ability to express their ideas within the group.

Edge Point 3: Usernames

Finally, the youth were encouraged, but not required, to create a public username that differed from their own when expressing themselves throughout the program through various public digital media tools. When using a thumbnail graphic to represent themselves online, particularly when leaving comments on VoiceThread, the guys chose to use their initials, either their real initials or the initials of their chosen username.

Not choosing one's real first and last name is not unique to the jail setting; it would be encouraged in a program given at the public library as well. One of the differences though is the impact it could create if there is information from their stories that talk about why they are in jail. We felt it was important to protect them from this by having them choose a username that is not their own. The pseudo-anonymity provided by these online social media tools allowed each youth to be identified with, and take pride in, their public expressions, yet provided distance from the work should its content prove damaging were it linked back to them in unintended ways in the future. This solution seemed to strike an effective balance between the edge formed by the inclination of a digital media program to publicly share work and the needs of incarcerated youth to maintain a level of anonymity.

3. Worked Example: Eyes without a Face—Videos

In order to communicate with the youth in uCreate, we planned for scheduled Skype video sessions, which would allow jail library staff and Global Kids staff to coordinate and allow the latter to interact in real time with the incarcerated youth. Since the technology didn't work at Jail North (it seemed to have been blocked), Global Kids created a video to introduce themselves, the organization, and the role they had in the program. The video can be watched here: http://tinyurl.com/ucreatevideo.

In response to viewing the video, Jesse, the librarian from the Madison Public Library who worked with the youth at the Dane County Jail, posted in the private section of uCreate web site the following:

> The MAD crew appreciated your video introduction so much they asked if they could record a response. After discussing how this could be done with the teacher, we had KB (the 16 year-old who cannot be filmed) record it and the other two talked. I just sent you the video and will not post here as the teacher expressed great concern that it not be posted online or shown outside of the uCreate program. I'm sure they'd dig any other chances you guys have to interact, whether it is another video or perhaps a live stream. It's nice that they now have a feel for who is responding to their posts too.
>
> *(http://projectedge.ning.com, February 3, 2010)*

To create this video, however, entailed working on the edge.

Edge Point: Self-Expression vs. Forced Anonymity

Note that Jesse described the youth known as KB as "the 16 year-old who cannot be filmed." These were not public videos to be shared on a site like YouTube. They were strictly designed for site-to-site communication. Yet still the correctional center would not give permission for an underage youth to show his face in a video. If it was live, and presumably unrecorded, Skype video would have been fine but recorded video was deemed pushing the envelope too far.

This was not our expectation at the outset. At Jail North, for example, we drafted a form for the youth to give their permission to be on camera if they wanted to record such things as their learning map or timeline while having their face visible. This form was preliminarily approved by the librarian at Jail North, but later rejected by the sheriff, even for those 18 and older, as this was such uncharted territory.

In the end, it was okay to bring in the Flip camera and film audio and video of the guys, just not their faces, even if they gave permission to do so. Recording their voice without showing their faces seemed like a workable solution. In fact, it encouraged the youth to not just be behind the camera but literally holding it, filming their program.

But whether it was the overage youth showing their faces or the underage youth revealing only their voice and viewpoint, we can't show you their video. In other words, the video for this segment of the worked example exists. It is the video produced by the youth. It was viewed by the intended audience. You, the reader of this worked example, unfortunately, cannot view it, as you were not part of that audience. And perhaps that's the point. It need not be publicly shared to have educational impact for the youth who produced it, as long as it was shared site-to-site. In fact, this worked example can best make this point by not showing you the artifact, by, in fact, highlighting its absence.

4. Worked Example: Protecting Privacy—Comics

Bitstrips is a dynamic online comic creator, where expression, background, and movement can be translated online and shared through its own social network. We thought it would be a perfect tool, towards the end of the six weeks, to explore comics and graphic novels as a form of storytelling. To develop some comic literacy we brought in examples from the public library, talked about the range of content graphic novels covered, and explored the variety of artistic expression.

Edge Point: Protecting Youth vs. Supporting Youth Decisions

Social media like Bitstrips are often used by people to explore their identities. Because the youth in the program were incarcerated, there were limitations on how far these typical aspects of digital media could be publicly explored. However, sometimes it seems that being in jail is the only thing they want to talk about. It is ever present and causes them to define who they are.

We always encouraged the youth not to use the reason why they were in jail as a subject matter or, if they did, to be vague about it. This was partly to protect them, as they were pre-trial, and if they revealed anything about their case, especially on the social space of the Internet, it possibly could be used against them in a court of law. Confidentiality about their charges was important. Another reason was to help them see themselves as part of a different future, one which had nothing to do with being in jail but, rather, being a productive member of society.

However, it wasn't always cut and dry regarding what they could and couldn't say, or should and shouldn't say, in regards to their lives as incarcerated youth. There wasn't much precedent to reference in regards to using digital media in this manner within these two jails, much less any jail facilities. To complicate it further, some of the youth were eighteen and over, rather than minors, who theoretically could give their permission to say or do what they wanted within reasonable boundaries, even if that meant referring to why they were in jail.

Throughout the project, we tried to remain cognizant of what the youth revealed about themselves without compromising either their identity or security. As we did not want to squash their ability to use digital media to represent themselves, this was often a fine line to tread. Laying down ground rules such as "choose a screen name that is not your real name" was something fairly easy to do and abide by. Most all of the participants knew what a screen name was and had already had one they used on sites such as YouTube or MySpace before they were incarcerated. Other times, the guys self-regulated themselves. During the session where they used GarageBand to come up with lyrics related to a critical choice, they found it difficult not to swear. Even though this wasn't mentioned as a ground rule before they began free-styling, they immediately came to the conclusion we desired, that it wasn't appropriate to incorporate swear words. Provided with the right opportunity and context it seems they could, at times, figure out an appropriate level of self-restraint and self-censorship.

5. What We Learnt

Previous to uCreate, Kelly Czarnecki, the librarian from the Charlotte Mecklenburg Library, had worked with the incarcerated youth at Jail North, during which the youth accessed Teen Second Life, created a MySpace page, and wrote blog posts. Yet before starting uCreate, she had concerns that accessing the Internet might be a problem, as it had been some time since the youth had accessed a computer. Could they reign in their pent-up passions, staying focused and on task? Would the actual work of the program be able to compete with the flash of the digital media? In fact, this proved not to be a challenge at all and, instead, protecting their privacy became a key issue that needed to be addressed quite frequently.

She had to deal with many of the questions explored above, such as if their screen name could include their real name, or if they could create a comic depicting why they were incarcerated. She and her colleagues were forced to ask, time and again, where should the line be drawn between personal expression and collaboration and personal safety. Upon reflection, Kelly said if she ran a similar program in the future, she would like to anticipate issues of privacy coming up more often in regards to communicating over such a public forum. She doesn't believe everything has to be decided in advance—there should be ample opportunity for discussions with the youth about their consequences of putting certain information online—but perhaps some could be more cut and dried regarding what is okay to share online and what is best to keep within the classroom.

The skills the youth developed throughout this six-week collaboration not only exposed them to skills needed for the 21st century workforce but also gave them the opportunity to play with media they might be interested in pursuing as a hobby, such as creating music or reading comics. The librarians hoped that, for both those who return to the public and those who remain in the system, the youth would increasingly view the public library as a positive place for them to pursue a broader range of skills and opportunities through digital media than they might previously have imagined.

In the beginning we posed the following question: How can a participatory culture be created within an institution where self-expression is discouraged, where the idea of collaborating with adults and fellow incarcerated youth in other jails challenges key assumptions and structural components of the institution's culture and practices? We hope these worked examples offered a variety of practical answers, perhaps of use to others, and demonstrated the negotiation of edge points that was required as essential steps towards building the participatory culture experienced by the incarcerated youth within the uCreate program. We would be pleased if these Examples offered hope to others who similarly struggle to use digital media, regardless of context, to create their own participatory learning cultures. Finally, to reiterate the goals of worked examples, as defined by James Paul Gee, they should "publicly display… methods of valuing and thinking about a specific problem, proposing them as examples of 'good work' in order to engender debate." Now that you have read these written words, please move online to WorkedExample. org, find this report, post your comments, and help shape the emerging fields of learning through digital media.

Let the debate begin.

References

Collins, A. and Halverson, R. 2009. *Rethinking education in the age of technology: The digital revolution and schooling in America*. New York: Teachers College Press.

Gee, J. P. 2010. *New digital media and learning as an emerging area and "worked examples" as one way forward*. Cambridge, MA: The MIT Press.

The Global Kids Edge Project. 2011. http://projectedge.ning.com/, accessed January 5, 2010.

The GoodPlay Project. 2011. www.goodworkproject.org/research/goodplay/, accessed January 5, 2010.

Jenkins, H., Clinton, K., Purushotma, R., Robinson, A. J., and Weigel, M., 2006. *Confronting the challenges of participatory culture: Media education for the 21st century*. Chicago, IL: John D. and Catherine T. MacArthur Foundation.

The Partnership for 21st Century Skills. 2004. www.p21.org/, accessed January 5, 2010.

24

THE EXPANDING ROLE FOR MEDIA LITERACY IN THE AGE OF PARTICIPATORY CULTURES

W. James Potter

The media literacy movement is primarily concerned with helping individuals understand more fully the nature of their interactions with the media and thereby to exercise more control over their exposures, their meaning construction, and the influences the media exert on their beliefs and behaviors (Potter, 2004). Each year these goals of the media literacy movement grow in importance as the media themselves have evolved into a new media environment that consumes our time, our attention, and even our lives to a much higher degree than ever before.

A key element in this new media environment is the expansion of participatory cultures that are coalescing around all kinds of interests—political, religious, economic, and purely personal. The new media environment offers a wide range of interactive platforms that allow people to move beyond merely accessing an enormously wide range of messages and to contribute their own messages. Thus people are no longer only receivers of professionally produced messages but they are also pulled into interactions with all kinds of message producers—some identifying themselves, some not; some credible, some not; some ethical, some not. Thus the interactive nature of the new media environment increases the challenge to the media literacy movement. This increased challenge forces us to confront two fundamental questions. First, what does "mass" media mean in this new media environment? Second, what are the additional challenges for media literacy in the new media environment? This chapter is structured to address each of these two questions.

What Does "Mass" Media Now Mean?

Scholars have struggled over the years with providing a definition for "mass" media and "mass" communication (Potter, 2009a, 2009b). In this section, I'll first show why it has been such a challenge to define "mass" media, then I'll analyze the new media environment for key characteristics that require a new conceptualization of the mass media. This task is important to establish a basis for recommendations about the expanding role of media literacy, which is addressed in the final section of this essay.

Development of the Idea of "Mass" Media

A common—and relatively simple—way of defining the mass media has been to list the major media of information dissemination. As each new medium has come along, it was easy to add them to the list, which grew from books, magazines, and newspapers to include film, recordings, radio, broadcast television, and cable television. However, in the past two decades with the rise of personal computers and the digitization of information, the boundaries that made each medium distinct have become significantly blurred. Now it is no longer useful to define the mass media simply by listing certain technological channels. Instead, we need to focus attention on the particular characteristics of communication technologies and how they are used in order to provide a useful definition of "mass" media.

What are the key characteristics of a technology that would make a channel of communication qualify as a "mass" medium? The answer to this question lies in how the technology makes it possible to disseminate information quickly to a relatively large number of people. Each new mass medium started with a technological development that gave senders of messages the ability to reach wider audiences and to do so more quickly than was previously possible (Innis, 1951; McLuhan, 1964; Noll, 2007). The earliest of these technological innovations was the printing press in the 15th century, which greatly expanded the reach of the printed word. Then, with the rise of newspapers and magazines, information was made available to people beyond elites to a more general population and did so more quickly.

At the turn of the 20th century, the new media of recordings and film continued to make all kinds of messages available even faster and to a wider range of people—even those who could not read. Then, with the introduction of radio and television, information access was no longer a problem; messages of all kinds were made available to everyone in the general population whether they could read or not. Now with the widespread use of personal computers followed by other new communication technologies, anyone in the general population can access any kind of information at any time.

New Media Environment

We now find ourselves in a media environment unlike any we have ever experienced before. The newest technological developments of personal computers, the Internet (with Wi-Fi and broadband fiber-optic connections), cell phones, and other handheld portable devices for connecting to messages and other people have not just changed society but have changed the older, more traditional media themselves. This new media environment is characterized by the four inter-related features of technological convergence, interactivity, information saturation, and a shift in marketing.

Technological Convergence

Media convergence is the movement away from distinct media channels toward a common platform where all kinds of messages are shared (Jenkins, 2006; Nayar, 2010). The common platform thus allows the user to access words, pictures, video, and audio as well as to send his or her own text and voice messages. Nayar (2010) argues that all media are now crossover media, which means that they all adapt and borrow from each other. "Movies merge into computer games, and computer games generate fan sites, movie plots, and toys; advertisers use computer gameworlds. … A cell phone serves as an email device … as a camera, a movie-making device, a conferencing facility, and a personal diary" (p. 2). Not only are the media reconfigured but society is also reconfigured where "computer-mediated communication becomes the dominant form of social interaction" (p. 3). This convergence has been made possible through a process of what Bolter and Grusin (2000) call remediation, where all media copy the functions and strategies of one another. That is, when one medium is successful in serving a particular audience need, the other media quickly try to follow suit by offering up the same types of messages and services.

This convergence is also a product of the conglomeration of media ownership. Jenkins (2003) explains: "Technological convergence is attractive to media industries because it opens multiple entry points into the consumption process and at the same time, enables consumers to more quickly locate new manifestations of a popular narrative" (p. 284). Thus companies who own many platforms of mass communication can achieve economies of scale by spreading out the cost of producing a message across many different outlets; that is, once they have paid to have a message produced they send it out through the newspapers, magazines, cable channels, and Internet sites they own or control and generate revenue through each of these channels.

Interactivity

With the introduction of personal computers and the innovation to network them, people began to use the mass media in interactive ways so they could correspond with other people who share their interests. More than two decades ago, Rice (1984a) recognized the profound change that computers represented to media communication due to their ability to allow audience members to interact. Thus the distinction between sender and receiver has broken down within the mass communication experience. Over the past two decades we have seen an increase in media platforms that allow people to function as both receivers and senders of messages. Now people can share their expertise (on platforms such as Wikipedia), share personal observations (blogs and Twitter), share all aspects of their personal lives (MySpace, Facebook), or create a new personal life (dating sites, Second Life). More and more people are using media platforms to participate in all kinds of activities, such as gaming, relationship building, and public activism. Now there are communication networks growing up on just about every possible human interest, and people use this interactive technology to network with others who share their interests.

Information Saturation

The potential for all kinds of interactions along with the digitization of information and increasingly high-speed access has touched off an explosion of information creation. Rice (1984b) pointed out that, by the early 1980s, "approximately half of the US gross national product is devoted to the creation, handling, and distribution of information" (p. 23). Now, in the US alone, there are more than 400,000 book titles published annually. Throughout the world, radio stations send out 65.5 million hours of original programming each year, and television adds another 48 million hours (Potter, 2010).

There is now so much information being produced each year that it is hopeless for anyone to keep up. It was estimated that in 2007 there were more than 281 exabytes of information produced in that one year alone (Infoniac.com, 2008). That is 28-million bytes produced *in that one year alone* for each byte of information stored in the entire Library of Congress, which houses more than two centuries' worth of books, magazines, films, TV, recordings, and documents of all kinds. Therefore it is even hopeless for huge libraries to keep up with all the information being produced each year. And each year the rate of growth in the amount of information dramatically increases.

The amount of information available has fundamentally changed the audience experience with the media. No longer is there a problem with information access; the problem is now how to adapt to a flood of messages aggressively competing for our attention.

How have we adapted to this information glut? People have been gradually increasing the time they spend with the media. According to Nielsen Media Research, the average American continues to increase the amount of time he or she spends watching television each year. While this is only an increase of a few minutes each year, it adds up over time. In the decade from the mid–1990s to 2006, Americans on average increased their viewership from 7:15 to 8:14—an increase of almost one hour per day! In addition people are also increasing the time spent with other media, like MP3 players for music and video, and the Internet, which they can access not just from their computers but also their phones (Angwin, 2009, p. 238). The use of these newer technologies is so prominent among people aged eight to eighteen, that a report generated by the Kaiser Family Foundation characterized them as the "M Generation" for their focus so strongly on media use. This report found that children and adolescents were spending forty–nine minutes per day with videogames and another sixty-two minutes with the computer (Kaiser Family Foundation, 2005). People now spend 70 percent of their day on average with the media (Ransford, 2005).

In order to handle this increase in time spent with the mass media, people frequently multi-task. The Kaiser Family Foundation report (2005) indicated that most of the M Generation frequently expose themselves to more than one medium at a time. And Ransford (2005) found the same multi-tasking with media messages across people of all ages. This multi-tasking during media exposures means that, when people split their attention across two or more messages at the same time, the level of concentration used in processing any one message is low or even non-existent. This means that most media messages are processed in automatic, unconscious routines.

The proliferation of information sources has changed the way we make our decisions about media exposures. To illustrate, if you had to make a choice between two magazines to read and there were no other magazines or any other media available, you would consider this a relatively important decision worthy of much thought. However, when you have 10,000 magazines, along with millions of web sites and other media, you likely do not think much about your decisions. When the number of choices is large, humans typically make quick, intuitive decisions based on prior conditioning rather than informed choice that requires more effort (Schwartz, 2004; Wright, 2007). This is clearly the case in the new media environment where there is an overwhelming number of choices every minute of every day. Therefore, people rely largely on automatic routines that have been conditioned by the mass media over the years (Potter, 2009a, 2009b).

This overwhelming number of exposure choices has increased the power of the mass media in terms of their ability to condition our exposure habits and then to control our future exposures through those habits. To illustrate the importance of unconscious habits, think about when you first learned to drive a car. Your parents or your driving instructor tried to condition you into developing good habits of wearing a seat belt, checking rear view mirrors, always using turn signals, and so on. Once these habits were conditioned, you perform them each time you drive without thinking, that is, without any conscious effort. These habits become very easy to perform and keep you safe. In contrast if you had a friend who conditioned you to perform unsafe habits, you would perform those habits each time you drive without thinking. We all engage in hundreds of routine habits each day; this is what allows us to get through all the decisions we face each day. With the media, the more choices we have (among media, among messages, among meanings of messages, etc.), the more we rely on our conditioned habits. Media literacy is therefore concerned with reminding you to examine your automatic routines periodically to make sure they direct you into positive habits that will help you meet your goals rather than negative habits that help others reach their goals to your detriment.

Shift in Marketing

The amount of information available has fundamentally changed how media companies market their messages. To survive in the new media environment with so many message alternatives constantly competing for audience members' attention, all mass media—the newer technologies as well as the more traditional older media—have been developing a particular marketing strategy. This strategy begins with identifying needs in some segment of the general population, then working to attract the attention of the people in that niche segment (Arens *et al.*, 2009; Hirsch, 1981). The strategy then directs the mass-media business to create or stimulate content that can attract members of that niche audience to their particular platform, where they can charge those people an access fee (such as a subscription to a newspaper, magazine, web site, Internet game, etc.), a usage fee (downloading music, video, texting, etc.), and also charge advertisers an access fee to their constructed audiences. The media businesses must also condition their audience members for repeat exposures so as to amortize the high cost of attracting those people over many repeat exposures and thus make the enterprise economically viable.

The mass media engage in a very risky business; the cost of producing messages is high and the chance of successfully attracting you is fairly low, given all the alternative messages competing for your attention. They must continually spend more money to construct their messages so that those messages have the ability to break through all the clutter and attract the attention of as many of their potential audience members as possible. The mass media want to be creative and present new kinds of messages such that those messages will be more appealing to you than the messages of competitors; however, they cannot be too creative and ignore the standard message formulas that have worked well in the past. The media must continually search for message designers (journalists, film-makers, novelists, musical composers, web designers, etc.) who are creative enough to attract audiences but not too creative to confuse audiences; this talent is in very short supply so the media businesses must pay a lot for it. Thus the cost of producing successful media messages is very high and this cost must be spread out over many exposures. So the mass media must condition audiences for repeated exposures.

The mass media know that there is little possibility of designing messages that will appeal to everyone. For example, the top-rated television program is watched by only about 10 percent of the total population of the country. Instead, mass-media businesses try to provide messages and services that appeal to small audiences (niche audiences) of people who all share some interest, such as a common taste in music, a political orientation, or a hobby. Then they design messages that strongly appeal to people in that niche.

The mass-media businesses have developed interactive platforms to offer users the ability to create and share their own messages. This too is niche oriented, that is, the mass media must find groups of people who all share a common interest, then attract those people together into a niche audience and condition them for repeat exposures. With the interactive platforms, there are blogs for all kinds of interest groups where people can post messages. People who want to feel like an expert on some topic post on Wikipedia. People who like to send very short messages on mundane topics are attracted to Twitter.

Whether the mass media design their own messages or provide interactive platforms for their audiences to design their own messages, the overall marketing strategy is the same. First, the media must identify some need that defines a potential niche audience. Next the media design a means (messages or platforms) to attract an audience. Finally and continuously, the media must condition their audience members for habitual exposures so that the audience is maintained over time and the media business can amortize its high attraction costs over repeated exposures.

New Conceptualization of Mass Media

Given the salient features of the new media environment, we need a definition of "mass" media that focuses on their special characteristics of technological channels, senders, and audiences.

It should include the newer media as well as the more traditional media. Such a definition is as follows: The "mass" media employ technological devices of message dissemination that make it possible for messages to reach audiences within a relatively short time, even simultaneously, and extend the availability of messages in time and space. Channels are not defined ostensively, because, while the ostensive form of definition has been useful in the past, it has lost its usefulness with the blurring of distinctions across channels.

With "mass" media, the sender of messages must have an awareness of specific niche audiences and actively promote itself in order to attract as many audience members of that niche as possible, then condition audience members for habitual repeated exposures. Given the nature of the sender along with the technological characteristics specified in the previous paragraph, we can reason that a person who sets up a Facebook page and creates messages to attract a certain niche audience may be very successful in attracting and conditioning visitors for repeat exposures, but it is Facebook and not the page designer who is the mass medium because it is the organization of Facebook that has created the technological and marketing platform that makes the pages possible. In this case, the sender of personal messages through his or her Facebook account is actually working for Facebook without pay by creating—along with millions of other Facebook users—the content.

With the "mass" media, the audience must be composed of people who 1) are widely dispersed geographically, that is not all in one place, 2) are aware that they share message exposures with others in the audience, and 3) encounter messages in a variety of exposure states but most often in a state of automaticity. Audience members are always receivers of messages and often also serve as creators and senders of messages.

Mass communication then is defined as the process of using the mass media to disseminate messages, that is, it is the process of designing, manufacturing, and marketing messages to specific niche audiences in a manner to maximize exposures within those niches and conditioning niche audience members for habitual repeat exposures to subsequent messages.

Given this updated definition of "mass" media and the process of "mass" communication, we need to reconsider what media literacy means. With the changes that are creating the new media environment, we need to think about expanding the role of media literacy.

Additional Challenges for Media Literacy

Scholars and citizen action groups have provided a wide range of definitions for media literacy over the years (for an analysis of those definitions, see Potter, 2004). What characterizes these definitions is that they regard the person almost exclusively as the receiver of messages. Therefore, the focus of media literacy in these definitions is on providing receivers with the tools to become better at processing the meaning of media messages and thereby protect themselves from negative effects.

Now that we have clearly moved into a new media environment, we need to recognize that people are often senders of messages and not only receivers. This necessarily expands the focus of media literacy. In this section, I will first lay out the essential components of media literacy that scholars and citizen activists have emphasized for decades. Then I will address the need for expanding the role of media literacy in the new media environment.

Essential Components of Media Literacy

A definition of media literacy that is broad enough to encompass most of the concerns expressed in the literature is as follows. Media literacy is a set of perspectives that we actively use to expose ourselves to the mass media to interpret the meaning of the messages we encounter. We build our perspectives from knowledge structures. To build our knowledge structures, we need tools, raw material, and willingness. The tools are our skills. The raw material is information from the media and from the real world. The willingness comes from our personal locus (see Potter, 2010). The three building blocks of media literacy exhibited in this general definition are personal locus, knowledge structures, and skills. Let's examine each of these in some detail.

Your personal locus is composed of goals and drives. The goals set up filters for what you seek out in media messages and what gets ignored. The more you are aware of your goals, the more you can direct the process of filtering. And the stronger your drives for information are, the more effort you will expend to attain your goals. However, when your locus is weak (i.e. you are not aware of particular goals and your drive energy is low), you will default to media control where you allow the media to exercise a high degree of control over exposures and information processing.

The locus operates in two modes: conscious and unconscious. When the locus operates in the conscious mode, you are aware of options and can exercise your will in making decisions. In contrast, when the locus operates in the unconscious mode, the decisions are made outside of your awareness and control. In both modes, knowledge structures can get formed and elaborated. However, when you are consciously using your locus, you are in control of the information processing and meaning making, but when your locus is operating in the unconscious mode, the media exert their most powerful effect.

Knowledge structures are sets of organized information in a person's memory. Knowledge structures do not occur spontaneously; they must be built with care and precision. They are not just a pile of facts; they are made by carefully crafting pieces of information into an overall design. To perform such a task, we rely on a set of skills. These skills are the tools. We use these tools to navigate through the constant flow of information, so that we can select the particular experiences we need and ignore the rest. Once we have selected the information we need, we make sense of it by shaping it into knowledge structures. The structure helps us see the patterns. We use these patterns as maps to tell us where to get more information and also where to go to retrieve information we have previously crafted into our knowledge structure.

With media literacy, we need strong knowledge structures in five areas: media effects, media content, media industries, the real world, and the self. With knowledge in these five areas, you will be much more aware during the information-processing tasks and therefore be better able to make good decisions about seeking out information, working with that information, and constructing meaning from it that will be useful in serving your own goals. The information that makes this awareness possible resides in knowledge structures.

Skills are tools that you develop through practice. They are like muscles; the more you exercise them, the stronger they get. Without practice, skills become weaker. The skills most relevant to media literacy are analysis, evaluation, grouping, induction, deduction, synthesis, and abstraction. These skills are not exclusive to media literacy tasks; instead, we use these skills in all sorts of ways in our everyday lives. We all have some ability with each of these skills, so the media literacy challenge is not to acquire these skills; rather our challenge is to get better at using each of these skills as we encounter media messages.

Expanding the Role of Media Literacy

Now that we find ourselves in a new media environment that is characterized by audience members being both the senders as well as receivers of media messages in participatory cultures, we need to expand the role of media literacy. Does this mean that media literacy should help you become a better sender of messages? I would answer no, it should not be the purpose of media literacy to help people write better tweets, design better graphics for their blogs, upload a more artistic collage of pictures for their Facebook page, or become more successful in playing games. Instead the expanded role of media literacy should be to help people understand the additional threats and opportunities to them now made possible in the new media environment.

Of course, learning to produce media messages can serve as a tool towards generating greater understanding of threats. For example, message production skills have been suggested in the past as being important to increase one's media literacy, but those skills have been mentioned only to help people become better receivers of media messages. That is, it is assumed that when people experience the process of producing a film, television program, radio show, or musical recording they will better understand how to process the meaning of those media messages so they can more easily spot manipulated messages and therefore protect themselves better from potentially harmful messages. Now, in the new media environment, it can be useful to train people to tweet, create blogs, and play games because these training experiences will reveal to them how easy it is to develop alternative personalities, present falsehoods as truth, and behave aggressively with no personal consequences. So when media literacy interventions train people to be message designers and disseminators, the purpose of the training is not to make them better artists and technicians as much as it is to make them more aware of the potential risks of entering into interactions on various media platforms. Central to this expanded awareness are three issues: managing identity, negotiating privacy, and improving skill sets. For each of these issues, I will show that the new media environment offers the opportunity for something positive as well as a risk for something negative. Becoming more media literate then involves understanding the opportunities and risks, and then being able as a sender of media messages to take advantage of the opportunities while avoiding the risks when using the "mass" media.

Managing Identity

The available mass media offer many opportunities for you to experiment with new identities as you create messages and disseminate them through the mass media. Livingstone (2010) points out that the Internet "is becoming an integral means of managing one's identity, lifestyle and social relations" (p. 469). She explains that young people are in the vanguard of social networking practices.

The way the media offer you an opportunity to manage your identity can be positive for many reasons. For example, if you are shy you can use social networking sites to build your confidence for real-world interactions. Also, you can explore many facets of your existing personality in anonymous environments where people don't know you and thus judge you on your history rather than on your current performance. You can try out different social techniques to see which work best at attracting friends and solving interpersonal problems. When you use interactive media platforms you can get immediate feedback and, if your messages did not work out for you, it's no big deal; you can start fresh and try something else. And when you find something that works well, you have the confidence to try it in face-to-face interactions away from the media platforms.

However, there is also a risk for negative consequences. The most obvious risk is being exploited by others who use the media to deliberately mislead you and hide their sinister motives. There are people who use the media platforms to take your money, your time, and your friendship under false pretenses. You must learn to be skeptical and defend yourself against such threats.

Another risk is depending too much on media platforms and thus seeming to live one's life more in the virtual world than in the real world. There is also a risk to senders who become so attracted to the allure of exploring the facets of their personalities that they create newer and more bizarre personae for the sake of continuing their exploration and in so doing lose touch with who they really are. And, shy people who become successful at establishing relationships online might become so emotionally involved with the relationships in their virtual worlds that they have no time to return to the real world and try to establish meaningful relationships there.

You need to be especially careful when you manage your identity with online games in virtual worlds, because the games allow a wide latitude of identity management tactics and they provide continual and immediate feedback that serves to condition game players very strongly. Internet games can pull people into a virtual world that consumes all their time and resources. With addictions, people become slaves to the games and cannot exercise self-discipline. They are playing not to lose certain experiences rather than to gain more experiences. At this point, the games control the player, and the player has no power. This has been found to be the case with MMORPGs (Massively Multiplayer Online Role Playing Games) where there is evidence that many players have become so addicted to the game and its virtual world that they would rather live in the game than in real life (Yee, 2002). The most profound effect of these games is that they create a cyberworld that often takes the place of a player's real world. For many players, the cyberworlds offer experiences they cannot get in their real world, so players move into the cyberworld and live their lives there, where they create economies, political systems, friendships, romantic attachments, and careers. In his book *Synthetic Worlds*, Edward Castronova argued the thesis that

> the synthetic worlds now emerging from the computer game industry … are becoming an important host of ordinary human affairs. There is much more than gaming going on there; conflict, governance, trade, love. The number of people who could be said to "live" out there in cyberspace is already numbering in the millions; it is growing and we are already beginning to see subtle and not-so-subtle effects of this behavior at the societal level in real Earth countries.
>
> *(2005, p. 2)*

Castronova conducted a study of users of these games and found that about 57 percent said they would quit their real-world job and work in the cyberworld if they could make enough money there to support themselves, and three quarters of players wish they could spend all of their time in the cyberworld of the game.

Negotiating Privacy

The new media environment offers many opportunities for people to become public figures by creating blogs or web pages that attract many visitors. This gives individuals a chance to influence the attitudes and beliefs of a much larger group of people than they could if they did not use mass-media platforms. When the messages are strategically designed and disseminated, they can be very effective at reaching a sender's goals.

However, when people digitize messages and put them on a mass-media platform, they are in danger of giving up some of their privacy in unplanned and even unforeseen ways. Privacy is about boundaries. We all share certain kinds of information with friends but not with strangers, so we draw a line between our circle of friends and everyone else. If one of our friends shares information about us with someone outside that circle, we often feel betrayed by our friend who violated our privacy. When we share information about ourselves with our friends on a mass-media platform, we need to consider that those messages can be copied and re-transmitted over and over again. While we may control who gets our original transmission, we have little control over subsequent transmissions.

Time is also a factor in privacy; that is, we might feel that it is okay to share information about us at one time but not another. For example, when we are in college we might post pictures on Facebook of us doing wild, risky things at parties every night and not care who sees these pictures. But then several years later we do not want prospective employers or a potential mate to see those images. However, once posted on an interactive platform, those messages are archived and can be accessed at any time. The platforms themselves might at any time take your images and re-transmit them. For example, when you open a Facebook account, you agree to allow the staff at Facebook to use any information you post there and to share it with other websites (Guynn, 2010). There is an opt-out feature that allows you to prevent Facebook from sharing your information, but you need to read the user agreement carefully in order to realize you have this option and learn how to exercise it. Some members of Congress have been trying to enact legislation that would require Internet sites to create opt-in as a default, that is, users would have their information automatically protected unless they gave sites explicit permission to share that information with others. Until that opt-in legislation is passed, users must realize that sites use an opt-out feature, which requires users to tell the sites they cannot use their content without the user's explicit permission. Therefore it is important to read user agreements and ask questions about privacy before opening up accounts on any Internet site.

Improving Skill Sets

The virtual world provides a wonderful opportunity for people to improve sets of skills that they feel are weak and to do so in a low-threat environment that provides immediate feedback. People can practice all kinds of skills on mass-media platforms (such as poker playing, investing in stocks, making friends, flying airplanes, shooting bad guys, etc.) in low-threat, high-feedback situations. Such practice can be very helpful in improving one's skills without losing money, face, or one's life.

These opportunities for building skill sets can be extremely helpful and therapeutic. But, beyond a certain point, these opportunities can turn into risks of negative effects, if people continue practicing their skills in virtual worlds and fear testing their skills in real-world situations. The practice becomes an end unto itself and the practice never translates into achieving the goal for which the practice was intended. Therefore if people are aware of their own goals and use the games as tools to achieve those personal goals, they are acting in a media-literate manner. However, media literacy is reduced to the extent that the games take over the person's personal goals and the person slavishly works to achieve the game's goals beyond the point where the game is bringing excitement or pleasure to the player.

Another risk is the development of antisocial skill sets. First-person shooter games are one such example. Another example is sharing one's harmful biases or beliefs on a blog where others write back and reinforce these harmful biases and beliefs. The mass media provide a means for strong reinforcement schedules as people send messages then immediately get positive feedback in a continuing iterative process. If this process is used to build constructive skills sets and prosocial attitudes, then it is positive; however, when its power is used to build destructive skill sets and antisocial attitudes, it becomes a negative influence. Becoming more media literate requires you to think about this distinction and then make good choices.

Conclusion

The new media environment is forcing us to re-examine some of our old assumptions and practices about the mass media. This chapter provides a critical analysis of what "mass" media now means. Then building on this newer conceptualization of mass media, the essay presents an expanded role for media literacy. The prevalence of interactive experiences with the mass media where audience members not only consume messages but also frequently produce them requires media literacy to expand its role to help people confront the new opportunities and risks offered in media interactions.

References

Angwin, J. 2009. *Stealing MySpace: The battle to control the most popular website in America.* New York: Random House.

Arens, W. F., Weigold, M. F., and Arens, C. 2009. *Contemporary advertising* (12th edn). New York, NY: McGraw-Hill/Irwin.

Bolter, J. D. and Grusin, R. 2000. *Remediation: Understanding new media.* Cambridge, MA: MIT Press.

Castronova, E. 2005. *Synthetic worlds.* Chicago: University of Chicago Press.

Guynn. J. 2010. "Senators ask Facebook to make privacy fixes to new features," *Los Angeles Times*, April 28: B1, B7.

Hirsch, P. M. 1981. "Institutional function of elite and mass media." In E. Katz and T. Szecsko (eds). *Mass media and social change.* London: Sage, pp. 187–200.

Infoniac.com. 2008. "The amount of digital information reached 281 exabytes (281 billion gigabytes)," March 13.www.infoniac.com/hi-tech/amount-digital-information-reached-281-exabytes.html, retrieved September 11, 2009.

Innis, H. A. 1951. *The bias of communication.* Toronto: University of Toronto Press.

Jenkins, H. 2003. "Quentin Tarantino's Star Wars? Digital cinema, media convergence, and participatory culture." In D. Thorburn and H. Jenkins (eds). *Rethinking media change: The aesthetics of transition.* Cambridge, MA: The MIT Press, pp. 281–312.

Jenkins, H. 2006. *Convergence culture: Where old and new media collide.* New York: New York University Press.

Kaiser Family Foundation. 2005. "Key findings from new research on children's media use," March. www.kaisernetwork.org/health_cast/hcast_index.cfm?display=detail&hc=137, retrieved August 23, 2009.

Livingstone, S. 2010. "Taking risky opportunities in youthful content creation: Teenagers' use of social networking sites for intimacy, privacy and self expression." In Nayar, P. K. (ed.). *The new media and cybercultures anthology.* Malden, MA: Wiley-Blackwell, pp. 468–482.

McLuhan, M. 1964. *Understanding media: The extensions of man.* New York: McGraw Hill.

Nayar, P. K. (ed.). 2010. *The new media and cybercultures anthology.* Malden, MA: Wiley-Blackwell.

Nielsen Media Research. 2006. September 21. www.nielsenmedia.com/nc/portal/site/public, retrieved October 30, 2006.

Noll, A. M. 2007. *The evolution of media.* New York: Rowman & Littlefield Publishers.

Potter, W. J. 2004. *Theory of media literacy: A cognitive approach.* Thousand Oaks, CA: Sage.

Potter, W. J. 2009a. "Conceptualizing the audience." In R. Nabi and M. B. Oliver (eds). *Handbook of media effects.* Thousand Oaks, CA: Sage, pp. 19–34.

Potter, W. J. 2009b. *Arguing for a general framework for mass media scholarship.* Thousand Oaks, CA: Sage.

Potter, W. J. 2010. *Media literacy* (5th edn). Thousand Oaks, CA: Sage.

Ransford, M. 2005. "Average person spends more time using media than anything else," September 23. Ball State University News Center. www.bsu.edu/up/article/0,1370,32363-2914-36658,00.html, retrieved October 30, 2006.

Rice, R. E. 1984a. "New media technology: Growth and integration." In R. E. Rice *et al.* (eds). *The new media: Communication, research, and technology.* Beverly Hills, CA: Sage, pp. 33–54.

Rice, R. E., 1984b. "Development of new media research." In R. E. Rice *et al.* (eds). *The new media: Communication, research, and technology.* Beverly Hills, CA: Sage, pp. 15–31.

Schwartz, B. 2004. *The paradox of choice: Why more is less.* New York: HarperCollins.

Wright, A. 2007. *Glut: Mastering information through the ages.* Washington, DC: Joseph Henry Press.

Yee, N. 2002. "Ariadne – Understanding MMORPG addiction," October. www.nickyee.com/hub/addiction/home.html.

PART VIII

Challenging the Boundaries of Participatory Culture

25

PARTICIPATION AND THE TECHNOLOGICAL IMAGINARY

Interactivity or Interpassivity?

Paul A. Taylor

> They find themselves shoved into an everyday life that turns them into henchmen of the techno-logical excesses.
>
> (Kracauer, 1995, p. 70)

> [Interactivity] … a purely ideological term, projecting an unfocused fantasy rather than a concept of any analytical significance.
>
> (Aarseth cited in Wilson, 2003)

There is a widespread tendency to treat digital technologies and the quality of interactivity synonymously. This paper argues that this has helped to foster an excessively uncritical attitude to new technologies—familiarity breeds consent. In this context, hackers and hacktivists are groups who, since hands-on engagement with technology is their *raison d'être*, have frequently been viewed as pioneering exemplars of "interactivity." I question that assumption by drawing upon my experience as one of the earliest sociological researchers of both hacking and hacktivism (see Taylor 1998, 1999; Taylor and Jordan 1998, 2004) and my ongoing interest in past and present critical theories of technology (see Taylor and Harris 2005, 2008; Taylor 2010).

The majority of social science literature dealing with hacking and hacktivism is premised upon the conventional wisdom whereby technology is deemed to be essentially neutral and, as the cliché goes, it is what we choose to do with it that really counts. In this light, hackers and hacktivists epitomize interactivity because:

- they interact with computers on a real-time basis
- at the forefront of hands-on technological involvement, they represent working proof of technology's purportedly neutral essence.

From a perspective informed by critical theory, both these forms of interactivity are profoundly suspect. Addressing the experiential narrowness of computer-based interaction is beyond the scope of this paper. It concentrates instead on a radical reinterpretation of the wider notion of hackers and hacktivists as emblems of technology's essential neutrality. Langdon Winner (1977) scathingly refers to this as the myth of neutrality … a truism striving to become a bromide.

In order to undermine this myth and to question radically the notion that hackers/hacktivists should be held up as positive role-models of interactivity, this paper presents a much fuller historical and cultural context. Readers are encouraged to check out additional online sources to flesh out the following inevitably brief explanations of themes such as cyberpunk fiction, the historical curiosity-figure of the *flâneur*, and the French philosopher Jean Baudrillard's notion of simulation (in a neat visual pun, the Keanu Reeves character Neo in *The Matrix* stores his discs in a hollowed-out copy of Baudrillard's book *Simulacra and Simulation*). Using such past and present examples to move beyond the false neutrality in terms of which technological issues are frequently analyzed, hackers and hacktivists are shown to represent a very different quality to rose-tinted interactivity; instead, they can be seen as embodiments of a much more disturbingly pessimistic quality—interpassivity.

The Ideology of Interpassivity

Interactivity serves a ubiquitous, yet equally generally unacknowledged, ideological function. From critical theory's perspective, interactivity should more accurately be labeled "interpassivity"—a situation in which technology undermines human agency in the very guise of claiming to enhance it. To illustrate the concept, Slavoj Žižek (1999) refers to the phenomenon of "canned laughter" one encounters whilst watching various TV programmes. Our emotional response to a programme is pre-emptively taken care of—laughter occurs even if we are too tired to laugh for ourselves. At first glance only a superficial feature, Žižek argues that canned laughter actually demonstrates the light-touch nature of interpassivity's pervasive ideological effects. As it applies to computer technology, this phenomenon of interpassivity works in two key forms.

1. Interactivity has become synonymous with point-and-click digital mediations despite the fact that, from a more "traditional" presence-privileging viewpoint, there are strong grounds to suggest that digital interactivity represents an ideologically motivated oxymoron.
2. Those groups (like hackers and hacktivists) who proactively engage with digital technology risk becoming false alibis for a more general loss of autonomy in the rest of society's technologically mediated interactions—meta-level interpassivity. Furthermore, not only do we over-rely upon technologically savvy groups to compensate for our own techno-deficiencies, but we also fail to recognize the more negative, disempowering aspects of those groups' own experiences.

In both these cases, the ideological effect of interpassivity occurs because there has been a flattening out of the discriminatory basis from which one could distinguish between "authentic" and "inauthentic" interactions. For example, it is indisputable that web-based forms of political activity make new kinds of civic engagement possible (a clicktorate?). However, the academic disciplines devoted to studying these novel forms of online democracy have significant theoretical limitations. They limit themselves to a transmission-oriented, sign-based understanding of communication that fails to account for the profound difference between symbols and signs. This failure creates a key distinction to be made between what I would call critical media philosophy, non-philosophical communications studies "proper" and semiotics. In the latter, symbols tend to be discussed merely as a form of sign. By contrast, critical media philosophy emphasizes how signs lack and exclude the much more richly ambiguous levels of resonance and allusiveness that exist within authentically symbolic communication. Signs are elements of communication pre-designed for ease of transmission and comprehension, derived as they are from the inherently predictable, standardized, nature of commodified culture. The capitalist media system, by its very nature, promotes the diffusion of eminently commodifiable signs to the corresponding detriment of symbol-based forms of exchange culture.

The now well-established discipline of political communication, even whilst adapting itself suitably to cater for new online environments, tends to be either unwilling or unable to contemplate the possibility that, far from being essentially the same as previous modes of communication (just much quicker and easily accessible), from a symbolic point of view new technologically mediated forms of political interaction are distinctly non-neutral. This analytical blind spot is demonstrated by the marginal status afforded to philosophical critics who do indeed emphasize the innately anti-communicational nature of highly technologized Western modes of political discourse. Within the broad church of media studies, for example, Jean Baudrillard's dogged insistence that, in practice, contemporary communications systems fabricate non-communication has meant that his "work has been largely ignored by the mainstream discipline, due to the latter's differing origins, interests, methodologies and theory" (Merrin, 2005, p. 3). Critical media theory highlights the largely inverse relationship that exists between the efficiency of interactive digital transmission processes in our increasingly "point and click polity" and the substantive nature of the political issues being clicked so readily upon. Mainstream communications studies, by contrast, either ignores the philosophical distinction or glosses over its profound implications. Even those writers who do at least engage with philosophy's relevance to our understanding of mediated interactions (see, for example, Scannell 1996 and Gauntlett 2009)—do so only by ignoring those uncomfortable, negative implications that require confronting the cages that our technologies create. They risk instead (in a self-circumscribing theoretical version of interpassivity) merely gilding the cage bars by their uncritical interpretation of interactivity as inevitably empowering.

Hackers and Hacktivists—(Not) Beating the System

From its earliest days, hacking had an ambivalent relationship with the Establishment. On the one hand, there was a patina of rebelliousness to these innovative pioneers as they routinely broke into laboratories and re-engineered various technologies to suit their own purposes, e.g. their ingenious manipulations of the phone system to "phreak" free calls (see Levy, 1984). On the other hand, it can be argued that, with the exception of avowedly anarchistic strands, hackers have always been susceptible to co-optation by the status quo because of their quasi-addictive need for access to technological systems for its own sake. Ultimately, this reliance upon techno-kicks makes them passively reliant upon, rather than an active challenge to, the overarching system—capitalism. This explains how the hippy-minded early computer hardware producers movement evolved from promoting an iconoclastic "Hacker Ethic" espousing "all information should be free," to a stock-holding corporate mindset. Alternative lifestyles soon seamlessly accommodated themselves with commercial structures—for example, the carefully self-cultivated bohemian persona of Apple Computers and the 'campus' environment of Microsoft.

Recourse to critical theory suggests that hacking and hacktivism's technical virtuosity consists of technological playfulness with little political purposiveness. Writing about radio hams (keen early amateur radio geeks—prototype hackers), Adorno was scathing in his assessment of, what in the end, proves to be their political timidity:

> At twenty, he is still at the stage of a boy scout working on complicated knots just to please his parents. This type is held in high esteem in radio matters. He patiently builds sets whose most important parts he must buy ready-made, and scans the air for shortwave secrets, though there are none. As a reader of Indian stories and travel books, he once discovered

unknown lands and cleared his path through the forest primeval. As radio ham, he becomes the discoverer of just those industrial products which are interested in being discovered by him. He brings nothing home that would not be delivered to his house.

(Adorno, 1991 [1938], p. 54)

With a similar level of scorn, Baudrillard also rejects the notion that widespread familiarity with technological gadgets is likely to lay the basis for the sorts of revolutionary social change that were claimed when computing was first developed:

> this "revolution" at bottom conserves the category of transmitter, which it is content to generalize as separated, transforming everyone into his own transmitter, it fails to place the mass media system in check. We know the results of such phenomena as mass ownership of walkie-talkies, or everyone making their own cinema: a kind of personalized amateurism, the equivalent of Sunday tinkering on the periphery of the system.
>
> *(Baudrillard, 1981, p. 182)*

Baudrillard critically characterises the contemporary communications environment as a "totalitarian semiotic order," an integral reality (2005) in which symbolic nuances are increasingly expunged by sign-based transmission-orientated interactions—the much lauded notion of digital "interactivity." Whilst "totalitarian" may be a provocative exaggeration, it nonetheless points to an essential truth, namely, the paucity of significant modes of symbolic resistance that might genuinely threaten to overturn this overwhelmingly dominant sign-based semiotic order.

Excessive dependency upon technology for its own sake and a lack of political purpose could be seen as a natural consequence of hacking's unashamedly apolitical and techno-centric origins. Hacktivism, by contrast, evolved from hacking with the express intent of applying hacking means for more overtly political ends, yet, from a Baudrillardian perspective, the totalitarian nature of the semiotic order prevents ready escape from its encompassing logic. Thus, although Baudrillard (1981) commented favourably on the oppositional motivation of graffiti writers during the 1968 Parisian protests, there are slim pickings in his work to suggest other forms of protest that go much beyond this relatively mild instance. Anything greater tends to succumb to the logic and language of Debord's (1983) *Society of the Spectacle* so that:

> Exciting pictures of Basque activists scaling the Millennium Dome in Greenwich, London may contribute to an "innovative and variegated type of politics" but only because as a spectacle their antics are suitable for the sign-off slot at the end of prime-time news. Full of energy and éclat, this sort of media event may still constitute a withdrawal of energy from traditional domains of citizen action and produce no substantive gain for its perpetrators.
>
> *(Axford and Huggins, 2001, p. 9)*

Or as Baudrillard puts it:

> the worst error, the one committed by all our revolutionary strategists, is to think they can put an end to the system on the real plane: that is … the imaginary the system itself imposes on them, a system that lives and survives only by getting those who attack it to fight on the terrain of reality, a ground that is always its own.
>
> *(cited by Turner in Baudrillard, 2005a, p. 4)*

Bearing in mind the paucity of real-world evidence of what critical theory would consider truly empowering forms of technological interactivity, literature provides a useful source for exploring how, unhindered by the awkward constraints of reality, interactivity has at least been imagined. It was, after all, a novel (William Gibson's *Neuromancer* [1984]) that gave us the highly culturally influential everyday concept of cyberspace and the über-interactive figure of the cyberpunk. In the 1980s and 1990s this created the whole cyberpunk genre of literature—science fiction set in the near future and whose focus was upon cyberspatial environments that were arguably exaggerated representations of already existing trends in computer technology.

In the Destructive Element Immerse—the Interpassivity of Fiction's Technological Wish-Fulfilment

A man that is born falls into a dream like a man who falls into the sea. If he tries to climb out into the air as inexperienced people endeavour to do, he drowns—*nicht wahr?* … No! I tell you! The way is to the destructive element submit yourself, and with the exertions of your hands and feet in the water make the deep, deep sea keep you up. So if you ask me—how to be? … I will tell you! … *In the destructive element immerse.*

(Conrad, 1971 [1900], pp. 163–164 [second emphasis added])

a book about order and disorder more of a, sort of a social history of mechanization and the arts, *the destructive element.*

(Gaddis, 2003 [1975], p. 244 [emphasis added])

Elsewhere (Taylor and Harris, 2005), I make an uppercase/lowercase-indicated distinction between the Matrix now generally understood as the specifically digital cyberspace created by the world's interconnected computer systems and the broader notion of a matrix conceived as the multifariously enframing features of technologically developed societies—as experienced via bureaucracies, the grid-like circumscriptions imposed on life by city structures, etc. Fiction is a valuable conceptual tool with which to trace the relationship between the Matrix of postmodernity and its predecessors, the various earlier matrices experienced during the development of the modern industrial world. The first of the above quotations is taken from Joseph Conrad's *Lord Jim*, as the trader Stein describes his philosophy of survival. The second is taken from William Gaddis's *JR*, at the point where the character Jack Gibbs replies to a question as to what type of book he is in the process of writing. Both highlight an earlier literary focus upon the destructive element of a rapidly modernizing world that later culminated in the cyberpunk genre and its fevered depictions of an invasive and pervasive technological environment that accompanies a society "organized" around the dog-eat-dog principles of social Darwinism. Unlike the focus of above quotations and the manifestly critical themes in cyberpunk, however, fiction is typically used to promote an ideological climate that sustains a more optimistic view of technology's cultural effects. Thus, even though Gibson's work (and cyberpunk fiction in general) contains deeply negative and dystopian portrayals, these tend to be strategically ignored as cyberpunk's breathless descriptions of accessing cyberspace are used to foster an uncritically infused celebration of all things digital.

Notwithstanding their genuine and innovative attempts to reassert human agency in the face of complex technological systems, viewed more pessimistically hackers and hacktivists represent the latest in a line of alchemical cultural figures who (only appear to) turn base interpassivity into a much more socially acceptable commodity—interactivity. The roots of this ideological co-optation of interactivity can be found in much earlier cultural theories of urbanization. For example, in the 19th century, the *flâneur* was a semi-fictional figure, a dandy who strolled in, but remained a detached observer from, the burgeoning crowds of the rapidly growing city of Paris. He (like hackers, an invariably male figure) savoured the crowds as an object to be observed for his own amusement—one based upon a desire (remarkably prescient in the light of the much later cyberpunk experience of entering cyberspace): "To be away from home and yet to feel oneself everywhere at home; to see the world, and yet to remain hidden from the world … the lover of universal life enters into the crowd as if it were an immense reservoir of electrical energy" (Baudelaire, 2003 [1859], pp. 9–10). A full appreciation of socio-technical change today requires an understanding of the continuities to be traced between these past and present phenomena. The dandyish nature of the *flâneur*, the hard-boiled characteristics of the noir detective/console cowboy, and the socially rebellious attitudes of hackers/hacktivists—all can be criticized for being based more upon posture than actual power.

This pessimistic appreciation is vividly illustrated in Robert Musil's novelistic paen to interpassivity, *Der Mann ohne Eigenschaften* (The Man without Qualities). Published in two volumes in 1930 and 1932, Musil provides an epic account of the end of the Austro-Habsburg Empire due to the irresistible incursions of modernity. In the following excerpt, Musil describes the context of the apparent (we do not learn of his actual fate) death of a pedestrian (who represents the by-now anachronistic position of the *flâneur*). He is knocked down by a lorry in a Vienna that is rapidly assuming a matrix-like, inhumanely anonymous and threatening scale/sense of sublimity:

> Motor-cars came shooting out of deep, narrow streets into the shallows of bright squares. Dark patches of pedestrian bustle formed into cloudy streams. Where stronger lines of speed transected their loose-woven hurrying, they clotted up—only to trickle on all the faster then and after a few ripples regain their regular pulse-beat … the general movement pulsed through the streets. … Like all big cities, it consisted of irregularity, change, sliding forward, not keeping in step, collision of things and affairs, and fathomless points of silence in between, of paved ways and wilderness, of one great rhythmic throb and the perpetual discord and dislocation of all opposing rhythms, and as a whole resembled a seething, bubbling fluid in a vessel consisting of the solid material of buildings, laws, regulations, and historical traditions.
>
> *(Musil, 1979 [1930], pp. 3 and 4)*

Musil's fictional format enables him to counterpose the human and biological (like blood the crowd "clotted up" and has a "regular pulse-beat") with the technological and its inhuman movement of increasing abstraction. He is thereby able to portray the otherwise unportrayable sort of immaterial (but no less real) new social forces and systems with which hackers later sought to interact as those forces assumed much more explicit technological forms. Like the geometric lattices of light used by Gibson to portray the Matrix ("and still he'd see the matrix in his sleep, bright lattices of logic unfolding across the colourless void'" [Gibson, 1984, p. 11]), in Musil, early antecedents of later informational flows can be read into the "stronger lines of speed" that transect and contrast with the more organic movements of the crowd to create the "seething, bubbling fluid" to which traditional forms are reduced. Musil's mode of expression resonates with Marx's description of capitalism's effect as one that creates a situation in which "all that is solid melts into air" (Marx and Engels, 1977 [1848], p. 38). The pedestrian/*flâneur*'s death in Musil thus represents more than just a literary curiosity, rather, it is a vivid fictional depiction of a very real phenomenon—the fatal implications that cybersociety's interpassive flows have for traditional life-worlds and their increasingly obsolete forms of less technologically mediated interactivity.

Musil's scene neatly encapsulates the literary point in history at which the *flâneur*'s fascination and desire to become one with Baudelaire's immense reservoir of urban energy is overwhelmed by the sheer intractable power of forces that do not lend themselves readily to conscious contemplation and bodily interaction. Musil describes a new form of technology-induced sublimity witnessed by the interpassive man-without-qualities from the balcony of his town house:

> for the last ten minutes, watch in hand, he had been counting the cars, carriages, and trams, and the pedestrians' faces, blurred by distance, all of which filled the network of his gaze with a whirl of hurrying forms. He was estimating the speed, the angle, the dynamic force of masses being propelled past, which drew the eye after them swift as lightning, holding it, letting it go, forcing the attention—for an infinitesimal instant of time—to resist them, to snap off, and then to jump to the next and rush after that. ... "It doesn't matter what one does," the Man Without Qualities said to himself, shrugging his shoulders. "In a tangle of forces like this it doesn't make a scrap of difference."
>
> *(Musil, 1979 [1930], pp. 7–8)*

In Gibson's novels, the cyberpunks' explicit confrontations with the buzz of information (extreme digital interactivity), originally encountered in *Neuromancer*, make way in his later work for deliberately vague allusions to much more subtle interactions with an overarching commodity matrix (interpassivity). In his later novels, there is a Walter Benjamin-like nostalgia for a physically oriented reality that no longer exists, which resonates with the passive resignation exhibited in *The Man without Qualities*. For example, Bigend is one of Gibson's characters who appears in *Pattern Recognition* (2003), *Spook Country* (2007) and most recently *Zero History* (2010). He is emblematic of the manner in which the explicit technological framework of the Matrix (with which we can still attempt to interact no matter how futilely) is but part of a less obvious, but all the more powerful, matrix (which now interpassively subsumes us all). Indicative of Gibson's changed literary emphasis from the Matrix to the matrix, the character Bigend appears in both *Pattern Recognition* and *Spook Country*. Bigend is an informational impresario who refers to "pre-ubiquitous media" to distinguish between a "state in which 'mass' media existed, if you will, within the world" rather than "comprising it" (Gibson 2007, p. 103). This is a further advanced manifestation of Jameson's (1992) conceptualization of postmodernity as a certain "waning of affect"—personified in another Gibson character, Laney from *All Tomorrow's Parties*:

> Laney is in drift.
> That is how he does it. It is a matter, he knows, of letting go. He admits the random.
> The danger of admitting the random is that the random may admit the Hole.
> The Hole is that which Laney's being is constructed around. The Hole is absence at the fundamental core. The Hole is that into which he has always stuffed things: drugs, career, women, information.
> Mainly—lately—information.
> Information. This flow. This ... corrosion.
> Drift.
>
> *(Gibson, 1999, p. 40)*

Laney's drift is a phrase that describes with fiction's unique "exaggerated clarity" a very real-world situation in which we are all reduced to a state of ur-interpassivity, contained as we now are within ever increasing circles of sign-transmitting abstractions.

The Integral Reality of Starbucks' Neighbourhoods

Jean Baudrillard's term "integral reality" conveys his notion of an interpassive world in which there is a surfeit of representational exposure but a deficit of meaning. An essential aspect of the M/matrix is its creation of an existentially empty, tensionless space—a quality that runs across both digitalized cyberspace and the physical world of commodity culture, and which for Siegfried Kracauer (writing in the first half of the twentieth century) could be clearly witnessed in the pseudo-social space of a hotel lobby:

> What is presented in the hotel lobby is the formal similarity of the figures, an equivalence that signifies not fulfillment but evacuation. Removed from the hustle and bustle, one does gain some distance from the distinctions of "actual" life, but without being subjected to a new determination that would circumscribe from above the sphere of validity for these determinations. And it is in this way that a person can vanish into an undetermined void, helplessly reduced to a "member of society as such" who stands superfluously off to the side and, when playing, intoxicates himself. This invalidation of togetherness, itself already unreal, thus does not lead up toward reality but is more a sliding down into the doubly unreal mixture of the undifferentiated atoms from which the world of appearances is constructed.
>
> *(Kracauer, 1995 [1922], p. 179)*

In this context, hackers and hacktivists can be viewed as our technologically savvy alibis. We compensate for our own feelings of technical ignorance by projecting onto these apparently masterful figures. They surf the Matrix whilst we remain interpassively submerged within the matrix. The suspicion is that hackers and hacktivists are merely the vanguard explorers (but, finally, just as disempowered as the rest of us) of a society-enveloping hotel lobby within which we all now loiter aimlessly.

The above account of the cultural manifestations of the underlying abstract code of the M/matrix may itself seem unduly abstract and other-worldly. However, and this is a key paradox, the interpassivity of today's culture is based upon abstractions that have very real, physical effects. This powerfully pervasive social trend is illustrated by Starbucks' recent efforts to present elements of its franchise as independent, neighbourhood coffee shops:

> In a diversion from its usual mixture of stripped wood decor and bland artwork, Starbucks is opening a store in its home city of Seattle intended to capture the vibe of a beatnik coffee hangout—and disguise the fact that drinkers are in a Starbucks. The store will be called 15th Avenue Coffee and Tea in an apparent attempt to mimic a local, independent coffee shop. A Starbucks spokeswoman says the place will have a "mercantile" look with open bins of coffee beans and manual grinding machines. There will be live music and poetry performances. At least two other re-hashed outlets are on the way in Seattle as chairman Howard Schultz tries pushing Starbucks back towards its artsy roots. Steve Gotham, an analyst at marketing consultancy Allegra Strategies, thinks this is a smart move as customers look for differentiation among branded coffee houses: "The issue of localness and local relevance has some way to go—it's a consumer trend more operators need to tap into.
>
> *(Clark, 2009)*

Both the marketing consultants and the customers availing themselves of the neo-mercantile atmosphere of carefully culturally re-engineered shops know that genuine "localness" and "local relevance" cannot be corporately generated, but both proceed as if it can, and in an ersatz sense the experience becomes a self-fulfilling prophecy as the simulation becomes more desirable and "natural" than any notion of an original. This is Baudrillard's notion of the hyperreal quality that dominates today's mediascape. The hyperreal is more real than the real itself. It consists of signs that have been freed from roots in any prior reality so that the distinctions between media representations and our direct experience of our lived environments become more tenuous and blurred.

Referring to a French reality TV programme *Loft Story*, Baudrillard describes it as: "both the mirror and the disaster of an entire society caught up in the rush for insignificance and swooning to its own banality" (Baudrillard, 2005a, p. 190) Any threat of symbolic ambiguity and tension is evacuated in the hotel lobby just at it is in the Loft where:

> this existential micro-situation serves as a universal metaphor of the modern being enclosed in a personal loft that is no longer his or her physical and mental universe but a tactile and digital universe … of digital humans caught in the labyrinth of networks, of people becoming their own (white) mice.
>
> *(ibid., p. 193)*

Kracauer's hotel lobby, Baudelaire's *flâneur*, Gibson's cyberpunk, and Baudrillard's caustic analysis of reality TV, all refer to an underlying, complex process of abstraction ("the labyrinth of networks") that informs both cultural and technological matrices—the matrix and Matrix. It is in the face of this M/matrix, whether interacting in a self-consciously local fashion as consumers of lattes, or technologically as hackers of computer systems, that we are all perhaps still ultimately passive.

References

Aarseth, E. J. 1997. *Cybertext: Perspectives on ergodic literature*. Baltimore: The Johns Hopkins University Press.

Adorno, Theodor. 1991 [1938]. *The culture industry*. London: Routledge.

Axford, B. and Huggins, R. 2001. *New media and politics*. London: Sage.

Baudrillard, Jean. 1981. *For a critique of the political economy of the sign*. St Louis: Telos Press.

Baudrillard, Jean. 2005a. *The conspiracy of art*. New York. Semiotext(e).

Baudelaire, Charles. 2003 [1859]. *The painter of modern life and other essays*. London: Phaidon Press.

Clark, A. 2009. "When is a Starbucks not a Starbucks?" *Guardian*, 22 July. www.guardian.co.uk/lifeandstyle/2009/jul/22/starbucks.

Conrad, Joseph. 1971 [1900]. *Lord Jim*. London: Penguin.

Gaddis, William. 2003 [1975]. *JR*. London: Atlantic Books.

Gauntlett, David. 2009. "Media studies 2.0: A response," *Interactions: Studies in Communication and Culture*, 1(1): 147–157.

Gibson, William. 1984. *Neuromancer*. London: Grafton.

Gibson, William. 1999. *All tomorrow's parties*. London: Viking.

Gibson, William. 2003. *Pattern recognition*. London: Viking.

Gibson, William. 2007. *Spook country*. London: Viking.

Gibson, William. 2010. *Zero history*. London: Viking.

Jameson, Fredric. 1992. *Postmodernism, or, the cultural logic of late capitalism*. London: Verso.

Kracauer, Siegfried. 1995. *The mass ornament: Weimar essays*. London: Harvard University Press.

Levy, Stephen. 1984. *Hackers: Heroes of the computer revolution*. New York: Bantam Doubleday Dell.

Merrin, William. 2005. *Baudrillard and the media*. Cambridge: Polity Press.

Marx, Karl and Engels, Friedrich. 1977 [1848]. *Manifesto of the Communist Party*. Moscow: Progress Publishers.

Musil, Robert. 1979 [1930]. *The man without qualities, vol. 1.* London: Picador.

Scannell, Paddy. 1996. *Radio, television, and modern life.* Oxford: Blackwell Publishers.

Taylor, Paul Anthony. 1998. "Hackers: Cyberpunks or microserfs?" *Information, Communication and Society,* 1(4): 401–419.

Taylor, Paul Anthony. 1999. *Hackers: Crime and the digital sublime.* London: Routledge.

Taylor, Paul Anthony. 2010. *Žižek and the media.* Cambridge: Polity Press.

Taylor, Paul Anthony and Harris, Jan. 2005. *Digital matters: Theory and culture of the matrix.* London: Routledge.

Taylor, Paul Anthony and Harris, Jan. 2008. *Critical theories of mass media: Then and now.* Berkshire: Open University Press.

Taylor, Paul Anthony and Jordan, Tim. 1998. "A sociology of hackers," *Sociological Review,* 46(4): 757–780.

Taylor, Paul Anthony and Jordan, Tim. 2004. *Hacktivism and cyberwars: Rebels with a cause?* London: Routledge.

Wilson, L. 2003. *Interactivity or interpassivity: A question of agency in digital play.* http://hypertext.rmit.edu.au/dac/papers/Wilson.pdf.

Winner, Langdon. 1977. *Autonomous technology.* Cambridge, MA: MIT Press.

Slavoj Žižek. 1999. *The sublime object of ideology.* London: Verso.

26

PARTICIPATORY CULTURE AND MEDIA LIFE

Approaching Freedom

The Janissary Collective: Peter Blank, Watson Brown, Mark Deuze, Lindsay Ems, Nicky Lewis, Jenna McWilliams, and Laura Speers

> All manners of writing are allowed, not just boring ones.
>
> (Voltaire)

In our supposedly participatory culture, the good citizen feels 'free to contribute' only in so far as he or she aligns with dominant societal power structures. Rather than being more involved than previous generations, people in today's 'participatory culture' seem primarily engaged in mutual and self-disciplining behavior. In the shift from a national control society to a global suspicion society, greater participation in contemporary culture does not equal greater freedom. Meet the new boss, same as the old boss. Only this time, we are (like a) boss.

Introduction

Participatory cultures simultaneously empower people and put up new barriers to community membership. A culture produces (and in the process reproduces) a more or less stable set of norms, beliefs, and values that can function as a power structure. The design, infrastructure, and use of media are therefore not necessarily liberating (nor unavoidably constraining) a community's participatory potential. It is always an expression of what "participation" in a given place, at a specific time, and enacted by particular people, means. Our needs and desires for using media remain largely unknown to the individual (Katz, 2009). We also remain blind to what media actually are, to how the technologies of media profoundly shape our interactions with media and each other through media (Kittler, 1999). Unless media break down or do not function the way they are supposed to, it is impossible to see them or know our desires related to them. The same must go for a contemporary participatory culture as expressed and advanced in media: to understand the role of media in participatory culture is to break participatory culture and assess whether we use our media to meet our expectations, or, instead, those of others.

The use of networked personal computers and handheld devices has become an important and habitual part of people's everyday lives. Human beings now have many ways to communicate with one another beyond and outside institutionally sanctioned channels, which contributes to a widely shared perception that the average person can make, or at the very least, co-create culture, politics, pedagogy, and economy. While new media allow ordinary people to directly voice opinions and tell stories in different ways, the perception of (making) a difference creates an illusion of democracy. Whereas in the late 19th and early 20th centuries such an illusion was produced by the modernist belief that large social groups or masses could bring about meaningful participation and change in all aspects of society, today that conviction (and corresponding expectation) has shifted onto the shoulders of the individual. Just as this belief one hundred years ago helped create the horrors of two world wars and an endless series of other mass-produced atrocities worldwide, our current cultural dogma fuels terror by the individual. Such a dogma can best be described as the translation and sanitization of participatory cultural citizenship into a voting individual—"One Person, One Vote" (by governments and political organizations), into a consumer or producer (by the market), and into personal profiles (by "social" media like Facebook and Twitter). The attacks of 9/11 benchmark the ultimate terror enacted by the individual—and one could additionally note how quickly any sense of collective agency dissipated after those horrible acts. The goal in this chapter is to articulate a way for the individual to detect the expectation of participatory culture in our time, to consider ways to opt out (and break it), and hopefully thus find a sense of purpose in everyday life. The material in this chapter can therefore be regarded as a set of tools for taking matters into one's own hand.

Towards Acceptable Participation

In Western societies, any notion of participatory culture tends to be heralded as an empowering and intrinsically democratic force, a means for offsetting social inequities and making it possible for a diversity of voices to be heard. A century ago, such glorification of participatory culture found its expression in the rapid rise of political movements, the gradual extension of voting rights, the rise of academic fields such as mass psychology (and later on mass communication), and the development of technologies whose success was defined by their mass sociable use, in particular the telephone and radio (Chapman, 2005, p. 218ff.).

Today, such optimistic assumptions about participatory culture are exemplified most clearly in the work of Henry Jenkins and colleagues (2006, p. 6), offering that in participatory culture not all members must contribute, but all should feel free to contribute when ready to do so, and that what they contribute will be appropriately valued. Thus, membership is a prerequisite to participation. By necessitating behavior that feels comfortable and familiar to people who are already members, a participatory culture is quite likely to reproduce the features of traditional media culture—as it is a similar disciplinary construct only enforced by a different policing mechanism. We argue that contemporary participatory culture is a form of power that aligns closely with existing values and norms, and that members in participatory culture are not so much free to contribute, but rather can be seen as compelled to contribute in a way that aligns with dominant norms and already established power structures. Specifically, we question whether feeling free to contribute really means that members actually are free in how, when, and why they contribute to participatory cultures.

An acceptance of participatory culture as the ultimate expression of a happy and fulfilling life seems to serve the highest purpose at this moment if one follows the well-intended advice of new media theorists, political consultants, corporate marketers, and technology enthusiasts. This is why people are supposed to be proactive everywhere: in restaurants, bars, and grocery stores we take over part of the work by fetching plates, silverware, food, walking to the bar and selecting products to consume. At the doctor's office we bring a stack of printouts from WebMD. In public transport hubs we have to buy our tickets at automated kiosks. Wherever we go, we are constantly reminded that nobody is responsible for whatever happens to us while we're there: in stores, at work, on the road. In journalism we are "citizen" reporters, and in marketing we are the accelerating agents of the industry's feverish attempts to go viral (Deuze, 2007). The videogame and software business relies on us to find, report, or even fix bugs, design our own custom versions of their products—over which the publishers involved retain sole custody. People worldwide spend most of our time in media at online and mobile social networks, which without our "participation" would be desolate and defunct—yet their terms of use read like informal labor contracts that last until the end of time. Businesses seem to benefit from an entire "net genera-tion" treating their online profiles like resumes in disguise. As the anthropologists in the "Digital Anthropology UK" study of 2009 concluded: "the extent to which people use social networking and promote themselves online will become more important in determining their careers than what school or university they went to" (p. 18). Governments outsource social security to individual citizens and social welfare to multinational corporations (which, legally speaking, are individuals). We participate by shouldering individual responsibility for what used to be collective endeavors. Amplified and accelerated through available media technologies, the extension of our participatory work becomes the latent norm. As a result, the participatory act that roots our media lives in ethics and aesthetics is fundamentally one of a self-serve/single-serve culture. And if you're uncomfortable, unwilling, or unable to participate? You're on your own.

On a microscale, the mediated remixing of our co-creative lives in contemporary participatory culture encourages a view of how we perceive our work as (making) a difference. A media life is a good and beautiful thing—in media, we can be anything we want, contribute to and find out about all knowledge of the world. Influential scholars such as Manuel Castells are at times exuber-ant in claiming that today's media are "so comprehensive, so diversified, so malleable that it absorbs in the same multimedia text the whole of human experience, the past, present, and future" (2010 [1996], p. 404). Henry Jenkins agrees: "[i]n the world of media convergence every important story gets told, every brand gets sold, and every consumer gets courted across multiple media platforms" (2006, p. 3). The digital divide makes way for the participation gap, mobile connectivity reaches every corner of the globe, the message of participatory culture hard-wired into its exoskeleton. Anything goes and everything is possible. At the same time and from a distance, we see the maintenance of the status quo through consolidation of economic power in multinational corporations, local/regional/national governance-bypassing multilateral policies (such as the proposed Anti-Counterfeiting Trade Agreement in the case of media), and a general deference towards otherwise indifferent technologies (specifically code; see Lessig, 2006) for the organization of everyday life (Silverstone, 2007).

A participatory culture-supercharged life as lived in media essentially requires a blind embrace of technology—up to the point that we cannot meaningfully distinguish between people and things anymore. Sean Cubitt (2005, p. 18) thus calls for a nuanced appreciation of the less-than-clear and increasingly dissolving boundaries between *polis*, *physis*, and *techne*: the human world, the green world (i.e. nature), and technological world. Media in Cubitt's work are conceived more broadly as "ecomedia": providing the essential communicative devices and interfaces for improved human–nature relationships. Technology's role has been to bond human beings with the planet as intertwined strands of story. It therefore does not stand between them—it dissolves the false dichotomy that separates them.

Faced with an increased intimacy with (and subsuming by) technology, one has to wonder if technology can be seen as, archaeologically, a human choice. If human evolution is culture, can every technological innovation be seen as a natural choice? It points attention to how cultures are evolved systems of innovation. Importantly, one's culture is now unmasked; its former presence as nation-based and shared communal identity loses primacy over its rootedness in personal tech-nologies. We do not become the media (as the thus titled 2000 spoken-word album of singer and activist Jello Biafra suggested), nor do the media become us (as film director David Cronenberg suggested in a 2005 interview with *Wired* magazine): we are, and always have been, media—and the kind of media culture we (are told to) embrace is thus an expression of the way we are supposed to be, ruling out the possibility of middle-ground positioning.

Attachment to such everything-in-moderation thinking means that one is not completely participating and thus disqualified for an increasing array of potential futures laid out by governments and corporations. On the other hand, one is also not entirely logged off, which disempowers one to really engage in anything—acquiescence or resistance—meaningfully. One cannot switch a delusion on or off—one either runs with it, or not. The mode of participatory culture is premised on today's interactive/co-creative ICTs. In our argument, the delusion of a life as lived in, rather than with media seems to be more inspiring in terms of its potential to redirect what Castells calls "communication power" (2009) to the individual.

We believe that participatory culture spotlights the individual in ways a traditional, premodern culture could not. It simultaneously disrupts and stabilizes the lifeworld in which the communicative mechanism is given unhindered play. The lifeworld is "the social domain of communicative action wherein we see intersubjective understanding for the purpose of coordinating our activities" (Farr, 2009, p. 154). The lifeworld is the world taken for granted—the world before reflection and representation, a "zero degree" state of affairs. It is this intuitive condition of everyday life that has become "multimediatized" (Sonesson, 1997).

The multimediatization of the lifeworld does not, as is often suggested, reduce people to solipsistic engagement with the world—living in their own personal information space or what Peter Sloterdijk describes as the bubble of our individualized "media sphere" (2004). Living in media we are as much part of others as their worlds are part of ours. The German philosopher-sociologist Jürgen Habermas devised the concept of communicative action, which is a deliberative democracy in a public sphere where individuals collectively come to agreement through argumentation and cooperation. In his description of the risk built into communicative action, Habermas (1998, p. 36) notes how there are certain modes of traditional attitudes and behaviors that have to be accepted without question because they are so entrenched and defy communicative logic that we are not even aware of them. Because they remain a background, they are intuitively accepted without question. We are incapable of distinguishing whether these behaviors and embedded certainties are accepted justifiably or merely the unquestioned acceptance of human norms and practices. If we conceptualize the human archive (Ernst, 2005) as the backbone of stored information that is continually updated while in use, it is the only factor that can be taken for granted in communicative action as it is capable of providing the inevitable taken-for-granted. The archive used to be understood as centrally controlled, top-down, and (therefore) relatively stable. Today's human archive, however, is increasingly based on the tenets of participatory culture, and thus resembles a more or less open, participatory, and user-generated organism. Nicholas Gane and David Beer therefore argue, "life today is increasingly being played out through the archive than simply stored within it" (2008, p. 82). In a participatory culture, the human archive is not only an invisible machine guiding and signposting our interactions and behaviors, but it is also subject to collective (not necessarily collaborative) editing and revision. However, due to no institution having final power over the archive anymore, the situation can arise of a real or perceived lack of boundaries and control. Instead of leading to emancipation and the freedom to create and collaborate, participants end up reproducing the set of norms, beliefs and values of a dominant power structure. Therefore, rather than creating an innovative and egalitarian participatory culture, the traditional top-down human archive is enforced, but by a different mechanism that has participants permanently police each other.

Archive of Our Own

The Organization for Transformative Works (OTW) recently established a project called Archive of Our Own, an archive for creative fan projects that is described as both non-commercial and non-profit. OTW is an online fanvidding community which describes itself as a group that envisions a future in which all fan works are recognized as legal and transformative and are accepted as a legitimate creative activity. Indeed, many such communities exist in direct challenge to corporate-capitalist norms, as to subvert the very idea that narratives and characters can be owned by people or corporations. Fanvidders challenge or simply ignore the copyright laws and litigation designed to allow only the original authors to profit from their creative works (Trombley, 2007).

Many fanvidding communities operate on the premise that fanvidders do not or should not profit from their work. In such goals, we see clearly a simultaneous rejection of capitalist norms and laws and an embrace of a capitalist approach that is designed to gain power and a voice in legal and legislative issues. There is no reason to object to this approach, since the majority of members of OTW tend to agree with the organization's stated goals; however, it is possible that fans who reject this approach are either marginalized and kept voiceless in the OTW community or choose not to participate in OTW activities at all. To remix, repurpose, and co-create tends to be understood in terms of the either/or discourse of utopian empowerment versus the legal and business quagmire of intellectual property rights in an information economy. Such binary oppositions (in which the poles constitute each other) potentially neglect the question of whether the individual is free to do any of this in the first place. As Habermas suggests, a way out of this predicament of the unknown is for the actors themselves "to come to some understanding about the normative regulation of strategic interactions" (1996, p. 26). If participatory culture becomes a norm, how does one who does not like to share his or her participatory convictions and attitude take part in such a process? A critical approach to find re-enchantment in detached contemplation of participatory culture could lead to a motivation to share stories and provide insight to others while remaining within (however temporary) social norms and self-reference.

Self-Reference in Participatory Culture

Any understanding of this lifeworld in participatory culture ideally includes a thorough investigation of the underlying material infrastructure, codes and protocols that make such a life possible. However, the problem of expressing anything meaningful about our life in media is that we rely on media to do so (Kittler, 1999). What is beautiful or feels right in the media sphere is interpreted as versions of the unknown self, or the self that also functions as other. Theodor Adorno (1973, p. 162) argued it is therefore not possible to know whether one is capable of individual thought. What occurs to an individual as their own thoughts must be their performance of the product(s) they are. New experiential forms may be strongly correlated to the often-observed preoccupation with the self in participatory media. We agree with Mark Poster (1989, pp. 82, 139) that interaction and engagement with varying "modes of information" in media enacts a fundamental change in experience. This is why the self must now be understood as continually constructed or constituted, instead of a stable, centered identity. Our "media self" is subject to the same supposedly empowering elements of remix and co-creation as participatory culture. Individuals are expected to continually choose their next version(s) of self—and in the process submit their selves to be re-constituted out of the interactions with (and thus the redaction of) others. Zygmunt Bauman (2005, p. 33) offers that this produces "a permanently impermanent self, completely incomplete, definitely indefinite and authentically inauthentic."

Furthermore, the self can no longer, as Erving Goffman could still assume, be traced back to one speaker behind typewriter or camera, but is increasingly blown to bits in new co-creations. An example of this would be animation films where hundreds of artists make the experience of one animated character possible (without any one creator holding or retaining copyright and authorship over the creation).

For an individual to exist outside of such self-evanescent forces, he or she may have to perform the ephemeral "own" archive. In strategic warfare, the individual could then exist in the emptiness inside the machine, unanticipated by it. The only outside to the participatory culture that is particular to our time is to perform selves internal to the machine; in other words: to deliberately and passionately live a media life (Deuze, 2010).

Farr (2009, p. 4) writes, following Marcuse, that freedom means much more than merely being left alone. One is free to the extent that one has the ability and resources to pursue the good for one's life. If the two types of citizen, the responsible and functional individual and the free, unbound communitarian, cannot be understood from the creative moment of emptiness, they are to be understood from within technology (Habermas, 1996, p. 494). For Sartre (2001, p. 71), human beings were free as long as consciousness was an opening to an undetermined world. This freedom allows human beings to meet basic needs of self-perception and reflection, and provides the basis for intellectuals to have an effect on the world. Media could function as mirrors of self, reflecting back to us behaviors, events, identities and social relations. Media could thus present images and imaginations of the self and other in one or more different forms. One could conceive of such differences as unclear and unrecognized yet new cultural activity, producing greater diversity. The traits of this cultural activity include a rhetorical concept about boundaries in a postmodern world. Postmodern theorists suggest that realities are only human constructs and are subject to change, making them plural and relative depending on who the interested parties involved are because of the endless possibilities of human existence. Jameson (1984, p. 87) mentions existence in the periphery as one of his seven features of postmodernity. Yet, postmodernism blurs the boundaries and reference points of mainstream society. As a result, postmodernism eliminates the possibility of not existing as "other"; whether you are in the center or the periphery, you are still part of the system (and determined as such). In Jameson's terms, distance has been very precisely abolished in the new space of postmodernism. Such a realization of contingent distance could be cultivated and developed for access to a new level or perhaps second-order reality.

If the freedom of the individual in participatory culture cannot be guaranteed by a withdrawal from, or an unreflected embrace of, participatory culture, how can we truly act ethically and aesthetically? As a first step, we propose that lived reality cannot be experienced separate, or outside of media. As Sybille Krämer states, "[e]verything we can say, find out and know about the world is being said, found out and known with the help of media" (1998, p. 73). Metaphorically speaking, we are all living inside our very own *Truman Show* (referring to the 1998 movie by director Peter Weir): a world characterized by pervasive and ubiquitous media that we are constantly and concurrently deeply immersed in, which dominate and shape all aspects of our everyday life. Importantly, in this world it is also up to each of us to navigate the largely unwritten rules and often hidden pathways of an ocean of media on our own. In the film, actor Jim Carrey portrays the life of a man—Truman Burbank—who does not know his entire life is one big reality television show, watched by millions all over the world. In the course of the movie it becomes clear that the only way out for Carrey's character will be his individual ability, as the only True Man, to figure out whether the people in his life are actors (and to what extent they act), and where the fine line between the studio (stage, décor) and the "real" world can be drawn. We have argued that the solution to this vexing dilemma can only be found by the individual. *The Truman Show* metaphor is appropriate insofar as it addresses people's complex and forced solipsistic engagement with participatory culture through media. When asked how the show can be so successful in convincing Truman that his world is real even though it so clearly features a fake reality, the director of Truman's reality show explains: "[w]e accept the reality of the world with which we are presented." It is important to note the implication of this narrative, as it does not seem to be premised on a notion that Truman's world is unreal. *The Truman Show* is just another version of the real, one that is carefully staged and completely mediated, much like Plato's Allegory of the Cave, as the people in the cave, watching the puppets, were unaware of any other lifestyle or world other than the one in which they were presented. Using *The Truman Show* as a metaphor for living a media life, we must additionally note that the ending of the movie— Truman escapes from the studio—might in fact be the only truly unrealistic aspect of the film's story, as, in our fully mediated existence, escape is impossible.

During the summer of 2008 psychiatrists Joel and Ian Gold made headlines around the world with their diagnosis of a new condition found in initially five of their patients. The brothers suggested that the combination of pervasive media, classical syndromes such as narcissism and paranoia, and an emerging media culture where the boundaries between the physical and virtual world are blurring produces a new type of psychosis: a "Truman Show Delusion" (TSD). People who suffer from TSD are more or less convinced that everything around them is a décor, that the people in their lives are all actors, and that everything they do is monitored and recorded. McGill University's Ian Gold attributes TSD in an interview with Canadian newspaper the *National Post* to "unprecedented cultural triggers that might explain the phenomenon: the pressure of living in a large, connected community can bring out the unstable side of more vulnerable people. […] New media is opening up vast social spaces that might be interacting with psychological processes" (July 19, 2008, p. A1). In *Newsweek,* his brother (affiliated with the Bellevue Hospital Center in New York) suggests that TSD "is the pathological product of our insatiable appetite for self-exposure" (August 11, 2008, p. 10). Earlier that week in a special report on the WebMD site, he links TSD more generally to the role media play in people's lives: "[w]e've got the 'perfect storm' of reality TV and the Internet. These are powerful influences in the culture we live in." The TSD additionally contains a belief that one's life has ceased being spontaneous, as one is always aware of (the possibility of) the scripted and broadcast nature of everything one does. In a special report about the TSD at the website of the American Psychological Association (on June 6, 2009), the brothers identify specific features of modern culture—"warrantless wiretapping and video surveillance systems […] widely accessible technology […] reality TV shows and MySpace"—as squaring with *The Truman Show*'s basic premise. In the APA report and in an earlier background story in the *International Herald Tribune* several experts are quoted who confirm the possibility of the TSD and suggest that "[o]ne way of looking at the delusions and hallucinations of the mentally ill is that they represent extreme cases of what the general population, or the merely neurotic, are worried about" (August 30, 2008, p. 7). We would argue that in our current version of participatory culture, as amplified in media life, the TSD provides the necessary context for survival. As Woody Allen states in an interview with the *New York Times* (of September 14, 2010): "we need some delusions to keep us going. And the people who successfully delude themselves seem happier than the people who can't."

Merleau-Ponty (1993, p. 129), following André Marchand, wrote that when he was in a forest, he felt suddenly that instead of him looking at the forest, it was the trees looking at him. The inanimate forest seemed present, more so than he himself. His sudden experience of the real outside of himself, existing independent of (and indifferent to) him is similar to the final scene of *The Truman Show*, where Truman Burbank in his attempt to escape life on his island runs into a cardboard sky. It is here that an irreversible switch occurs. Once Truman realizes the nature of his existence, there is no going back. He cannot displace the dichotomy created by the revelation of his fabricated life. The question is whether Truman would not be more empowered to then return to his island—to the trees—and live a life in between the poles of fake and real, in Slavoj Žižek's (2006) parallax view living an uncanny existence as both a product of participatory culture as well as a producer of an essentially different mode of it. In short: we need to embrace our delusion in order to truly see and experience our reality. In a phone interview (on March 7, 2011) Ian Gold confirms, that if one considers delusion as a certain "bias" towards reality and experience, it can lead to greater happiness—for example if one deliberately adopts the positive predisposition that people are good. Seen as such, a *Truman Show* delusion can be turned into a co-creative use of the (real and perceived) cameras pointed at us.

Campaign Plan: Seizing the Ironic Moment of Liberty

Awareness of participatory culture as distinct from participation, as a derivative of it, requires a free choice to participate according to one's own strategies. We have emphasized the individual's potential awareness of participatory culture and capacity for ethical conduct and worldly re-enchantment through participation. Attitudes leading to behavior that not only reproduces but also creates systems of production can be termed self-inventive (Hofkirchner *et al.*, 2005, p. 89), even though, in media, they may be delusional. Technology may then be used to shift evolution of consciousness to conscious evolution: as we become aware, we can gain control over our mediatized evolution by letting it go (not by switching off or logging out).

The other option (that of accepting and conforming to technology's participatory norms) stands in the way of mindful, meaningful contribution to aspects of our existence. Rather, in the performance of one's position as digital immigrant (born before 1982), as contrasted by the coming age of digital natives (born after 1982), one has the "unique freedom from habitual rights and duties … to construct them anew, either on return home or in committing to a new place" (Cubitt, 2005, p. 139). The Czech philosopher Villém Flusser describes the migrant as forced into a void where meaning can no longer arise from habit or habitus; what remains is "to seize the ironic moment of liberty and commit herself to using it in the context of the culture where she lands. Only in that engagement with change, that grasping of responsibility, does the migrant achieve her freedom" (Cubitt, 2005, p. 140).

Participatory culture can never provide the basis for the good life—in fact, it can be its worst enemy.

References

Adorno, T. 1973 [1966]. *Negative dialectics*. London: Routledge & Kegan Paul.

Bauman, Z. 2005. *Liquid life*. Cambridge: Polity.

Castells, M. 2009. *Communication power*. Oxford: Oxford University Press.

Castells, M. 2010 [1996]. *The rise of the network society* (3rd edn). Cambridge, MA and Oxford: Blackwell.

Chapman, J. 2005. *Comparative media history*. Malden, MA: Polity Press.

Cubitt, S. 2005. *Eco media*. Amsterdam, New York: Rodopi.

Deuze, M. 2007. *Media work*. Cambridge: Polity Press.

Deuze, M. 2010. "Media life." In Stylianos Papathanassopoulos (ed.). *Media perspectives for the 21st century*. London: Routledge, pp. 181–195.

Ernst, W. 2005. "Not seeing the Laocoön? Lessing in the archive of the eighteenth century." In J. Bender and M. Marrinan (eds). *Regimes of description. In the archive of the eighteenth century*. Stanford, CA: Stanford University Press, pp. 118–134.

Farr, A. L. 2009. *Critical theory and democratic vision: Herbert Marcuse and recent liberation philosophies*. Plymouth: Lexington Books.

Gane. N. and Beer, D. 2008. *New media*. Oxford, New York: Berg.

Habermas, J. 1996. *Between facts and norms: Contributions to a discourse theory of law and democracy* (Studies in Contemporary German Social Thought). Cambridge, MA: MIT Press.

Habermas, J. 1998. *The inclusion of the other*, edited by Ciaran Crinin and Pablo de Greif. Cambridge, MA: MIT Press.

Hofkirchner, W., Fuchs, C., and Klauninger, B. 2005. "Informational universe. A praxeo-onto-epistemological approach." In E. Martikainen (ed.). *Human approaches to the universe*. Interdisciplinary Studies. Helsinki: Luther-Agricola-Seura, pp. 75–94.

Jameson, F. 1984. "Postmodernism, or the cultural logic of late capitalism," *New Left Review*, 146: 53–92.

Jenkins, H. 2006. *Confronting the challenges of participatory culture: Media education for the 21st Century* (John D. and Catherine T. MacArthur Foundation Reports on Digital Media and Learning). Boston: MIT Press.

Katz, J. E. 2009. "Social structure, new communication technology and citizen journalism." In K. Nyíri (ed.). *Engagement and exposure: Mobile communication and the ethics of social networking*. Vienna: Passagen Verlag, pp. 27–36.

Kittler, F. 1999. *Gramophone, film, typewriter*. California: Stanford University Press.

Krämer, S. 1998. "Das Medium als Spur und als Apparat." In S. Krämer (ed.). *Medien, Computer, Realität*. Frakfurt am Main: Suhrkamp, pp. 73–94.

Lessig, Lawrence. 2006. *Code*. http://codev2.cc/.

Merleau-Ponty, M. 1993 [1961]. "Eye and mind." In Galen A. Johnson (ed.). *The Merleau-Ponty aesthetics reader*. Evanston: Northwestern University Press, pp. 351–378.

Poster, M. 1989. *Critical theory and poststructuralism. In search of a context*. Ithaca, NY: Cornell University Press.

Sartre, J. P. 2001 [1956]. *Being and nothingness. An essay in phenomenological ontology*. New York: Kensington Publishing Corp.

Silverstone, R. 2007. *Media and morality: On the rise of the mediapolis*. Cambridge: Polity Press.

Sloterdijk, Peter. 2004. *Sphären*. Berlin: Suhrkamp Verlag.

Sonesson, G. 1997. "The multimediation of the lifeworld." In Winfried Nöth, (ed.). *Semiotics of the media: State of the art, projects, and perspectives*. Proceedings of an international congress, Kassel, March 1995. Berlin, New York: Mouton de Gruyter, pp. 61–78.

Trombley, S. 2007. "Visions and revisions: Fanvids and fair use," *Cardozo Arts and Entertainment Law Journal*, 25: 647–683.

Žižek, S. 2006. *The parallax view*. Cambridge, MA: MIT Press.

27

LEGAL CONSTRAINTS ON PARTICIPATORY CULTURES IN THE UNITED STATES

Anonymity, Concealment, and Revelation

Clay Calvert

Questions regarding anonymity and the concealment or revelation of identity or information are at the heart of contemporary First Amendment litigation in the United States. Even in a country that prides itself on protections of free speech and press, the United States' courts are grappling with where or if to draw the lines regarding how individuals can or should interact in participatory cultures.

The First Amendment to the United States Constitution generally protects freedom of speech against censorship by federal, state, and local government entities and officials; it does not, however, prevent censorship by non-governmental entities or officials. It provides, in relevant part, that "Congress shall make no law … abridging the freedom of speech, or of the press," with the term "Congress" including not only the US Congress, but also any and all government actors and entities, from the local school board or town mayor to the senate and governor of any state. Indeed, it is the time-tested safeguard and shield of the First Amendment, adopted more than two centuries ago in 1791, that allows participatory cultures and virtual communities on the Internet to develop and flourish in various online forms and forums, from blogs and social networks to newspaper apps and entertainment fan sites.

Although the framers of the First Amendment never could have envisioned or imagined the advent of the Internet as a venue for participatory spaces and cultures, the United States Supreme Court has made it clear that expression conveyed through this medium receives the same level of protection as speech printed in old-fashioned newspapers and even more protection than is given to the speech of over-the-air television broadcasters. In particular, the Supreme Court is the body that gives ultimate meaning to the forty-five words in the First Amendment. In Reno v. ACLU (1997), the Court described the Internet as a "new marketplace of ideas" when it struck down a federal law that regulated sexually explicit content on the then-emerging Internet. The nation's high court emphasized the unique communicative aspects of this medium, opining that "it constitutes a vast platform from which to address and hear from a world-wide audience of millions of readers, viewers, researchers, and buyers" (Reno, p. 853).

An important corollary of the right to engage in free speech is the right to engage in that speech anonymously. The Supreme Court has long recognized an unenumerated or implicit First Amendment right to engage in anonymous speech, particularly when the speech at issue concerns politics. As the Court wrote in a 1995 case that protected the right to engage in anonymous political leafleting, "an author's decision to remain anonymous, like other decisions concerning omissions or additions to the content of a publication, is an aspect of the freedom of speech protected by the First Amendment" (McIntyre v. Ohio Elections Commission, 1995).

It is this First Amendment-protected cloak of anonymity that arguably allows many of the participatory cultures on the Internet today to thrive. Indeed, if traditional hallmarks of participatory cultures are "low barriers of entry for artistic expression and civic engagement" (Jenkins *et al.*, 2005, p. 7), then digital anonymity arguably reduces the barriers even further by lessening the anxiety some people may feel about participating if their identities were known to other participants. Many people feel more comfortable posting their honest opinions and frank feelings, for instance, in response to an online newspaper story if they are anonymous. In stable political systems such as the United States, anonymity may have a liberating effect on participation while, under repressive regimes, anonymity may be the only way participation can occur.

Yet, as University of Florida Law Professor Lyrissa Barnett Lidsky observes, "anonymity is a double-edged sword. Anonymity frees speakers from inhibitions both good and bad. Anonymity makes public discussion more uninhibited, robust, and wide-open than ever before, but it also opens the door to more trivial, abusive, libelous, and fraudulent speech" (Lidsky, 2009, p. 1383). Masks of anonymity facilitate a more vibrant and vigorous discussion because anonymous posters do not fear reprisals or retributions from others; they believe that no one knows their identities or can discover them. Or, at least, so they think.

The reality is that the right to engage in anonymous speech is not absolute. For example, anonymous participants in online cultures can be unmasked when their postings contain content that is false and defamatory such that it harms another participant's reputation. There are actually a number of categories of speech that the Supreme Court has determined fall outside the scope of First Amendment protection. These exceptions come despite the amendment's straightforward words stating "Congress shall make no law … abridging the freedom of speech" that appear to signal an impenetrable barrier against government censorship.

Current categories of unprotected expression include, among others, obscenity, child pornography, fighting words, true threats of violence, incitement to violence, false advertising, and defamation. Speech that comes within the confines of these groupings, each of which has a precise legal definition, receives no constitutional protection and, in turn, can be censored and punished.

Therefore, participants in online cultures that convey such messages may face legal repercussions. They might, for instance, be sued for defamation in civil courts by the individuals they libel with false statements. Alternatively, they may be criminally prosecuted by states and/or the federal government for possessing and swapping child pornography in the online micro-communities in which pedophiles traffic their illicit content. In brief, while participatory spaces of all sizes and interests exist on the Web, there are limits to what can be said and transmitted within them.

New media do not necessarily mean or entail new laws or new legal principles. For instance, although libel law is centuries old, the same general elements or ingredients of a libel suit that have been applied for years to disputes centering on statements made in print media—books, newspapers, and handbills—apply today to statements posted in participatory spaces on the Internet, as well as to texts and email. A libelous statement is one that tends to expose a person to public scorn, hatred, contempt, or ridicule, thereby discouraging others in the community from having a good opinion of, lowering the reputation of, or associating with, that person.

The elements of a libel suit require the person who files the suit to prove that: 1) the defendant published and communicated the message to at least one person other than the plaintiff and defendant; 2) the message is the kind that would harm the plaintiff's reputation by, for instance, attacking the plaintiff in his or her occupation, by suggesting the plaintiff engaged in criminal wrongdoing or by imputing misconduct in the plaintiff's personal life, such as sexual transgressions; 3) the message is false (if the message is true, there is no libel and the lawsuit will fail); and 4) the plaintiff indeed suffers reputational injury as a direct result of the defendant's publication of the message.

Finally, it is important to understand that it makes little difference in libel law whether a message is read by one person or 100,000 people. All it takes is one person in addition to the author and the person mentioned to read the message to create libel in the eyes of the law. Likewise, even if the message is quickly removed or taken down from a blog or other participatory online venue, it still has been published and a libel action may result.

With this background in mind, this essay centers on the legal constraints imposed on anonymous participation in Internet cultures and, in particular, when the interests in revelation of the identity of the participants, due to their publication of libelous statements about others, trump the need or desire for concealment and secrecy. In order to understand this tension between secrecy and revelation in the context of libelous statements in participatory spaces, it is useful to consider a fairly common scenario: A hypothetical social networking site for college students called CollegeHottiesConfidential.com includes a message board where students can post comments about "the students who are the biggest losers on campus." It is one of those participatory spaces where a college student posts a message and other students from the same college respond to it, engaging in an online dialogue that riffs off of the initial posting.

Jane Smith, carefully cloaking her real identity by using the pseudonym "KeepingItRealGirl," posts the following message:

"Suzi Tuscadero is such a little whore. She sleeps with all the frat guys on campus and now she's got so many diseases I can't believe they even touch that skank. And get this—she also deals drugs on the side to make a little extra cash. She definitely is the biggest loser at Southeast Metro State University. Suzi T. is going nowhere in life fast."

Someone points out the message to Suzi, and Suzi is rightfully livid. In fact, she does not sleep around. She is monogamous and has been going out with the same guy for three years. What's more, she also does not sell or even use drugs. She thus wants to sue KeepingItRealGirl for defamation because the statements are false and harm her reputation, lowering her in the eyes of others at Southeast Metro State University and possibly hurting her chances of landing a good job after graduation if potential employers surf the web for "dirt" on job applicants, as they often do today.

Because the statements about Suzi on CollegeHottiesConfidential.com are false and would damage her reputation, Suzi would have an excellent chance of winning a defamation lawsuit against KeepingItRealGirl. But the problem, of course, is that Suzi doesn't know who KeepingItRealGirl really is and thus she doesn't know who to sue. Suzi, as the plaintiff, would have to name the defendant as "John Doe" until she can determine the defendant's true identity. At this stage, her lawsuit would be called Suzi Tuscadero v. John Doe.

The question becomes: Can Suzi use the legal system to discover the identity of KeepItRealGirl and unmask Jane Smith in order to sue her?

Courts across the country are grappling with this issue, and they are fashioning various tests that allow people like Suzi to force web sites such as CollegeHottiesConfidential.com to reveal the IP address and/or the identity of anonymous posters like KeepingItRealGirl. These tests typically require someone like Suzi to go to court and to prove several things before they will compel a social networking site, online newspaper, or forum moderator to give up KeepingItRealGirl's identity.

In creating these tests, courts are trying to strike a balance between the competing interests. As one federal appellate court wrote in 2009, "the tension between a speaker's desire for anonymity and the right of the plaintiff to protect his reputation or property arises in a variety of contexts, including defamation, copyright infringement, harassment, and malicious gossip" (Solers, Inc. v. Doe, 2009, p. 951). It added that

> when faced with the clash of such valued interests, we must strike a balance between the well-established First Amendment right to speak anonymously, and the right of the plaintiff to protect its proprietary interests and reputation through the assertion of recognizable claims based on the actionable conduct of the anonymous, fictitiously-named defendant.
>
> *(2009, p. 951)*

The first step that most courts would require of someone like Suzi is to attempt to provide notice to KeepingItRealGirl that Suzi wants to learn her identity and intends to file a lawsuit against her. How might such notice be served by Suzi? Suzi could post a responsive message to KeepingItRealGirl on CollegeHottiesConfidential.com stating something along the lines of:

"To KeepingItRealGirl: Your statements about me are false, and they have harmed my reputation. Please reveal your identity to me. If you fail to do so, I will go to court to compel the operator of this web site to reveal your name and IP address to me."

Why do courts require people like Suzi to take this "notice" step? Because if the poster voluntarily identifies herself, then it spares the web site or Internet Service Provider (ISP) from having to reveal the identity and, in the process, spares it from potentially losing the confidence of other members of its service who believe their own identities are private and confidential. Courts therefore require that Suzi give KeepingItRealGirl a reasonable amount of time to reply to the notice.

If KeepingItRealGirl, however, refuses either to respond or to reveal who she is to Suzi, then Suzi still must prove a few more things to a court before it will order CollegeHottiesConfidential.com to release the name of Jane Smith and/or Smith's IP address, allowing Suzi to trace back the offending message to Jane's computer. In particular, Suzi will need to prove to the court that she actually has a legitimate cause of action or legal theory against KeepingItRealGirl for defamation. In essence, she would have to show she has a good shot at winning her case, except for not knowing who to sue. The court requires this step because it wants to make sure that Suzi's threatened lawsuit is not frivolous or meritless. Forcing a web site to reveal the identity of an anonymous poster when the reasons for revealing the identity are devoid of any legal merit would represent an unnecessary encroachment on the First Amendment right to engage in anonymous speech.

For instance, if KeepingItRealGirl had only said something like "Suzi Tuscadero is the worst dresser. Her sense of fashion sucks," then Suzi would not have a legitimate case for defamation. Why? Because those statements are matters of opinion—they cannot be proven true or false. One person's sense of bad fashion is another person's sense of fabulous fashion. Statements of opinion thus typically cannot form the basis of a defamation suit. Defamation lawsuits must be based on false factual assertions, not opinions. It is, however, a false factual assertion that Suzi is a whore; she can prove that she is monogamous, that she only sleeps with one person, and that she doesn't take money in exchange for sex. It also is a false factual assertion that she deals drugs; she can prove that she never sells them.

Finally, some courts will balance the competing interests of the parties involved—the need for Suzi to obtain the information in order to seek redress for reputational harm versus the First Amendment right to speak anonymously in unfettered manner. This last step provides courts with much discretion to weigh the interests of the parties and to consider the specific facts of the case. For instance, in the hypothetical suggested here, there would seem to be very little reason to protect the identity of KeepingItRealGirl. Why? Because she is not engaged in political speech, and she is not some anonymous whistle-blower attempting to expose corporate graft or wrongdoing while cloaking her identity. She also apparently has no larger purpose of serving a public good or societal need. Her sole goal is to trash and tarnish the reputation of Suzi. By comparison, Suzi does have a vested interest in gaining compensation for the reputational harm that might be caused by KeepingItRealGirl's posting. As noted earlier, Suzi might not be able to land a good job after graduation because prospective employers often scour participatory spaces on the Internet for incriminating information about possible hires.

The bottom line is that there are legal constraints on both speech and anonymity in the multitude of participatory cultures and spaces on the Internet. Although the Internet seems, at first glance, to be an anything-goes, no-holds-barred marketplace of ideas for individuals of all varieties and interests to congregate, it does have its limits. In the hypothetical described above, the defamatory statements of KeepingItRealGirl are not protected by the First Amendment and, in turn, Suzi will be able to obtain KeepingItRealGirls' identity if she can first prove several things.

But what about the potential liability of CollegeHottiesConfidential.com, the site on which KeepingItRealGirl posted her message about Suzi? Shouldn't the web site have some legal responsibility or liability to Suzi since it supplied the online venue of which KeepingItRealGirl took advantage?

The answer to that question is no, at least as long as CollegeHottiesConfidential.com did not either create or control the messages posted on its web site. This is the case because of a federal law adopted in 1996 that provides that "no provider or user of an interactive computer service shall be treated as the publisher or speaker of any information provided by another information content provider" (47 U.S.C. § 230). This means that interactive computer services like CollegeHottiesConfidential.com are exempt from civil liability for content posted by other information providers. In the hypothetical above, KeepingItRealGirl is the information provider.

Congress created this so-called Good Samaritan provision to protect ISPs and other interactive computer services in order "to preserve the vibrant and competitive free market that presently exists for the Internet and other interactive computer services, unfettered by Federal or State regulation" (47 U.S.C. § 230). By exempting ISPs from civil liability in situations like that in this hypothetical, Congress wanted to ensure that ISPs would continue to "offer a forum for a true diversity of political discourse, unique opportunities for cultural development, and myriad avenues for intellectual activity" (47 U.S.C. § 230). This would be like suing the owner of a magazine stand for the content of an article in *Time*.

It is highly doubtful, of course, that Congress today would consider all of the content that circulates in participatory spaces on the Internet, such as hate speech, explicit pornography, and hurtful gossip, to constitute either "cultural development" or "intellectual activity." There is a disconnect between the legislative intent behind the federal law granting Good Samaritan immunity to ISPs and the reality that it has wrought years later. If it wants, Congress can amend this provision or scrap it altogether by adopting a new law that specifically allows for civil liability in defamation suits to be imposed on ISPs for content posted by others.

As new problems with free expression arise in participatory places on the Internet—consider, for instance, cyberbullying as one such problem—there will be fresh efforts by states and the federal government to impose further legal constraints on expression. The bottom line is this:

- Without freedom of expression and the First Amendment, there would be no participation, no engagement, and no interaction in the spaces and places that flourish today in the online world; and
- There will always be a tension between those who exercise that freedom responsibly and those who abuse it. The legal system in the United States will step in to keep in check certain

types of abusive content, from obscenity and child pornography to defamation and threats of violence.

While the distinguishing qualities of participatory cultures are low barriers to civic engagement and venues where members of a culture believe that their contributions to it matter, members of online communities who abuse the "civic" part of that equation via the posting of harmful anonymous messages face legal constraints. Thus the true "cost" of participation—at least the monetary cost—goes way up when a lawsuit is filed.

Ultimately, it is useful to keep in mind the following words from the United States Supreme Court discussing freedom of the press—words that suggest we must sometimes put up with and tolerate speech we don't always like when trying to find the proper balance between responsibility and abuse of free expression:

> It is better to leave a few of its [the press's] noxious branches to their luxuriant growth, than, by pruning them away, to injure the vigor of those yielding the proper fruits. And can the wisdom of this policy be doubted by any who reflect that to the press alone, chequered as it is with abuses, the world is indebted for all the triumphs which have been gained by reason and humanity over error and oppression; who reflect that to the same beneficent source the United States owe much of the lights which conducted them to the ranks of a free and independent nation, and which have improved their political system into a shape so auspicious to their happiness?
>
> *(Near v. Minnesota, 1931)*

The remaining question for readers to consider as this essay comes to a close is this: If people engaging in online participatory cultures knew that their identities could be revealed—if they understood, in other words, that their right to hide behind a mask of anonymity is not absolute—would that deter their participation in these cultures or would it encourage more civil engagement?

References

47 U.S.C. § 230 (2010).

Jenkins, Henry, Clinton, Katie, Purushotma, Ravi, Robison, Alice J., and Weigel, Margaret. 2009. *Confronting the challenges of participatory culture: Media education for the 21st century*. Chicago, IL: John D. and Catherine T. MacArthur Foundation. www.newmedialiteracies.org/files/working/NMLWhite-Paper.pdf.

Lidsky, Lyrissa B. 2009. "Anonymity in Cyberspace: What can we learn from John Doe?" *Boston College Law Review*, 50(5) (November): 1373–1391.

McIntyre v. Ohio Elections Commission, 514 U.S. 334 (1995).

Near v. Minnesota, 283 U.S. 697 (1931).

Reno v. ACLU, 521 U.S. 844 (1997).

Solers, Inc. v. Doe, 977 A.2d 941 (D.C. Cir. 2009).

28

TOWARD AN ETHICAL FRAMEWORK FOR ONLINE PARTICIPATORY CULTURES

Jennifer Jacobs Henderson

The potential of participatory cultures—spaces where thoughtful, engaged world citizens tackle complex problems, build creative networks, and contribute to political decision-making—is seemingly limitless. In these spaces, the pace of scientific discovery could speed up and misunderstandings could subside. In these spaces, individuals with little power or voice could gain acceptance because of their ideas and creativity rather than their pocket books. And in these spaces, geopolitical boundaries could be erased.

For these potentialities to come to pass, however, ethical scaffolding must be erected to support developing cultures and undergird established ones. For participatory cultures to flourish, online and off, we must address five fundamental areas of ethical concern: *access*, *rule making*, *connectedness*, *contribution*, and *freedom*.

Access

In the past, access to participatory culture was primarily limited by a combination of income and geography. If you lived in the village, you could attend the council meeting and (when allowed) voice your concerns. If you lived too far outside of town, or across the river or the mountains, your opportunities to participate in council decisions were limited. Your barriers to access were physical and economic. It was expensive (physically, emotionally, and monetarily) to travel.

While technology has created new opportunities for participation across greater physical spaces, in many ways very little has changed in a thousand years regarding access to spaces of participation. It is still about geographic location and economic status. We know that some nations can boast near universal access to the Internet—Iceland, Greenland, Bahrain, Sweden, New Zealand, the Netherlands—while many others remain virtually unconnected—Iraq, Liberia, Bangladesh, Cambodia, East Timor (Internet World Stats, 2011). Unlike many discussions of technology adoption and development, this is not a tale of North and South. It is, as it always has been with participatory cultures, a tale of rich and poor.

In countries with high Internet penetration rates, we know governments and the wealthy overwhelmingly control points of access to the Internet. In the United States, media conglomerates Comcast, AT&T, and Time Warner control most broadband connections. Internationally, government-owned and operated ISPs such as China Telecom, China Unicom, Deutsche

Telekom, and France Télécom have jurisdiction over most broadband Internet access (Malik, 2010).

For more than two decades, public interest organizations have fought for physical access to digital grids with scholars noting gaps in access based on race, ethnicity, income, and geographic location (Hoffman and Novak, 1999; Ebo, 1998; Norris, 2001; Eamon, 2004) And, while battles against "information redlining" and "the digital divide" might seem a relic of the last century, the core issue of access still remains. Low-income citizens in nations have limited access; this is equally true in nations with the highest-penetration rates. The issue of children's access to digital participation is particularly important. In their study of youth engaged with digital media, James *et al.* (2010) concluded that "while new media are technically open to all, digital divides persist. Access is increasingly available in spaces such as public libraries, but some young people don't have consistent access to the new media or to support structures that guide their use or participation" (p. 265).

Access in many nations is also limited by governmental barriers. Freedom House (2011), a non-profit organization concerned with global speech and press freedoms, in its report *Freedom on the Net 2011* rated nations based on "obstacles to access," which they defined as "infrastructural and economic barriers to access; governmental efforts to block specific applications or technologies; and legal, regulatory and ownership controls over internet and mobile phone access providers" (p. 1). Freedom House ranks countries such as Iran, Burma, Cuba, and Ethiopia highest among those who impede access to the Internet.

These discrepancies in access due to governmental policies were directly addressed in May 2011 by the United Nations General Assembly's Human Rights Council when it declared that access to the Internet was a "basic human right" and, if restricted, would be a violation of international law. While progress has surely been made, access is still an ethical issue that

FIGURE 28.1 This Internet cafe is located in Kafountine—a small Senegalese fishing town
Source: Malcolm Smith, 2007. Creative Commons Attribution—ShareAlike 3.0 Unported Licence)

must be addressed. For a participatory culture to be equal, fair, and productive, it must allow *meaningful* access to all.

But what does meaningful access entail? It begins with providing a universal infrastructure for connectivity. At most basic, this includes free or low-cost hardware and software needed to access the Internet, free or low-cost high-speed broadband connections, and universal policies such as those suggested by the United Nations that protect unhindered connection to the Internet, and, by extension, online participatory cultures. It also requires education so everyone may have the productions skills and creative knowledge needed for vibrant participation. As Schradie (2011) concludes, physical access alone is not enough to level the participatory playing field. A "digital production gap" also exists, one in which those who are have more educational opportunities and easier access to online technologies are more likely to engage in digital production and distribution.

Written out, these "basics" seem to be overly idealistic, unneeded luxuries for those who have no food, water, shelter, or whose friends and family are being jailed and tortured. But universal access to participatory cultures is an ethical necessity. These should not simply be communal spaces for the wealthy and educated to think, play, and plan. Universal access would provide everyone with a voice to investigate, invent, and shape his or her own future.

Rule Making

Participatory cultures are often considered to be places of collective decision making (see for example: Sandercock, 1998; Jankowski and Nyerges, 2001) and, by extension, collective rule making (McLaverty, 2002; Noveck, 2004) The philosopher Jürgen Habermas (1995) argues that, as morality resides in the communal rather than the individual, there must be an "inclusive and noncoercive rational discourse among free and equal participants" to determine the common good (p. 117). Christians (2009) explains Habermas's position in this way: "The moral claims we make on one another are the glue that holds communities together" (p. 8). Therefore, Christians (2007) argues, "Information networks on a global scale cannot be served by an ethics centered on individual decision making" (p. 122).

Participatory cultures are bounded by the rules of the culture—including who has the power to set the topics of discussion and organize the contributions—and the technology itself. As Gibson (2009) explains in an analysis of distance learning discourse, "both the title and the subject heading are pre-specified and built-in characteristics of how a post will be represented when a contributor replies to a given thread" (p. 714). On the other end of the spectrum, Mitrović and Tadić (2010) describe Belgrade radio B92 Blogs as having an "internal structure of posts" that is "self-organized" through "user interactions on posts and comment-on-comment actions" (p. 297). Rules regarding participation, as well as decisions regarding organization, must be made collectively with the widest amount of participation allowed. Clearly developed and articulated rules are an important consideration of an ethical online participatory culture. As James *et al.* (2010) warn, "Communities themselves may dissolve if their members do not create standards of behavior and codes of conduct that are agreed on and well understood" (p. 266).

The rules of participation, however, are not universal. Rules that govern online interaction, for example: posting, commenting, uploading, sharing, inviting, are unique to each participatory culture. Where one culture may support members who write long, footnoted posts, others may balk at the formality. In some cases, visuals and videos are rewarded over text. In others, words are clearly preferred. Even in text-based cultures, each values or degrades certain words, grammar, or spelling differently. Learning the rules of one certainly does not mean learning the rules for all.

Many participatory cultures—in the realms of both work and play—are created by corporations and overseen by moderators. These moderators patrol interactions, ensure rules have been followed, and level penalties when rules are broken. For the online social networking site, Facebook, hundreds of User Operations Analysts enforce rules set forth in a legal User Agreement. Rules are changed regularly and without user input. This model is replicated in many of the spaces where participatory cultures reside—MMORPGs, video-sharing sites, fan blogs, health forums, and virtual worlds. While these rules are presented in the form of a legal contract, in fact most of the rules are baselines of ethical behavior set forth by the company and overseen by company employees.

On the other hand, in cultures founded and preserved by collective input, there is a different, though not always more equal, rule-making structure. The rules of many grassroots participatory cultures are not formalized. Norms for interactivity and engagement are bound into rules by participants, but not equally so. Many are developed, administered, and reinforced by those with the loudest voices and longest tenures. As others in this volume have argued (Jenkins, 2012; Scott, 2012), "founders," "creators," "big-name fans," and "big-name bloggers" determine how and what should get done.

Members of top-down and bottom-up cultures learn the rules and the skills for participation not just by reading legal commandments but also by interacting with others in those spaces. Jenkins *et al.* (2006) describe this as "mentorship whereby what is known by the most experienced is passed along to novices" (p. 3). Gee (2004) explains that in many creative online communities learning takes place informally with new members interacting with other artists at varying levels of competency, expertise, and completion. He refers to these as "affinity spaces." Much like Bandura's (1962, 1977) Social Learning Theory, new members of online creative communities learn by interacting with and observing the behaviors of others.

It is important to note that strictness with which rules are enforced does not necessarily correlate to the formality of the rules. We've all heard tales of take-down notices (formal) for YouTube videos as well as felt the sting of reprimand for violating the unwritten rules (informal) of posting on Craigslist. Take for example students in my First Year Seminar course, "The Fandom of Harry Potter." To get students engaged in the fandom, they are required to post on one of three highly popular fan websites, MuggleNet.com, the-leaky-cauldron.org, or veritaserum.com. Each year, at least one person ends up in tears from negative responses he or she received to posts. In very rare cases, a respondent will explain why the original post was inappropriate ("too long," "repeated an earlier question that had already been answered," "interrupted a conversation thread that was not finished," etc. ...) thus engaging in the mentorship (Jenkins) and learning (Gee) saw reflected in these participatory cultures. But, more often than not, students are heckled and/or bullied out of the space ("newbie get lost," "don't you read?"). On these sites, informal rules are vigorously enforced through public reprimand. Learning takes place here, but not always through positive feedback.

Control over engagement or input imposed by rules (formal or informal) must be wielded infrequently and judiciously if the culture is to thrive. To meet an ethical standard of participation, rules must be developed by members, enforced equally, and taught consistently to new members. Community mentors, a participatory tutorial, or even an informal encouragement of new participant contributions ("hey, great idea!") would support the passage of behavioral rules to the next "generation."

Connectedness

In their description of participatory cultures, Jenkins *et al.* (2006) observe that members "feel some degree of social connection with one another (at the least they care what other people think about what they have created)" (p. 7). Social connectedness is apparent in many online participatory cultures. Members in these spaces show and feel support. For example, on the online comic creation site, Pixton, community members recently came together to support an online friend with a serious illness. In fact, support has grown from cultures as diverse as World of Warcraft guilds and collaborative YouTube videos. United States military families use websites such as ourfallensoldier.com to remember those killed in war, just as Rwanda-geonocide.org serves as a compilation of historical primary source documents related to those atrocities.

Within participatory cultures, however, there are varying degrees of "support for creating and sharing one's creations," (Jenkins *et al.*, 2006, p. 7) and this is not always the "strong support" Jenkins and his co-authors envisioned when *Confronting the Challenges of Participatory Culture*.

Most commonly, exclusion in participatory cultures is based on a cultural expectation of expertise or specialized knowledge. Growing up, my father used to tell me that it was hard because he couldn't talk about his work outside of the biochemistry lab. "Only four people on the planet know what I'm talking about," he'd insist. While his sentiment may have been overstated, those who engage in complex scientific experimentation may understand. Only recently have participatory cultures arisen to link together individuals with these kinds of specialized knowledge (see, in this collection, Pearce and Venters, 2012). And, it is clear that these cultures have generated significant contributions to the advancement of science in many areas. These cultures, however, have tightly controlled admissions. Don't have a Ph.D. in chemistry? Not invited to the party.

On the other hand, many global research projects exist solely because happily "average" citizens have chosen to participate in the gathering, analysis, and reporting of data. Citizen science projects such as setiQuest, the National Audubon Society's "Christmas Bird Count," and IceWatch USA are all excellent examples of the power of distributed, engaged thinking applied to scientific problems.

This atmosphere of exclusion is also not limited to the realm of scientific inquiry. Other creative cultures also engage in these practices. In some creative communities, expertise can be either a welcoming hand *or* a slamming door. For example, there are several blogs designed for graduate students pursuing an MFA in Creative Writing. On some of these blogs, only people who hold the proper credentials are allowed to participate. The numbers of people who qualify are only a minute fraction of those who enjoy writing. They can lurk, but they cannot fully join.

Of course, there is nothing wrong with specialized blogs. In fact, I've learned quite a bit from them over the years—everything from the proper way to create a mosaic tabletop to how to design a valid survey question. The point is that many of these online spaces are not nearly as welcoming as they could be. Whenever possible, people should not be turned away at the gates of knowledge, or, in this case, the gates of participation. We cannot possibly know where the next great writer will come from. Why limit the opportunities of the many for the benefit of the few?

Ward and Wasserman (2010) call this virtue of welcoming, "hospitality," and conclude it is an important condition for discourse surrounding questions of media ethics. Hospitality, they write, is "a 'positive' inclusivity which seeks out different viewpoints and unheard voices" (p. 288). In the most vibrant participatory cultures, expertise and hospitality are defined broadly, allowing the voices of anyone who has a contribution to join in the discourse or endeavor.

Contribution

Participatory cultures are comprised of individuals with varying degrees of belonging, interaction, and contribution. De Cremer and Tyler (2005) found that the need to belong was not equal among all participants in a group because "people differ in the extent to which they desire to strengthen their connections with others" (p. 149). "Not every member needs to contribute," Jenkins and Bertozzi (2008) explain, "but all need to feel that they are free to contribute when they are ready and what they contribute will be appropriately valued" (p. 174).

Members of participatory cultures, like those of other mediated audiences (and even more so), are "active" and participation in the cultures is "goal-directed" (Katz *et al.*, 1974). Engagement in some online participatory cultures flares up and dies down much like it does in real-world projects and activities. Engagement levels rise nearer grant deadlines, comic book releases, political crises, and events of natural devastation. In others, a steady stream of contribution marks the interactions.

Respect must be at the core of valued participation. Hill (2000) writes that respect is "something to which we should presume every human being has a claim, namely full recognition as a person, with the same basic moral worth as any other" (p. 59). Respect is not self-situated; rather, it arises from interactions with others in the group. Tyler (1999) notes that an individual does not come to a group with respect, but must first interact with the group to be treated with respect.

Respect in participatory cultures is often attained through recognition by others. When a participant—whether recognized by username, avatar, or "real" name—constructively contributes to a participatory culture, then he or she gains respect. The more regular and helpful those contributions, the more well respected he or she becomes. Take, for example, a regular poster on a cooking Do-It-Yourself (DIY) blog who explains how to build contraptions that will remove wine stains, cook sous vide beef, or slice grapefruit. She is "known" in that participatory culture. Now consider her best friend, a lurker who reads every post and consults every recipe. He is respected not because of his input, but because he actively engages in the knowledge community. In both cases it is the *action*—not the kind of activity—that makes them significant members of this DIY culture.

Some participants' real-world credibility and fame bring them instant "knowability" in an online participatory culture, but not instant respect. National leaders, sports heroes, authors, and entertainment celebrities may be seen as providing contributions that have value in the short run simply because they are identifiable. The value of their contribution, however, is not solely based (thank goodness) on celebrity. Even those whose voices are immediately heard because they are "known" do not have instant respect. This is the great leveling of online participatory cultures. Like shaking a pan of cake batter, online participatory cultures provide a creative and intellectual leveling. Kids who master videogame levels, pastors who salsa dance, and grandmothers who introduce new tire-changing techniques become known and respected through their contributions.

The paired concepts of the "known" and respect relate directly to the concepts of the anonymous and untrustworthy in online participatory cultures and much has been written about the potential moral hazards of anonymity. There are valid ethical concerns regarding responsibility for words and actions, and the ease with which anonymity allows avoidance of these responsibilities. Hateful contributions to participatory cultures (cyberbullying, death threats, racial profiling) are serious and undeniably harmful, but fear should not guide rulemaking in these spaces. In the land of participatory cultures, the value of the contribution should not be confused with the transparency of the participant. A protester in Egypt or Syria or Libya who tweets updates to let compatriots know the extent of violence in the city center is "known" around the world by @ (name) but remains anonymous to protect the cause, his family, and his life. The contributions to the participatory culture are significant; his identity is much less so.

One of the additional difficulties in determining the value of engagement is the reality of time. In a world comprised of participatory cultures, time becomes a highly sought after and valuable commodity. McGonigal (2011) refers to the bounded limits of our online participation as our "participation bandwidth"—"our individual and collective capacity to contribute to one or more participatory networks" (p. 226). She explains that "across serious crowd projects, our participation resources are increasingly being spread too thin" (p. 226).

As we begin to assign value to contributions and bestow respect upon our colleagues in participatory cultures, it is essential to remember that it is not time or status alone that determines worth. Participatory cultures need all kinds of intellectual insights and creative visions to thrive— not just the learned proclamations of the select few. Individual contributors must feel respected enough to participate freely in whatever ways they choose.

Freedom

More than 350 years ago, John Milton (1644) wrote: "Where there is much desire to learn, there of necessity will be much arguing, much writing, many opinions; for opinion in good men is but knowledge in the making." He could very well have been writing an article on participatory cultures.

Indeed, he was.

A fundamental value of participatory cultures must be freedom of expression. While at first this may seem antithetical to a collective culture, the protection of individual expression is essential to a robust and respectful discourse and is at the heart of all creative endeavors.

At their best, participatory cultures encourage a wide range of voices. Milton's (1644) original argument for a "free and open encounter" among men with unlimited access to unlimited ideas and John Stewart Mill's (1859) "marketplace of ideas" where the best ideas rise to the fore through free and open debate are at the heart of many participatory cultures. As Supreme Court Justice Oliver Wendell Holmes, Jr. (1919) contended, "the best test of truth is the power of the thought to get itself accepted in the competition of the market" (Abrams v. United States, p. 630).

The ability to speak freely is fundamental to the human condition. "The marketplace theory justifies free speech as a means to an end," Smolla (1992) writes, "But free speech is also an end itself, an end intimately intertwined with human autonomy and dignity" (p. 9). In this theoretical vein, the United Nations' most recent declaration (2011) regarding access to the Internet is a part of a larger report "on the promotion and protection of the right to freedom of opinion and expression" and begins by outlining the rights provided for in article 19 of the International Covenant on Civil and Political Rights. They are: "the right to hold opinions without interference," "the right to seek and receive information and the right of access to information," and "the right to impart information and ideas of all kinds" (p. 5).

Dissent can be, but is not always, given value in a participatory culture. Dissent for the sake of dissent is often rejected by other members, and dissent perceived as violating the cultural norms such as flaming, rejected even more roundly (for example, by denying future privilege of access to the community). Ward and Wasserman (2010) also call for a virtue of "sincerity" of practice in the facilitation of open media discourses, thus ensuring that the "hospitality" described above "does not merely constitute the token incorporation of dissent in order to sustain hegemonic control" (p. 289). Take, for example, the case of a chat group comprised of academics the majority of whom don't agree with the lengthy and often acrid postings of a colleague. To resolve the issue, the group bans the verbose member because of trolling—purposefully antagonizing participants. Several other members leave the group in protest, noting that they believe this colleague's views should be heard. Now the group discourse may be more pleasant, but its *potential* is exponentially smaller.

Conclusion

The rise of participatory cultures has ushered in a new, complex web of ethical considerations. Where ten years ago communication scholars fretted over the control of media content by a few large corporations, scholars of participatory cultures today are concerned with the creation, sharing, and interaction of media content by the many. This shift both expands and distributes the ethical burden. In today's participation environment, there must be a constant weighing of the potential of participation (e.g. finding a cure to cancer) and the banal way in which connectedness is often put to use (e.g. messages from intoxicated celebrities and digital photos from disgraced politicians). We can recalibrate, remind, and reinforce.

We must become champions of ethics in our participatory cultures. We have all allowed participants in our online communities to mock and chide others, to disparage their thoughts, their looks, and their identities. We have stood by while others were silenced. But we have the collective power to stand up to the bullies and the hate mongers. To do so only requires a simple sentence of support: "Glad you could join the conversation."

If participatory cultures are to reach their full potential, it is not enough for us to post our own videos, data, comic strips, and short stories. We must also acknowledge disparities in access and rulemaking, and work to promote equality, respect, and freedom in our engagements. These values constitute the ethical core of participatory culture.

References

Abrams v. United States. 1919. 250 U.S. 616.

Bandura, Albert. 1962. *Social learning through imitation*. Lincoln, NE: University of Nebraska Press.

Bandura, Albert. 1977. *Social learning theory*. Englewood Cliffs, NJ: Prentice Hall.

Christians, Clifford G. 2009. "Philosophical issues in media convergence," *Communications and Convergence Review*, 1(1): 1–14.

Christians, Clifford G. 2007. "Utilitarianism in media ethics and its discontent," *Journal of Mass Media Ethics*, 22(2&3): 113–131.

De Cremer, David and Tyler, Tom R. 2005. "Am I respected or not? Inclusion and reputation as issues in group membership," *Social Justice Research*, 18(2) (June): 121–153.

Eamon, Mary Keegan. 2004. "Digital divide in computer access and use between poor and non-poor youth," *Journal of Sociology and Social Welfare*, 31(2): 91–112.

Ebo, Bosah (ed.). 1998. *Cyberghetto or cybertopia? Race, class and gender on the Internet*. Westport, CT: Praeger Publishers.

Freedom House. 2011. *Freedom on the Net 2011: Global scores*. www.freedomhouse.org/images/File/FotN/MainScoreTable.pdf.

Gee, James Paul. 2004. *Situated language and learning: A critique of traditional schooling*. New York: Routledge.

Gibson, Will. 2009. "Negotiating textual talk: Conversation analysis, pedagogy and the organization of online asynchronous discourse," *British Educational Research Journal*, 35(5): 705–721.

Habermas, Jürgen. 1995. "Reconciliation through the public use of reason: Remarks on John Rawls's political liberalism," trans. C. Cronin, *The Journal of Philosophy*, 42(3): 109–131.

Hill, T.E., Jr. 2000. *Respect, pluralism, and justice*. Oxford, UK: Oxford University Press,

Hoffman, Donna L. and Novak, Thomas P. 1999. "The growing digital divide: Implications for an open research agenda." http:/ecommerce.vanderbilt.edu/.

Internet World Stats, 2011. *List of countries classified by Internet penetration rates.*

James, Carrie, Davis, Katie, Flores, Andrea, Francis, John M., Pettingill, Lindsay, Rundle, Margaret, Gardner, Howard, 2010. "Young people, ethics, and the new digital media," *Contemporary Readings in Law and Social Justice*, 2(2): 215–284.

Jankowski, Piotr and Nyerges, Timothy, 2001. *Geographic information systems for group decision making.* New York: Taylor & Francis.

Jenkins, Henry. 2012. "The guiding spirit and the powers that be: A response to Suzanne Scott," *The participatory cultures handbook.* New York: Routledge.

Jenkins, Henry and Bertozzi, Vanessa, 2008. "Artistic expression in the age of participatory culture." In Steven J. Tepper and Bill Ivey (eds). *Engaging art.* New York: Routledge, pp. 171–195.

Jenkins, Henry, Clinton, Katie, Purushotma, Ravi, Robison, Alice J., and Weigel, Margaret. 2009. *Confronting the challenges of participatory culture: Media education for the 21st century.* Chicago, IL: John D. and Catherine T. MacArthur Foundation.

Katz, E., Blumler, J. G., and Gurevitch, M. 1974. "Utilization of mass communication by the individual." In J. G. Blumler & E. Katz (eds). *The uses of mass communications: Current perspectives on gratifications research.* Beverly Hills: Sage, pp. 19–32.

McGonigal, Jane. 2011. *Reality is broken.* New York: Penguin Press.

McLaverty, Peter (ed.). 2002. *Public participation and innovations in community governance.* Aldershot UK: Ashgate Publishing, Ltd.

Malik, O. 2010. "Who is the biggest broadband company? Find out." *Gigom.* 28 July.

Mill, John Stewart. 1859. *On Liberty.*

Milton, John. 1644. *Areopagitica.*

Mitrovi , M. and Tadi B. 2010. "Bloggers' behavior and emergent communities in Blog Space," *The European Physical Journal B*, 73: 293–301.

Norris, Pippa. 2001. *Digital divide: Civic engagement, information poverty, and the Internet worldwide.* Cambridge: Cambridge University Press.

Noveck, Beth Simone. 2004. "The electronic revolution in rulemaking," *Emory Law Journal*, 53: 433–518.

Pearce, Sarah and Venters, Will. 2012. "How particle physicists constructed the world's largest grid: A case study in participatory cultures." *The participatory cultures handbook.* New York: Routledge.

Sandercock, L. 1998. *Towards Cosmopolis. Planning for multicultural cities.* Sussex: John Wiley.

Schradie, Jen. 2011. "The digital production gap: The digital divide and Web 2.0 collide," *Poetics*, 39(2): 145–168.

Scott, Suzanne. 2012. "Who's steering the mothership? The role of the fanboy auteur in transmedia storytelling." *The participatory cultures handbook.* New York: Routledge.

Smolla, Rodney A. 1992. *Free speech in an open society.* New York: Vintage Books.

Tyler, T. R. 1999. "Why people cooperate with organizations: An identity-based perspective," *Research in Organizational Behavior*, 21: 201–246.

United Nations General Assembly Human Rights Council. 2011. *Report of the Special Rapporteur on the promotion and protection of the right to freedom of opinion and expression, Mr. Frank LaRue.* 16 May. www2.ohchr.org/english/bodies/hrcouncil/docs/17session/A.HRC.17.27_en.pdf.

Ward, Stephen J. A. and Wasserman, Herman. 2010. "Towards an open ethics: Implications of new media platforms for global ethics discourse," *Journal of Mass Media Ethics*, 25(4): 275–292.

INDEX

1968 uprisings 10, 13, 14, 15, 116, 250
9/11 258

Access: addictive need for 249; alternative media
and 177; anonymity and 134; application
programming interfaces and 187; barriers to 272;
comic making tools and 82; computer network
19, 111, 273; cost of 236, 273; cultural production and 57; cultural works and 86, 233;
democracy and 166; denial as punishment 88,
278; digital hardware and 158, 198, 220;
disability and 124; disparities in 279; effects of
deprivation 4; ethical concerns 272–274;
financial limits on 127; Geographic Information
Systems and 187; hacker ethic and 5; human
knowledge and 186, 223, 233, 278; human
rights and 273, 278; intellectual property laws
effects upon 4; Internet service and 67, 88, 159,
198; open 36; Japanese games and 61–2;
participatory culture and 11; participatory media
218; prerequisites of 274; public information and
156, 168; public libraries and 223; social media
and 201; source files and 80; steady employment
and 175; surveillance data and 201; voting 24;
youth and 228, 273
Adorno, Theodor 249–50, 261
aesthetic action 262
aesthetic consistency 44
aesthetic tyranny 127, 178
aesthetics 149, 259
affinity spaces 275
Afghanistan 115,154, 202
ALICE 131
alternative media 16–19, 172, 176–79
amateur aesthetics 48
Amazon 5, 112, 122, 126, 133
Amazon Mechanical Turk 30, 122, 126
animation 74, 77–8

anime 39, 60, 62, 63, 66
anonymity 4; crowdsourcing and 121; First
Amendment protections of 266–71; forced 229;
moral hazards of 277; open publishing and 177;
relative 37, 39, 228
Apache 27, 216
Apple Computer 17, 18, 28, 249
appropriation 56, 86, 95, 109
Arab Network for Human Rights Information 199
Arendt, Hannah 13
ARPANET 4, 18
Astérix 82
ASTRA 133
ATLAS 131, 134
attention: as basis of public participation 25, 27,
126; as commodity 46, 116, 234, 236;
management 101
audience: active 5, 8, 10, 23, 48–51, 55, 110;
interactive 234; passive 5, 10, 44, 110;
productive 49, 55, 94, 110–112, 177, 218,
236, 242
authenticity 112–13, 117
authorship 36, 37, 44–51, 53–5, 57–8, 80, 262
avian flu 133

Ba 106, 107
Babylon 5 47, 54
Bahrain 197, 272
barackobama.com 23
Battlestar Galactica 47–50, 54, 56
Bechhold. Dennis 207
Berkman Center for Internet and Society 4
Berners-Lee, Tim 131
big-name fans 275
Benkler, Yochai 4, 7, 23, 30, 121, 216, 217
BitTorrent 6
Black Power 28
blogger 6, 115, 116